Contemporary issues in health, medicine, and

social policy · *General Editor: John B. McKinlay*

Women, health, and healing

Edited by Ellen Lewin and Virginia Olesen

Women, health, and healing
Toward a new perspective

Tavistock Publications · New York · London

First published in 1985 by
Tavistock Publications
in association with Methuen, Inc.
733 Third Avenue, New York,
NY 10017
and
Tavistock Publications Ltd
11 New Fetter Lane, London
EC4P 4EE

© 1985 Tavistock Publications Ltd

Printed in the United States of
America

*Library of Congress Cataloging
in Publication Data*
Women, health, and healing
(Contemporary issues in health,
medicine, and social policy)
Bibliography: P.
Includes index
1. Women – Health and hygiene –
Addresses, essays, lectures
2. Women – Health and hygiene
– Sociological aspects –
Addresses, essays, lectures
3. Women's health services –
Addresses, essays, lectures
I. Lewin, Ellen
II. Olesen, Virginia L.
III. Series
RA778.W72   1984   362.1'088042
84-16214
ISBN 0-422-78020-0
ISBN 0-422-78030-8 Pbk

*British Library Cataloguing in
Publication Data*
Women, health and healing –
(Contemporary issues in health,
medicine, and social policy)
1. Women – Diseases
2. Women – Health and hygiene
I. Lewin, Ellen
II. Olesen, Virginia
III. Series
618   RG101

ISBN 0-422-78020-0
ISBN 0-422-78030-8 Pbk

Contents

List of contributors   vii

Acknowledgements   x

1 Women, health, and healing: a theoretical
   introduction   1
   Virginia Olesen and Ellen Lewin

2 Providers, negotiators, and mediators: women
   as the hidden carers   25
   Hilary Graham

3 Occupational health and women: the case of
   clerical work   53
   Ellen Lewin and Virginia Olesen

4 The frail elderly woman: emergent questions
   in aging and women's health   86
   Helen Evers

5   Estrogen-replacement therapy: the production
    of medical knowledge and the emergence of
    policy   113
    Patricia A. Kaufert and Sonja M. McKinlay

6   Abortion in the 1980s: feminist morality and
    women's health   139
    Rosalind Pollack Petchesky

7   Struggle between providers and recipients: the
    case of birth practices   174
    Shelly Romalis

8   Women and sports: reflections on health and
    policy   209
    Mary Boutilier and Lucinda SanGiovanni

9   Women and the National Health Service: the
    carers and the careless   236
    Lesley Doyal

10 Women and health: the United States and the
    United Kingdom compared   270
    Margaret Stacey

    Name index   304

    Subject index   311

List of contributors

Editors

Ellen Lewin After completing a PhD in Anthropology at Stanford University in 1975, Ellen Lewin served on the research faculty at the University of California, San Francisco. Her research has focused on issues in the anthropology of gender and has included work with Latina immigrants, nurses, and lesbian and heterosexual single mothers. She is currently completing a book on single motherhood in America.

Virginia Olesen is Professor of Sociology in the Department of Social and Behavioral Sciences, School of Nursing, University of California, San Francisco. With Ellen Lewin and Sheryl Ruzek she co-directs the Center on Women, Health and Healing. Her current research focuses on gender related aspects of self-care and socialization issues in lives and careers of mid-life professional women.

Contributors

Mary A. Boutilier is Professor of Political Science at Seton Hall University. She received her PhD in Government from Georgetown University. Her publications include *The Sporting Woman* (with Lucinda SanGiovanni), *The Making of Political Women* (with Rita Kelly), and several articles in the area of political socialization, sport, and public policy. Her recent research interests include political theory and public administration.

Lesley Doyal is a Senior Lecturer in Sociology at the Polytechnic of North London. She is the author of *The Political Economy of Health* and co-author of *Cancer in Britain: The Politics of Prevention*. She is on the organizing collective of the Women's Health Information Centre in London and is currently working on a book about what makes women sick.

Helen Evers is a Senior Research Fellow in the Department of Sociology, University of Warwick. She has been doing research on care of the elderly, both in hospital and at home, since 1978.

Hilary Graham is a Lecturer in Social Policy at the University of Bradford. She is currently on Leave of Absence from Bradford at the Open University where she is engaged in research into the division of health responsibilities and resources in the home. Her previous research concerned the experience of pregnancy, childbirth, and early motherhood among mothers of young children. She has written a book and a number of articles on issues relating to women's health and informal health care within the family, current development in health policy, and research methodology.

Patricia A. Kaufert received her PhD from the Centre of West African Studies at the University of Birmingham. After moving to Canada her interests shifted toward medical sociology and she is now in the Department of Social and Preventive Medicine at the University of Manitoba. Her current interests are in the area of women's health, particularly with respect to the menopause.

Sonja M. McKinlay As a statistician and epidemiologist, Dr McKinlay has had major involvement in research on cancer of the cervix, the causes of low birth weight, the use of prenatal services, and issues related to the menopause. She is presently directing a longitudinal study of the menopause on a sample of healthy women.

Rosalind Pollack Petchesky is the author of *Abortion and Woman's Choice: The State, Sexuality and Reproductive Freedom*. An Associate Professor of Political Theory and Women's Studies at Ramapo College of New Jersey, Professor Petchesky lives in New York City, where she has been active in the feminist movement for reproductive rights.

Shelly Romalis received her PhD in Anthropology from McGill University in 1968. She is now Associate Professor of Anthropology at York University in Toronto as well as a certified ASPO (Lamaze) Instructor. Romalis is the editor of *Childbirth: Alternatives to Medical Control*. Her current teaching and research interests center on women and health care systems and women's movements of protest and resistance.

Lucinda SanGiovanni is Professor of Sociology in the Department of Sociology and Anthropology at Seton Hall University. She received a PhD in Sociology from Rutgers University. Her publications include *Ex-Nuns: A Study of Emergent Role Passage* and *The Sporting Woman* (with Mary A. Boutilier) as well as articles in the areas of sexuality and role passage. Her current research interests center on white collar and corporate crime and public regulation.

Margaret Stacey is a Professor of Sociology at the University of Warwick, where she specializes in the sociology of health and healing focusing on the division of labor in health care. Her insights into problems associated with women and health derive not only from her research but from her experience as woman, wife (now widowed), mother of five children and grandmother of six, in the women's movement, and as woman in the male public world. With Marion Price she is author of the Fawcett Prize winning book, *Women, Power, and Politics*.

Acknowledgements

We are pleased to acknowledge colleagues, students, and associates who helped make this book possible. Sheryl Ruzek, a friend and colleague, was instrumental in obtaining the invitation for us from Tavistock. We hope that the volume will be as fine as the one she might have done. It was a pleasure to work with John McKinlay, the series editor, and our publisher, the general editor. Their guidance and suggestions assisted greatly. Various colleagues suggested contributors in fields where our networks did not reach: Carole Browner, Arlene Kaplan Daniels, Fred Davis, Linda Gordon, Janet Harris, Joan Hult, Brigitte Jordan, John MacAloon, and Margaret Stacey.

Very useful comments on the outline and purpose of the volume came from members of a Feminist Research Seminar organized by Dr Beverly Hall, now of the University of Texas School of Nursing. Participants, all students in the Doctorate of Nursing Science program at UCSF, were Robin Whidden, Robin Cameron, Andrea Renwanz, Peggy Wilson (and her new daughter Catlin), Chris Vourakis, Susan Browne, Merrie Kaas, Sally Bisch, and Barbara Limandri. We acknowledge with particular gratitude two colleagues whose support has been especially valuable: Dr Carroll L. Estes, chair of the Department of Social and Behavioral Sciences, School of Nursing, UCSF, and Dr Margaret Clark, chair, Medical Anthropology Program, School of Medicine, UCSF. The Department of Social and Behavioral Sciences generously provided staff time for manuscript processing, done, as always, with great skill and care by Sally Maeth. Finally, our contributors bore with good grace the necessary editing and lengthy processes of bringing their work and ours into print.

One

Women, health, and healing:

a theoretical introduction

Virginia Olesen and Ellen Lewin

During the late 1960s and early 1970s feminism emerged in both Britain and the United States from the slumbers of the four preceding decades. Much as they had in the earlier suffrage struggle, agendas of concerns included efforts to bring women into full and equitable participation in every domain of society, questioning, in the process, the future of traditional roles. With the new movement, however, a theme surfaced which had been only minimally present during the earlier feminist movement: women's experiences as recipients of health care, and, to a lesser extent, their work as providers of health care began to receive attention.[1] Although activists often dealt with each of these issues – those of providers and those of patients – separately because of the particular context of their concern, the new movement has come to include an overall attention to the roles women play in health and healing systems broadly construed. Feminists, thus, began to question both the level of women's health status and the quality of care they received, linking these problems to the extreme sexual segregation of the health-care labor force (e.g. male doctors and female nurses) as well as to some of the broader questions of political economy which they saw as having influenced these developments. Very early in the new era of feminist organizing, health-care critics and their supporters argued that these matters were proper foci both for political action and for scholarly inquiry. Early statements of these positions include the classic *Our Bodies Ourselves* (Boston Women's Health Book Collective 1973) and the writings of Seaman (1969, 1972), Ehrenreich and English (1972, 1973), Chesler (1972), and Frankfort (1972).

This volume takes its place in the history of feminist scholarship and activism amidst heightened public and academic attention to the overall issues of health: a growing contentiousness over the quality and cost of care for everyone, the impact of technology on the practice and delivery of care, and the future distribution of shrinking resources. Along with these problems, several themes particularly relevant to women have also emerged. Demographic predictions point to the elderly becoming a more prominent segment of the population and one which is predominantly female. At the same time, observers of epidemiological and service-utilization trends have shown that women make more frequent use of health services and seem to experience illness more often than do men. The importance of these themes to the future direction of health-care delivery as well as to the quality of life of the female population mandates a fresh approach to the analysis of women's health issues, one which places them in a broad societal context.

This approach is particularly timely not only because of the trends just noted, but also because of the existence of a considerable body of recent scholarship in women's health which facilitates enlarging our analytical framework. The earliest writing on health produced since the rise of the new feminist movement – by committed feminists and sympathetic outsiders alike – has reflected the initial criticisms raised by the women's movement and the perceived urgency of calling attention to inequitable and dehumanizing conditions for women receiving care. Those early writings ranged widely in their concerns: the negative imagery of female patients used in drug advertising (Prather and Fidell 1975); the tendency to diagnose women's physical ills as psychogenic (Lennane and Lennane 1973); the indiscriminate use of mastectomies in cases of breast cancer (Cope 1971); the difficulties faced by female providers in nursing (Clelland 1971) and medicine (Lopate 1968; Campbell 1973); the excessive prescription of tranquilizing and psychotropic drugs for women (Castleman 1974); and of course, a large body of writing on every aspect of women's reproductive life, ranging from the risks of contraceptive devices and medications (Seaman 1972) through dehumanizing aspects of pregnancy and delivery (Haire 1972; Shaw 1974; Arms 1975) and gynecological care (Scully and Bart 1973). These writings helped to highlight specific, critical issues, often leading to specific reforms. They were followed by other work in a similar vein and enlarged later by works which placed the topic of women's health (or some aspect of it) in a comprehensive, sociocultural context (Gordon 1974; Luker 1975; Ruzek 1978). The essays in this volume continue that last tradition, in that they argue that women's experience in the health-care system is not an isolated phenomenon, but one which is influenced by and in turn influences wider societal themes.

A concern with considering women's health issues in their broadest context had informed our thinking for some years before Tavistock invited us to prepare this volume. Throughout several years of teaching together in this area, we found that treatment of women's health issues as discrete topics permitted some new information to be generated but ultimately served neither our students nor our own interests well. Further, our earlier collaborative research on socialization to a woman's profession (nursing), as well as our individual research – Lewin on single mothers and Olesen on devalued occupations – sustained the conviction that the broader view would be essential to a meaningful analysis of women's health issues (Olesen and Katsuranis 1978; Lewin and Olesen 1980; Lewin 1985, forthcoming). This early collaboration across our home disciplines of social anthropology and sociological social psychology had also persuaded us of the necessity for an interdisciplinary stance in approaching these complex issues.

History of the volume

The Tavistock invitation, however, challenged us. To meet the specifications laid down for this series (Contemporary issues in health, medicine, and social policy), we would have to extend this viewpoint in ways relevant for policy and include British, as well as North American, colleagues. It was clear to us from the beginning that this venture would entail not a few difficulties. In particular, while British and American feminist scholars share many concerns and methods, they have tended not to address or develop the same key issues, or, even when working on similar questions, to approach them in the same way. These divergences derive from the differing histories of the various academic disciplines which have been applied to women's issues and women's health issues on the two sides of the Atlantic as well as from the particular sociopolitical contexts which obtain in the two societies (see Stacey Chapter 10).

The American interest in athletics, fitness, and sport is a good example of these disciplinary differences. In the United States, the sociology of leisure and sport and the anthropology of play are both well-recognized fields within their respective disciplines. At the same time, the social sciences in the US have extensively penetrated the field of physical education, where a considerable body of work on women, athletics, and fitness has been produced (Gerber *et al.* 1974). This emphasis is largely absent from British social science and writing of British feminists, one notable exception we know of being an historical essay on nineteenth-century feminism and fitness (Atkinson 1978). On the other hand, perhaps because feminist critiques of classical theories of the division of labor have been pursued more acutely in British sociological circles (Stacey 1981), scholars in Great Britain have attended rather carefully to the issue of "hidden providers" in health-care systems (Finch and Groves 1982; Ungerson 1983; Graham, this volume Chapter 2). American analyses of domestic work, where "hidden" health care is provided, have tended until recently[2] to overlook this critical problem, focusing instead on the organization and execution of domestic tasks (Lopata 1971; Berk 1980).

The basic political and historical differences between the two societies are well illustrated by the kind of work which has been undertaken on abortion. American feminists quickly took the issue as a critical one, very likely because events and litigation which led to the 1972 US Supreme Court decision on abortion coincided with the early years of the American women's movement (Hayler 1979). Indeed, as Ruzek (1978) points out, the feminist victory in the legalization of abortion constituted the first major success of the reborn feminist movement. In contrast, British law had made abortion legal in 1967, just prior to the emergence of the women's movement in Britain, making abortion a right British women would have to defend rather than struggle to obtain (Stacey Chapter 10).

These differences between British and American feminists are often matters of degree, rather than kind, as the British literature does contain many informed and critical works on abortion (Macintyre 1977; Sims 1981). However, until very recently, American feminists have tended to leave less well analyzed the effects of race and class on women's health (Davis 1983). These are issues, particularly the impact of social-class membership, which are well developed in British writing, probably because living in a highly stratified society sharpens British sensitivity to its importance. The more loosely divided American system, on the other hand, tends to blunt perceptions of social class, despite powerful effects exerted on women's health and on the health-care system in general.

Mindful of these national differences, and of the still different emphases of the Canadian system, we decided to select for strength in scholarship, but along lines which would provide readers with insights into topics relatively unfamiliar or poorly developed until now. Our overall mandate to all the authors, British, American, or Canadian, was, however, that they develop their specific topics to reflect salient women's health themes in their own societies, a critical point raised by Stacey in another context (1982).

Beyond the matter of the cross-Atlantic differences, we also confronted vexing issues of familiarity, urgency, and contemporaneity. Should we include, for example, well-known issues in reproductive health because of the keen interest in that topic in both Britain and North America? Here we worried that by strongly emphasizing reproductive questions we would run the risk of obscuring the view of women in other critical social roles and as providers or patients in other health domains. Beyond this, we struggled with the problem of whether we should invite a chapter on abortion, a very familiar topic for most of us, as against taking up the new and compelling problems presented by such obstetrical technologies as electronic fetal monitoring.

We finally returned to our overall theme – that women's

health be considered in relation to other aspects of the societies under discussion – and were thus able to determine the three topics relevant to women's reproductive life we would include. The new political movements surrounding abortion in the US, and to a lesser extent in Britain, are critical to an understanding of wide national developments. Controversies over birth practices in Canada have evoked struggles which highlight the broader problem of how providers and recipients of health care may conceive differently of their fundamental interests. And the debate over estrogen-replacement therapy which took place in the United States has implications not only for specific therapeutic policies but for the sociocultural construction of the menopause and of the professionals in whose sphere it falls.

This same overall perspective also guided selection of topics which fall outside the reproductive arena: the care ot the frail elderly, women's occupational health, race and class in the organization of health care. It also led us to select new topics, previously little studied by women's health scholars. These include women and athletics, women as "hidden providers" of health care, and the comparative analysis of the British and American health-care systems as they affect women. Our invitation to the authors emphasized this perspective:

> This volume will present analysis of these various themes not only in their own right, but, further, as they reflect on broad characteristics and changes within these two societies. As you can see, a number of the issues are indicative of features of these societies and reveal those societies to us, as well as informing us about the particular theme as important to women. It is this overall theme of reciprocal influence, if you will, between women's issues considered in their own right and what they reflect about the actual construction of gender and health in society, as well as the nature of the society itself that we wish to stress, since we see these links as integral for the sound analysis of policy relevant for women's health.

There are, of course, many other topics to which this same perspective might have been applied with good results but which we could not, by virtue of the limitations of a single volume, handle in these pages. Our readers will doubtless be able to list many others of equal or greater significance; we would hope that such analysis will be advanced by authors who continue to work from this perspective.

The conceptual basis of this volume

Much social-science literature on health assumes meanings for critical matters such as health, illness, healing, the nature of care delivery, and, particularly important for our purposes, the nature of women's participation in all of these. In contrast to this literature, qualitative sociologists and anthropologists interested in health and healing have attempted to challenge these deeply rooted assumptions. This work has shown, for example, how individuals' material condition influences their conception of health and illness (Kelman 1975) while their social location, especially their class position, contributes to both how they define responsibility for health (Pill and Stott 1982) and how they conceive of health itself (Blaxter and Patterson 1982). Comparative and crosscultural analyses, further, have indicated the range of variation which exists in the meanings attached to illness, the interpretation of etiology, and the action to be taken in dealing with illness of all kinds (Landy 1977). This body of research has demonstrated, moreover, that even western "medical knowledge" is shaped by students' experiences as they move through training programs (Atkinson 1983), by the ongoing interactions of patients and physicians (Hayes-Bautista 1978) and by the percolation of lay knowledge into the domain of "scientific" medicine (Helman 1978).

At the same time that these and other writings show how variously health and illness can be constructed, another body of work has led us to question the static models of care systems envisioned in much sociological writing. Unlike the sharp divisions of participants into "recipients" and "providers," some recent studies suggest that these roles may instead blur and shift situationally. The comparative data provided by anthropologists can be especially instructive on this point in that they demonstrate how roles of "caregivers" may, for some groups, be tied to the way meanings of illness are constructed (Lewis 1976). Applying similar insights to western settings, a number of authors have described the existence of lay consultation systems as both related to and separate from the formal operation of care systems (Freidson 1961; Robinson 1971; Zola 1973; McKinlay 1973; Dingwall 1976; Locker 1981; Scambler, Scambler, and Craig 1981).

In devising the overall perspective of this volume, we have drawn our inspiration, in part, from these lines of thought of anthropology and qualitative sociology. As the foregoing review suggests, these traditions posit knowledge as a human accomplishment, arguing that it is socially constructed and distributed (Berger and Luckman 1966; Rabinow and Sullivan 1979). Actors in particular social and cultural loci, seeking to realize and maximize their particular goals under a variety of conditions and constraints, construct meanings on which they act and which in turn provide lines of action for others. As a number of anthropologists have noted (Leach 1954; Barth 1969; Geertz 1973), these processes also engender boundaries and distinctions which themselves become part of the process of constructing knowledge and acting upon it. This very simple statement of a complex epistemological position reminds us that women in health and healing systems function as social actors who assign meanings to their situations which reflect cultural themes. Their actions, based on these meanings, lend form to both social organization and particular relationships and can become the focus of action for both providers and policy-makers. In short, this perspective enables us not only to understand how cultural meanings attach to facets of women's health, but how to go about analyzing the action taken by individuals in light of those meanings.

While these views have been present in the social sciences of health for at least two decades, they have never constituted the dominant stance of these disciplines. Rather, a more static, structural–functional outlook has prevailed, predicated on unquestioning assumptions of the meanings of situations and institutions, as can be readily observed by a review of the tables of contents of some of the major textbooks.

This may explain why the early statements of women's health movement spokeswomen failed to exert any noticeable influence on social scientists concerned with health. From the very start of the new feminist movement those who took up health issues advanced the seemingly incredible claim that even ordinary women's own knowledge of their bodies was as legitimate as the expertise of the medical profession. The political implications of these positions were radical in that they invited women to use this knowledge to take control of their bodies and to assume or even create active roles in their own health care (Kleiber and Light 1978; Ruzek 1978). However, while this stance was influential in the women's movement, leading to the formation of various kinds of self-help organizations, the statement remained fundamentally political and insulated from scholarly focus (Olesen 1980). Its epistemological implications and their resonance with major emphases within the interpretive social sciences went largely unnoticed. Jordan's investigation of lay competence in the self-diagnosis of pregnancy is an outstanding, but rare, example of scholarship which noted and developed the implications of women's knowledge of their bodies as a means to action and control (1977).

Along with the failure to explore the analytic potential of feminist political perspectives, the examination of women's roles in care systems failed to take these statements into account. Traditional conceptualizations of patient and provider continued to dominate even feminist research, thus perpetuating a static view of the health-care system, not as participatory and processual, but as one characterized by a "post office model" of receipt and delivery (Nelson 1975). These limitations notwithstanding, feminist scholars managed even within this narrow context to generate a large corpus of data about particular features of health-care systems, for example whether gender or professional status was more salient in health-care encounters (West 1984). These explorations opened up a host of new questions at the same time that some significant phenomena, notably those related to the informal and "hidden" aspects of health-care delivery, remained underinvestigated because the traditional conceptualizations failed to recognize them. Further, because of the unconscious incorporation of certain misogynist biases into even feminist thought, some critical topics – notably nursing – were largely overlooked by women's health researchers (Lewin 1977).

Thus, while feminist scholarship on health continually developed new conceptualizations and insights, as well as considerable new knowledge, these researchers rarely examined women's roles as constructors of knowledge or considered what women's participation in the health domain might reveal about the wider society. Ruzek's (1978) work was a notable exception in this period. Using a qualitative approach and building on the implications of the women's health movement rallying cry to "take control of our bodies and our care," Ruzek looked at the new knowledge women generated with this statement and showed how this led to the formation of a new type of social organization, the self-help gynecological clinic, which in turn made vital contributions to the direction of the women's health movement. Her analysis was relevant not only to the specific features of the women's health movement, but amplified our understanding of the dynamics of social movements in American society.

Perspectives in the book

To one degree or another all the chapters in this volume build on this interpretive tradition. Although the particular subject-matter of each chapter is different, and the intellectual roots of the contributors varied, each reveals women not as passive creatures who can only be acted upon by others, but as active constructors of contexts and meanings which both reflect and affect their society. Some of the chapters also deal with the ways in which others – not necessarily women – also engage in the business of constructing meanings and lines of actions relevant to women to shape the definition of problems and the direction of our understanding. Beyond this, all the chapters tell us something about the specific problem at issue and about the wider society within which that problem is situated.

How the very definition of what constitutes women's health can be called into question and new meanings constructed through alterations in the political climate are at the heart of Petchesky's analysis of recent trends in US thinking about abortion (Chapter 6). Using judicial opinion as well as an analysis of positions on both sides of the issue, she shows that the medicalization of abortion narrows our ability to understand its meaning in the fuller context of health. She argues for an expanded definition of health which would include individual wellbeing and choice as essential elements. Even more profoundly, she demonstrates the connection between a medicalized definition of abortion and the types of organization and policy that emerge in the debate surrounding it.

Social movements which give rise to controversy also shape definitions of women's reproductive health. Romalis explores this dynamic in her review of a public debate in Canada over what would constitute "safe" birth practices and appropriate facilities for delivering them (Chapter 7). She presents the positions of the various protagonists, namely those who favored a preventative emphasis and those who favored high-technology, regionalized hospital care, to show how the intense struggle which ensued, initially a matter of differing definitions, emerged as a political dispute over the dispersal of resources. Romalis' analysis, like Petchesky's, shifts our focus of concern from the plight of individual females and groups of women to the larger social and political contexts within which basic definitions are shaped.

If women's health plays a part in social movements, such as those which Petchesky and Romalis analyze, other social trends may also influence conceptions of health and alter our understanding of it. Boutilier and SanGiovanni illustrate this in their discussion of women and fitness (Chapter 8). They argue that increased participation in athletics and exercise has led to new definitions of women's mental and physical health. Beyond this, they present the view that an understanding of women and sports is best accomplished by examining their multiple roles and commitments, thus placing the apparently narrow issue of athletic participation in a much wider social context. According to this formulation, a woman's involvement in exercise may act on the other roles she performs, just as these other areas influence the meaning of sport and fitness in her life.

Viewing women's health through multiple roles is a perspective which also characterizes the Lewin and Olesen chapter on women's occupational health (Chapter 3). They begin with a consideration of ongoing technological change in a predominantly female occupation, clerical work, but move from this to a critique of the narrow framework within which conceptualizations of women's occupational health have generally been cast. Technological change in the workplace has raised some provocative questions about occupational health, to be sure, but this process of change is suffused with ambiguity, requiring that investigators extend their concern beyond "working conditions" narrowly construed. Lewin and Olesen propose that the meanings women attach to their work and the complex situational contexts, personal and public, within which work is imbedded must be examined. Women are, in this perspective, neither healthy nor unhealthy apart from the context in which such meanings are produced.

Kaufert and McKinlay's account of the origin and history of debates over estrogen-replacement therapy takes this perspective in a somewhat different direction (Chapter 5). They analyze materials from medical journals and media documents and thereby define not only the history of the controversy but the ways in which the controversy defined the relationships among a complex set of participants – the popular and professional media, medical researchers and clinicians, female patients and their physicians. Rather than using the complicated dispute which unfolded merely to approach the manifest question of the risks and benefits of estrogen replacement, Kaufert and McKinlay move to the problem of how legitimate issues of investigation are defined and how this epistemological process acts upon health care for women and women's own perceptions of what constitutes good health and good care. Feminists, they show us, no less than other scholars, are drawn to topics as they become defined as important; thus the "discovery" of the menopausal woman is revealed as an issue in the sociology of knowledge.

The Kaufert and McKinlay chapter points, as well, to how the dissection of a controversial issue may generate understandings of larger themes. Their history of the conflict reveals the latent tensions between major social institutions and the interplay among these. Similarly, Romalis' review of the struggle between providers and recipients of birth practices shows the trajectory a public conflict assumes when protagonists of a consumer movement and public officials clash. Boutilier and SanGiovanni's chapter alerts us to the factors of culture change which may come into play as new behaviors are defined, while Petchesky's scrutiny of the anti-abortion forces focuses on the contrasting currents which may shape any social movement. Finally, Lewin and Olesen provide glimpses into the difficulties of understanding the social impact of any sort of technological change when ambiguity is an essential part of such change.

The four British contributions also examine how knowledge of women's health is constructed in a particular societal context. Graham's work on women as "hidden providers," for example, clarifies how static notions of women's roles in health-care systems and of the difference between public and domestic domains come to determine our understandings of the informal contributions of women to health-care work. She advances the important idea that these informal structures in the private sphere are not merely an adjunct to the "real" medical-care system, but provide the material conditions in which health comes to be. At the same time, and rather ironically, the state is shown to assume the existence of these "hidden" providers, following from traditional gender-role expectations, and to mount efforts to use their integral contribution in order to limit public services.

Evers addresses a similar problem, that of female relatives' care of frail elderly mothers, aunts, or sisters (Chapter 4). At the same time that shared understandings define this work as "normal, natural, and traditional," there is in fact a subtle process of recruitment for this population into care roles. Evers' own research on frail elderly women clearly indicates that frailty alone does not determine how these care roles will be defined; rather, she distinguishes two types of frail elderly women according to lifelong social styles and clarifies how these styles set the tone for emergent care delivery.

Both Graham (Chapter 2) and Evers alert us to aspects of the division of labor in British society, particularly as it is defined and sustained in the health-care system. Doyal's examination of the National Health Service, taking a somewhat different angle of attack, looks at the influence of other systems of stratification – those of race and class – and how these intersect with gender in defining the experience of British women as patients and health workers (Chapter 9). Her history of women's participation in the National Health Service shows that the idea of adequate care for all women must be revised in the light of the impaired access of poor women and women of color to the system. Doyal shows, interestingly, how the current debate over these definitions has led to the seemingly paradoxical situation of feminists simultaneously defending and criticizing the health-care system.

Utilizing a comparative perspective rarely employed in

writings about women's health, Stacey outlines key structural and cultural properties of women's lives in both British and American societies (Chapter 10). She notes similarities and differences in women's lot in the two societies, suggesting ways in which these contrasts and similarities shape the definition of women's health issues. Stacey shows not only how different forms of feminist participation in women's health debates derive from different health-care institutions, i.e. a nationalized service versus fee-for-service, but suggests that these matters reflect differing core values in the two societies.

Viewed together these chapters have a number of implications. They question the very nature of participation in health and healing, examining it in various contexts and thereby showing how it is shaped by cultural and social change and how the definitions generated around it provide the basis for action, protest, and policy. Health and women's health particularly are therefore not taken for granted but revealed as dynamic aspects of women's lives which alter and are altered by other societal themes. The essays also suggest that topics ordinarily thought to stand outside the "realm of health" may not only have an impact on it but be integral to it. It is in this way that the chapters offer a perspective on the understanding of policy and policy analysis.

The perspective of this volume and policy

As many analysts have noted, policy is a complex social process in which individuals in different roles interact more or less extensively with one another in seeking an informed basis for framing or taking action on issues of importance to them. The kinds of issues which provide the focus for such activity are sometimes characterized by considerable ambiguity and/or conflict (Rivlin 1971; Rein 1976; Heighton and Heighton 1978; Lipman-Blumen and Bernard 1979; Nakamura and Smallwood 1980; Estes and Edmonds 1981). Needless to say, not all the parties involved in a policy interaction share the same views. The process can and does occur in a variety of settings usually thought of as policy contexts, including municipal councils, city halls, state houses, federal agencies, and legislative bodies such as the Houses of Parliament. However, the policy process is also enacted in other less "appropriate" settings: the chair of a university physical education department which has women's athletic programs, a trade union's health committee which considers time off for women with sick children, a senior citizens' organization board which looks into home health care for elderly widows. Indeed, feminists who are concerned about women's health and the very women who receive or deliver health care also play a part in this process.

A critical aspect of policy, wherever it is made or enacted, and one which this volume seeks to address, is the knowledge which participants require, whatever their role in the policy process. Each of these chapters makes a substantive contribution on a particular topic, thus potentially informing a wide range of policy-makers. For example, individuals associated with the Food and Drug Administration (FDA) (or its British parallel) will find much to inform them in the Kaufert and McKinlay chapter about the controversy over estrogen-replacement therapy, but so will women who take estrogen or are considering doing so. In this respect, the chapters are "intrinsically relevant," for they inform policy participants about women's health, whether or not those participants regard the topic as worthy of consideration (Weiss 1976).

However, the chapters also move beyond this purely informational level. Because each author has attempted to treat women's health as a key domain in the societies under consideration, each has also outlined how cultural and social dynamics shape these issues and knowledge about them. Thus, in illustrating dynamic properties of the construction of knowledge, the chapters suggest different variables relevant for various stages of policy analysis (Boneparth 1982: 13).

Some detail how certain issues arose. Kaufert and McKinlay's account of the arguments of the contending parties in the estrogen-replacement debate shows how that dispute created an issue not only for those directly involved, but eventually for feminist scholars. Boutilier and SanGiovanni depict the slowly emergent trend in women's fitness as both integral and tangential to the women's rights movement and reveal how women's participation in athletics and sports became an issue of health as well as equity. Petchesky's discussion of the recent social history of abortion policy discloses how sociopolitical trends can alter critical issues for women in their roles as service recipients and for feminists concerned with that care. Similarly, Lewin and Olesen's account of the impact of computer-mediated office work shows how this technological change and decisions about its deployment have seemingly created a new occupational health problem which mainly affects women. Doyal's chapter on women and the National Health Service, further, informs us on how issues are revised as women experience particular care systems and how expectations about race and class differences are woven into the definition of ongoing policy.

The perspective advanced here, that women's health is not a static issue, brings us to the consideration of a key point which a number of analysts have raised, namely that it is crucial for participants in the policy process to understand the origins, as well as the potential outcomes, of specific issues (Scott and Shore 1974; Estes and Edmonds 1981). Most of the chapters therefore tell us a story about how the issues they consider emerged, were altered or redefined:

> Neither science nor applied science provides an adequate model for social understanding. What matters in social understanding is the overall effect of a complex of behavior. This understanding cannot be reached by aggregating known regularities in the behavior of discrete events. Rather, social understanding in this situation depends on telling relevant stories: that is, deriving from past experience a narrative which interprets the events as they unfolded and draws a moral for future actions, suggesting, for example, how the future might unfold if certain steps were taken.
>
> (Rein 1976: 265)

What readers can take away from these pages is, then, not only information, but a perspective on the dynamics of women's health-care issues. A sense of these dynamics, complex and variegated as they appear in the chapters, can be transferred to the examination of women's health issues not discussed here. Graham's analysis, for instance, of "hidden" care roles which women play and how they have emerged as an issue in some circles might well be instructive in anticipating what other dimensions of women's health careers might be similarly obscured. Evers' review of the assumptions which inform policies concerning frail elderly women and their caregivers, and which persist in spite of variations within the frail elderly population, bids us to be aware of those interpretations which have their origins in stereotypes and conceptions of "normal" behavior. Her chapter indicates that these assumptions need to be carefully questioned if responsive policy is to be generated.

Sensitivity to these dynamics and their influence on defining and shaping issues is clearly more than an interesting academic or historical exercise. Rather, the perspective advanced in these pages moves toward constructing the issues in ways which lead to more subtle characterizations of the "problems" and their implications for women. Thus we seek to avoid the tendency to cast women's health issues as individual problems, as has sometimes been the case with certain feminist constructions (Guettel 1974: 45). Further, our approach helps us to resist premature conceptualization of a particular women's health issue as one either of role-equity or of role-change (Carden 1977: 40–3; Gelb and Palley 1982: 7).[3]

Although the distinction between role-equity and role-change has undergirded a great deal of feminist writing and has proven useful in many instances in evoking and focusing issues (particularly as regards changes in the nuclear family), it has the potential, largely because of its binary nature, to hide some features of women's participation in health and healing systems. In the case of occupational health, for example, a number of issues are not easily characterized as reflecting either "change" or "equity." Attentiveness to how the issue has emerged in a post-industrial society under conditions of rapid technological change may help us to avoid premature foreclosure on the issue; that is, the kind of contextual approach we propose will show us, we believe, that the shifting situation of women's occupational health contains elements of *both* change and equity. In a similar· vein, other issues, such as abortion, may seem at first glance to be clear instances of role-change, particularly as they involve the arrangement of decision-making roles. However, as one reads the Petchesky account of recent historical and political developments in this area, it becomes clear that the question of role-change is only a part of the issue. Access to abortion is also an issue in role-equity.

Finally, some awareness of how women's health issues emerge in a sociocultural context can surmount the tendency to regard certain features of women's health careers as deriving from a "natural" moral foundation. Any policy which relates to gender issues, of course, carries implications of "naturalness," but it is precisely the necessity to avoid labelling women's health issues as emergent from nature that is at issue here. Evers' chapter on the recruitment of female relatives, particularly daughters, to the care of the frail elderly in general, and frail elderly females in particular, shows clearly that culturally mediated notions of naturalness can be very costly and burdensome for women. However, Evers argues that most policies do not recognize the substance of this burden and in fact base continuation of current programs on an underlying assumption of what is "right, proper, and natural."

A number of challenges to convenient understandings about women's participation in health and healing systems thus run through these pages: women's potential as decision-makers in the outcomes of their own reproductive status; the conceptualization of women in multiple roles related to health and not merely as "victims" in domestic or public situations; the reservoir of talent and energy from which women perform their hidden care roles; the genesis and outcomes of controversies and their influence on health delivery and therapeutic policy; and the powerful effects of society's multifaceted systems of social stratification on provisions made for health care.

Will these or other challenges lead to changes which reflect the perspectives which we have put forward in this volume? The answers are elusive, though the challenges we have presented all have policy implications. Reflecting what has generally been a modest (at best) pace of reorganization of gender structures, the roles of female participants in the domain of health will probably be slow to change, and sometimes with consequences unanticipated by those who forward the new challenges (Ruzek 1980). It may well be that a kind of "cognitive lag" will best describe the coming flow of events as the reconceptualization of women's participation advances far more rapidly than the social arrangements in which the current situation is imbedded (Haber 1965).

Even under these conditions of uncertainty, tempered no doubt with a dose of realistic pessimism, it seems to us that some of the answers (or fragments thereof) we need are to be found in the discussions which appear in this volume. No less than policy-makers, concerned feminists and others involved in every phase of the policy process – no matter how minute – can profit from consideration of these processes. In particular, the type of discussion attempted here, insofar as it has argued throughout that none of these issues stand as discrete topics, insulated and isolated, leads us to query how sexual stratification and the processes of constructing gender take shape in one major social domain – health – and beyond that, in the society of which that domain is a vital part.

The domain of health

The domain of health includes the entire range of issues which touch on illness, sickness, disease, wellness, wellbeing, as well as those activities of preventing, diagnosing, healing, caring, and curing. More than any other in contemporary industrialized societies, the domain of health embodies almost all the crucial elements necessary to achieve an understanding of the society itself: life and death, strength and weakness, fear and suffering, production and reproduction, work and play, separation and unification. Examination of health permits the revelation of most of the elements of western cultures which bear most directly on the construction of gender and its consequences for women, men, and the larger social order. While the analysis of other domains, such as religion and law, also can yield far-reaching insights about the wider culture and society, these do not take us as far as does the study of health, precisely because health is so encompassing.

Thus questions about women's participation in this domain, though of profound and immediate concern to women, are also fundamentally moral issues which involve the shaping of roles and selves. Activists, critics of all persuasions, policy-makers, and participants in these processes – no less than women themselves – shape women's place and hence construct the society even as they address pressing issues in health. The questions about women's health within the larger domain of health which are raised in this volume are therefore, in their most vital aspect, questions about the place of women in society and ultimately about the transformation of gender and society (Bologh 1984).

Notes

1 The American suffrage movement of the late nineteenth century strongly advocated equal access to medical education for women. It was also intertwined with the Popular Health Movement which emphasized hygiene and dress reform (Shryrock 1966: 117, 178–80).

2 Nona Glazer is currently analyzing the political economy of health care in domestic contexts, thus bringing American interests in housework into this sphere (Glazer-Malbin 1976).

3 Role equity involves extending rights held by other groups to women, whereas role change implicates alterations in traditional female roles and implies greater independence in both social and sexual spheres. As some policy analysts have noted, "The latter issues are fraught with greater political pitfalls, including perceived threats to existing values, in turn creating visible and often powerful opposition" (Gelb and Palley 1982: 8).

References

Arms, S. (1975) *Immaculate Deception: A New Look at Women and Childbirth in America*. Boston: Houghton-Mifflin.

Atkinson, P. (1978) Fitness, Feminism and Schooling. In S. Delamont and L. Duffin (eds) *The Nineteenth Century Woman*. London: Croom Helm.

—— (1983) *The Clinical Experience*. Westmead: Gower Publishing.

Barth, F. (1969) *Ethnic Groups and Boundaries*. Boston: Little Brown.

Berger, P. and Luckman, T. (1966) *The Social Construction of Reality*. New York: Doubleday Anchor.

Berk, S.F. (1980) *Women and Household Labor*. Beverly Hills: Sage Publications.

Blaxter, M. and Patterson, E. (1982) *Mothers and Daughters: A Three Dimensional Study of Health Attitudes and Behaviors*. London: Heinemann.

Bologh, R.W. (1984) Feminist Social Theorizing and Moral Reasoning: On Difference and Dialectic. In R. Collins (ed.) *Sociological Theory*. San Francisco: Jossey-Bass Publishers.

Boneparth, E. (1982) A Framework for Policy Analysis. In E. Boneparth (ed.) *Women, Power and Policy*. Elmsford, NY: Pergamon Press.

Boston Women's Health Book Collective (1973) *Our Bodies Ourselves*. New York: Simon & Schuster.

Campbell, M. (1973) *Why Would a Girl Go into Medicine? Medical Education in the United States: A Guide for Women*. Old Westbury, NY: Feminist Press.

Carden, M.L. (1977) *Feminism in the Mid-1970s*. New York: Ford Foundation.

Castleman, M. (1974) Men Get Cured . . . Women Get Drugged. *Her-Self* 3: 12–13.

Chesler, P. (1972) *Women and Madness*. Garden City, NY: Doubleday.

Clelland, V. (1971) Sex Discrimination: Nursing's Most Pervasive Problem. *American Jounal of Nursing* 71: 1542–547.

Cope, O. (1971) Breast Cancer: Has the Time Come for a Less Mutilating Treatment? *Psychiatry in Medicine* 2: 263–69.

Davis, A.Y. (1983) Racism, Birth Control and Reproductive Rights. In A. Davis (ed.) *Women, Race and Class*. New York: Random House.

Dingwall, R. (1976) *Aspects of Illness*. London: Martin Robertson.

Ehrenreich, B. and English, D. (1972) *Witches, Midwives and Nurses – A History of Women Healers*. Old Westbury, NY: Feminist Press.

Ehrenreich, B. and English, D. (1973) *Complaints and Disorders: The Sexual Politics of Sickness*. Old Westbury, NY: Feminist Press.

Estes, C.L. and Edmonds, B.C. (1981) Symbolic Interaction and Social Policy Analysis. *Symbolic Interaction* 4: 75–86.

Finch, J. and Groves, D. (1982) By Women, For Women: Caring for the Frail Elderly. *Women's Studies International Forum* 5: 13–20.

Frankfort, E. (1972) *Vaginal Politics*. New York: Quadrangle Books.

Freidson, E. (1961) *Patients' Views of Medical Practice*. New York: Russell Sage Foundation.

Geertz, C. (1973) Religion as a Cultural System. In C. Geertz *The Interpretation of Cultures*. New York: Basic Books.

Gelb, J. and Palley, M.L. (1982) *Women and Public Policies*. Princeton: Princeton University Press.

Gerber, E., Felshin, J., Berlin, P., and Wyrick, W. (1974) *The American Woman in Sport*. Cambridge, MA: Addison-Wesley.

Glazer-Malbin, N. (1976) Housework. *Signs* 1: 905–22.

Gordon, L. (1974) *Women's Body, Women's Right, A Social History of Birth Control in America*. New York: Penguin Books.

Guettel, C. (1974) *Marxism and Feminism*. Toronto: Canadian Women's Educational Press.

Haber, A. (1965) Cognitive Lag. *Social Research* 32: 42–70.

Haire, E. (1972) The Cultural Warping of Childbirth: Special Report of the President of the International Childbirth Education Association. *International Childbirth Education Association News*, Special Issue, Spring. (Reissued with postscript, 1975.)

Hayes-Bautista, D. (1978) Chicana Patients and Medical Practitioners: A Sociology of Knowledge Paradigm of Lay-Professional Interaction. *Social Science and Medicine* 32: 83–90.

Hayler, B. (1979) Abortion. *Signs* 5: 307–23.

Heighton, R.H., Jr, and Heighton, C. (1978) Applying the Anthropological Perspective to Social Policy. In E. Eddy and W. Partridge (eds) *Applied Anthropology in America*. New York: Columbia University Press.

Helman, C.G. (1978) "Feed a Cold, Starve a Fever" – Folk Models of Infection in an English Suburban Community and their Relation to Medical Treatment. *Culture, Medicine and Psychiatry* 2: 107–37.

Jordan, B. (1977) The Self-Diagnosis of Early Pregnancy: An Investigation of Lay Competence. *Medical Anthropology* 1: 1–38.

Kelman, S. (1975) The Social Nature of the Definition Problem in Health. *International Journal of Health Services* 5: 625–41.

Kleiber, N. and Light, L. (1978) *Caring for Ourselves: An Alternative Structure for Health Care*. Vancouver, Canada: University of British Columbia School of Nursing.

Landy, D. (ed.) (1977) *Culture, Disease and Healing: Studies in Medical Anthropology*. New York: Macmillan.

Leach, E.R. (1954) *Political Systems of Highland Burma*. Boston: Beacon Press.

Lennane, K.J. and Lennane, R.J. (1973) Alleged Psychogenic Disorders in Women – A Possible Manifestation of Sexual Prejudice. *New England Journal of Medicine* 288: 288–92.

Lewin, E. (1977) Feminist Ideology and the Meaning of Work: The Case of Nursing. *Catalyst* 10 and 11: 78–103.

—— (1985) By Design: Reproductive Strategies and the Meaning of Motherhood. In H. Homans (ed.) *Power and Reproduction*. London: Heinemann.

—— (forthcoming) *The Contours of Single Motherhood*. Ithaca, NY: Cornell University Press.

Lewin, E. and Olesen, V. (1980) Lateralness in Women's Work: New Views on Success. *Sex Roles* 6: 619–29.

Lewis, G.L. (1976) A View of Sickness in New Guinea. In J. Loudon (ed.) *Social Anthropology and Medicine*. New York: Academic Press.

Lipman-Blumen, J. and Bernard, J. (1979) *Sex Roles and Social Policy*. Beverly Hills: Sage Publications.

Locker, D. (1981) *Symptoms and Illness*. London and New York: Tavistock Publications.

Lopata, H. (1971) *Occupation: Housewife*. New York: Oxford University Press.

Lopate, C. (1968) *Women in Medicine*. Baltimore: The Johns Hopkins University Press.

Luker, K. (1975) *Taking Chances: Abortion and the Decision Not to Contracept*. Berkeley: University of California Press.

Macintyre, S. (1977) *Single and Pregnant*. London: Croom Helm.

McKinlay, J. (1973) Social Networks, Lay Consultation and Help-Seeking Behavior. *Social Forces* 51: 275–92.

Nakamura, R.T. and Smallwood, S. (1980) *The Politics of Policy Implementation*. New York: St Martin's Press.

Nelson, C. (1975) Reconceptualizing Health Care. In V. Olesen (ed.) *Women and Their Health: Research Implications for a New Era*. National Center for Health Services Research, DHEW Publication No. (HRA) 77-3138.

Olesen, V.L. (1980) Gender and Medicine: A Critique of Contemporary Medical Sociology in the United States. Unpublished plenary address to the British Sociological Association Medical Sociology Group, University of Warwick.

Olesen, V.L. and Katsuranis, M.F. (1978) Urban Nomads: Women in Temporary Clerical Services. In A. Stromberg and S. Harkess (eds) *Women Working*. Palo Alto, CA: Mayfield.

Pill, R. and Stott, N.C.H. (1982) Concepts of Illness Causation and Responsibility: Some Preliminary Data from a Sample of Working-Class Mothers. *Social Science and Medicine* 26: 43-52.

Prather, J. and Fidell, L.S. (1975) Sex Differences in the Content and Styles of Medical Advertising. *Social Science and Medicine* 9: 23-6.

Rabinow, P. and Sullivan, W.M. (1979) *Interpretive Social Science*. Berkeley: University of California Press.

Rein, M. (1976) *Social Science and Public Policy*. New York: Penguin Books.

Rivlin, A. (1971) *Systematic Thinking for Social Action*. Washington, DC: The Brookings Institution.

Robinson, D. (1971) *The Process of Becoming Ill*. London: Routledge & Kegan Paul.

Ruzek, S.B. (1978) *The Women's Health Movement. Feminist Alternatives to Medical Control*. New York: Praeger.

—— (1980) Medical Response to Women's Health Activities: Conflict, Accommodation and Cooptation. *Research in the Sociology of Health Care* 1: 335-54.

Scambler, A., Scambler, G., and Craig, D. (1981) Kinship and Friendship Networks, Women's Demand for Primary Care. *Journal of the Royal College of General Practitioners* 31: 746-50.

Scott, R. A. and Shore, A. (1974) Sociology and Policy Analysis. *The American Sociologist* 9: 51-9.

Scully, D. and Bart, P. (1973) A Funny Thing Happened on the Way to the Orifice. *American Journal of Sociology* 74: 1045-050.

Seaman, B. (1969) *The Doctors' Case Against the Pill*. New York: Avon.

—— (1972) *Free and Female*. New York: Coward, McCann & Geoghegan.

Shaw, N. (1974) *Forced Labor: Maternity Care in the United States*. New York: Pergamon Press.

Shryrock, R.G. (1966) *Medicine in America*. Baltimore: The Johns Hopkins University Press.

Sims, M. (1981) Abortion: The Myth of the Golden Age. In B. Hutter and G. Williams (eds) *Controlling Women*. London: Croom Helm.

Stacey, M. (1981) The Division of Labor Revisited, or Overcoming the Two Adams. In P. Abrams, R. Deem, J. Finch, and P. Rock (eds) *Practice and Progress: British Sociology: 1950–1980*. London: Allen & Unwin.

—— (1982) Comment on the paper "The Political Economy of Sexism in Industrial Health" by Marcia Felker. *Social Science and Medicine* 16: 3–13.

Ungerson, C. (1983) Women and Caring: Skills, Tasks and Taboos. In E. Gamarnikow, D. Morgan, J. Purvis, and D. Taylorson (eds) *The Public and the Private*. London: Heinemann.

Weiss, J. (1976) Using Social Science for Social Policy. *Policy Studies Journal* 4: 234–38.

West, C. (1984) *Routine Complications: Troubles With Talk Between Doctors and Patients*. Bloomington: Indiana University Press.

Zola, I.K. (1973) Pathways to the Doctor: From Person to Patient. *Social Science and Medicine* 7: 677–89.

Two

Providers, negotiators, and mediators:

women as the hidden carers

Hilary Graham

Introduction

This chapter describes the informal, unpaid work which women
do to protect and promote the health of others. It examines the
domestic activities which sustain, literally and symbolically,
what we know as the British way of life.

Like the formal systems of health care in Britain – the
National Health Service (NHS) and the expanding industries of
private medicine – the informal health service is geared to the
swift and efficient delivery of specialist skills to those in need
(Litwak 1965: 310). Yet, despite its social and economic significance, the organization of this most fundamental system of
health care has not been centralized. The informal services of
women are distributed neither through the market nor through
the welfare state. Instead, informal health care has remained
part of the domestic economy, molded by the relations which
govern everyday life in the family and community. In particular, it is seen to be shaped by two convergent sets of social
relations: first, by a sexual division of labor in which men make
money and women keep the family going, and second, by a

spatial division of labor whereby the community becomes the setting for routine care and maintenance and the institutions of medicine are the location for the acquisition and application of specialist skills. These two dimensions have been closely related historically, with the process of male domination converging with the process of professionalization to define the health work of women (Gamarnikow 1978; Hearn 1982).

To understand the experience of caring we therefore need a perspective which addresses the factors both of gender and of privacy. This chapter contributes to this perspective, by identifying three aspects of women's health work: providing for health, teaching for health, and, in times of crisis, mediating professional help.

As the providers of health, women are responsible for securing the domestic conditions necessary for the maintenance of health and for recovery from sickness. Women's health work involves the provision of a materially-secure environment: a warm, clean home where both young and old can be protected against danger and disease, and a diet sufficient in quantity and quality to meet their nutritional needs. It involves, too, the provision of a social environment conducive to normal health and development. It is a woman's job to orchestrate social relations within the home, and to minimize the health-damaging insecurities and anxieties which can arise when these relations go awry. The second dimension of the informal health service, the negotiation of health, springs from the first. In laboring for their families' health, women are also teaching it. In setting standards of diet and discipline, women not only facilitate health in a biological sense; they transmit a culture in which health and illness can be understood. Women's health work is not exclusively private, restricted to the confines of family and community. Women also serve as mediators of outside services. Their responsibilities within the domestic health service unavoidably bring them into contact with professional welfare workers: the doctor and health visitor, the social worker and the district nurse. Their caring role places them at the interface between the family and the state, as the go-betweens linking the informal health-care system with the formal apparatus of the welfare state.

The nature of this health work is explored in three sections. The first considers the way in which it has been represented within the two disciplines most deeply committed to the study of health and welfare, namely medical sociology and social policy. The second examines the experience of informal caring, focusing on women's role as health providers. The third sets this experience in a wider political context, looking at the recent devclopments in health policy which shift the burden of caring from the public to the private domain.

Perspectives on women's health work within medical sociology and social policy

The informal organization of care has long had its place on the agenda of medical sociology. Freidson argued over twenty years ago that both "the organization of medical practice" and "the organization of community life" must be addressed when seeking answers to questions about health behavior (1961: 11). The conceptual framework he advocates involves "two major structures, the lay and the professional, in interaction, meshing at some points and failing to mesh, or clashing at others" (1961: 13).

Writers on social policy, too, have recorded the significance of the informal institutions lying beyond and beneath the welfare state. A quarter-century ago Titmuss argued that an appreciation of both the formal and informal systems of welfare should be a hallmark of the new discipline (Rose 1981). He noted that state intervention was predicated on the existence of a network of caring relationships linking family, friends, and neighbors. The discipline, he concluded, therefore required a dual focus:

> On the one hand, we are interested in the machinery of administration which organizes and dispenses various forms of assistance; on the other, in the lives, the needs and the mutual relations of those members of the community for whom the services are provided.   (Titmuss 1958: 14–15)

Despite such appeals for a broad perspective, the boundaries of both disciplines have followed those of the formal institutions of health and welfare. Medical sociology and social policy concern themselves with the social relations which operate within medicine and the social services (Stacey with Homans 1978; Rose 1981). In consequence, the informal sector features as the site for the consumption and not the production of services. It is represented, not as an arrangement for the provision of care, but as a reservoir of individuals waiting, in varying states of readiness, to take up their allotted places in the professional domain. Individuals thus appear not as wives and husbands, mothers and daughters, sisters and brothers, linked to each other through a complex set of gender and generation-based relations: they feature as cases and clients, patients and recipients, attenders and defaulters on their way to what in Britain is tellingly called "the *primary* health-care team."

Perhaps this is too harsh a characterization of the two disciplines. Indeed, a major realignment of medical sociology and social policy is in progress, a realignment specifically concerned with the impact of gender and the organization of lay care on the provision of welfare (Stacey 1981). Nonetheless, as within sociology as a whole, the two dimensions remain separate. Rather than confronting the integration of gender and privacy, social scientists have evolved two modes of analysis: one to explain the sexual division of labor within medicine and welfare; and the other to explain the division between the public and private domain.

First, there are the recent studies examining gender divisions (for example, Navarro 1976; Levitt 1977; Leeson and Gray 1978). However, while each seeks to illuminate the position of women as the providers of health services, the illumination is restricted to the professional sphere. Thus when Navarro seeks to uncover "the problems encountered by all women who are producers of services in the health sector" (1976: 170), he includes only those health workers who sell their skills on the market. "All women" and "the health sector," it seems, are embracive and unproblematic categories. Similarly Levitt, in her review of *Men and Women as Providers of Health Care*, is concerned exclusively with the public domain. While noting that "women are the overwhelming majority of health care providers" (1977: 395), her analysis does not take her into the family and community where that majority is most visibly concentrated. Again, Leeson and Gray in *Women and Medicine* clearly state their interest in "all women health workers" (1978: 9), and devote a major section of their book to "women providers of health care." However, their concern is with the exclusion of women from the domain of professional medicine in the past, and their position as doctors, nurses, and ancillary workers in the medical institutions of the present.

These studies have undoubtedly illuminated the nature of women's contribution to health. Yet, by equating health work with professional care, they extend our vision on one dimension only. While giving priority to gender, they eclipse the private domain. As a result, their perspectives on women's health work tend to be framed through categories designed for the public sector of medicine and welfare. This tendency manifests itself in a variety of ways. First, rather than seeing women's health work as part of an autonomous and authentic structure of care, researchers have sought to identify those women who, in pre-industrial societies, occupied positions analogous to the professionals of today. Women feature not as mothers and neighbors routinely engaged in the business of maintaining health, but as midwives, old wives, wise women, and handywomen who, like their professional equivalents, offer help and advice in times of crisis (for example, Ehrenreich and English 1976; Oakley 1976; Donnison 1977). Second, and relatedly, studies of women's health work display an orientation to the management of illness (and childbirth) rather than the production of health. Like the NHS in whose shadow it sits, lay care is seen as a service for the sick. For example, Ehrenreich and English define their project in *Witches, Midwives and Nurses* as "a beginning of the research which will have to be done to recapture our history as health workers" (1976: 21). But theirs is a project wholly concerned with women as healers: diagnosing and curing in the guise of witches, midwives, and nurses. Third, as Versluysen (1980) notes, this concern with the preprofessional components of women's health work has led to an emphasis upon those moments in history where the traditional healing and nursing functions of women have been absorbed into the male-dominated structures of professional medicine. As a result, the routine business of keeping individuals alive and functioning has gone uncharted. We still know little about the ways in which women have provided, negotiated, and mediated health throughout history; we can only guess at the division of resources and responsibilities within the community on which this health work rested.

To some extent, a second group of studies concerned with what Titmuss called "the lives, the needs and mutual relations of the community" (1958: 15) remedies these deficiencies. These studies place the separation of the private and public domains at the center of analysis, viewing them as two mutually dependent but distinct systems of welfare. The most significant contributions have been Freidson's model of the lay referral system (Freidson 1960, 1961) and the Marxist feminist accounts of reproduction (McIntosh 1979).

Freidson's concept of the lay referral system provides a way of integrating an analysis of informal health care into mainstream functionalist sociology. As a corrective to the dominant paradigm which defines health care in terms of the practice of professional medicine, Freidson argues that there is not one but two systems which determine health beliefs and practices. He identifies (1960: 374) "the lay referral system, which consists in a variable lay culture and a network of personal influences . . . and the professional referral system of medical culture and institutions." The lay referral system encompasses important features of informal health care, outlined in the previous section. Its role in the negotiation of health, in the transmission of a culture in which health can be understood, is explicitly referred to by Freidson (1961: 147). The mediating role that women play, in facilitating the involvement of professionals at times of crisis, is also accommodated within Freidson's model. He notes (1961: 146) how the lay referral system provides "a network of consultants" who "impose form on the process of seeking help."

While Freidson spells out the negotiating and mediating functions of the lay referral system, he does not expand upon its role in providing the material conditions for health. From our point of view this is a significant omission. In identifying the cultural rather than the material dimensions of the lay referral system, Freidson comes to define it as a typical, but not essential, component of everyday life. Rather than providing the preconditions for health, the system is seen as an atavistic feature of industrial society which modern communities can do without. His typology thus extends from communities with a "highly extended" referral structure to those with a "severely truncated" structure or with "none at all" (1960: 377).

Freidson's interest in the private domain springs from his concern with professional dominance and the division of labor within health care which sustains it. Marxists, by contrast, have sought to incorporate the private domain within their analysis of class domination and the economic division of labor from which it derives. Here we find the material dimension of health work, obscured in Freidson's schema, given primary attention. The emphasis shifts from the diagnosis of illness to the maintenance of health: it is reproduction and not referral that is the phenomenon to be explained. The private domain is given a more precise location in the structures of the family, with its contribution measured in both material and cultural terms.

At first glance, the change of emphasis looks promising. Like Freidson's concept of referral, reproduction seems to encompass many features of women's health work. As McIntosh notes (1979: 153), the concept refers to the "processes whereby people are replaced, repaired and replenished from day to day as well as from generation to generation." Such a definition neatly incorporates much of what women do in the private domain as the providers, negotiators, and mediators of health. The identification of the family as the primary unit of reproduction, too, seems a useful advance on the more nebulous concept of the lay referral system, and serves to highlight the economic contribution which women make in caring for their kith and kin (Delamont 1980: 101).

But despite these advances, a Marxist analysis of informal health work remains unsatisfactory. Different in origin and orientation, it none the less contains the same basic limitations as Freidson's scheme. These limitations lie beyond the relative weight the two perspectives give to the material and cultural components of caring. They are found, instead, in their failure to adequately confront the social divisions in which caring occurs. Neither adequately deals with the dual and intersecting forces of the public and the private on the one hand and gender on the other.

First, in both perspectives, the private sphere is defined in terms of its subordination to and functions for the public domain. In Freidson's model, the primary orientation is to the world of professional medicine. The concept of the lay referral system is introduced not to understand the structure and organization of the informal health service but, as he notes himself, to identify "aspects of client experience that may significantly affect medical practice" (1960: 375). Although the focus is on the private domain, individuals are defined through their relationship to the formal structures of medicine: as "more or less organized potential clients" and "prospective patients." The lay referral system is located through its cultural and spatial proximity to professional medicine, and not in terms of the social relations of gender and generation which underpin family life.

Interestingly, a similar criticism can be levelled against Marxist accounts of the private domain. Again, activities within the family are defined through and in terms of the activities of the public domain. Reproduction, like referral, is introduced as the concept which specifies the nature of the relationship between the two spheres (McIntosh 1979: 155). The family is cast as the setting in which the reproductive work of capitalism gets done, work defined in categories with a direct and measurable relationship to the productive domain. Like Freidson's vocabulary of potential clients and prospective patients, these categories have the effect of distancing and sanitizing women's health work. Lost is the daily reality of caring. Housework, once described as "a worm eating away at your ideas . . . a compulsive circle like a pet mouse in its cage spinning round on its exercise wheel, unable to get off" (Peckham Women's Liberation Workshop, quoted in Rowbotham 1973: 71), is transformed into "a cheap way of servicing the worker" (Wilson 1977: 62). Caring for children, "a complicated, rich, ambivalent, vexing, joyous activity" (Elshtain 1981: 234), emerges simply as the means of "ensuring the adequate reproduction of the labour force," with marriage providing men with "relief from the alienation of the workplace" (Foreman 1977: 102). Lost, too, is the psychology of caring, a feeling for the sense of responsibility which propels women into reproducing the labor force and overcoming its alienation. As Stacey and Price (1981) have argued, we need a perspective which takes account of the social relations of intimacy and family loyalty if we are to understand women's work within the home.

Beginning our analysis with the experiences and social relations of the carer involves the articulation of her gender. Here we confront the second limitation of the Marxist and Freidsonian accounts of lay care. For both accounts are "sex blind": neither explains (or even records) the gender of the carers. Although Freidson's data (1961: 145) and the findings from more recent studies (Litman 1974) suggest that the "friends" and "relatives" who people the referral structure are typically women, an appreciation of sexual divisions is lost in an analysis couched in the gender-neutral terminology of "lay referral," "lay men," and "lay consultants." A similar myopia has been detected within Marxism (Bruegel 1978; Hartmann 1981). They argue that the Marxist account of the private domain is one of "empty places": like Freidson, Marxists can explain why a lay structure of consultants and carers exists, but give us no clues as to why these positions should be occupied by women. "Marxist categories, like capital itself, are sex-blind. The categories of Marxism cannot tell us who will fill the empty places. Marxist analysis of the woman question has suffered from this basic problem" (Hartmann 1981: 11).

Sex-blindness has particularly serious consequences for our analysis of women's health work. A way of understanding gender, a way of understanding women's subordinate position in the private and public domain, is essential if we are to understand why there is an informal health-care system at all. The logic of capitalist development has involved the collectivization of work, with more and more areas of life organized through the machinery of the market. Health care has not been exempt from this process. Yet as noted in the introduction to this chapter, the development of the National Health Service and private medicine has excluded the provision of basic care during health and illness. The provision of food, warmth, and comfort continues to be organized on an informal, individual, and unpaid basis within the home. The possibilities for the socialization of these essential caring services are limited, it seems, because the family can provide them more cheaply than either the state or private industry. This is true only because women's labor in the home is "free." It is "a given feature of life and a factor which does not have to be taken into account in economic calculations" (Thomas and Shannon 1982: 7).

But it is a factor which has to be taken into account in an analysis of women's health work. For this, we need to recognize the forces within our social structures which make women's labors "free." We need, further, to find a way of giving voice to the experiences of individuals locked by those forces into the role of carer.

Women as providers, negotiators, and mediators

Although the social-scientific perspectives on health and welfare have traditionally distanced themselves from the private world of women's work, the experience of caring has not gone unrecorded. There is an extensive, though largely untapped, legacy of historical data contained in diaries, handbooks, and letters (Versluysen 1980). There are, in addition, the historical and contemporary writings collected as part of political campaigns to improve the working conditions of the nation's carers (for example, Women's Cooperative Guild 1978; Spring Rice 1981; Equal Opportunities Commission 1981, 1982). The tradition of research into poverty, too, provides another source of data on the harsh reality of caring (for example, Rowntree 1901; Wilson and Herbert 1978; Townsend 1979; Blaxter and Paterson 1982). This tradition, now a century old, presents something of a paradox. For it seems that, although we lack a theoretical framework through which to understand women's role in health and welfare, it. is one which has been incorporated into the design of empirical research. As a *sine qua non* of survey investigation, social scientists recognize that collecting data on the conditions of health and the organization of care means going "down among the women" (Weldon 1973). It was a principle built into the nineteenth-century investigations. Rowntree (1901), for example, in his study of the health of the people of York, relied on information collected from housewives: over 11,000 of them representing 46,000 people. In contemporary studies, too, women are assumed to be the family caretakers. For example, Blaxter and Paterson conclude in their study of the transmission of health beliefs (1982: 194) that they were "right to anticipate that it would be the women of the families who would be eager to talk about health matters," noting that "similar interviews with an older generation of men would have been much more difficult."

What can be learned about the caring role from women who have been "eager to talk about health matters"? The investigations of social scientists and political campaigners document the subjective dimensions missing from the theoretical accounts considered in the previous section. They highlight, too, the social forces which mold the experience of caring. They detail the way in which the division of labor between the sexes converges with that which separates the public from the private domain. Margery Spring Rice, for example, in her study of working-class women in the 1930s, brings out clearly how gender and privacy intersect to create the specific conditions of women's health work:

> It is abundantly clear from the accounts given by the women themselves in this investigation that they are subject to many hardships from which circumstances or they themselves protect their husbands. To begin with, the working mother is almost entirely cut off from contact with the world outside her house. She eats, sleeps, "rests" on the scene of her labor and her labor is entirely solitary.
>
> (Spring Rice 1981: 105)

These observations are echoed in contemporary accounts concerned with the plight of those who labor within the home. One recent study of childrearing, for instance, noted that "the demands of caring for young children are met very largely by mothers. . . . Much of this working time must be spent at home, away from other adults" (Hughes *et al.* 1980: 15, 17). Similarly, a study of community care concluded that "the family is very much at the center of the caring function. . . . Family care generally means care by women, and as things stand the caring role can, and frequently does, restrict severely their opportunities in the wider society" (Equal Opportunities Commission 1982: 1 and 2).

In seeking to understand how gender and privacy intersect to structure women's experience and identity, Dahl and Snare introduced the notion of "the coercion of privacy." Women's commitments within the private domain, they suggest, restrain them "to the extent that we might speak of them living their lives in a private prison" (Dahl and Snare 1978: 21). In this prison, experiences become personalized, with problems seen as self-inflicted and failures seen as a cause for self-recrimination and blame. Caring becomes an experience in which women identify themselves as "the person beyond whom there is no recourse or appeal" (Hughes *et al.* 1980: 18).

> Over and above the physical demands and restrictions that mothers face, there is the added burden for most of feeling continually and ultimately responsible for the health,

development and happiness of their children. However
much help a mother may get in bringing up her children, she
is still likely to feel that she is the person beyond whom there
is no recourse or appeal, and who is answerable for whatever
happens.   (Hughes *et al.* 1980: 18)

This sense of responsibility appears as the central motif in
women's accounts of caring. It seems to be the concept through
which women speak of their work in the private domain (Gavron
1966; Graham 1976, 1979, 1982; Rapoport and Rapoport 1977).
Belief in women's responsibility for health underlines, too, the
organization of paid health work and the administration of the
welfare state. Whether we look at community care or social-
security benefits, at the history of women nurses and doctors or
the development of social work, we find enshrined the principle
that women care for the family (see, for example, Adams 1971;
Gamarnikow 1978; Land 1978; Finch and Groves 1980).

When put into practice, this principle means more work for
women. Caring is a highly labor-intensive role (Oakley 1974).
Even for those who escape into the public world of paid employment, health work remains hard work. As one carer in a recent
survey of women factory workers explains, ''I get up at about
quarter to five . . . and I never really do sit down. . . . I can't sit
down if I know something has to be done, I'd rather get stuck
into it. I go to bed between 10 and 11'' (Shimmin, McNally, and
Liff 1981: 347).

Within this relentless schedule, it is possible to detect the
kind of responsibilities which structure the carer's day. In the
introduction, I suggested that the carer acts simultaneously as
the provider, negotiator, and mediator of health within the
home. Of the three, the provision of health is the most life-
sustaining and labor-intensive aspect of caring. It is the one,
moreover, which provides the context in which both education
and professional intervention occur. Yet it is the least well-
documented area of women's health work. It is here, close to
the reproductive heart of family life, that the coercion of privacy seems to operate most effectively, locking carers in and
researchers out. Social-scientific interest in health intensifies
the further we move from the point of reproduction towards the
intersection of the private and public domain. Thus the work of
negotiation and mediation has been incorporated through the

concept of the lay referral system into studies of health beliefs and patterns of utilization. By comparison, we know very little about the physical and psychological labor of sustaining human life. It is this area that social scientists need to analyze if they are to increase their understanding of the processes which govern health within the home.

Much of the scientific literature on health provision relates to household patterns of food consumption. Like shelter and warmth, food is a basic requirement for health. But while housing and fuel are relatively fixed items in the family budget, spending on food can be controlled (at least in theory) by the carer. It is therefore the item most likely to be cut when resources are limited (Burghes 1980). In such circumstances, it tends to be the wife–mother who restricts her food consumption in order to maintain standards for the rest of the family. Observers in the nineteenth century noted repeatedly that "the wife, in very poor families, is probably the worst fed of the household" (Oren 1974: 227). In the early twentieth century, the Women's Cooperative Guild recorded that "in a working class home, if there is any saving to be done, it is not the husband and children, but the mother who makes her meals off scraps which remain over, or 'plays with meatless bones' " (1978: 5). Even in more affluent households today, women's responsibilities as providers involve them in planning menus and preparing meals which rarely reflect their own food preferences (Kerr and Charles 1982; Murcott 1983).

The patterns of responsibility which underlie the organization of the family meal appear to reflect principles on which family health as a whole is organized. In the provision of other health resources, women again have been found to act as buffers, maintaining the health of others by absorbing the shortages themselves. Land, in her study of large families, noted how the scarce resources of space, warmth, and clothing were also unevenly allocated, with the women carrying a disproportionate burden. She concludes:

> The impact of a low income, bad housing, and insufficient food, is not borne equally by all members of the family. Resources are allocated by reference to custom or tradition and the interests of some members of the family are sacrificed to the interests of others. In particular, it is noticeable

that in many respects the mother of the family puts the needs of her husband and her children before her own.

(Land 1977: 174–75)

Women's responsibilities for health clearly involve them in the careful budgeting of finite physical resources. But being a provider involves more than ensuring an adequate supply of food and warmth. It involves the giving of time, attention, and affection to those in your charge. These less tangible resources are commonly regarded as the crucial ones which mothers provide for their children, their husbands, and their dependent relatives. Yet these are the resources for which the demand can appear infinite, and where shortages are not so easily contained by self-sacrifice. As Rowbotham observes, "the housewife tries to save time, she tries to accumulate space and time in order to push out the boundaries [but] the attempt disintegrates continuously" (1973: 71). The arrival of a handicapped relative, an elderly parent, or a new baby places additional demands on the mother's time and energy, restricting the areas in which further savings can be made. As one new mother, searching to find the rest-time necessary for successful breast feeding, put it:

> Well, I try to rest, but I don't manage it. Everybody says "rest as much as you can," but you never get a chance. If there isn't his nappies to wash, he's crying, he wants feeding. And then you've got your own housework to get in round it, and dinners to get ready for Dads and teas ready for Dads.

(Graham 1980: 173)

A coercion of privacy again results in women lacking both the material support and the personal inclination to seek outside assistance. State policies in the field of health and welfare have sought to ensure that material support does not threaten "the nineteenth century doctrine of the spheres, which made women's proper place the home" (Lewis 1980: 447; see also Land 1978). Lack of inclination stems from the ideology of caring itself. Caring, it seems, whether for a young baby, a handicapped child, or an elderly relative, means shouldering alone a "constant burden" (Voysey 1975). It involves organizing both the labor of caring, and the accounts one gives of it to outsiders, in such a way that the respectability and sanctity of the family is maintained (Voysey 1975). Whatever the personal costs, outsiders must remain convinced that the family is coping (Graham 1982). The situation demands that carers find ways of reconciling the responsibilities of the caring role on their own. The strategies, however, invariably prove contradictory in their effects, jeopardizing health in order to protect it.

Sometimes these solitary strategies involve sacrificing the health of one dependent in order to promote the health of another. In our study of motherhood, for example, women found the benefits that breast-feeding brought to the new baby were measured in costs for the rest of the household (Graham and McKee 1980). The cost-saving alternative, bottle-feeding, was similarly problematic, with the baby's needs subordinated to those of older family members (Graham 1980).

More typically, it appears that the burden of sacrifice falls not on others, but on the woman herself. The labor of caring is sustained by a finely tuned repertoire of habits and hobbies, woven deep into the structure of the health worker's day. Some of these undoubtedly assist the carer without harming her. Listening to the radio, for instance, brings solace to millions of housewives but carries no government health-warning. Other habits, although undeniably sustaining, are also destructive. Cigarettes, psychotropic drugs, and alcohol offer women this contradictory kind of support, helping and hurting them at the same time. Here we see the complex nature of women's role as provider depicted in sharp relief. The physical and emotional resources necessary for caring, it seems, are secured through an edifice of health-threatening habits necessary for her own survival.

Smoking, for example, provides a way of coping with the constant and unremitting demands of caring, a way of temporarily escaping without leaving the room. One mother in my study of pregnancy described the importance of cigarettes in the following way:

> After lunch, I'll clear away and wash up and put the telly on for Stevie [her son]. I'll have a sit down on the sofa, with a cigarette and maybe a cup of tea. It's lovely, it's the one time in the day I really enjoy and I know Stevie won't disturb me.
> (Graham 1976: 403)

Another mother pinpointed the functions of smoking more succinctly: "I couldn't stop, I just couldn't. It keeps me calm. It's me one relaxation is smoking.'' This theme has been amplified in a recent report on women smokers, where Jacobson (1981) argues that smoking provides a means of containing (and surviving) the conflicts that spring from women's caring role. As the nature of this role becomes more complex and more anxiety-producing, women have turned to smoking "as a safety valve, an alternative to letting off steam. They smoke not to accompany expressions of frustration and anxiety, but *instead of expressing these feelings*" (Jacobson 1981: 32; italics in original).

These kinds of coping strategies can be seen as a response to the coercive privacy of the home by those left to provide for the health needs of the family on their own. The coercion of privacy shapes, too, the way in which women tackle their responsibilities as negotiators and mediators, although, for reasons of space, it is possible only to outline the processes involved.

The wife–mother is thought to be the primary agent in health socialization (Litman 1974).[1] However, "teaching about health" is unlikely to be a formal part of the carer's day. Instead, health education seems to be a ubiquitous and unavoidable feature of the everyday strategies that women employ to keep themselves and their families going (Graham 1983). "Bad" habits like smoking, as professional health teachers are at pains to publicize, provide a model for the rest of the family. Being an effective health educator therefore means not only taking responsibility for the education of others, but, somehow, adjusting one's coping strategies in order to "lead by example." The Flora Project for Heart Disease Prevention, for example, lists what are optimistically labelled "simple precautions" to help wives reduce the risk of heart attack in their husbands. The precautions, however, add up to a change of life-style for the carer as profound as that advocated for the spouse. Moreover, while promoting the health of the husband, these precautions may prove incompatible with the fragile arrangement of coping strategies on which the caring role rests. Domestic routines to ensure the long-term health of husbands may thus only be achieved at the cost of the short-term health of their wives. The authors advise their female readers that:

> It is highly unlikely that you will persuade your husband to give up smoking if you smoke yourself. Show your husband that you intend to deal firmly with the smoking habit. . . .

The sensible wife will first decide whether her husband should lose weight, and then plan his menu accordingly. Pressure and pace at work, family responsibilities and general worries can be controlled to some extent by the man himself. . . . But perhaps more important is the tolerance and understanding of his wife. Let your husband talk about his worries, and whenever possible take the work from him – draft letters, pay bills, arrange for the plumber to come yourself. (Flora Project n.d.: 5–6)

The coercion of privacy, and the coping strategies to which it gives rise, also structure the way in which women tackle their tasks as mediator. Social scientists concur that it is the wife–mother who, as the principal carer, acts as the gatekeeper between the family and the outside world. She is the one who makes the decision about the utilization of lay and professional services (Carpenter 1980: 1213); she is also the one with whom outsiders negotiate (Cockburn 1977: 58). These transactions typically occur at the point where the resources of informal caring are exhausted; where, in Zola's schema (1973), the accomodation of symptoms breaks down. This breakdown is often imbued with moral significance; a symbol that the woman has failed to find private and solitary ways of fulfilling her health responsibilities. As a result, women appear to be particularly vulnerable to labelling by professionals when the welfare of their family is at risk (Dobash and Dobash 1980).

The process of mediation implies that there is a limit to women's responsibilities. It implies that, on certain terms and conditions, the agents of the public domain will shoulder the burden of meeting the health needs of the family. Over the last decade, the boundaries of private and public responsibility have been redrawn, with the care of the elderly and mentally handicapped, for example, increasingly located in the private domain. With these boundary changes go major alterations to the job description of the nation's hidden carers. It is these alterations, and the ideology to which they speak, which are addressed in the final section of this chapter.

Caring and the new health policies

The social divisions of gender and privacy not only mold the personal experiences of caring. They provide the framework in which state policies have evolved. In the legislation on maternity services and family allowances, social security and invalidity care, British governments have built a welfare state which assumes (and prescribes) a traditional nuclear family in which "women care for the young, the sick and the old, and, most important, for able-bodied men (their husbands)" (Land 1978: 257; see also Davin 1978; Finch and Groves 1980; Lewis 1980).

Lacking an explicit family policy, the assumptions about women's unpaid role have remained more deeply buried within the fabric of British welfare practice than within that of other western countries (Land and Parker 1978). However, in the current period of retrenchment, this doctrine is being publicly stated. The present government began its term of office with a series of prescient statements about the preservation of the patriarchal family and the unpaid roles which women perform within it (see Coussins and Coote 1981). The field of health and welfare, clearly, offers great potential for restructuring along these lines, with the state withdrawing services in order to enable the family to assume its rightful place as "the front line when Gran needs help" (Patrick Jenkin, when Secretary of State for Health and Social Services, quoted in Coussins and Coote 1981: 8).

This restructuring has been viewed by some social scientists as indicating a radical departure from the welfare principles of the postwar period (for example, David and Shaw 1980; Coussins and Coote 1981). The assertion of women's domestic responsibilities is seen as a response to the particular political conditions of the 1980s, as an expedient way of controlling public expenditure. These conditions, in turn, are traced back to tendencies apparent since the early 1970s, when political concern with the cost of the welfare state began to dominate social policy (Conference of Socialist Economists 1979). While not denying that the laissez-faire doctrines of the present government, and the cuts in welfare services in particular, have adversely affected the nation's unpaid carers, it is important to recognize that the changes are of degree rather than kind. It should not be forgotten that the family has traditionally provided the ideological and material context in which state policy has evolved. It is not "the cuts" which have created women's caring role; they have served only to highlight the way in which state policies have always worked to sustain a particular family form and a particular set of responsibilities for the women who labor within it.

This style of mediation between the public and private domains is well documented in the fields of prevention and community care (Graham 1979; Finch and Groves 1980). Both concepts have a long history, which can be traced back to the origins of western medicine (Dubos 1960). Both were recognized, at least in principle, in the National Health Act of 1946, with community care receiving a further impetus in the 1959 Mental Health Act and the 1968 Seebohm Report. However, both concepts have enjoyed a renaissance in the last decade. Since the mid-1970s, successive governments have searched for ways to control social-policy expenditure in the face of economic recession. Prevention and community care have served as "low cost solutions" (Department of Health and Social Security 1976a: 12) to the seemingly insatiable demand for professional medical care. Prevention, in advocating a self-help approach to health care, is seen as a way of combating the so-called "diseases of affluence"; community care is identified as a cut-price option for the treatment of its victims. Both place the responsibility for health and health care on genderless "individuals" and "communities" in the private domain. As the policy document *Care in Action* states:

> We all have a personal responsibility for our own health. We also have a duty to help one another. . . . The prevention of mental and physical ill-health is a prime objective, and an area in which the individual has clear responsibilities. . . . It has been a major policy objective for many years to foster and develop community care for the main client groups – elderly, mentally ill, mentally handicapped and disabled people and children.
>
> (Department of Health and Social Security 1981a: i, 11, 21)

Other documents spell out these proposals in more detail. In the field of community care, for example, the White Paper on the elderly, *Growing Older*, makes it clear that the private domain is to provide both the context and the resources for the day-to-day care of dependents. It notes "the primary sources of support and care for elderly people are informal and voluntary. . . . Care *in* the community must increasingly mean care *by* the community" (Department of Health and Social Security 1981b: 1, 9: italics in original). Empirical studies have indicated more precisely the nature of this community. Abrams notes "the bulk of helping that is reported as community care turns out on closer scrutiny to be kin care" or, more precisely, as the Equal Opportunities Commission found in their study, care by female kin (Abrams 1977: 134). The report concludes that "most carers are women and . . . most women will at some time in their lives become carers" (Equal Opportunities Commission 1982: 4).

Becoming a carer involves meeting the needs of those who fall victim to illness and invalidity. It involves, too, preventing the onset of ill-health in the young and able-bodied. Prevention, and the health education which accompanies it, have been major platforms of government strategy in the last decade, as anticipated in the 1976 consultative document *Prevention and Health: Everybody's Business* (Department of Health and Social Security 1976b). Although presented as "Everybody's Business," the policy has an implicit gender bias. For women in the home, the campaign to "Look After Yourself," championed by the Health Education Council, implies not only self-care. As the Flora Project for Heart Disease Prevention makes clear, it demands that women "Look After Them" as well. This gender bias is particularly marked in the field of child health, where the rhetoric of parental and family responsibility quickly gives way to specific advice aimed at mothers. It is they who are encouraged to breast-feed and give up smoking, to attend the child-health clinic and teach children good habits (Graham 1979, 1983). The logic of prevention implies major changes in the personal habits of the nation's carers, habits evolved, within the constraints of the private domain, to promote the health of the family. Further, as we saw in the previous section, the unhealthy activities which women are being asked to sacrifice – from smoking to going out to work – may be the very ones necessary for the health of the carer and her family. The paradox is compounded when we realize that, while it is the organization of women's labor in the private domain which is claiming the attention of policy-makers, it is the organization of labor in the public domain which is increasingly recognized to be the major source of ill-health (Doyal with Pennell 1979).

Interest in the private domain as the setting for health care does not end with prevention and community care. These concepts, dominant in the policy debates of the 1970s, have now been supplemented by two others. Like prevention and community care, these new policies seek to develop alternative non-government sources of health care, as so-called low-cost options which transfer the cost of caring from the state to the individual. The first, voluntary service, represents a logical extension of self-help and kin care. It expands them into a "voluntary sector" of unpaid workers who, individually or in organized groups, can be drawn into the caring process (see Department of Health and Social Security 1981a: 15, 48). Again, such policies presume (and relabel) the social networks and support services of women, with the examples making explicit what the gender-neutral vocabulary serves to hide. Thus while *Care in Action* talks of "volunteers," "neighbors," and "mutual aid groups," it cites the playgroup movement, a movement run by women, as "a magnificent example of what can be achieved with only limited support from the services: some 350,000 children can now go to playgroups organized by the community" (Department of Health and Social Security 1981a: 15).

The mobilization of volunteer labor raises questions not only for women working unpaid in the home, but for other groups of workers who are displaced from the labor market. Clearly, the specter of mass unemployment haunting Britain creates the possibility of a reserve army of carers, deployed to take over the tasks which were previously performed on a paid basis by health workers in the public domain. Voluntary work is already an accepted feature of government programs for unemployed school leavers, and is receiving increased financial support (Bulletin on Social Policy 1982). Its political implications were succinctly conveyed by the leader of the select committee on social services, William Rees-Davies, when he explained the place of voluntary work for the young unemployed:

> Those that are not involved in other training schemes should be offered this kind of work. Women would tend to go for work in the health service. Men's schemes would be much

wider, including work on farms and roads. If they did not
accept the job offered, they would not be paid. We have very
high waiting lists in the NHS. This is a very good source of
labor to tap.   (Rees-Davies 1981)

The politics of caring is implicated again in a second policy
option favored by the present government, private medicine.
The label "private medicine" fits uneasily, and perhaps confus-
ingly, into a discussion of the private and public domain. While
organized through the machinery of the public domain, private
medicine is paid for by individuals acting as private citizens and
not, as is the case with the NHS, by individuals in their public
role of taxpayers. However, the label is a useful one, for it
causes us to question the role of gender in the design and delivery
of private medicine. The recent blueprint for a British health-
care system based on private insurance, *The Litmus Papers*,
indicates that gender is essential to the plans to dismantle the
NHS (Seldon 1980). Private medicine, the authors argue, is more
in line with the realities of a profit-based economy and the
psychological needs of "ordinary people." "Ordinary people,"
it emerges, are men with family responsibilities:

> More and more ordinary people will be able to express the
> elemental instinctive urge to ensure the comfort of a child in
> pain, reassure a wife anxious about a symptom or save a
> parent neglected in a large ward. And they will put these
> intensely personal anxieties before the political appeal to
> continue supporting a system that *prevents them acting as
> human-beings* – as parents, husbands or children.
>   (Seldon 1980: 145; italics in original)

Despite such clues to the patriarchal character of private
medicine, the debate has been concerned primarily with class
divisions and the market place. Argument has hinged on the
question of whether private medicine rations the supply of
medical care as fairly and efficiently as the state (for example,
Counter Information Services 1980; Politics of Health Group
1981). What has been left unexplored is the likely impact of
private medicine on the informal sector in Britain. Unques-
tioned is how private medicine relates to the crisis in the
"other" national health service.

The development of private medicine assumes, and has particular implications for, the sexual division of labor within the

private domain. First, it is acknowledged that private medicine will intensify the bias towards surgical and hospital-based treatment (Counter Information Services 1980). However, the need for health care is greatest among those suffering from chronic conditions requiring long-term care rather than short-term cure. Fourteen per cent of Britain's population is over 65 and although the vast majority (over 90 per cent) live in "the community," nearly 50 per cent of NHS beds are occupied by this age-group. While private medicine enhances the power and earning capacity of hospital specialists, it has little to offer that other band of skilled workers who care for the elderly at home.

The health-care packages offered to private patients take advantage of the organization of informal caring in a second and more obvious way. Private insurance is expressly designed for medical care, not health care: it meets the costs of surgical and pharmacological repair but not the costs of full convalescence. The British United Provident Association (BUPA) offers restricted cover for individuals with chronic disorders not requiring "active treatment," while Private Patients Plan (PPP), BUPA's main competitor in the British market, notes that its benefits are designed to provide "good cover for the surgical and inpatient treatment required to cure a medical condition or to relieve acute episodes of a long-term illness." However, they are not intended "to meet the costs of a residential stay in hospital or nursing at home not directly related to the treatment of a medical condition" (Private Patients Plan 1980). It is difficult to see how a political program aimed at replacing the National Health Service with such private insurance schemes can avoid putting additional burdens on those who provide nursing at home for "free" (*Economist* 1982).

Private medicine, like the other apparently new solutions to the crisis in health care considered in this section, appears to be highly traditional in its sexual politics. It conforms to a formula which underlies the development of prevention, community care, and voluntary service, a formula which has governed the design of social policy throughout the twentieth century.

It is only recently that social scientists have uncovered this formula. For like the policy-makers they study, their perspectives, whether informed by structural functionalism or Marxism, have misrepresented the nature of informal caring as a specifically female and private activity. To understand caring, we must take account of the social relations of gender and privacy which place those who care in a private prison to cope alone with their responsibilities. From here, we can begin to grasp the complexities of women's hidden role as the providers, mediators, and negotiators of health within the home. We can begin to chart, too, the way in which the caring role has been molded by policies formulated in the public domain. With these insights, social scientists will be better equipped to engage in the debate about health and welfare, a debate which is set to occupy the political stage of the western world for the rest of the twentieth century.

Note

1 The fact that women take responsibility for health teaching does not mean that mothers and children hold identical perceptions about health and illness. As Campbell (1975a, 1975b) has demonstrated, a mother's health beliefs are a poor predictor of those of her child. However, as in other areas of child development, while women cannot determine what their children believe and do about health, they are likely to assume – and be ascribed – responsibility for health education in the home.

References

Abrams, P. (1977) Community Care: Some Research Problems and Priorities. *Policy and Politics* 6: 125–51.

Adams, M. (1971) The Compassion Trap. In V. Gornick and B. Moran (eds) *Women in Sexist Society*. New York: Basic Books.

Blaxter, M. and Paterson, E. (1982) *Mothers and Daughters: A Three Generational Study of Health Attitudes and Behaviour*. London: Heinemann.

Bruegel, I. (1978) What Keeps the Family Going? *International Socialism* 2 (1): 2–15.

Bulletin on Social Policy (1982) Unemployed. *Bulletin on Social Policy* 10 (Winter): 29–30.

Burghes, L. (1980) *Living from Hand to Mouth: A Study of 65 Families Living on Supplementary Benefit*. Poverty Pamphlet, 50. London: Child Poverty Action Group.

Campbell, J. (1975a) Attribution of Illness: Another Double Standard. *Journal of Health and Social Behavior* 16 (1): 114–26.

—— (1975b) Illness Is a Point of View: The Development of Children's Concept of Illness. *Child Development* 16 (1): 92–100.

Carpenter, E. (1980) Children's Health Care and the Changing Role of Women. *Medical Care* 18 (12): 1208–218.

Cockburn, C. (1977) *The Local State*. London: Pluto Press.

Conference of Socialist Economists State Apparatus and Expenditure Group (1979) *Struggle over the State*. London: CSE Books.

Counter Information Services (1980) *NHS – Critical Condition*. London: CIS.

Coussins, J. and Coote, A. (1981) *The Family in the Firing Line*. Poverty Pamphlet 51. London: Child Poverty Action Group and National Council for Civil Liberties.

Dahl, T. and Snare, A. (1978) The Coercion of Privacy: A Feminist Perspective. In C. Smart and B. Smart (eds) *Women, Sexuality and Social Control*. London: Routledge & Kegan Paul.

David, M. and Shaw, J. (1980) Women and Children First. *Marxism Today* April: 21–3.

Davin, A. (1978) Imperialism and Motherhood. *History Workshop* 5 (Spring): 9–67.

Delamont, S. (1980) *The Sociology of Women*. London: Allen & Unwin.

Department of Health and Social Security (1976a) *Priorities for Health and Social Services: A Consultative Document*. London: HMSO.

—— (1976b) *Prevention and Health: Everybody's Business*. London: HMSO.

—— (1981a) *Care in Action*. London: HMSO.

—— (1981b) *Growing Older*. Cmnd 8172. London: HMSO.

Dobash, R.E. and Dobash, R. (1980) *Violence Against Wives*. New York: Free Press.

Donnison, J. (1977) *Midwives and Medical Men*. London: Heinemann.

Doyal, L. with Pennell, I. (1979) *The Political Economy of Health*. London: Pluto Press.

Dubos, R. (1960) *The Mirage of Health*. London: Allen & Unwin.

Economist (1982) Thatcher's Think Tank Takes Aim at the Welfare State. *The Economist* 284 (9255): 25–6.

Ehrenreich, B. and English, D. (1976) *Witches, Midwives and Nurses: A History of Women Healers*. London: Writers & Readers Publishing Cooperative.

Elshtain, J.B. (1981) *Public Man, Private Woman*. Oxford: Martin Robertson.

Equal Opportunities Commission (1981) *The Experience of Caring for Elderly and Handicapped Dependents: Survey Report*. Manchester: Equal Opportunities Commission.

—— (1982) *Who Cares for the Carers?* Manchester: Equal Opportunities Commission.

Finch, J. and Groves, D. (1980) Community Care and the Family: A Case for Equal Opportunities. *Journal of Social Policy* 9 (4): 498.

Flora Project for Heart Disease Prevention (undated) *Coronary Disease: How To Protect Your Family*. London: The Flora Project.

Foreman, A. (1977) *Femininity as Alienation*. London: Pluto Press.

Freidson, E. (1960) Client Control and Medical Practice. *American Journal of Sociology* 65 (4): 374–82.

—— (1961) *Patients' View of Medical Practice*. New York: Russell Sage Foundation.

Gamarnikow, E. (1978) Sexual Division of Labor: The Case of Nursing. In A. Kuhn and A. Wolpe (eds) *Feminism and Materialism*. London: Routledge & Kegan Paul.

Gavron, H. (1966) *The Captive Wife*. Harmondsworth: Penguin Books.

Graham, H. (1976) Smoking in Pregnancy: Attitudes of Expectant Mothers. *Social Science and Medicine* 10: 399–405.

—— (1979) "Prevention and Health: Every Mother's Business": A Comment on Child Health Policy in the Seventies. In C. Harris (ed.) *The Sociology of the Family: New Directions for Britain*. Sociological Review Monograph 28, University of Keele.

—— (1980) Family Influences in Early Years on the Eating Habits of Children. In M. Turner (ed.) *Nutrition and Lifestyles*. London: Applied Science Publishers.

—— (1982) Coping: Or How Mothers Are Seen and Not Heard. In S. Friedman and E. Sarah (eds) *On the Problem of Men*. London: The Women's Press.

—— (1983) Health Education. In A. Anderson and A. McPherson (eds) *Women's Problems in General Practice*. Oxford: Oxford University Press.

Graham, H. and McKee, L. (1980) *The First Months of Motherhood*. Research Monograph No. 3. London: Health Education Council.

Hartmann, H. (1981) The Unhappy Marriage of Marxism and Feminism: Towards a More Progressive Union. In L. Sargent (ed.) *Women and Revolution*. London: Pluto Press.

Hearn, J. (1982) Notes on Patriarchy, Professionalism and the Semi-Professions. *Sociology* 16 (2): 184–202.

Hughes, M., Mayall, B., Moss, P., Perry, J., Petric, P., and Pinkerton, G. (1980) *Nurseries Now: A Fair Deal for Parents and Children*. Harmondsworth: Penguin Books.

Jacobson, B. (1981) *The Ladykillers: Why Smoking is a Feminist Issue*. London: Pluto Press.

Kerr, M. and Charles, N. (1982) Food as an Indicator of Social Relations. Paper presented at the British Sociological Association Conference on *Gender and Society*, University of Manchester.

Land, H. (1977) Inequalities in Large Families – More of the Same or

Different? In R. Chester and J. Peel (eds) *Equalities and Inequalities in Family Life*. London: Academic Press.

—— (1978) Who Cares for the Family? *Journal of Social Policy* 7 (3): 257–84.

Land, H. and Parker, R. (1978) Family Policies in Britain: The Hidden Dimensions. In J. Kahn and S. Kammerman (eds) *Family Policy*. New York: Columbia University Press.

Leeson, J. and Gray, J. (1978) *Women and Medicine*. London and New York: Tavistock Publications.

Levitt, J. (1977) Men and Women as Providers of Health Care. *Social Science and Medicine* 11: 395–98.

Lewis, J. (1980) The Social History of Social Policy: Infant Welfare in Edwardian England. *Journal of Social Policy* 9 (4): 463–86.

Litman, T. (1974) The Family as a Basic Unit in Health and Health Care: A Socio-Behavioural Overview. *Social Science and Medicine* 8: 495–519.

Litwak, E. (1965) Extended Kin Relations in an Industrial Society. In E. Shanas and G. Streib (eds) *Social Structure and the Family: Generational Relations*. Englewood Cliffs, NJ: Prentice-Hall.

McIntosh, M. (1979) The Welfare State and the Needs of the Dependent Family. In S. Burman (ed.) *Fit Work for Women*. London: Croom Helm.

Murcott, A. (1983) "It's a Pleasure To Cook for Him," Food, Mealtimes and Gender in Some South Wales Households. In E. Gamarnikow, D. Morgan, J. Purvis, and D. Taylorson (eds) *The Public and the Private*. London: Heinemann.

Navarro, V. (1976) *Medicine Under Capitalism*. London: Croom Helm.

Oakley, A. (1974) *The Sociology of Housework*. Oxford: Martin Robertson.

—— (1976) Wisewoman and Medicine Man: Changes in the Management of Childbirth. In J. Mitchell and A. Oakley (eds) *Rights and Wrongs of Women*. Harmondsworth: Penguin Books.

Oren, L. (1974) The Welfare of Women in Laboring Families. In M. Hartman and L. Banner (eds) *Clio's Consciousness Raised: New Perspectives on the History of Women*. New York: Harper & Row.

Politics of Health Group (1981) *Going Private: The Case Against Private Medicine*. London: POHG.

Private Patients Plan (1980) The British Universities Private Health Insurance Plan, P771 a/11, 80. London: PPP.

Rapoport, R. and Rapoport, R.M. (1977) *Fathers, Mothers and Others*. London: Routledge & Kegan Paul.

Rees-Davies, W. (1981) Quoted in *Times Health Supplement*, 6 Nov.

Rose, H. (1981) Re-reading Titmuss: The Sexual Division of Welfare. *Journal of Social Policy* 10: 477–501.

52   Women, health, and healing

Rowbotham, S. (1973) *Woman's Consciousness, Man's World.* Harmondsworth: Penguin Books.

Rowntree, B.S (1901) *Poverty: A Study of Town Life.* London: Macmillan.

Seldon, A. (1980) *The Litmus Papers: A National Health Dis-Service.* London: Centre for Policy Studies.

Shimmin, S., McNally, J., and Liff, S. (1981) Pressures on Women Engaged in Employment. *Employment Gazette* Aug. 344–49.

Spring Rice, M. (1981) *Working Class Wives: Their Health and Conditions.* London: Virago (first published by Penguin Books, 1939).

Stacey, M. (1981) The Division of Labour Revisited or Overcoming the Two Adams. In P. Abrams, R. Deem, J. Finch, and P. Rock (eds) *Practice and Progress: British Sociology 1950–1980.* London: Allen & Unwin.

Stacey, M. with Homans, H. (1978) The Sociology of Health: Its Present State, Future Prospects and Potential for Health Research. *Sociology* 12 (2): 281–307.

Stacey, M. and Price, M. (1981) *Women, Power and Politics.* London and New York: Tavistock Publications.

Thomas, G. and Shannon, C. (1982) Technology and Household Labor: Are the Times A-Changing? Paper presented at the British Sociological Association Conference on *Gender and Society,* University of Manchester, England.

Titmuss, R. (1958) *Essays on the Welfare State.* London: Allen & Unwin.

Townsend, P. (1979) *Poverty in the United Kingdom.* Harmondsworth: Penguin Books.

Versluysen, M. (1980) "Old Wives Tales": Women Healers in English History. In C. Davies (ed.) *Rewriting Nursing History.* London: Croom Helm.

Voysey, M. (1975) *A Constant Burden: The Reconstitution of Family Life.* London: Routledge & Kegan Paul.

Weldon, F. (1973) *Down Among the Women.* Harmondsworth: Penguin Books.

Wilson, E. (1977) *Women and the Welfare State.* London and New York: Tavistock Publications.

Wilson, H. and Herbert, G. (1978) *Parents and Children in the Inner City.* London: Routledge & Kegan Paul.

Women's Cooperative Guild (1978) *Maternity: Letters from Working Women.* London: Virago (first published by Bell & Sons, 1915).

Zola, I. (1973) Pathways to the Doctor: From Person to Patient. *Social Science and Medicine* 7: 677–89.

Three

Occupational health and women: the case of clerical work

Ellen Lewin and Virginia Olesen

Despite the growing participation of women in extra-domestic work throughout the economy, the study of the relationship between conditions in the workplace and the health of workers has not been broadly developed with respect to the woman worker. On one level, this may reflect the usual focus of occupational health scholars on the most dramatic threats working conditions pose to workers' health; that is, considerable attention has been directed to those who work in industrial settings where threats to health are always present and extremely severe (cf. Cralley 1972; Bridbord and French 1978; Hunter 1978; Gardner 1979). Such diseases as black lung and dangers presented by interaction with hazardous equipment or toxic substances have been a major concern in this literature. Since women workers are infrequently present in these settings (with obvious exceptions in, for example, the textile and electronics industries), little of this work has been directed to the health of women.[1]

When women workers and their health have been considered, however, investigators have tended to do so within a narrow reproductive context. Here, the focus has been on the real or potential reproductive hazards presented by work with various substances or by work which unduly strains women physically (Bingham 1977). It would not be unreasonable to suggest that this focus mirrors a more general concern about the appropriateness of women's participation in work outside the domestic sphere. Occupational conditions believed to threaten women's reproductive capacity may be of special concern to those who consciously or unconsciously question the right of women to move freely in the wider world of work and who view women primarily as reproducers of the species (Bell 1979; Hunt 1979; Petchesky 1979; Wright 1979).

More recently, in the wake of some apparent gains for women in various professional and managerial fields, concern has come to surround the health effects of stress to which women in higher-level jobs are presumably vulnerable (Waldron 1978; Lemkau 1980; Rice *et al.* 1981; Haw 1982).[2] These concerns parallel, to some extent, those which have emerged in discussions of reproductive hazards in the workplace, in that they often focus on the interface between women's public, productive roles and those they occupy as wives and mothers. Thus a seemingly limitless literature on "role strain" and the lack of fit between work and home has been generated (including a highly developed subfield on "dual-career families"), suggesting that analysts possess a heightened sensitivity to the possibility that women are not well suited for the stresses and strains present in demanding occupations (Rice *et al.* 1981). While the "hazards" investigated in this latter literature do not bear on reproductive health in the way that lead poisoning or chemical contamination might (by harming the fetus, that is), the kinds of stress under consideration are presented as posing a threat to family functioning and to the performance of maternal responsibilities (see, for instance, Fogarty, Rapoport, and Rapoport 1971).

Some notable gaps emerge as one delves into this literature. First, clerical work, in which women workers have been concentrated in numbers beyond their participation in other sorts of work, has received minimal attention, possibly because it lacks some of the more dramatic possibilities for injury in the workplace. At the same time, it is clear that the occupational health literature has rarely looked beyond the workplace itself as the locus of work-related health issues. With the exception of the concern of scholars with the role strains experienced by women in the professions, occupational health, like other fields of sociological inquiry, has suffered from a tendency to encapsulate domestic and public, family and work concerns (or to cast them narrowly in terms of "reproduction"). It has thus lost opportunities to generate a broader conceptualization of the factors which impinge on the health of both male *and* female workers. Finally, the sociological literature on women and work has tended to address itself to women in either high-status or unusual occupations (cf. Lopate 1968; Epstein 1970; Kundsin 1974; Mandelbaum 1981; Walshok 1981), which leaves us with little beyond conjecture when considering the many women who work in clerical fields. Even this literature says little about health.

We will argue in this chapter that one reason for the present scarcity of data on the health of women clerical workers derives from an overly narrow conceptualization of the parameters of "occupational health." We will use the case of the health of women clerical workers, now beginning to emerge in the occupational health and sociological literatures, to suggest that the study of women's occupational health requires an extension of concern beyond the boundaries of the workplace. Such an extension would add to the study of "intrinsic" workplace characteristics consideration of such "extrinsic" factors as women's domestic experience and the meaning and values they invest in their activities as workers (cf. Leira 1983).

We will use this approach not only to enrich our general understanding of the impact of work on women, but to examine specific problems arising from the introduction of massive technological change in clerical workplaces. We will describe the historical outlines of clerical work as a women's field, the broad shape of technological change now underway in this domain, and the varied theories and interpretations which have been brought to bear by scholars concerned with the impact of such changes. This will lead us to a discussion which considers both the impact of work on women and the specific effects of the rapid introduction of advanced electronic technology into women's workplaces, areas still characterized by considerable speculation in the social sciences. Finally, we will suggest that this approach necessitates a wider perspective on occupational health, one which applies both to men and to women.

Clerical work in America

Clerical work, nowadays thought to be women's work *par excellence*, has not always been the province of women. Prior to the Civil War, male clerks performed the tasks then carried out in offices (usually as a way of learning the business), and it was not until the end of the Civil War, when the number of clerical jobs increased sharply, that women began to enter clerical fields.[3] Women's entry into clerical work in large numbers was clearly tied to the introduction of the typewriter and other efficiency-oriented business equipment during the 1880s. This trend was repeated again between 1910 and 1920 when changes in business practice related to "scientific management" created a second expansion in clerical opportunities.

By the 1930s, women constituted 52.5 per cent of the clerical force, and such employment was widely regarded as "women's work," a designation which (along with low pay levels) doubtless deterred males from seeking employment in a field they had once dominated.[4] Thus, when women, including married women and mothers of young children, began to enter the labor force in the years following World War II, and especially after 1960, clerical work provided an opening in the non-professional occupational structure to which they had special access and for which they had often received special preparation. It is not surprising, then, that most women who entered or returned to the labor force during this period went into clerical work. By 1980, 35.1 per cent of all working women in America held clerical positions, the largest single category of women workers (Bureau of the Census 1981: 401). At this writing, 80.1 per cent of all clerical workers, including typists, stenographers, secretaries, and bookkeepers, are women (Bureau of the Census 1981: 673). In some job categories, the figures are even more dramatic: 96.1 per cent of typists, for instance, are female.[5]

Contemporary women clerical workers differ in important ways from their counterparts in the late 1800s and early 1900s. Though some married women took up clerical occupations in earlier times when extreme conditions demanded that they assume responsibility for the support of their families, most clerical workers at the turn of the century were young, single, and self-supporting women living with their families prior to marriage (Davies 1982: 76–7). Few, if any, of these women were college-educated, although some had obtained specialized clerical training in so-called "business colleges" of the day. Clerical workers were predominantly white.

In contrast, the clerical worker of today is more likely to be married (58 per cent), in her 40s, and a mother.[6] This reflects wider trends in the labor-force participation of women, which since 1960 has been increasingly characterized by married women and women with small children (Bureau of the Census 1981: 388).[7] The majority of female clerical workers have finished high school, though increasingly they come from the ranks of the college-educated. Because of declining opportunities in the professions, some labor-force analysts now anticipate that "increasing proportions of women college graduates will start and probably end their careers in clerical jobs" (Best and Stern 1977; Rumberger 1983). High educational levels also are characteristic of black and hispanic women who have entered the clerical world, although their total participation in this field is still low; in 1979, only 29 per cent of all employed black women and 30.8 per cent of all hispanic women worked in clerical occupations (Hult 1980: 23).

Women who do clerical work not only earn less than do men in other fields requiring comparable skills[8] but make substantially lower wages than the few men who work in clerical positions, including typists (Rytina 1982: 27). If they work full-time, for example, women can expect to earn only 60 per cent of what males in their job categories do (Bureau of the Census 1981: 405).

Clerical workers and health

Although the clerical worker, the nature of her work, and her health have, as we have shown, rarely been of interest to students of occupational health or the sociology of occupations, recent technological changes affecting the clerical workplace have begun to draw attention to this group of workers.[9] During the past decade the advent and diffusion of microelectronics and computers have precipitated a rapid and pervasive "revolution" in the American office (Hult 1980: 10). While the direction these changes will take and the ultimate impact they will have on the shape of future clerical occupations are still unclear, they have promoted considerable discussion among social scientists, feminists, and students of occupational health. In the context of continuing disputes about the rapidity with which the changes are occurring and the kinds of offices which have been affected, more important debate surrounds the question of how technological innovations in the clerical workplace will affect the job status of the worker and her health.

Despite the fact that thorough research on the health effect of new technological equipment has yet to be carried out (such studies have been more common in Europe but are glaringly absent from the United States) and that, in particular, evidence on their long-term effects does not yet exist, there are indications that the use of video display units and other new equipment can produce a variety of deleterious effects including eye strain, headaches, and pains in back, neck, and shoulder (Harman 1979; Murray, Moss, and Parr *et al.* 1981; NIOSH 1981; National Association of Working Women 1981: 22). What has not been established with any certainty is the degree to which these health problems differ from problems workers may have faced in the offices of the past and the extent to which the problems documented may have have long-term consequences. Further, it still remains difficult to distinguish the untoward effects of working with computerized office equipment from the less specific impact of doing any sort of routinized work without sufficient opportunity for rest or variation. However, various observers (Driscoll 1981; Menzies 1981; Morgall 1983) have pointed to the way in which the new technology is organized, suggesting that it is used to increase control of the work force and to widen the gap between skilled (men's) and unskilled (women's) tasks.

Work and stress: clerical work as a complex domain

Any type of work engenders stress. Simply transporting oneself to and from the workplace, regardless of what takes place during the eight-hour day, can be a stressful experience. Even without considering the significant changes now underway in the organization of the office, including those related to the introduction of computerized technology, clerical work appears to be particularly stressful for women. Clerical work is low-paid, low-status work; it presents few opportunities for women to fully utilize their abilities or to make meaningful decisions, a situation identified as causing occupationally related stress for women (Lemkau 1980). Moreover, complexity in work, which recent studies have demonstrated to have a significant relationship to job satisfaction, is typically lacking in clerical occupations (Bowen 1973; Miller *et al.* 1979). When one considers the relatively high educational standards employers impose on clerical workers (Oppenheimer 1970), the potential of this type of work to be frustrating and demoralizing is obvious.[10]

The findings of the prospective Framingham study are particularly useful for showing the complexities which emerge in trying to trace the relationship between clerical work and stress (Haynes and Feinleib 1980). In attempting to identify risk factors associated with the development of coronary heart disease, the Framingham study isolated occupational stress as one salient factor. While clerical workers in this study were not further differentiated in terms of job-related factors,[11] workers were distinguished in terms of a variety of non-work or extrinsic factors which also contributed to the general stress relevant to future rates of CHD. The Framingham study reveals that the women at the greatest risk for coronary heart disease are in fact clerical workers, but that, beyond that, the highest rates appear among women who are also married to blue-collar men, who are raising children, and who are identified as having an "unsympathetic boss." In contrast, female clerical workers *without children* are at no greater risk for coronary heart disease than other women workers; nor do clerical workers married to white-collar workers face excess CHD risks. It appears, then, that it is the combination of intrinsically stressful work in the clerical field and the addition of particular extrinsic features from the women's domestic and work situations which contribute to elevated risk levels (Haynes and Feinleib 1980: 140). These findings did not consider further sources of job-related stress, such as the introduction of new technology.[12]

What the specific mechanisms are which mediate the flow of stress back and forth from home to workplace or regulate the ways in which such strains are additive or mutually cancelling cannot currently be determined with any precision. The existence of these relationships on an empirical level, however, suggests that not only aspects of the occupational environment but aspects of the domestic situation need to be carefully differentiated before their impact on the worker's health can be assessed with any accuracy. Not only marital status, then, but factors such as partner's occupational status and social class, the presence of children and the number and ages of children, all have implications for the way in which a woman's occupational obligations are coordinated with her domestic duties, as well as the values and priorities that are likely to characterize her orientation to work.

As we demonstrate below with data from a study of temporary clerical employees, it is equally important to consider meanings which workers themselves bring to their work and use to locate their labor in the broader structure of their lives. Anthropologists have placed great emphasis on recording informants' own words and have analyzed the ways expressed meanings interrelate. This approach, termed "emic" by some,[13] mirrors the perspectives of sociologists whose roots are in the school of symbolic interaction, in that these investigators also focus their analytic energies on detailed examinations of what people say about themselves and their experience. These experientially based approaches may supplement, rather than supercede, studies which begin with the public level of work, using the fundamental structural and organizational realities of particular work situations as their point of departure. On the one hand, such organizational perspectives are quite useful for directing our attention to the issues that are likely to be of concern to broad classes of persons engaged in particular kinds of work; on the other hand, these perspectives may involve hidden hazards in that they obscure the ways in which different individuals may invoke distinct meanings in evaluating the place of work in their lives.

New approaches

The approach we advocate here recognizes the ways in which women coordinate work and domesticity but also departs from the traditional organizational study of work. As the Framingham data suggest, enhanced understanding of the relationship

between work and health is to be achieved through a consideration of both "intrinsic" (work-related) and "extrinsic" (non-
work-related) factors as they exist and/or are perceived by
workers – whether men or women. This understanding
becomes especially crucial when examining workers in occupations where a great deal is known about the presumed high or
low status of the work. In these cases, a careful evaluation of
the intersection between intrinsic and extrinsic factors must be
woven into a recognition of the meanings and beliefs that
workers themselves hold about themselves and their work.
This approach will do much in helping us to avoid the unfortunately mechanistic pitfalls of an externally measured, quantitative assessment of stress. The Framingham data, though
imprecise on many levels, indicate that the health effects of
stress (whether produced in the home or in the workplace) are
not strictly additive; rather they derive from the meanings
which attach to all of these activities in relation to one
another.[14]

In this approach we regard women as purposeful actors, as
strategists, who operate deliberately in the world and make
decisions based on what they perceive to be their best options.
While particular strategies may not succeed in meeting all the
needs of those who enact them, the choices and behaviors
women (and other actors) use may enable them to make the
best of a compromised and complex situation. Real-life
decision-makers, as Simon (1957) has pointed out, "make do"
with the options that present themselves and make decisions
on the basis of limited and incorrect information in many cases.
In some situations, optimizing one goal may compromise
another, and many real-world decisions represent an effort, in
essence, to reduce these conflicts while still maximizing some
valued goals.

An example of this approach can be seen in a study of temporary service employees, familiarly known as "Kelly girls" or
"office temps" (Olesen and Katsuranis 1978). This research
shows that some respondents valued temporary clerical work,
which is accorded low status even within the clerical realm, for
providing greater levels of independence and autonomy than
are typically available in permanent clerical employment.
Rather than exacerbating the alienation clerical workers may
feel when their work is repetitive and apparently meaningless,

many of the temporary workers interviewed felt that they had the ability to avoid unpleasant work assignments because they had no obligation to any particular employer. Further, respondents valued this work because it provided an avenue to earn income which could support other pursuits more central to the workers' self-image, such as primary, but unremunerative, careers as writers and artists.

In other instances, temporary work presented an opportunity for older women, whose skills were outdated, to reenter the labor market and to refresh their knowledge of office equipment and procedures. At the same time it was not unusual for respondents to reveal a keen awareness of the exploitative aspects of their work. They understood that they were used by employers as interchangeable pieces of equipment and a number of temporary workers reported ways in which they had been shunned and ignored by their co-workers, or had experienced loneliness on the job. Nevertheless, these workers tended to view their work positively in that it fits comfortably within the context of their particular round of life. That is, the workplace features of temporary work, both good and bad, were evaluated within the context provided by the workers' lives outside the workplace; intrinsic and extrinsic features were inexorably intertwined.

The understanding that intrinsic and extrinsic factors are not, in practice, divisible is essential if we are to clarify the ambiguity which surrounds current speculations about clerical workers and technological change. For one thing, this perspective points to new approaches to the issue of stress for women employed in clerical occupations which do not present themselves through narrow analyses of changes in the nature of the job, on the one hand, or changes in the personal arena, on the other. We recall that in the Framingham study it was neither clerical work itself, having children in itself, being employed, or any other of the single variables which was associated with higher levels of morbidity, but instead the apparently cumulative effect of several of these factors acting in concert.

The importance of the Framingham findings, for our purpose, lies in their complexity: they underscore the importance of avoiding uni-causal explanatory models and point to the dangers of underestimating the ways in which even powerful stress-inducing factors may be modified by their cultural and social context. The question of how the women of the Framingham study may have evaluated and understood the meaning of their work goes beyond the scope of that project, though we can certainly speculate on this a bit from the information provided by the survey data. The presence of a blue-collar husband and several children as a combined risk factor points, very likely, to the impact of a traditional articulation of sex roles apt to be stressed in working-class families (Komarovsky 1962; Rubin 1976). (In very few families do men perform as many household tasks as women, hence the blue-collar family is but an extreme example of conjugal-role arrangements throughout the society.) For example, this may mean that women returning home from work will not be able to count on their husbands to share or even help with domestic and childrearing tasks, with the obvious result of a heavier workload for the employed wife. Nor are the burdens falling on these women solely composed of domestic labor; in families where women bear the major responsibility for domesticity they are also likely to be accountable for a variety of decisions affecting the family. From this perspective, it is the planning and the thinking, the "kin-keeping," that must be undertaken in families that fall to women and must be coordinated with their activities as workers, homemakers, and mothers (Firth, Hubert, and Forge 1970).

Taking a different perspective, the "unsympathetic boss" risk factor suggests that it is not merely the nature of women's work in clerical settings, but a number of other work-related factors which are apt to have an important impact on health. Certainly, the personal characteristics of the supervisor reveal little about what have been thought to be the really "important" factors in the workplace, that is the alienation of the worker and the intrinsic characteristics of the task with which she is charged. We might expect that both sympathetic and unsympathetic bosses are to be found in a variety of clerical and other workplaces, independent of other factors which may or may not be conducive to good or bad health. What the personal characteristics of the employer reveal, of course, is the element of meaning as an influence on health, operating in concert with other, non-workplace-related factors.

Technological change in clerical work

As we discussed briefly above, technological changes, particularly those associated with the introduction of. computer-mediated information transmission, have begun to occur at a rapid pace in office settings, and have stimulated a wide variety of reactions from observers. Regardless of technology, of course, the basic work performed by the clerical employee involves the transformation or transmission of information, whether by pen, typewriter, or word-processor.

Recent advances, however, are marked by their effects on the speed with which information transmission is achieved: whereas in the office of the 1950s the secretary or typist worked at her desk, probably not too far from her supervisor and her filing cabinets, used a typewriter to transmit information, and used carbon paper to reproduce copies of these transmissions, to be physically placed in file cabinets, nowadays the scene can be quite different. The clerical worker may still sit at a desk, but the equipment she uses and her potential for transmitting and acquiring information has changed greatly. Instead of a typewriter, she may use a keyboard connected to a display feature like a video screen on which she can see what she herself has entered and on which she can summon information from the departed file cabinets now stored in computer banks. If she needs to produce a paper (or hard) version of her work, she can turn one out on the printer connected to her terminal, which may or may not be accessible to her. Copies of printed work are produced at high speed on photocopy equipment, which can collate automatically large numbers of copies of whatever is needed. Tasks which once required judgment and precision skills, such as planning the layout of typed documents, can now be carried out automatically by the word-processor and special features not possible on ordinary typewriters, such as justification of right margins, have become expected in professionally produced written material. The operation of the word-processing equipment requires different skills and information than the skills needed to operate a conventional typewriter, and the degree to which workers on new equipment will need to use the kind of judgment formerly required of them remains unclear (Morgall 1983).

The new workplace of the clerical worker – called a

"station" – and her information-processing equipment – called a "terminal" – need not be physically proximate to those of her supervisors or co-workers. Indeed, one of the significant potentials in the new technology is the possibility for large portions of the labor force to conduct their business without leaving their homes. At the same time, not only the clerical worker herself, but also a variety of supervisors may have access to similar equipment. This means that the supervisor may have the same information displays available, and may use these to request specific tasks, set the pace for the work being carried out, and even monitor and observe the progress of employees (Barron and Curnow 1979; Morgall 1983).

The technological changes that have been outlined have begun to touch women in all sorts of settings, from the smaller "one girl" offices through those with large, differentiated staffs. These changes influence clerical workers at all levels of prestige, from the file clerk (a job which will very likely soon pass into history) to the elite private secretary, and are being introduced into all kinds of settings at a rapid pace (Murphree 1981). Some estimate that by 1990 between 40 per cent and 50 per cent of all workers, including clerical employees, will perform computer-mediated work at 38 million terminal-based work stations, in addition to 34 million home terminals and 7 million portable terminals (Giuliano 1982; see also Uhlig and Farber 1981).

Observers of these changes, which have occurred very rapidly in some sectors, have generated a variety of perspectives and interpretations of the consequences of computer-mediated work for workers' experience, for the structure of work environments, and for the health of the clerical work force. Because computer devices promote greater efficiency in clerical work, as well as the potential for monitoring clerks and controlling the pace of work completed, some have viewed the new technologies in terms of their impact on the rationalization of office work. That is, the use of computer-mediated technology will permit the division of clerical tasks into component parts, with the subsequent definition of the job solely in terms of the performance of the rationalized parts (Braverman 1974). Thus each job could be reduced to its lowest common denominator, much as some jobs are in industry, eliminating or limiting relational elements of the division of labor. As has been mentioned, microcomputer technology offers management increased capabilities for monitoring and controlling the work process itself. Using a device called a "prompter" machines can be programmed to present a new typing job as each one is completed. Beyond this, the machines can be equipped with counters which register the number of key depressions made per day and which measure the speed and accuracy of each worker (Morgall 1983: 221). Thus, if used to their fullest potential, word-processors can intensify the rationalization of work, reducing each task to particular motions and limiting the time allotted for its performance. The potential of this technology for the introduction of piecework, as well as for the division of jobs into part-time components, is clear. Morgall (1983) has pointed to the potentially ironic effects of concerns with occupational health hazards within this emerging system. Employers may respond to demands that workers be limited to four hours per day exposure to visual display units by dividing full-time jobs into part-time positions. Such a change would, clearly, have serious implications for women's already disadvantaged economic status, as well as for their ability to achieve any sort of occupational mobility.

Those who have expressed concern with the possible emergence of these trends have advanced the argument that efficiency realized through implementation of new technology will result in the elimination of existing jobs and the substitution of human clerical workers by "intelligent" machines (Sleigh *et al.* 1979; Nora and Minc 1980; Crompton, Jones, and Reid 1982). These contentions follow the results of a much earlier study of the impact of the introduction of electronic information-processing; this earlier, classic study by Hoos (1960) indicated that job loss and shrinkage of employment opportunity comes in the wake of new technology.

Countering the claims that computer-induced employment will throw large numbers of clerical workers out of their jobs, others have contended that technological advances will stimulate white-collar employment. These observers claim employment opportunities will expand at the end of the century, with the greatest growth at the managerial level, but with substantial increases as well for clerical workers (Hult 1980: 16). In suggesting that technological changes will create rather than destroy opportunities in the long run, these commentators make much of the likelihood that new kinds of jobs, not currently of great importance in clerical settings, will emerge with the growth of computer technology, and that these new jobs will, in fact, be more challenging and require more expertise, than the clerical jobs more typical of the pre-computer scene (Goldfield 1980). For example, new types of relatively creative work in the area of compiling information relevant to particular sorts of problems could be instituted, providing a mechanism for upgrading some clerical positions (Sleigh *et al*. 1979). Exploration of the mathematical capabilities of word-processing equipment could, as well, offer enhanced opportunities to workers now limited to editing activities (Morgall 1983). These discussions fall into the futuristic approach mentioned earlier, insofar as they demand that one discard old conceptions of the nature of clerical work and remain open to the production of new images.

While some observers have predicted that workers displaced by computer-mediated work will eventually find other employment in an economy energized by the promise of new technology, few have considered the kinds of problems which finding a job "elsewhere" may generate. Although new jobs may in fact be created by these changes, individuals may not learn about those located at some geographical distance, or may not be able to take advantage of "opportunities" which require pulling up stakes and moving their families (Hoos 1960: 78). For women who are married, such moves may be precluded by the occupational situation of their mates; for those who are heads of household or single parents, a move may involve separation from established networks of support essential to the family's wellbeing. Such networks are difficult to replace and, in the case of networks based upon kin ties, may be irreplaceable. Thus, while in the aggregate new technology may not lead to a general decrease in the number of jobs available, the potential for such changes to produce widespread dislocation and individual misfortune still exists, particularly for displaced women workers (Hult 1980: 12).

The potential impact of technological change in clerical employment may not, however, be felt exclusively in terms of the numbers of jobs available in the offices of the future. Closely related to arguments that technological change will lead to widespread unemployment are claims that it will result in the "proletarianization" of clerical work (Glenn and Feldberg 1977; Arnold, Birke, and Faulkner 1981). An examination of the effects of the introduction of electronic data-processing equipment in the 1950s does tend to support this contention: not only were clerical positions downgraded in that needed skills were not sufficient for women using them to advance, but middle managers in these same establishments were downgraded as well (Hoos 1960: 79–80). In parallel fashion, the introduction of new technology has begun to deskill even the more high-status clerical workers such as the legal secretary by permitting their rationalization into component, lower-status tasks (Murphree 1981). These alterations in the kinds of aspirations which clerical workers might realistically hold follow from a pattern such as that described by Glenn and Feldberg (1977). Their study of five large companies revealed that "the main avenues for clerical workers were either horizontal or downward," though the total number of clerical positions remained constant as work in preparing data for processing continued to expand (1977: 206).

In analyzing the alternations which are reported for the clerical opportunity structure, however, there is a danger that the previous era will be romanticized, creating a mythological pre-computer golden age in which clerical work was meaningful and varied and in which clerical workers enjoyed real opportunities for occupational advancement. As we saw earlier, clerical work, particularly once it became firmly entrenched as a woman's occupation, has offered few upward pathways and had been characterized, instead, as one of the fields in which the concept of women's serving as a reserve labor force has been most applicable (McNally 1979: 178). Moreover, clerical work has historically tended to be boring, repetitive, alienating, and devalued. Technology, at least in its current forms, did not introduce these elements; rather, it may heighten them in some instances even while it reduces them in others.

Thus the new technology may alter both the tasks which clerical workers perform and the social context in which these tasks are enacted. On the one hand, preliminary, somewhat limited studies, have indicated that some work is "deskilled" with the introduction of new technology, becoming more repetitive and boring than it was before (Glenn and Feldberg

1977). These studies also suggest that computer-mediated office work alters clerical tasks in terms of opportunities for workers to differentiate themselves according to their skills and accomplishments. Whereas in the pre-computer office, the typist could measure her competence in terms of her ability to execute tasks such as centering and planning the appearance of typed materials, the modern word processor accomplishes these tasks automatically. Thus the perfectly centered and exquisitely organized typed product can now be produced by a typist of minimal skills as easily as by one with years of experience and considerable esthetic sensibilities. Individual human skill has little value when it is leveled by the readily accessible and broader resources of the machine (Glenn and Feldberg 1977).

Other preliminary evidence, on the other hand, points to different possible interpretations of the impact of technological change on clerical workers. Some workers surveyed have reported that new equipment made their jobs more interesting (National Association of Working Women 1980: 12), and many cite the reduction in meaningless repetition (e.g. typing the same letter to different addresses) made possible with word processors as eliminating much of the frustration which once characterized their jobs.

Possibly more significant in terms of the potential health impact of these changes are the new pressures workers experience because of the high speed at which the new equipment functions. The technical capabilities of computers not only make it possible for vast quantities of information to be managed quickly, but often exert new pressures on the managers for more rapid output of work (McCartney 1979). These managers, in turn, pressure their subordinates to produce ever-increasing quantities of work under conditions in which the managers have new opportunities to control the flow of work and the pace at which clerical workers process it. Because work can now be routed to clerical workers electronically, the ability of the worker to determine her own pace and to relieve monotony by standing up, walking to pick up new work, or deciding when to take breaks may be significantly impaired (Glenn and Feldberg 1977; National Association of Working Women 1980; Cohen, Smith, and Stammerjohn 1981; Zuboff 1982). As one observer puts it: "Stress *is* the occupational hazard of the computer age

much in the way that loss of limb was the characteristic occupational hazard of the industrial age'' (Nussbaum 1982: 91).

Social relationships of work

The changes in the technology of office work may also have an
impact on the kinds of social relationships which surround
clerical work. Whereas the traditional clerk we described
earlier could and did move about to carry papers from manager
to typing pool, to chat with others, or at the very least to have
contact with office messengers, the equipment now being
introduced can change this organization. Individual terminal
operators have been reported as being caught in an ''uncomfortable isolation'' (Zuboff 1982: 146) in which such mediating
tasks are no longer performed mechanically by human beings
but are carried out electronically. In remarking on this same
feature, others have commented on the apparent breakdown of
social relationships in the office and the deterioration of social
interaction which once lent a comforting humanness to the
clerical workplace (Glenn and Feldberg 1977: 61; National
Association of Working Women 1981: 9). However, at the same
time that the workers may no longer be physically proximate to
one another and have a work-related need to engage in communication, the very equipment which has distanced them physically may come to permit new modes of communication. We
would suggest that very much as the telephone facilitated links
between workers at an earlier time, the introduction of data
terminals may come to be adaptable for this purpose as well.

A further social change which has been predicted has even
more dramatic potential effects on the social atmosphere
within which clerical work is carried out. It is not inconceiv-
able that many clerical workers will eventually work at home
or in a variety of non-office environments, using terminals connected to larger computer systems. (Such work is already the
case in some fields.) This alteration of the social context of
work is potentially both more isolating and more satisfying. On
the one hand, the possibility exists that the shift of clerical
work into the home could lead to a piecework mentality not
unlike that experienced by garment workers who work at home.
Such workers might labor on individual, distanced terminals

without benefits, raises, or promotions, while also performing domestic tasks which interrupt their work.

On the other hand, the transformation of the home into a workplace might mitigate many of the problems women face in attempting to maintain full-time employment, especially if they have young children. As has been shown in several studies, employed women are no less obliged to carry out the full range of domestic and childcare tasks than women not in the paid labor force. For women who must arrange paid child care in order to maintain a job outside the home, the costs of such care can decimate their earnings, often placing them periodically at or just slightly above the standard of living they would achieve on welfare. To the extent that computer technology may enable women to work at home, the possibility that they might vary their hours, and that they might be able to work without incurring the expenses of childcare, transportation, lunches, and clothing for work, such technology could represent an unprecedented opportunity for economic independence.

While such hypothetical benefits can give rise to rather elaborate fantasies of the utopian possibilities offered by "telecommuting," however, recent research suggests that office work in the home may instead increase stress for workers. Olson (1981) found that homeworkers could not, in fact, care for children at the same time that they worked at their terminals. Additionally, work in the home setting clearly presents more opportunities (Olson 1981) for social isolation and may, as well, provide fewer possibilities for communication with other workers essential to labor organizing and the sharing of essential information (Hope, Kennedy, and DeWinter 1976). This latter point is, as we have shown, still in dispute, as it is unclear to what extent the isolation of dispersed workplaces may be relieved by the very technology which created it.[15]

A further factor which remains in question is the extent to which the introduction of new technology may begin to reverse the feminization of clerical work which began with the introduction of the typewriter and instead make the office a more attractive setting for men seeking employment. While no clear trends have emerged to date, there appears to have been a recent small, but distinct, increase in the numbers of men engaged in the formerly solidly feminine occupations of typing, stenography, and other low-status clerical fields, possibly the result of depressions elsewhere in the labor market.

At the same time, one of the interesting results of the new role of the computer in offices has been the arrival of the terminal on the desk of the middle manager; use of this equipment has meant that these higher-level personnel have had to master some typing skills and even, in some cases, that they are now expected to develop drafts of communications on the word-processor, eliminating the need for dictation. These changes, where they have been effected, have met with mixed receptions, apparently because of the associations men have of typing with "women's work." Others, however, enjoy entering and editing materials (McCartney 1979). These changes point to a possible merging of "women's" and "men's" work in the office of the future as use of keyboards becomes less resolutely sex-typed. How such changes would finally affect the status of the woman clerical worker remains unclear.

Thus, with respect to potential job loss, the downgrading of work, the alteration of the nature of clerical tasks, and the changes which technology might mean for social relationships among clerical workers, the picture is as yet ambiguous, with commentators predicting positive, negative, and mixed outcomes apparently according to their status as social critics or business enthusiasts. Despite the uncertainty of the picture with respect to the social impact of the new technology, however, clear negative effects have now been documented as regards short-term health of workers who use the new equipment (NIOSH 1981; National Association of Working Women 1981; Stellman and Henifin 1983).

Ambiguity and the health of clerical workers

If one attribute can be said to characterize the impact of the computer revolution on clerical work, that would be ambiguity. Despite some indications that machine-monitoring of work has begun and that coding and data-entry jobs are assigned to new and often non-white employees as deadend positions, the long-term implications of these shifts remain unclear. Feldberg (1982), for example, has commented that we don't currently know how technology actually is being used to redesign jobs, what kinds of new jobs are being created, what proportion of these jobs will depend on particular computer-based skills, how new jobs will be classified in terms of skill levels and wages, what kinds of job ladders are being created, and whether new jobs are being linked to existing clerical areas.

This means that many workers now contemplating impending changes have no way to predict the form such change will have and the effect it may have on other aspects of their lives. The high probability that change will occur, however, even in the absence of information about its attributes, is apt in itself, then, to engender stress, quite apart from whatever stress attaches to the work or office conditions themselves. Clerical workers are having to imagine themselves beginning new kinds of jobs (though they don't know what sort), terminating old relationships and beginning new ones (also unknowns), and possibly facing some sort of status change, though the direction of this, too, remains mysterious.

Even the prospect of future advancement within the context provided by the new technology may be stressful for women clerical workers who are hesitant about leaving the familiar, supportive work groups characteristic of the traditional ''social office'' (Kanter 1977). Simply dealing with the new technology *qua* technology may produce strains of its own: learning to use the word-processor, for example, can be especially discouraging for women who have already achieved competence on traditional office equipment. For these women, the learning period presents a situation in which they are thrust back from a position of expertise into the status of a novice; the fears that this will mean downward job mobility just as younger, ''computer-literate'' competitors come on the job can similarly engender anxiety.

While we must as yet remain speculative about some of the kinds of stress which arise in changing office environments, some research has shown that job stress is a reality among clerical workers working with the new equipment. One study, for example, showed that job stress among video-display terminal operators was higher than among any other occupational group studied, including air-traffic controllers (National Association of Working Women 1981: 4). These findings, however, are both recent and sparse, raising more questions in many instances than they answer.

This brings us back to the model we presented earlier in our discussion of temporary clerical workers and of the findings of the Framingham study. These data point to two essential understandings. First, the meanings and contexts workers associate with their work experience must be considered at the same time that more "objective" factors such as working conditions, pay, and the status attached to the work are analyzed. Second, the health impact of any particular occupation can rarely be understood outside of an analysis of those associated social factors, both intrinsic to the work and extrinsic to it, which may contribute to a particular outcome.

The matter of ambiguity which attaches to the introduction of new technology in the clerical workplace can be examined in this broader framework as well. Change and uncertainty are not likely to have uniform effects on every worker, just as boring, repetitive work is not seen as alienating in all circumstances.[16] To the extent that familiar social ties are disrupted by the new technologies, furthermore, we might expect sequelae from the loss of supportive social networks, long known to be associated with better management of stressful life circumstances (Levine and Scotch 1970).

This approach has particular relevance in finding our way through the ambiguity which currently surrounds the introduction of computer-mediated technology into clerical work settings. First, as we have seen earlier, no clear outcomes in terms of the upgrading or downgrading of jobs can yet be discerned, as claims for both sorts of trends have appeared in the literature. Similarly, the impact of the new technology on rates of employment remains difficult to assess during the transitional period, as some new employment connected to working with computers begins to emerge. Whether such employment will provide opportunities for women equivalent or superior to those which have traditionally existed in clerical work remains to be seen.

These are the issues which have particular importance for an understanding of women's position in the occupational world as a whole, in relation to wider social and economic development. But, as we have asked earlier, what are the ways in which individual women find their way through the restrictions that these conditions impose on them as they attempt to earn a living, meet their obligations to their families, and achieve a sense of worthiness and accomplishment for themselves? First, the data suggest that women view greater complexity on the job in a positive light and show, with some clarity, that such complexity is associated with greater job satisfaction (Miller *et al.* 1979). On this issue, the introduction of computer technology may have two sorts of effects. For some women, the change may mean that they no longer carry out relatively interesting and creative work, such as planning the design of letters and other typed materials. In some cases, the shift to word-processing and computerized data banks may eliminate opportunities that once existed to move around on the job, to pace oneself and vary one's activities over the course of the workday. For others, in contrast, the change may have drastically different effects: new opportunities to become familiar with complex machinery may occur, along with hitherto unknown ways to communicate with unseen colleagues. In both of these scenarios, it must be remembered, we have focused on the change between how it used to be and how it is now; for new workers, of course, this change is increasingly non-existent as a whole generation of neophyte clerical workers enters the office assuming the normality of what we have here labeled changed working conditions. In this instance, clearly, change will not emerge as a stressor and the opportunity to examine the impact of the working conditions themselves, i.e. the direct impact of high technology equipment on the mental and physical health of workers, will be possible for the first time.

Even considering the fact that the new technology will not affect all workers similarly, and that change itself will not be a factor for all workers, we must still move a step closer to the individual to understand how the meaning she brings to her work situation intervenes with other factors in determining how she will respond to office technology. As has been seen earlier, even while workers may view themselves as exploited, they may also evaluate their work positively because it facilitates the optimization of some other valued goal. This is no less likely to be the case in the office of the future than it is in the office of today.

What are the implications of these developments for the long-term health concerns of women workers? The ambiguities which still surround the direction of change mean that our discussion must be speculative in its broad outlines; nevertheless, some basic issues stand at the center of the debate and these are likely to retain their importance in the years to come.

First, the possible health impact of computer-mediated work itself continues to be debated, and it will probably be some time before we know whether or not the equipment in and of itself has deleterious effects on clerical workers' health. In any case, the results of investigations into such matters as eye strain from VDT (visual display terminal) use or emotional exhaustion from rapidly paced work will have consequences of some economic significance for future health insurance policy and for possible sex differences in cost and coverage. Employers seeking to avoid or ease such expenses may well figure recreational time for workers using these machines into their overall costs, particularly if they have or wish to retain a stable group of employees. For employers who depend on or prefer temporary workers, however, the protection of workers' health may be a less vital goal than short-term production objectives. In either case, employer policy may be influenced in important ways by clerical workers' perceptions of their work and its role in their lives, as workers with a continuing stake in a particular job are more apt to make health-related demands than those committed to more transitory relationships with their employers.

This latter point suggests the potential importance of health issues as pivotal questions for the development of worker consciousness and for labor organizing among clerical workers. Clerical workers have historically been resistant to union organization,[17] and women workers have also been less involved in unions, presumably because of their lesser identification with their roles as workers. As women's jobs in offices, however, become lifetime occupations rather than short-term commitments, workers' concerns about safety on the job may develop into the basis for union organization, as occurred with flight attendants (Lessor 1982). While the health issues which affect clerical workers are unlikely to be as serious as those which follow from years of constant air travel, the implications for the growth of worker consciousness may be comparable.

Perhaps most vexing, however, are the still unanswered questions around the future organization of work in office settings and the relative involvement which men and women will have in those contexts. As was discussed earlier, there are some indications that the "high tech" mystique which is beginning to surround some formerly routine clerical tasks may be drawing men into this once all-female preserve. This trend appears to be enhanced by recent reductions in employment opportunities in traditionally masculine occupations such as manufacturing, as well as by redefinition of some management activities to include use of the computer keyboard; whether this nascent masculinization of the office will persist, or whether it reflects a temporary accommodation to economic crisis, cannot yet be determined. Clearly, however, the extent to which men move into clerical occupations and the levels at which they settle have important implications for women's futures in these jobs. To the extent that women may experience reduced opportunity in the clerical arena, at the same time that their options in non-traditional occupations have not really expanded substantially, the technological revolution now underway may have drastic consequences for women's economic roles even though the total number of clerical jobs is not reduced. Substantial evidence already exists that women, especially those who head households, are coming to constitute the poorest segment of American society (Pearce 1979). We suspect that any developments which restrict women's access to clerical work and which further impede their ability to move up within those occupations will exacerbate these trends, with direct effects on the health of both the women workers and their families. Such possibilities do not even begin to consider the impact of stress, both physical and psychological; clearly more empirical research will be needed if we are to be able to identify such patterns.

We have argued that the health impact of job stress cannot be understood without a consideration of the personal context in which the worker is situated; that is, the factors intrinsic to the job which influence morbidity are mediated by a complex of extrinsic factors. This approach can potentially be applied to the study of the computerization of the office, but only if epidemiological data and work-related information are considered in the context of the wider structure of women's lives and with respect to meanings, beliefs, and values that govern their appraisal of their experience as workers. While such research may provide us with a deeper understanding of the ways in which technological change affects the experience and health of workers, it also holds out the possibility of broadening our thinking with respect to general questions of occupational health for both men and women. While it is the study of women's health that has led us to consider the importance of "extrinsic" factors, this new understanding should lead us toward more meaningful, and hopefully predictive, studies of the relationship between work and health.

Notes

1   These emphases in the field of occupational health, which tend to disregard women, parallel the concern in the sociology of work with industrial workers. This approach has not only failed generally to consider women workers but has led to relatively little attention being paid to white-collar and crafts occupations (Walshok 1981).

2   It is ironic that concern with women's occupational health has been stimulated by interest in the impact of high-stress jobs. Recent figures show that despite the recent movement of women into some non-traditional fields (medicine and law being good examples) overall women's employment situation has not improved. Women continue to work in a sex-segregated labor market, with the results that most women work in a few female-dominated fields and that women still earn far less than men in comparable jobs (Truman and Hartmann 1981).

3   Rotella (1981) and Davies (1982) provide excellent historical accounts of the feminization of the American office between 1870 and 1930.

4   The phrase "male secretary," like "male nurse," reveals the sex-typing of these occupations as clearly as do expressions such as "woman doctor," "female lawyer," and "lady executive."

5   Clerical work provides one of the clearest examples of the sex segregation of the American labor market (Hartmann 1976).

6   Because there are few statistical portraits of clerical workers which show age, sex, marital status, and ethnicity, we have based our inferences here on a 1980 National Secretarial Association study of secretaries, realizing that some of these inferences may not reflect adequately characteristics of typists, clerks, and other clerical workers (National Secretarial Association 1980). Elsewhere, wherever possible, we have specified the type of clerical work to which we refer, since one of the analytic issues here is the nature and diversity of clerical work, hence the necessity to avoid assuming that all clerical workers are alike or similarly influenced by technological change.

7 In 1960, 34.8 per cent of all American women were employed, while by 1980, this figure had increased to 51.1 per cent. The increasing participation of mothers of younger children is even more startling. In 1960 18.6 per cent of married women with children under six were working; in 1980 that figure was 45 per cent (Bureau of the Census 1981: 388).

8 Recent litigation on employment discrimination has stressed the issue of "comparable worth" as essential to establishing compensation parity in a segregated labor market.

9 Though there were some studies of women's occupational health in the 1930s, as Hunt's massive bibliography shows (Hunt 1977), the health of males, being productive workers, was of greater interest. Even after women came into the labor force in large numbers, this issue was still overlooked, probably because, as we have pointed out here, they largely went into clerical work, which, being in an office and being women's work, was thought "safe." As environmental concerns have grown, and as more women during reproductive years have remained in the labor force, health of working women has become problematic (Petchesky 1979).

10 At the same time, however, it should be remembered that employed mothers (as we have shown, an increasingly important segment of the female labor pool) tend to score better than either housewives or women with part-time employment on a number of measures of physical and mental health (Hoffman and Nye 1974), findings which suggest that even with the increased burden of employment and domestic responsibility, women's health is enhanced when they are employed. These studies did not, of course, differentiate women by type of employment, but considering the large proportion of the female work force in the clerical category, it must be assumed that these positive effects attach, to some extent, to clerical work (cf. also Nathanson 1980).

11 The clerical category in the Framingham studies includes clerical and kindred workers with secretaries, stenographers, bookkeepers, bank clerks, cashiers, and sales personnel in the majority of those interviewed (Haynes and Feinleib 1980). It would be important in future investigations to separate these jobs, since the pressure in sales is clearly different than in bookkeeping.

12 In a contrasting interpretation, Verbrugge (1984) suggests that epidemiological data point to ongoing improvements in working conditions for clerical workers. She points to the fact that the women followed in the Framingham study had been employed some years prior to the study, whereas women clerical workers followed in two more recent projects were at markedly lower risk for CHD and other stress-related ailments.

13   The linguistic categories "emic" and "etic" used in anthropology refer respectively to whether the knowledge presented in an ethnography is derived from the structures individuals being studied use to understand their own actions or whether it reflects the investigator's "objective" description of behavior. The ultimate test of the efficacy of the "emic" approach lies in the power of ethnography to predict future behavior, much as a grammar provides instructions which permit adequate language performance (Pike 1954; Harris 1968; Burling 1969). This approach parallels the epistemology of symbolic interaction which argues that data gathering and interpretation must attend carefully to interpret ("verstehen") the acting individuals' own realities, avoiding at all costs the imposition of investigator interpretation (Blumer 1969).

14   "Whether men or women are subjected to more work-related stress is debatable. Secretaries may be subjected to more stress than their bosses. The evidence is that working women still spend more time on household work than working men, and when we evaluate work-related stress, we must develop ways to include that extra work in the analyses. At the moment, based on cross-sectional data, we have little evidence that work outside the home is contributing to the morbidity and mortality among women" (Rice *et al.* 1981: 23).

15   For instance, the possibility exists that the shift of clerical work into the home might lead to the exploitation of child labor.

16   One might predict that for the large number of single mothers and other heads of households in the clerical labor force the unpredictability that accompanies the reorganization of clerical work may be a source of particularly severe stress, with probable deleterious effects on the health of workers.

17   A lack of "class consciousness" may well be a major reason why clerical workers in some places have resisted unionization. As Kanter points out, many secretaries identify with their bosses' careers, seeing this as the way to further their own self-interest (Kanter 1977).

References

Arnold, E., Birke, L., and Faulkner, W. (1981) Women and Microelectronics: The Case of Word Processors. *Women's Studies International Quarterly* 4: 321–40.

Barron, I. and Curnow, R. (1979) *The Future with Microelectronics: Forecasting the Effects of Information Technology.* London: Frances Pinter.

Bell, C. (1979) Implementing Safety and Health Regulations for Women in the Workplace. *Feminist Studies* 5 (2): 286–301.

Best, F. and Stern, B. (1977) Education, Work and Leisure: Must They Come in That Order? *Monthly Labor Review* 100 (7): 3–10.

Bingham, E. (1977) *Proceedings: Conference on Women and the Workplace.* Washington, DC: Society for Occupational and Environmental Health.

Blumer, H. (1969) The Methodological Position of Symbolic Interaction. In H. Blumer, *Symbolic Interactionism, Perspective and Method.* Englewood Cliffs, NJ: Prentice-Hall.

Bowen, D.D. (1973) Work Values of Women in Secretarial–Clerical Occupations. *American Journal of Community Psychology* 1: 83–90.

Braverman, H. (1974) *Labor and Monopoly Capital: The Degradation of Work in the Twentieth Century.* New York: Monthly Review Press.

Bridbord, K. and French, J. (1978) *Toxicological and Carcinogenic Health Hazards in the Workplace.* Proceedings of First Annual NIOSH Scientific Symposium. Park Forest South, IL: Pathotox Publishers.

Bureau of the Census (1981) *Statistical Abstract of the United States.* Washington, DC: US Government Printing office.

Burling, R. (1969) Linguistics and Ethnographic Description. *American Anthropologist* 71: 817–27.

Cohen, B.G.F., Smith, M.J., and Stammerjohn, L.W., Jr (1981) Psychosocial Factors Contributing to Job Stress of Clerical VDT Operators. In *Machine-Pacing and Occupational Stress.* London: Taylor & Francis.

Cralley, L.V. (ed.) (1972) *Industrial Environmental Health: The Worker and the Community.* New York: Academic Press.

Crompton, R., Jones, G., and Reid, S. (1982) Contemporary Clerical Work: A Case Study of Local Government. In J. West (ed.) *Work, Women and the Labour Market.* London: Routledge & Kegan Paul.

Davies, M. (1982) *Woman's Place Is at the Typewriter.* Philadelphia: Temple University Press.

Driscoll, J.W. (1981) *Office Automation: The Dynamics of a Technological Boondoggle.* Cambridge, MA: Sloan School of Management, MIT.

Epstein, C.F. (1970) *Woman's Place.* Berkeley: University of California Press.

Feldberg, R. (1982) Notes on Issues and Approaches to the Problems of Clerical Work, A Female-Dominated Occupation in a Period of Major Technological Change. In C.H. Chertos, L. Haignere and R.J. Steinberg (eds) *Occupational Segregation and Its Impact on Working Women: Report of a Conference Held at the Ford*

Foundation. Albany, NY: Centre for Women in Government.

Firth, R. Hubert, J. and Forge, A. (1970) *Families and Their Relatives*. New York: Humanities Press.

Fogarty, M.P., Rapoport, R., and Rapoport, R.N. (1971) *Sex, Career, and Family*. Beverly Hills: Sage Publications.

Gardner, A.W. (ed.) (1979) *Current Approaches to Occupational Medicine*. Bristol: John Wright & Sons.

Giuliano, V.E. (1982) The Mechanization of Office Work. *Scientific American* 247: 149–64.

Glenn, E.N. and Feldberg, R.L. (1977) Degraded and Deskilled: The Proletarianization of Clerical Work. *Social Problems* 25: 52-64.

Goldfield, R.J. (1980) The Automated Office in the 1980s. *Dun's Review* 115: 129–49.

Harman, C. (1979) *Is a Machine After Your Job?* London: Socialist Workers Party.

Harris, M. (1968) Emics, Etics and the New Ethnography. Chapter 20 in *The Rise of Anthropological Theory*. New York: Thomas Y. Crowell.

Hartmann, H.I. (1976) Capitalism, Patriarchy and Job Segregation by Sex. *Signs* 1 (2): 137–69.

Haw, M.A. (1982) Women, Work and Stress: A Review and Agenda for the Future. *Journal of Health and Social Behavior* 23: 132–44.

Haynes, S.B. and Feinleib, M. (1980) Women, Work and Coronary Diseases: Prospective Findings from the Framingham Heart Study. *American Journal of Public Health* 70: 133–41.

Hoffman, L.W. and Nye, F.I. (1974) *Working Mothers*. San Francisco: Jossey-Bass.

Hoos, I.R. (1960) When the Computer Takes Over the Office. *Harvard Business Review* 38: 102–12.

Hope, E., Kennedy, M., and DeWinter, A. (1976) Homeworkers in North London. In D.L. Barker and S. Allen (eds) *Dependence and Exploitation in Work and Marriage*. London: Longman.

Hult, M. (1980) *Technological Change and Women Workers: The Development of Micro-electronics*. New York: World Conference of the United Nations Decade for Women. Report Number 80–14948.

Hunt, V.R. (1977) *The Health of Women at Work*. Evanston, IL: The Program for Women, Northwestern University. Occasional Papers no. 2.

—— (1979) A Brief History of Women Workers and Hazards in the Workplace. *Feminist Studies* 5 (2): 274–85.

Hunter, D. (1978) *The Diseases of Occupations*, Sixth edition. London: Hodder & Stoughton.

Kanter, R.M. (1977) *Men and Women of the Corporation*. New York: Basic Books.

Komarovsky, M. (1962) *Blue-Collar Marriage.* New York: Random House.

Kundsin, R.B. (ed.) (1974) *Women and Success.* New York: William Morrow.

Leira, A. (1983) Women's Work Strategies: An Analysis of the Organisation of Everyday Life in an Urban Neighborhood. In A. Leira (ed.) *Work and Womanhood: Norwegian Studies.* Oslo, Norway: Institute for Social Research.

Lemkau, J.P. (1980) Women and Employment: Some Emotional Hazards. In C.L. Beckerman (ed.) *The Evolving Female.* New York: Human Sciences Press.

Lessor, R. (1982) *Unanticipated Longevity in Women's Work: The Career Development of Airline Flight Attendants.* Doctoral dissertation, University of California, San Francisco.

Levine, S. and Scotch, N. (1970) *Social Stress.* Chicago: Aldine.

Lopate, C. (1968) *Women in Medicine.* Baltimore: The Johns Hopkins University Press.

McCartney, L.D. (1979) Putting It All Together. *Dun's Review* 114: 70–72.

McNally, F. (1979) *Women for Hire. A Study of the Female Office Worker.* London: Macmillan.

Mandelbaum, D.R. (1981) *Work, Marriage and Motherhood: The Career Persistence of Female Physicians.* New York: Praeger.

Menzies, H. (1981) *Women and the Chip.* Montreal: Institute for Research on Public Policy.

Miller, J., Schooler, C., Kohn, M.L., and Miller, K.A. (1979) Women and Work: Psychological Effects of Occupational Conditions. *American Journal of Sociology* 85: 66–94.

Morgall, J. (1983) Typing Our Way to Freedom: Is It True That New Office Technology Can Liberate Women? *Behavior and Information Technology* 2 (3): 215–26.

Murphree, M. (1981) *Rationalization and Satisfaction in Clerical Work: A Case Study of Wall Street Legal Secretaries.* PhD thesis, Columbia University.

Murray, W.E., Moss, C.E., and Parr, W.H. *et al.* (1981) *Potential Health Hazards of Video Display Terminals.* DHHS-NIOSH Publication No. 81–129. Washington, DC: US Department of Health and Human Services.

Nathanson, C. (1980) Social Roles and Health Status Among Women: The Significance of Employment. *Social Science and Medicine* 14A: 463–71.

National Association of Working Women (1980) *Race Against Time: Automation of the Office.* Cleveland, OH: National Association of Office Workers.

—— (1981) *Health Hazards for Office Workers.* Cleveland, OH: Working Women Education Fund.

National Secretarial Association (1980) Secretarial Statistics. *The Secretary* 40: 17–20.

NIOSH (1981) Potential Health Hazards of Video Display Terminals, Cincinnati, June.

Nora, S. and Minc, A. (1980) *Computerizing Society.* Cambridge, MA: MIT Press.

Nussbaum, K. (1982) Office Automation: A Potential Solution to the Female Job Ghetto. In C.H. Chertos, L. Haignere, and R.J. Steinberg (eds) *Occupational Segregation and Its Impact on Working Women: Report of Conference Held at the Ford Foundation.* Albany, NY: Center for Women in Government.

Olesen, V.L. and Katsuranis, M.F. (1978) Urban Nomads: Women in Temporary Clerical Services. In A. Stromberg and S. Harkess (eds) *Women Working.* Palo Alto, CA: Mayfield.

Olson, M. (1981) CAIS Working Paper no. 25, New York University.

Oppenheimer, V.K. (1970) *The Female Labor Force in the United States.* Westport, CT: Greenwood Press.

Pearce, D. (1979) Women, Work, and Welfare: The Feminization of Poverty. In K.W. Feinstein (ed.) *Working Women and Families.* Beverly Hills: Sage Publications.

Petchesky, R. (1979) Workers, Reproductive Hazards, and the Politics of Protection: An Introduction. *Feminist Studies* 5: 233–45.

Pike, K. (1954) *Language in Relation to a Unified Theory of the Structure of Human Behavior,* 1. Glendale: Summer Institute of Linguistics.

Rice, D., Hing, E., Rovar, M.G., and Prager, K. (1981) Sex Differences in Disease Risk. In E.B. Gold (ed.) *The Changing Risk of Disease in Women.* Lexington, MA: Collamore Press.

Rotella, E.J. (1981) The Transformation of the American Office: Changes in Employment and Technology. *Journal of Economic History* 41: 51–7.

Rubin, L.B. (1976) *Worlds of Pain: Life in the Working Class Family.* New York: Basic Books.

Rumberger, R.W. (1983) *The Job Market for College Graduates, 1960–1990.* Stanford, CA: Institute for Research on Educational Finance and Governance, Stanford University.

Rytina, N.F. (1982) Earnings of Men and Women: A Look at Specific Occupations. *Monthly Labor Review* 105: 25–31.

Simon, H.A. (1957) *Models of Man: Social and Rational.* New York: Wiley.

Sleigh, J.M., Boatwright, B., Irwin, P., and Stanyon, R. (1979) *The Manpower Implications of Micro-electronics Technology.* London: HMSO.

Stellman, J. and Henifin, M.S. (1983) *Office Work Can Be Dangerous to Your Health*. New York: Pantheon.

Truman, D.J. and Hartmann, H.I. (eds) (1981) *Women, Work and Wages: Equal Pay for Jobs of Equal Value*. Washington, DC: National Academy Press.

Uhlig, R. and Farber, D.J. (1979) *Office of the Future*. New York: Elsevier.

Verbrugge, L. (1984) Physical Health of Clerical Workers in the U.S., Framingham and Detroit. *Women and Health* 9 (1): 17–41.

Waldron, I. (1978) The Coronary-Prone Behavior Pattern, Blood Pressure, Employment and Socio-Economic Status in Women. *Journal of Psychosomatic Research* 22: 79–87.

Walshok, M.L. (1981) *Blue Collar Women*. New York: Anchor Books.

Wright, M.J. (1979) Reproductive Hazards and "Protective" Discrimination. *Feminist Studies* 5 (2): 302–09.

Zuboff, S. (1982) New Worlds of Computer-Mediated Work. *Harvard Business Review* 60: 142–52.

Acknowledgements

We gratefully acknowledge support for work on this paper from the Century Fund and the Office of Nursing Research of the University of California, School of Nursing, San Francisco, and from the Department of Social and Behavioral Sciences, also at UCSF. We received able assistance from Barbara Bowers, Lydia Jensen, Sally Maeth, Ann Merrill, and Marvin Prosono. The following colleagues offered helpful criticism at various stages in the preparation of the paper: Roberta Lessor, Carol Shepherd McClain, Ann Merrill, and Sheryl Ruzek. Carole Browner's extensive comments deserve special recognition, as they helped us to clarify our thinking and to focus our argument. A preliminary version of this paper was presented at the 1983 meetings of the Society for Applied Anthropology, San Diego, California.

Four

The frail elderly woman: emergent questions in aging and women's health

Helen Evers

Aging and elderly women, in particular frail elderly women, have until quite recently been virtually invisible in feminist, sociological, and gerontological literature. In the early 1980s British literature on the subject remains sparse, but shows some signs of development (Fairhurst and Lightup 1981; Phillipson 1981). Many frail elderly women have to contend with various difficulties including ill-health, low income, poor housing, social isolation, and their own dependency and perhaps that of close kin. As with many other social issues, the analysis of dependency reveals discrepancies between the aims and operations of social and health policies in Britain and women's needs and experiences. Policy on community and long-term institutional care illustrates this particularly well.

This chapter will attempt to redress the lack of knowledge about elderly women which currently exists. The discussion will show the need to pay closer attention in research and theory development to clarifying the relationship between macrolevel social arrangements and individual subjective experience, and will review some work which is beginning to do this. A demographic portrait of elderly women and research in progress which primarily concerns the subjective side of the equation will serve as the basis for the discussion. Themes from that research which will be discussed are old women's activity and passivity in relation to organizing their own lives, and shared and contrasting perceptions of support relationships held by supporters and supported.

Portraits of elderly women in Britain: demographic issues

In 1979, 14.8 per cent of the population of the United Kingdom was aged 65 or over, comprising 8,047,000 people; 2,997,000 of these were aged 75 or more. From ages 65 to 74, women outnumbered men by 1.3:1, and for the population over 75 years of age, by more than 2:1 (Central Statistical Office 1979).

This preponderance of women, which increases with age, is one of the most significant features of the elderly population. Three important characteristics go along with this: first, widowhood is extremely common among elderly women. According to the *General Household Survey* for 1980, 75 per cent of men over 75 were married and 17 per cent widowed, as compared with 38 per cent of women who were married and 49 per cent who were widowed (Office of Population Censuses and Surveys 1982).[1] Rowlings (1981) cites data showing that the percentage of elderly women who are widows rises with increasing age. Second, since women tend to marry men older than themselves, 92 per cent of women over 65 living only with their spouses were married to men who were also aged 65 years or more. Only 71 per cent of men over 65 were married to women who were also 65 years old or more. Third, it is far more common for women to be living alone than it is for men: 45 per cent of women and 17 per cent of men over 65 lived alone in 1980 (Office of Population Censuses and Surveys 1982). About a third of those living alone – whether men or women – had no relative living nearby.

Abrams' study provides a useful foundation for considering recent research on the social life of the elderly. For example, his (1980) second report on the elderly, based on a sample of 844 subjects over 75, contains a section specifically about women. The report notes differences between those living alone and those living with others with regard to family life, leisure, and economic conditions. It was found that 79 per cent of those living alone were widows as opposed to 38 per cent of those living with others. Thirty-nine per cent of those living alone, but 26 per cent of those who lived with others, had never had children. At the same time 22 per cent of those living alone and 39 per cent of those not living alone lived very near an offspring. To generalize, those living alone had fewer and more tenuous family ties than those living with others. They were also far more likely to feel the lack of someone with whom to discuss personal matters and to feel lonely. Jerrome's (1981) British study of friendship of elderly middle-class women shows that friends – old and new – are important not only in relation to maintaining continuity and identity, but also as practical helpers, confidantes, and companions.

Apart from these demographic trends, elderly women are subject to a number of important disadvantages. Ermisch notes that in older age men tend to have higher income than women while spinsters have higher income than widows (1982: 42). These figures reflect the fact that fewer women than men receive occupational pensions. Ward (1981), too, shows how women, especially married women, are systematically at a disadvantage regarding access to pensions, particularly occupational pensions. The DHSS White Paper *Growing Older* (Department of Health and Social Security 1981) reports that the state pension is the main source of income for half of people past retirement age. Abrams (1980) suggested that this is true for the vast majority of people over 75. Almost everybody in Abrams' research sample claimed to have a secondary source of income: 28 per cent of men living alone were receiving supplementary benefit,[2] 18 per cent of men not living alone, 14 per cent of women not living alone, and a hefty 44 per cent of women living alone.

Joshi and Ermisch (1982), in looking at trends for the future and the likely impact of actual and possible changes in pensions provided and pension rights, as well as work-force participation of women and conditions of employment for both men and women, express cautious optimism regarding improvements for women in retirement, at least with respect to income. These analyses tend toward oversimplification in that they ignore the consequences of both ethnicity and social class[3] for the economic situation of elderly women. The evidence shows that a majority of older women, particularly widows, are less well off as regards material resources and income than men of roughly equivalent occupationally derived social class. In some cases this may be mitigated by access to family or other resources.

Turning next to women's disadvantages with respect to health, Sheldon's now classic study showed that elderly men living at home were more likely to be either extremely well or acutely ill than were women, whereas women were much more likely to suffer limiting but non-acute illness (1948: 13). In a different vein, the *General Household Survey* for 1980 (Office of Population Censuses and Surveys 1982) shows women are more likely than men of comparable ages to report long-standing illness and also more likely to see illness as limiting their activities. This sex difference is particularly marked among those elderly people who live alone. That is, lone women as compared with lone men of the same age group are far more likely to report limitations on their activities as a result of long-standing illness.[4] In another important study, Hunt shows that a relatively higher proportion of women than men of comparable ages suffers some loss of mobility. She suggests that "possibly this shows that women can continue to live at home with disabilities that might cause men to go into institutions" (1978: 69). Another possible interpretation of these data is that women are simply expected to be able to put up with limiting disabilities to a greater extent than are men.

The *General Household Survey* for 1980 contains the most recent data on capacity for self-care. Some interesting sex differences emerge in reported ability to perform a range of household tasks. Ability was age-related, but within that, men were more likely to be able to perform some domestic tasks such as household shopping than women, doubtless reflecting their generally better mobility. However, sex-role stereotypes, and a lifetime of gender-based division of labor in the home may be reflected in the *General Household Survey*'s findings: men were twice as likely as women to say they could not manage small amounts of washing, nor manage to prepare a main meal. As many as 23 per cent of women over 75 who live alone, as compared with 11 per cent of lone men over 75, report problems with going out alone (Office of Population Censuses and Surveys 1982). Possibly the tendency for women to be more likely to report problems in going out alone is related to gender-based lifestyle differences as well as to actual mobility problems.

Standards of housing are clearly relevant in relation to mobility and capacity for self-care. Tinker and Brion (1981) cite evidence that elderly women have a higher incidence of housing problems than do elderly men. At the same time, women perhaps require housing not just of equivalent, but of a better standard than men, given Hunt's findings regarding women's relatively more common loss of mobility. Tinker points out as well that proportionately more old women suffer from arthritis, a condition which creates imperatives for housing design and adaptation (Tinker 1981).

Although only a minority (around 5 per cent) of the elderly population is in institutional care at any particular time, women greatly outnumber men in residential homes and long-stay geriatric wards, as indeed would be expected from the wider demographic picture. The feminization of the institutional environment has implications for both men and women occupants, as I will discuss below.[5]

The demographic picture I have presented shows a preponderance of women in the elderly population and suggests they have certain needs and suffer from particular disadvantages which differ from those of men and are directly related to the issue of dependency. The next section will look at women's own perceptions of and reactions to their circumstances. Discrepancies between women's needs and experiences and social and health policies will then be taken up.

Portrait of the elderly women: subjective assessments

Research which I am now conducting on the experiences of elderly women in receiving support and services is generating case material which will illustrate two emergent themes relating to dependency: passivity, and activity in relation to control over daily life and the shared and contrasting perceptions of supportive relationships of women and their primary supporters. They are, as I will show below, interrelated.[6]

Control over daily life: activity or passivity?

The women interviewed to date constitute two broad groups with respect to their perceptions of being in control of their own lives. One group, whom I call the passive responders (PR), appear to lack positive control over the organization of their lives. The other group, the active initiators (AI), appear to be and feel themselves to be very much in charge of life. The two groups, thus far, do not seem to have discrete characteristics regarding health or physical and mental dependency, and none of the twenty-two women interviewed to date appear to suffer marked loss of intellectual capacity. At first glance, one might expect AI women to be more physically and mentally robust than PR women. However, while more of the AI women to date have relatively better health and less disablement than is the case with the PR group, some AI women are frail, and while they receive in some cases a great deal of outside support, they see themselves as being "in charge" of their helpers. Some PR women, in contrast, are apparently very fit, suffer little or no disablement, and receive little or no support from other people.

At present there is no obvious link between level of activity or passivity and social class, whether judged by the women's own or their husbands' occupations, by education or relative affluence, past or present. However, because of the area of the city in which I am sampling, the upper classes have not been represented thus far in the sample. A further set of variables which might be expected to relate to the activity–passivity dichotomy is that of current family structure and contact, although the nature of such relationships can be extremely complex. For example, having kin at hand who might be seen as potential supporters could reinforce any tendency towards passive behavior. Alternatively, relatives close by might engender opportunities for elderly women to be active initiators: sharing enjoyable activities or providing services such as child-minding or doing household chores for an elderly sibling. Absence of available kin might also relate to activity and passivity. For some women solitude may be their usual way of life or a glorious release from obligations, prompting a change to AI behavior. For others, unaccustomed or unwelcome solitude may engender apathy. But in this research, there are as yet no simple or obvious links between activity/passivity and patterns of family relationships.

With the caveat that these three factors, health, class, and family relationships, may yet emerge as significant as the research proceeds, my present working hypotheses as to the bases for the differences between PR and AI women relate to other factors. Namely, AI women have shared characteristics in that they have either initiated new interests and activities relatively recently or have sustained lifelong interests and activities. They thus feel a sense of purpose about and positive involvement in life. The PR women, in contrast, share an apparent lack of definite purpose in life. Thus far, such a distinction is not new: the AI women bring to mind the notion of "engagement"; the PR women, "disengagement" (Cumming and Henry 1961). But there are further, rather subtle, distinctions between the life histories of these two groups of women which may explain their self-perceptions of relative passivity or activity in late life.

PR women tend to have engaged in unpaid "care work" for a substantial proportion of their lives; they did not find time and space in their lives to invest energy in other activities and interests. Now at least 75 years old, these women have all lost their husbands (all but one had been married), and although they may have family nearby, these women generally do not have regular commitments to care work for their relatives; indeed, they may instead receive support from them.

In contrast, the AI women are more likely to have worked outside the home and to have found fulfillment from their work beyond the additional income it provided. AI women are also more likely to have had hobbies or interests which they pursued over many years, alongside their commitments to care work in the home and sometimes also paid work. AI as compared with PR women thus appear to be better able to maintain a positive stance towards life, a feeling of being in control of decisions, whether major or trivial, which affect their lives from day to day. Some short case histories illustrate this. First, AI women.

Active initiator: Mrs Beatrice B

At the time of the interview Mrs B was almost 82. Her husband had died thirteen years earlier after a long and happy marriage. He had been an engineering worker at a large car factory. There were no children. Mrs B had worked all her married life: nineteen years in manufacturing industry, then laundry work, and, after her husband's death, she worked as a cleaner for eight years at an old people's home. She had stopped work to help a sister who was ill. Living only on her old age pension, she had been left her house by a friend who had died twelve months earlier. Mrs B felt herself to be in good health, although she suffered from arthritis in her knees. Despite this, Mrs B had a very busy life. She had redecorated her house since moving in, worked the large garden herself, went out each day, provided regular help to a friend by looking after her 90-year-old mother, went to church each week, and still found time to make many of her own clothes. She had always enjoyed going out and about, gardening, sewing, and knitting, and took some pride in her new-found do-it-yourself skills. Mrs B felt herself to be very much in charge of her own life.

Active initiator: Mrs Florence J

Mrs J, a 95-year-old, had had four children, and had been living alone since her husband's death at the age of 93 five years before. He had died at home, a council flat, after a twelve-month illness. Mrs J looked after him with a great deal of help from services. This was as she had wished. Mrs J had not had paid work outside the home during her married life but had helped her husband with paperwork to do with his job as a self-employed decorator. The family had never been particularly affluent and Mrs J's main source of income was her old age pension. At the time of the interview, she was receiving considerable support from a home help, two neighbors, and her children. She and her husband had been very keen on the theater and on travel, making cycling trips and visits to many parts of the country. These leisure pursuits, cycling excepted, continued to figure importantly in Mrs J's life despite her now considerable frailty. When I first called at her house, she was away on holiday with her daughter. She reported going on many outings with her children and grandchildren by car and visiting the theater each Saturday night. Mrs J was a woman very much in control of her own life, who expressed contentment. One comment of hers was, "If you moan, people don't want to know you. As long as you're cheerful and enjoy a joke, you'll always have plenty of friends."

Although very different from each other in terms of physical robustness, age and family relationships, these two "active initiators" both had a continuing interest in activities which they had enjoyed all their lives and which were not directly related to care work.

Passive responder: Mrs Edith H

This woman, aged 86, had been living alone for twenty-five years, since her husband's death. She had given up paid work after marriage, and although she had been keen on photography as a hobby, had given this up too when her daughter was born, saying she had no time for herself once she had a child as well as her husband to look after. Her husband had had his own small coach-building business, and although obviously not affluent, Mrs H owned her own flat and had some savings which provided her with income over and above her old-age pension. (Even so, she said she could not afford to have a telephone installed, although she would have liked one.) She appeared somewhat frail, walking with a stick, and reported that she had not gone out unaccompanied for many years. Mrs H spent most of her waking hours at her married daughter's house, being collected in the mornings and returned at bed-time. Her daughter took care of all Mrs H's household tasks. Mrs H said, ''I couldn't even manage to boil an egg without ruining it.'' This had been going on for a number of years, and Mrs H seemed to take it entirely for granted. Her daughter Olivia saw it as her duty to provide this help, but resented the fact that she had not felt able to take up paid work as her own children grew up. Mrs H expressed contentment with her life at present, saying, ''I have always spent so much of my time just waiting for people and keeping myself to myself – waiting to be talked to, waiting for my husband to come home, waiting for my daughter to come or my neighbor to fetch my shopping.'' She needed other people to control her life, and was quite happy that this should be so.

Passive responder: Mrs Mabel E

Mrs E, aged 80, had been living alone since her husband's death eight years earlier. She had had ten children, two of whom had died. Some of her children lived nearby, her daughter Irene, in particular, providing a great deal of help. Mrs E lived in a ground-floor council flat, and received only her old-age pension as income. Her health had not been good for some years. She suffered from arthritis, chronic bronchitis, and hypertension. Besides help from several members of her family, Mrs E was visited weekly by a home help and a district nurse, the latter to wash her feet and cut her toenails as she was unable to do this herself. These formal helpers had become involved only after persistent and determined pressure on service providers by family members. She had had various unskilled jobs for short spells during her married life, including munitions work, but the greater part of her time and energy had been devoted to her family. She had had no particular hobbies or outside interests, apart from the church. Watching television was her main pastime, and she said that she often felt lonely and "down," and was always waiting for one of the family to visit or take her out in the car. She felt her physical problems affected her life in that it was difficult for her to go out alone for fear of falling. She felt very dependent on others to organize her life and her dearest wish was for more visits from the family. However, according to her daughter, she had at least one family visitor six days a week.

These case histories show that AI women perceive themselves as having control over their own lives. While some are fit and healthy and others frail, they share a sustained involvement in activities and interactions apart from their commitments to "women's work" as carers. Many of them have histories of work outside the home and indicate that this work was the source of more than purely financial rewards. In contrast, PR women do not see themselves as being in positive charge of their lives. Their life histories show they lack any sustained commitment to activities over and above care work and that they are less likely than AI women to have worked outside the home. Although some may be physically frail, others are relatively robust.

Mothers' and daughters' perspectives on supportive relationships

While those of the women in my sample who are receiving support may have it from various sources, the most commonly mentioned helper is a daughter. This accords with the evidence from a large number of other studies of help to old people (for example, Equal Opportunities Commission (1980) and Nissel and Bonnerjea (1982) both show that daughters and daughters-in-law are the most usual main carers for elderly people). Although the sample so far is too small to permit generalizations, and each dyad presents diverse relationships with respect to help with household chores, personal care, and financial and emotional support, there are some common threads that run throughout the stories.

First, let us consider the insidious onset of the support relationship. Both mothers and daughters in all cases found it hard to pinpoint a particular incident or date from which the support relationship had developed. This is perhaps surprising, but it must be remembered that the women of the sample are all non-institutionalized, and further that they live "successfully" alone. Therefore, extremes of physical and mental dependency are by definition less common among such a group. One daughter, Barbara, told of how she had "always" helped with the washing, first for both her parents after her own marriage and removal from home and later for her mother. The contact over the washing had, it seems, provided a context to which other tasks had sporadically, then regularly, attached themselves. Her mother, Mrs Hilda H, said that Barbara had always been "a golden daughter, good to her mother," and had been doing the "washing, the shopping, sometimes a bit of cleaning and this and that, for I don't know how long." It was the same for Olivia and her mother. Olivia recounted how her widowed mother had, to Olivia's trepidation, moved to live very close to her and how gradually as her mobility had decreased, Olivia's part in organizing her mother's life had increased. Mrs Edith H, a passive responder described above, could not remember how long she had been almost totally reliant on Olivia. Thus support relationships had grown up gradually between these women and their daughters. Beyond this, all the dyads believe that it is normal, natural, and perhaps inevitable that support would be provided in this way. For these women, the dominant social values which underlie public policies concerning family care and women's roles are also strong imperatives for actions and interactions of particular kinds.

It is clear that some daughters have perhaps never consciously thought about the emotional cost, not to mention lost opportunities, of providing care for their mothers; this means that in some cases the interview itself was an occasion for seeing the situation with new eyes.[7] The gradual development of the support relationship, then, and the "naturalness" of daughters' obligations requires that support be done alongside, though sometimes in deep conflict with, their other obligations – usually care of their own families and paid work. So strong is the feeling of "natural obligation" that conflicts seem to be accepted and somehow survived.

From the mothers' point of view, there are some who, like the daughters just mentioned, have apparently never consciously thought about the significance to themselves or their daughters of the support relationship, so "natural" is the obligation. They have never consciously considered alternative strategies whereby they might have met their needs for support.

For other old women, as for several of the daughters, there are overt personal conflicts, sometimes intense, associated with reliance on daughters. Although they see it as inevitable and natural that they should turn to their daughters first and foremost, some feel worried lest their requirements become a "burden." In some instances, although the mothers appreciate and indeed depend greatly on the help daughters provided, they do not get on with their daughters, and are even afraid of them. Mrs Maggie H, for example, described in glowing terms how wonderful her daughter Jenny was at providing meals and housework help and doing the washing. She wished she could see more of her, that the daily visits could be longer. Yet she also said she was afraid of her daughter: "She shouts at me, she's got no patience, I'm always afraid of what she'll say." This suggests the support relationships and obligations between old mothers and middle-aged daughters may be fraught with ambivalence and conflicts for both parties. Thus Walker's (1983) argument that both have a common interest in a challenge to structurally enforced dependency carries much weight.

The contrasting self-perceptions of the two categories of women discussed here have some practical implications. AI women see themselves as people who make their own decisions and control their own lives. They do not see themselves as dependent upon and subordinate to others, despite, in some cases, the fact that they receive various kinds of essential support from a number of people. In contrast, PR women see themselves as circumscribed by and dependent on the routines of their lives, whether or not their lifestyles are influenced or controlled by other people. A change in health status or usual social network, e.g. the death of a family member or close friend, may trigger the initiation or review of service provision, whether by lay or official supporters, some or all of whom may be strangers. A first contact with health professionals – health visitors, district nurses, consultant geriatricians – is more likely to occur when the woman is "not herself," which may pose difficulties in discovering something about her "normal" or usual self. The woman is very likely to present symptoms and be treated as sick, dependent, and passive.

An acute episode of illness may appropriately prompt authoritative intervention, but it would seem very important that the woman's usual self is discovered early on if services are to be provided sensitively and appropriately. For instance, if her self-perceptions are not taken into account, the AI woman may find this painful, and it may indeed be counter-productive. She may be rendered dependent by the well-intentioned ministrations of so-called "care professionals"; or she may resist to the point of becoming labeled a "difficult" patient or client with consequent detriment to herself.[8]

Similarly, for a woman who, when her usual self, is used to being dependent on routines and on other people for the organization of life, overzealous encouragement towards establishing autonomy may be painful, unwelcome, and inappropriate. Again, there may be negative consequences for the services providers as well. The PR patient/client may again come to be labeled as "difficult," though in a different way from the AI patient/client, and professionals' attempts to achieve therapeutic aims are very likely to be frustrated. Thus the practical implications of the nuances of old women's self-perceptions of relative autonomy do not necessarily fit in a commonsense way with usual levels of physical autonomy, as in the case of the physically frail AI woman, Mrs J (described above).

The next section will discuss aspects of United Kingdom policy on care of the elderly and some features of practical care provision by paid and unpaid supporters. The inherent anomalies with respect to the preceding portraits of frail elderly women will be drawn out. The discussion will show, for example, how the demographic preponderance of women over men tends to be ignored and how the possibility of different needs, experiences, and perceptions among elderly women, as between AI and PR women for example, has not been considered in official policies.

Policies on care of the elderly in the community and in institutions

Community care

Central to British policy on the elderly is the assumption that "community care" is the preferred mode of providing support to those elderly people who need it. Walker (1981b, 1981c) analyzes the different senses in which the term "community care" has been used in government policies. At one extreme, it can be taken to mean help provided by lay members of society, from lay care in the home supported by welfare workers to total care in any of a range of settings "in the community," even including residential homes or hospitals. The White Paper of 1981, *Growing Older* (Department of Health and Social Security 1981), together with other recent DHSS policy documents (1976, 1977) state government aims as being, crudely speaking, to maintain old people in their own homes as long as possible. *Growing Older* makes it clear that services are supposed only to support primary-care provision by families and other lay people and not to replace it. The clear assumption is that women, the traditional carers in the family, will routinely take on the job of supporting elderly kin. For women there are profound implications from this policy and its manifestations in patterns of service provision. The effects of economic recession and demographic trends on the financial and other costs of this policy, which must be borne not just by the state, but largely by families, mean that these implications must be seriously considered.

These policies affect women of all generations in various ways. Bond (1980) suggests that home-help organizers apply different decision criteria when assessing potential needs of men and women for home-help services. Often a woman is assumed to be more capable of looking after herself and her home than a man having apparently comparable limitations or disablement. Hunt (1970: 178) found that for a comparable level of incapacity men were more likely than women to receive a home help. It seems that so far as the home-help service is concerned, implementation of community-care policy embodies assumptions about the naturalness of old women's greater affinity for domestic and self-care work as compared with old men. Unfortunately, evidence about service allocation and need in relation to sex is scarce. Research data and official statistics may document utilization of services, but information about providers' decision criteria are seldom made explicit. Usually we know nothing either about potential clients who were rejected, or about those whose needs were never reflected in services.

Further, many married women face increased requirements for home care from elderly spouses who become ill. This happens more often to women than to men, since they tend not only to live longer, but to marry men who are older than they are. For those whose spouses survive into extreme old age, the likelihood of this situation arising is very high, given the increasing probability of disability with greater chronological age. Community-care policy assumes that these women, perhaps facing frailty themselves, should and will cope, as indeed did Mrs Florence J described earlier. Bowling and Cartwright (1982) studied the experiences of caring for a dying spouse by means of interviews with surviving partners. This illustrates some of the stresses: coping with mental confusion of the sick person, physical exhaustion, lack of practical help and emotional support among other things. However, we know too little about elderly women who take care of their sick elderly spouses, with the exception of those cases where arrangements break down and services, including the hospital, become involved. Indeed, Isaacs and Neville (1974) write of "the defeated" as those whose care requirements cannot be met by family carers faced with intolerable strain. Community-care policy may serve as well to mask an enormous area of personal and financial stress borne in private by elderly couples. One woman in my research sample, for example, felt extremely bitter about the indifference of health professionals to her difficulties in caring for her dying husband, the strain of which had taken a lasting toll on her vitality.

Thinking about women more generally and not just about old

women caring for old spouses, the reliance of community-care policy on unpaid female kin and low-paid women workers, e.g. home helps, has been well documented (Taylor 1979; Bond 1980; Equal Opportunities Commission 1980; Finch and Groves 1980; Ungerson 1981; Walker 1981b; Durie and Wilkin 1982; Equal Opportunities Commission 1982a and b; Finch and Groves 1982; Rossiter and Wicks 1982; Wright 1983). A detailed analysis of care work done by twenty-two families and of social, psychological, and financial costs shows that in all cases women were the main carers, often devoting several hours a day to direct care activities (Nissel and Bonnerjea 1982). The women and not their husbands often reorganized or gave up paid work outside the home in order to cope. Help from outside sources was not distributed equally between those families with similar problems; gaining access to services often depended instead on knowing how to "work the system" and on great persistence. Those seen to be coping were left alone to get on with the job. The case of Mrs Mabel E and her daughter Irene comes to mind here: dogged determination had been vital in instigating service provision. The costs of this are illustrated in Nissel and Bonnerjea's study (1982); carers suffered several forms of stress arising from physical work, mental effort, feelings of total and sole responsibility, and isolation. For some, this affected their self-concept: two-thirds of the women reported their estimation of their own worth had been adversely affected. These findings indicate, then, that family relationships are apt to be affected for the worse when care of an elderly relative is taken on.

The fact that married women who feel unable to take up or resume work, or who give up work to look after a relative receiving attendance allowance, are not eligible to claim the invalid care allowance illustrates a policy assumption that women's unpaid care work is normal, natural, and traditional. Yet any man or *single* woman who gives up work for the same reason is entitled to make such a claim. In the case of Olivia H, discussed above, who resented having to forego paid work in order to care for her aged mother Edith H, the inability to receive an allowance presented a real financial burden.[9]

Nissel and Bonnerjea (1982) conclude that the supposed benefits of home care for dependent elderly people may be nothing more than a rationalization by the state. The benefits to the state lie in saving public money better spent on services, including residential services, and ensuring that elderly dependent people, their problems and those of their carers, remain invisible in the private world of the home.

The growing concern about carers for elderly people, and the realities of community-care policies for them, represents a positive step towards challenging the status quo, although of course such a challenge carries potentially tremendous implications for resources as well as questions about current structural arrangements which restrict women's choices regarding participation in the labor market. In an economic climate of industrial decline, inflation, and unemployment and under a government committed to reducing public expenditure, it is unlikely that any major policy changes will be considered in the near future.

The literature on carers does not attempt to analyze the perspectives of the elderly people who are potential or actual recipients of care. This means that the cared-for are in danger of being relegated to the status of work objects. It also means that the realities of community-care policies are not well understood by those to whom they are directed, and further, that we can only speculate on the differences and similarities of old men's and women's expectations and experiences. The work of researchers in the United Kingdom who focus on carers and do not include the concerns of the cared-for may reflect a real lack of choice for the old people who want or need support. Arguments about the social creation of dependency, powerlessness, and reduced status all suggest that old people who want help of some kind may have real difficulties in making their preferences known, let alone translating them into practice.[10]

Moreover, the term "care," its uses and meanings, which has until recently received rather little attention, is an issue which should be central to any analysis of policy or care of the elderly and its practical implications. Some criticize the rhetoric of care in the context of social work (e.g. Anderson and Hewitt 1982). They argue that the term may be empty and meaningless, or, worse, a disguise for social control.

The term mystifies the social worker's activities, just as it excludes outsiders from scrutinizing them: "care talk" can be used to silence criticism or bargain for resources. Walker (1983) notes the confusion surrounding the term "care", and, again from within social work, Parker (1981) suggests that "care" can be disaggregated into a series of specific tasks, collectively described as "tending." Nissel and Bonnerjea (1982) develop a useful series of categories for analyzing care work of families for their elderly relatives. Graham (1983) argues that the perplexities associated with "caring" may derive in part from a failure to recognize its separate components: certainly it incorporates physical and mental work, e.g. planning and organizing daily life, but it can also be understood as an act of concern or love. She shows how sociological and psychological analyses of the caring activities of women need to come together to address both components and some of the inherent tensions and contradictions between them. It is beyond the scope of this paper to review the arguments in detail, but it is important to note the conceptual problems concerning the meaning of "care." Their further clarification would constitute a significant contribution to the analysis of relationships among policies on care of the elderly, the social and service infrastructure in relation to these, and their meanings for individual recipients and providers of care.

Institutional care

Although only about 5 per cent of the elderly population in the United Kingdom are in hospital or residential care at any time, the probability for the individual of experiencing some period – perhaps even permanent – of institutionalization increases with age. Townsend and Wedderburn (1965) showed that the socially isolated, those living alone, and those having no surviving children nearby (particularly female children) were more likely to enter residential care. The vast majority of long-term residents of either hospital wards or residential homes are, of course, women, since they account for the greater proportion of the elderly. Nevertheless, policies on institutional care take no account of the possible significance of the preponderance of women residents, or indeed of women workers in institutions. Men and women are implicitly regarded as members of the same category and as therefore having the same sorts of problems, which may work to the detriment of the male residents of these feminized environments, as well as to the female residents and those who care for them.

Further, current government policies say little about long-term institutional care. There is mention, in passing, of the rights of people in residential homes to dignity, privacy, and freedom of choice and of the need to mobilize members of the community to help patients "to adjust and respond to hospital treatment" (Department of Health and Social Security 1981: para. 8.25). However, the pervasiveness of the "medical model" in hospitals, which highly values active treatment and cure and relegates care work to the lowest-status categories, may act to the detriment of both patients and staff participating in long-term hospital care settings (Evers 1981a).

Current thinking associated with institutional care, whether in hospital or residential home, is essentially negative in that it is seen as a fall-back option in case community care fails. Finch and Groves (1982) point out that the institutional sector, like the community sector, relies primarily on care work by women, who are generally low-paid, low-status, part-time workers with family commitments. One objective of community-care rhetoric, and the avowed but scarcely fulfilled intention to divert a greater proportion of resources to it, is to keep the costs of residential care to a minimum. This assumes the continuing willingness of large numbers of women to work in low-status, physically and mentally stressful, low-paid jobs. However, there is very little literature which focuses on gender as an issue in residential care, with respect either to residents or to care-givers, just as public policy documents have little to say about long-term institutional care.

One exception appears in a national study of 100 local authority homes for the elderly. Willcocks (1982) reports that of 1,000 residents surveyed, 73 per cent were women, of whom nearly half were 85 years old or more. The men were younger on average and only a quarter of them were over 85. In general, though, the men had spent slightly longer in residence than the women. Willcocks suggests that the preponderance of female residents may have a key influence on the nature of the service provided, and furthermore that the circumstances leading to admission may differ between men and women, with the latter being perceived as able to cope for longer. Willcocks also found that only a minority of residents was offered any choice of residential home prior to admission and that the proportion of women who were offered choice was even less than that of men.

Bereavement was a much more common precipitating factor for admission among men, lending support to the assumption that men are perceived as less able to look after themselves. Among her other findings, Willcocks reports that women were much more likely to have experienced homesickness and difficulty in adjusting, and suggests that giving up the home and domestic responsibilities, so central to the lives of many women, may be more traumatic than is the case for men. (But perhaps men interviewed might have felt it "unmanly" to admit to homesickness.) Willcocks concludes by suggesting that residential facilities and regimes should create opportunities for residents, particularly women, to exercise greater autonomy over their own lives.

Research I conducted on the organization of work in geriatric wards also showed the importance of gender in relation to strategies used, albeit unconsciously, by nurses to care for and control their patients (Evers 1981b). These strategies varied not only in relation to how well nurses liked the patients, mediated by their compliance, cheerfulness, truculence, state of dementia, and so on, but also with the patient's sex. I argued that in some ways women patients posed a greater threat to nurses' professional control of care work in the ward. The bulk of such work is so-called "basic" care, a field in which elderly women patients have themselves often been great experts. The nurses' work is therefore open to criticism and sabotage by women patients of quite a different order than a potential male critique. Part of the nurses' control strategies included depersonalizing and devaluing the women to a far greater extent than men, whose identities were so often tied up with their pre-retirement work roles. The nurses often simply knew far less about the women, or ascribed to them the status of "just housewives" or "just widows." I would suggest, as does Willcocks (1982), that in hospital and residential homes alike, the deprivation of the freedom even to make a cup of tea, and the general lack of choice over the ordering of the domestic round, may be even more devastating for women patients than for men, and serve to reinforce their usual status in the institution as non-persons. The suspension of personal autonomy would be felt particularly keenly by women who tended to be more akin to the active initiators described earlier.

No simple solutions present themselves. Creation of

extended freedom of choice for patients would tend to create additional stresses for staff who are working within a bureaucratic system where smooth running and predictability are highly valued. More choice for patients could so easily become enforced choice in a bureaucratic organization. Women akin to the passive responders described earlier might then particularly suffer. However, it is time that policy-makers and practitioners took a more active interest in institutional care, particularly long-term care, and paid attention to the importance of gender in the residential process, its social relations, and the interface between community care, so-called, and residential care. Along these lines, further research is needed on the impact of gender-related variables on both recipients and providers of care.

Summary and conclusion

In this chapter, I have attempted to develop a picture of the frail elderly woman using demographic data and case material from research in progress. The former show the distinctive characteristics and disadvantages regarding health, income, housing, and dependency of members of the majority sex among elderly people. The latter, by identifying two types of women, active initiators and passive responders, shows something of the complexity of women's experiences and needs. A consideration of two areas of current United Kingdom policy, care of the elderly in the community and long-term care in institutions, shows built-in assumptions about gender. In practice these assumptions not only fail to take account of the distinctive experiences and needs of women, but also lead in many cases to active discrimination against them. Because of these characteristics of policy, the state system of care provision for frail elderly women features many anomalies, some of which the preceding discussion has sought to document.

   What are the implications for future developments in both policy and practice? This could be a subject for lengthy consideration but some thoughts can be suggested quite briefly. First, there is a need to develop and strengthen the data base, particularly regarding demographics, and to reveal further the range of subjective experiences and needs of frail elderly women and members of their networks of supporters and confidantes.[11]

Second, policy-makers' and care-providers' awareness of the issues should be fostered through appropriate education in the light of this developing knowledge base. Third, the rights of elderly people and those who care *about* and *for* them to choose the nature and mode of service provision should be incorporated into social and health policy if the needs of both populations are to be met in a way which recognizes their values and diversity.

Notes

1 The *General Household Survey* was started in 1971, and is a continuous survey based on a sample of the general population living in private households. In 1980, almost 14,000 households were sampled. The aim of the survey is to monitor relationships among the major variables with which social policy is concerned. It covers population, housing, employment, education, and health, as well as particular social groups. In 1980, for example, an extensive section on the elderly is included, based on a representative sample of 4,510 people of 65 or over.

2 The supplementary benefit can be claimed by pensioners whose weekly disposable income after payment of housing costs is below a state-defined minimum level and who have at 1983 rate savings of less than £2,500.

3 Many feminist writers, e.g. Delphy (1981), have argued forcefully that notions of social class relating to occupational status are very dubious when applied to women, who do not occupy an equivalent status to men either in the labor market or in the domestic sphere. The convention is to classify married women by the husband's occupation. This process becomes even more dubious for elderly women. Many of them have lost their husbands, perhaps many years ago. Others' husbands have retired from their main occupation, some having perhaps taken up other work, often part-time and/or of lower status than that which occupied them before retirement age.

Cartwright and O'Brien (1977) suggest that cultural position and lifestyle of elderly people of both sexes may well be related to previous occupation, but that their prestige and economic position are bound up with their status as pensioners. Townsend, in his study on poverty remarks on the problem of class analysis of the elderly, particularly women (1979). He goes on, however, to use class of origin and own or spouse's occupation as indices for married women. He shows that means and resources of late life for both women and men bear a relationship to their status as retired people with restricted access to the labor market as well as to class of origin and occupational class. For example, retired professional people and their spouses are likely to continue to be in a relatively advantageous position in old age.

4 Mental illness has not been singled out as a distinctive category in the *General Household Survey*. While there are numerous British analyses of the problems of mental illness in old age (e.g. Norman 1982) there appears to be a dearth of information about morbidity in relation to sex. Brice Pitt (1982) observes that the chance of admission to a psychiatric bed increases sharply in old age, particularly for women, but does not elaborate further. Mortimer, Schuman, and French (1981), writing of dementia, observe that a discrepancy in its incidence between the sexes would have important implications. Such evidence as there is seems equivocal.

5 *General Household Survey* data on use of services shows that more than one-third of the sample had seen a doctor during the month before interview, with women being more likely than men to have seen the doctor and the district nurse or health visitor. This is consistent with the higher incidence of reported long-standing illness among women. Almost 10 per cent had been in contact with the home-help service during the month before interview. Women were more likely to have had home help, probably due to their greater propensity to be living alone. Almost 20 per cent of those living alone had a home help, as compared with under 5 per cent of those living with others. Hunt's study, however, showed that of men and women with comparable disabilities, the men were more likely to be receiving home help (1970: 178).

6 The subjects of the research are fifty women, all aged 75 or over, who live alone. They have been identified through the age/sex registers of two general practices in different parts of the same large Midlands city. The sample is therefore not necessarily statistically representative of the elderly lone female population of the city. Extended interviews, lasting up to three hours, cover the patterns of their daily lives, including health and other problems, and strategies for coping with these. The respondent's background, and the development of social and family relationships and of lifestyle over the years, are also discussed. I take a particular interest in any supportive relationships the women may be engaged in, how they developed, and the women's feelings about these relationships. With the women's permission, up to three of their prime supporters are interviewed separately concerning their perspectives on the nature, history, and prognosis for the support relationship and their feelings about the relationship. I reinterview the women and their carers again after six to nine

months (or earlier, if any marked change occurs in their circumstance) in an effort to pick up any new decisions about support relationships, how these came about, and particularly the women's part in decision-making. The scale of the research discussed here is too small to permit any meaningful statistical comparisons given the complexities of the variables involved in the study. Fieldwork is still in the early stages and only a few follow-up interviews have been carried out as yet.

7 This raises methodological and ethical questions which I will not discuss here.

8 I have written elsewhere (Evers 1981b) about nurses' sometimes punitive control strategies directed towards "Awkward Alices" in geriatric hospital wards.

9 The Equal Opportunities Commission is campaigning for an end to this archaic discriminatory practice.

10 For analyses of the social creation of dependency mediated by macrosocial arrangements and social and health policy, see Walker (1980, 1981a, 1982, 1983), Townsend (1981), and Phillipson (1982), all of whom develop the analysis with respect to the position of elderly women.

11 An international review of the demographic position of elderly women has been carried out by Peace (1981). An important American study focusing on the characteristics, expectations, and experiences of middle-aged daughters caring for elderly mothers is being undertaken by Brody and her associates (Brody 1981). Both of these studies embody imperatives for further research and policy development.

References

Abrams, M. (1980) *Beyond Three-Score and Ten. A Second Report on a Survey of the Elderly*. Mitcham: Age Concern.

Anderson, D. and Hewitt, N. (1982) Careless Talk. *The Guardian*, 20 October.

Bond, M. (1980) *Women's Work in a Woman's World*. MA dissertation, Department of Applied Social Studies, University of Warwick.

Bowling, A. and Cartwright, A. (1982) *Life after a Death*. London and New York: Tavistock Publications.

Brody, E. (1981) "Women in the Middle" and Family Help to Older People. *The Gerontologist* 21 (5): 471–80.

Cartwright, A. and O'Brien, M. (1977) Social Class Variations in Health Care and in the Nature of General Practitioner Consultations.

In M. Stacey (ed.) *The Sociology of the NHS*. Keele: University of Keele.

Central Statistical Office (1979) *Social Trends 1980* no. 10. London: HMSO.

Cumming, E. and Henry, W. (1961) *Growing Old*. New York: Basic Books.

Delphy, C. (1981) Women in Stratification Studies. In H. Roberts (ed.) *Doing Feminist Research*. London: Routledge & Kegan Paul.

Department of Health and Social Security (1976) *Priorities for Health and Personal Social Services in England: A Consultative Document*. London: HMSO.

—— (1977) *Priorities in the Health and Social Services: The Way Forward*. London: HMSO.

—— (1981) *Growing Older*. London: HMSO.

Durie, A. and Wilkin, D. (1982) *Gender and the Care of Dependent Elderly People*. Paper presented at British Sociological Association Annual Conference, Manchester.

Equal Opportunities Commission (1980) *The Experience of Caring for Elderly and Handicapped Relatives: A Survey Report*. Manchester: EOC.

—— (1982a) *Caring for the Elderly and Handicapped: Community Care Policies and Women's Lives*. Manchester: EOC.

—— (1982b) *Who Cares for the Carers? Opportunities for those Caring for the Elderly and Handicapped*. Manchester: EOC.

Ermisch, J. (1982) Resources of the Elderly – Impact of Present Commitments and Established Trends. In M. Fogarty (ed.) *Retirement Policy: The Next Fifty Years*. London: Heinemann Educational for Policy Studies Institute.

Evers, H. (1981a) The Creation of Patient Carers in Geriatric Wards: Aspects of Policy and Practice. *Social Science and Medicine* 15A: 581–88.

—— (1981b) Care or Custody? The Experience of Women Patients in Long-Stay Geriatric Wards. In B. Hutter and G. Williams (eds) *Controlling Women: The Normal and the Deviant*. London: Croom Helm.

Fairhurst, E. and Lightup, R. (1981) *The Menopause: Trauma on the Road to Serenity?* Paper presented to Women in Later Life Conference, London.

Finch, J. and Groves, D. (1980) Community Care and the Family: A Case for Equal Opportunities? *Journal of Social Policy* 9 (4): 487–511.

Finch, J. and Groves, D. (1982) By Women for Women: Caring for the Frail Elderly. *Women's Studies International Forum* 5 (5): 427–38.

Graham, H. (1983) Caring: A Labour of Love. In J. Finch and D. Groves (eds) *A Labour of Love*. London: Routledge & Kegan Paul.

The frail elderly woman   111

Hunt, A. (1970) *The Home Help Service in England and Wales.*
London: HMSO.
— (1978) *The Elderly at Home.* London: HMSO.
Isaacs, B. and Neville, Y. (1974) *The Measurement of Need in Old
People.* Scottish Health Service Studies no. 34. Edinburgh: Scottish
Home and Health Department.
Jerrome, D. (1981) The Significance of Friendship for Women in Later
Life. *Ageing and Society* 1 (2): 175–97.
Joshi, H. and Ermisch, J. (1982) The Trend to Increased Female Labour
Force Participation and Women's Pension Rights in the Transition
to Maturity. In M. Fogarty (ed.) *Retirement Policy: The Next Fifty
Years.* London: Heinemann Educational for Policy Studies Institute.
Mortimer, J., Schuman, L., and French, L. (1981) Epidemiology of
Dementing Illness. In J. Mortimer and L. Schuman (eds) *The
Epidemiology of Dementia.* Oxford: Oxford University Press.
Nissel, M. and Bonnerjea, L. (1982) *Family Care of the Handicapped
Elderly: Who Pays?* London: Policy Studies Institute.
Norman, A. (1982) *Mental Illness in Old Age.* London: Centre for
Policy on Ageing.
Office of Population Censuses and Surveys (1982) *General Household
Survey 1980.* London: HMSO.
Parker, R. (1981) Tending and Social Policy. In E.M. Goldberg and S.
Hatch (eds) *A New Look at the Personal Social Services.* London:
Policy Studies Institute.
Peace, S. (1981) *An International Perspective on the Status of Older
Women.* Washington, DC: International Federation on Ageing.
Phillipson, C. (1981) Women in Later Life: Patterns of Control and
Subordination. In B. Hutter and G. Williams (eds) *Controlling
Women: The Normal and the Deviant.* London: Croom Helm.
— (1982) *Capitalism and the Construction of Old Age.* London:
Macmillan.
Pitt, B. (1982) *Psychogeriatrics – An Introduction to the Psychiatry of
Old Age,* Second edition. Edinburgh: Churchill Livingstone.
Rossiter, C. and Wicks, M. (1982) *Crisis or Challenge? Family Care,
Elderly People and Social Policy.* London: Study Commission on
the Family.
Rowlings, C. (1981) *Social Work with Elderly People.* London: Allen &
Unwin.
Sheldon, J.H. (1948) *The Social Medicine of Old Age.* Oxford: Oxford
University Press for The Nuffield Foundation.
Taylor, J. (1979) Hidden Labour and the National Health Service. In P.
Atkinson, R. Dingwall, and A. Murcott (eds) *Prospects for the
National Health Service.* London: Croom Helm.
Tinker, A. (1981) *The Elderly in Modern Society.* London: Longman.
Tinker, A. and Brion, M. (1981) Is There Equality for Women in
Housing? *Housing and Planning Review* 37 (2): 7–9, 19.

Townsend, P. (1979) *Poverty in the United Kingdom*. Harmondsworth: Penguin Books.

—— (1981) The Structured Dependency of the Elderly: A Creation of Social Policy in the Twentieth Century. *Ageing and Society* 1 (1): 5–28.

Townsend, P. and Wedderburn, D. (1965) *The Aged in the Welfare State*. London: Bell.

Ungerson, C. (1981) *Women, Work and the "Caring Capacity of the Community": A Report of a Research Review*. Unpublished report to Social Science Research Council.

Walker, A. (1980) The Social Creation of Poverty and Dependency in Old Age. *Journal of Social Policy* 9 (1): 49–75.

—— (1981a) Towards a Political Economy of Old Age. *Ageing and Society* 1 (1): 73–94.

—— (1981b) Community Care and the Elderly in Great Britain: Theory and Practice. *International Journal of Health Services* 2 (4): 541–57.

—— (1981c) The Meaning and Social Division of Community Care. In A. Walker (ed.) *Community Care: The Family, the State and Social Policy*. Oxford: Basil Blackwell and Martin Robertson.

—— (1982) Dependency and Old Age. *Social Policy and Administration* 1(2): 115–35.

—— (1983) Care for Elderly People: A Conflict Between Women and the State. In J. Finch and D. Groves (eds) *A Labour of Love*. London: Routledge & Kegan Paul.

Ward, S. (1981) *Pensions*. London: Pluto.

Willcocks, D. (1982) *Gender and the Care of Elderly People in Part III Accommodation*. Unpublished paper presented at the British Sociological Association Annual Conference, University of Manchester.

Wright, F. (1983) Single Carers: Employment, Housework and Caring. In J. Finch and D. Groves (eds) *A Labour of Love*. London: Routledge & Kegan Paul.

Acknowledgements

The ongoing research discussed in this chapter is funded by the Nuffield Foundation. Thanks are due to the women I interviewed, and to Margaret Stacey and Rae Harrison for their helpful comments on earlier drafts.

Five

Estrogen-replacement therapy: the production of medical knowledge and the emergence of policy

Patricia A. Kaufert and
Sonja M. McKinlay

Introduction

This chapter will discuss the impact of health policy and research on women's health using as its material the debate over the safety of estrogen-replacement therapy (ERT) which took place between 1970 and 1980. This debate had an impact on three different areas: the external relationships of the medical profession with the government, the press, and the pharmaceutical industry; the relationships within the profession between the researcher and the clinician; and the relationship between the physician and the patient. In each area, the outcome of the debate was influenced by the fact that estrogen was prescribed exclusively for women and had implications which were particular to women and to their health care. Tracing the history of the controversy is also an exercise in understanding how the production of medical knowledge is determined by ideological and sociopolitical factors among which women's own needs and interests have low priority.

Background

By the early 1970s, estrogen therapy had been in use for approximately forty years (Hoover *et al.* 1976a: 402). It had become one of the top five prescription drugs in the United States with the dollar value of the annual market in estrogen being nearly $70 million (Weiss, Szekely, and Austin 1976: 1261). According to Waldron (1977), the number of prescriptions per capita increased by 130 per cent between 1950 and 1972. The expanded use of estrogen is, therefore, to be understood within the context of a general and rapid increase in the use of medication. Nevertheless, the increase in sales of estrogen was particularly dramatic: by 1973, the market value was 3.8 times what it had been in 1963 (Weiss, Szekely, and Austin 1976); a survey in Washington carried out in the same year estimated that 51 per cent of women had taken estrogen for at least three months and that the median use was ten years.

The use of estrogen in the treatment of menopausal women was not without a research base, but it was formed by clinical trials in which the primary objective had been to demonstrate its ability to relieve menopausal symptoms and not its long-term safety. Neither the question of its safety nor of its efficacy had been adequately addressed and the majority of these studies had contained serious methodological flaws according to the review by McKinlay and McKinlay (1973). Yet, despite the lack of solid evidence, most clinicians believed that estrogen therapy worked and that estrogen was safe.

Neither the major medical journals nor the fraternity of epidemiologists had shown much interest in either the menopause or in estrogen therapy. There were no government regulations on its use, and the pharmaceutical industry had had an open market in which to promote ERT, using either direct contact with physicians or working indirectly through the medical and popular media, particularly the women's magazines. Physicians were encouraged to prescribe estrogen and women to ask for it; both were essentially passive recipients of information fed to them by the industry. The changes in the relationships among the pharmaceutical industry, the media, clinicians, and their women patients between 1970 and 1980 form the subject-matter of this chapter.

Methods

The material to be used in this discussion is taken from the *New England Journal of Medicine* (*NEJM*) or the *Journal of the American Medical Association* (*JAMA*). These journals were chosen because they are widely accessible within both the research and clinical communities of medicine and are unquestionably legitimate – characteristics which make them ideal as sources through which to monitor the debate over estrogen as presented within the medical profession itself. The indices of both journals were searched under the following headings: menopause, climacteric, estrogen, osteoporosis, endometrial cancer. Not only research papers, but review articles, letters, and editorials were retrieved by this method. They are used to reconstruct a summary history in which the debate is divided into three parts. The first describes the widespread acceptance of estrogen as a legitimate therapy for the menopause and post-menopause. The second part introduces the work of the researchers and follows the sequence in which the different studies were published in the *NEJM* and *JAMA*. While there will be some methodological criticism of this research, the primary aim is to trace the case against estrogen as it was made by the research community. The third part presents the response of the clinicians and the first movement towards a rehabilitation of estrogen therapy.

Debate

Neither the menopause nor its management by estrogen therapy received much attention in either the *NEJM* or *JAMA* between 1970 and 1973. There was one reference in the *NEJM* (a discussion of estrogen–progesterone in the treatment of cancer (Richardson 1972), and nine in *JAMA*; six of which dealt with questions of clinical management, such as dose levels, side-effects, the appropriateness of use with different patient groups. The general tone of this material is that estrogen is both a safe and a legitimate therapy. The slight whiff of quackery, associated with ERT as the result of Wilson's (1966) over-enthusiastic endorsement of its powers, had been dispelled by this time.

Attitudes towards estrogen therapy between 1970 and 1973 were well summarized in a *JAMA* editorial (Kase 1974) which appeared in January, 1974, as a commentary on two reports published in the previous year. These were the products of conferences on the menopause to which the conclusion, according to Kase, was that high-dose estrogen replacement was inconclusive, and he advised that physicians could and should continue its prescription. This editorial made three points relevant to understanding the widespread use and popularity of estrogen therapy in the late 1960s and early 1970s. First, the menopause was defined as a deficiency disease which had potentially serious implications for women's health. Second, estrogen was the therapeutically logical method of managing this estrogen deficiency. Third, although the demand for estrogen by women was labeled as foolish (the product of media publicity touting its value as a "youth drug"), the widespread physician adoption of hormone therapy was based on "a sensible" assessment of its therapeutic worth.

Enter the Researchers

Researchers became interested in ERT, not from a concern with the menopause and its treatment, but because estrogen was a topical issue in medical research on cardiovascular disease and on cancer. In the late 1960s and early 1970s, reports had linked the contraceptive pill with an increased risk of thrombo-embolic accident and myocardial infarction (MI) (Vessey and Doll 1968). Furthermore, when estrogen was used relatively successfully to treat prostatic cancer in men, the trials had to be discontinued because of an observed increase in heart disease among those treated. In terms of cancer, estrogen was associated with the growth of tumors in animal experiments but the first evidence linking hormones with tumor growth in young women implicated the drug DES with cancer (Herbst, Ulfelder, and Poskanzer 1971).

The menopause itself was incidental to the research published in the *NEJM* and *JAMA* between 1974 and 1980. The objective was to inquire into the positive and negative effects of estrogen on major disease processes such as endometrial cancer, breast cancer, and coronary heart disease.

The first paper in the series reported an association between ERT and gall-bladder disease (Boston Collaborative Drug Surveillance Study 1974). It provoked relatively little response in comparison with the reaction to four subsequent papers which linked estrogen with endometrial cancer. The first pair were the most controversial. Smith *et al.* (1975) included both menopausal and post-menopausal women in 317 cases and matched cancer controls, but did not attempt to control this variable. Ziel and Finkle (1975) included 94 cases and 188 matched controls with intact uteri. Thirteen cases were labeled as pre-menopausal (undefined) – too small a number for separate analysis – and no conclusions as to the role of menopause could be drawn. These studies also used a less than optimal design – pair matching. It is important to note, however, that the estimated increase in cancer risk due to estrogen, as reported in these articles, ranged between 500 and 800 per cent – a risk too high to be explained away by even major methodological flaws.

The second pair included another case-control, retrospective study (Mack *et al.* 1976), but Weiss, Szekely, and Austin (1976) took a different approach. After examining the data on endometrial cancer rates for eight areas in the United States, they found that ''after many years of relative stability incidence rates had risen sharply in the 1970s'' (Weiss, Szekely, and Austin 1976: 1259); an increase which ran parallel with the expansion in the market for estrogen. Despite the methodological problems inherent in these four studies, the debate over the safety of estrogen therapy was triggered by their publication.

The correspondence columns of the *NEJM* carried a series of criticisms of the four papers, but the first serious challenge to their argument – that estrogen was associated with endometrial cancer – came from Horwitz and Feinstein (1978). Two issues were raised. First, the choice of controls had been incorrect; second, that as women taking ERT received closer supervision, their cancers were more likely to be detected and at an earlier stage. An editorial in the same issue of the *NEJM* criticized Horwitz and Feinstein's arguments and their own methodology. The journal also published three further papers which reconfirmed the link between estrogen and endometrial cancer, each claiming freedom from the biases of which Horwitz and Feinstein (1978) had accused their predecessors (Antunes *et al.* 1979;

Jick *et al.* 1979; Shapiro *et al.* 1980). The final pair of papers in the set of ten on endometrial cancer agreed that the association was present, but argued that it was not significant when the dose was low and use limited to two years (Weiss *et al.* 1979) or three and a half years (Hulka *et al.* 1980). (These two, together with the Horwitz and Feinstein (1978) paper, represent a move to rehabilitate estrogen therapy which began in the late 1970s and which will be discussed in the next section.)

Given a higher disease incidence, any suggestion of an association between estrogen and breast cancer was potentially a more alarming prospect. Yet the question received less prominence in either the *NEJM* or *JAMA* than endometrial cancer. There were greater methodological difficulties to research on breast cancer, but the *NEJM* may also have been reluctant to set off another controversy, given the criticism it had received for publishing the Ziel and Finkle (1975) and Smith *et al.* (1975) studies. Out of the thirteen papers on ERT and breast cancer listed in a review by Jick *et al.* (1980), only three had appeared in the *NEJM* and all before 1976 (Boston Collaborative Drug Surveillance Program 1974; Mack *et al.* 1975; Hoover *et al.* 1976a). An association with breast cancer was not confirmed by either the Boston Collaborative Drug Surveillance Study (1974) nor by Mack *et al.* (1975). However, in 1976, Hoover *et al.*, reporting on a twelve-year follow-up of women who had taken estrogen, claimed that "Estrogen use was related to an especially high risk of breast cancer among women who had developed benign breast disease after they had started the drug" (Hoover *et al.* 1976a: 401).

The one paper appearing after 1976 was published in *JAMA* in 1980 (Ross *et al.* 1980) but was simultaneously criticized in an editorial by Meier and Landau (1980). The Ross *et al.* (1980) paper was later praised in the WHO review of menopause research as the first in a series of "methodologically sounder case-control studies" which "have provided repeated but not invariable indications that a relationship exists between estrogen use and breast cancer" (WHO Scientific Group 1981: 74). However, their numbers (138 matched cases and controls) were too small for adequate control of many intervening variables. The roles of age at and type of menopause were considered briefly, although the role of age at menopause was not adequately described or discussed. An earlier case-control study, in contrast, specifically investigated the pre- and post-menopausal risk (Stavraky and Emmons 1974). The numbers were adequate (278 cases, 106 pre-menopausal and 480 post-menopausal controls), and an increased risk with atypically late natural menopause (fifty-five years) was demonstrated.

The third issue raised by researchers in this period was the possibility of an association, whether positive or negative, between estrogen use and coronary heart disease. Rosenberg and co-workers published two papers (Rosenberg *et al.* 1976, 1980) in which they explored the association among women with non-fatal MI. Using further data from the Boston Collaborative Drug Surveillance Study, Rosenberg *et al.* found no evidence of a "statistically significant association between current regular use of estrogen and non-fatal myocardial infarction" (Rosenberg *et al.* 1976: 1256). Their final conclusion was that estrogens "neither increase nor decrease the risks of MI appreciably" (Rosenberg *et al.* 1980). On the other hand, an earlier paper by Jick, Dinan, and Rothman (1978) had reported that women who both smoked and took estrogen were at increased risk, while a study in *JAMA* reported that women were at greater risk if they took estrogen, when risk was assessed according to their "high plasma triglyceride levels and systolic and diasystolic blood pressures" (Stern *et al.* 1976: 811). Following the example of Stern *et al.* (1976), two papers examined the association between replacement therapy and the various risk factors for coronary heart disease, including blood pressure and cholesterol levels (Bradley *et al.* 1978; Barrett-Connor *et al.* 1979). The results were inconclusive, but an undeterred Barrett-Connor continued to argue that the risks of endometrial cancer should be weighed against the possibility (even if unproven) that estrogen might protect against coronary disease. In all of these studies, age at or type of menopause were not adequately considered as potential intervening or confounding factors. In particular, no distinction was made between those women with artificial and natural menopause – two very different groups with respect to disease risk.

To summarize the case against estrogen as presented to clinicians in the *NEJM* and *JAMA* – at least by the end of 1976 – these papers had linked estrogen therapy with gallbladder disease, endometrial and breast cancers and with higher levels of the risk factors for coronary disease, but not with myocardial infarction. The case against estrogen was certainly not unequivocal. Aside from their particular methodological flaws (cf. Hulka 1980), the case-control retrospective method followed by the majority of these researchers was not capable of settling questions of causation in any definitive sense (Jick 1977: 485). The limitations inherent in this design are not unique to work related to the menopause and post-menopause, but they were compounded by: (1) lack of consistent definition of the menopause, and (2) inclusion of subjects of widely varying menopausal status with no attempt to control this variation.

The clinical response and the move to rehabilitate estrogen therapy

Other material on ERT published simultaneously with this research tends to belong to one of two camps; either they are sober and careful appraisals of the evidence or they attack the research, defend ERT, and work towards its eventual rehabilitation. The editorials and research review articles published in the *NEJM* tended to fall into the first camp. At the beginning of the debate, Ryan (1975) and Weiss (1975), assessing both the Ziel and Finkle (1975) and Smith *et al.* (1975) papers, tried to set the risk of endometrial cancer in perspective. At the end of the period, Weinstein (1980) constructed an equation in which he attempted to quantify the costs and benefits of estrogen therapy. His conclusion was that it is not cost-effective ''as a prophylactic measure in an asymptomatic woman'' with an intact uterus; for symptomatic women, its value depended on the importance the individual and/or society attached to the relief of menopausal symptoms. Weinstein argued that:

> For the individual patient, the benefits of symptomatic improvement and reduced mortality and moribidity from hip fractures must be weighed against the risks, such as endometrial cancer and gallbladder disease.
>
> (Weinstein 1980: 308)

Writing in the *NEJM*, both Quigley and Hammond (1979) and Weinstein (1980) argued that only women could balance their need for symptom relief against the risks of therapy.

In contrast to the relatively moderate position adopted in the *NEJM*, articles in *JAMA* (Lipsett 1977; Shoemaker, Forney, and MacDonald 1977; Landau 1979; Meier and Landau 1980) tended towards support of ERT. They play down, while not denying, the risks of endometrial cancer and they extol the benefits of estrogen for women's health. Meier and Landau (1980), for example, list the diseases attendant on menopause against which they claim estrogen would offer effective protection:

> Osteoporosis, a potential crippler, can be arrested; and further attacks prevented with estrogen therapy. Genitalia can be preserved in functional state. It is conceivable that the progression of atherosclerotic disease can be delayed.
>
> (Meier and Landau 1980: 1658)

This catalogue of preventable diseases implied an obligation on the physician to prescribe estrogen, regardless of whether or not the patient experiences symptoms or whether or not she asks for therapy, and despite the risk of endometrial cancer.

The rehabilitation of estrogen therapy depended on research demonstrating that either the risks of endometrial cancer could be reduced or that the benefits of estrogen might outweigh the apparent risks. In terms of endometrial cancer, it was suggested that the risk would be reduced if progesterone were added to the therapeutic regime, a practice common in Europe, but not in the United States. Writing from London to the *NEJM*, Studd and Thom blamed the unopposed use of estrogen (which they called a "bizarre therapy" (Studd and Thom 1979: 923)) for the American rates of estrogen-related endometrial cancer. The campaign to encourage the addition of progesterone made some appearance in the correspondence columns of the *NEJM*, including the letter from Studd and Thom and one from Greenblatt (1979), a prominent American advocate of estrogen therapy. It was countered by a letter from Gastel, Cornoni-Huntley, and Brody (1980) reporting on a National Institutes of Health (NIH) conference at which the use of progesterone had been rejected. While agreeing that the risk of cancer might be reduced, the conference cited experience with the contraceptive pill, and argued that progesterone might increase the risk of thromboembolic accident. The NIH recommendation against progesterone delayed the introduction of combined estrogen–

progesterone therapy for general use in the United States and effectively closed off the first option: namely, to reduce endometrial risk.

As an alternative to discrediting its risks, the benefits of estrogen were promoted. Two arguments were favored. First, estrogen might protect women against cardiovascular disease, and second, it might protect women against osteoporosis. For those who favored the continued use of estrogen, the first hypothesis was the most attractive. Cardiovascular disease was the second major killer of post-menopausal women after cancer; a significant lowering of this risk would effectively counterbalance the now accepted risks of endometrial cancer. As discussed earlier, the research on this question published in the *NEJM* and *JAMA* between 1970 and 1980 had found no significant association, either positive or negative, between estrogen and cardiovascular disease. Nevertheless, undeterred by the quality of the evidence, both Shoemaker, Forney, and MacDonald (1977) and Meier and Landau (1980) claimed this as one of estrogen's benefits.

The probability that estrogen might protect against osteoporosis was also used to argue for its continued use. In terms of actual research this hypothesis had received more attention in Europe than in the United States; the first study on osteoporosis to appear in either *JAMA* or *NEJM* was not published until 1980. In that paper, Weiss *et al.* (1980) argued that the risk of fractures was lower among women who took estrogens, but that the reduction in risk was small. It also had to be weighed against the risk of endometrial cancer, particularly as prolonged use of estrogen, which would be required to protect against osteoporosis, would increase the risk of endometrial cancer according to the studies by Weiss *et al.* (1979), and by Hulka (1980).

A review of the debate

So far we have outlined the debate over estrogen therapy between 1970 and 1980. We have largely ignored material published outside the *NEJM* and *JAMA* and have been selective in the amount of detail with which each study has been discussed. There are some general methodological criticisms which can be made not only of these papers, but of other research in the area reported during the same period; criticisms which also apply to many ongoing projects. Research is primarily medical and oriented to the management of the post-menopausal period, rather than focusing on an understanding of the menopause itself. Clinical trials as well as clinical series investigating hormone and bone-density levels continue to be fragmentary and non-cumulative in character. They use small numbers, highly selected subjects of widely varying menopausal or post-menopausal status. Women experiencing natural or surgical menopause are repeatedly included in the same studies without controlling for the very different health status and symptom response in these two groups. There have been no population-based studies focusing on the menopause and post-menopause with large samples undertaken in the United States or North America until those being currently conducted by the authors which were funded in 1981.

In looking at research after 1980, it is evident that the move to rehabilitate estrogen therapy is an ongoing one. While the risks of endometrial cancer are not denied, there has been a major increase in U S research on osteoporosis and estrogen treatment within the last three years. While there is debate over whether estrogen can give more than temporary protection, the risks of osteoporosis and the beneficial effect of ERT are widely promoted. The other argument, that ERT protected women against cardiovascular disease, received a major boost from the publication of results from the Lipid Research Project (Bush *et al.* 1983). These results have been severely criticized on methodological grounds, but despite this they have encouraged claims that estrogen is beneficial to health.

Given the level of health risks involved in both cardiovascular disease and osteoporosis, any evidence that estrogen was protective would have important implications for women's health. Yet, given the past history of estrogen, attempts at its rehabilitation are inevitably suspect. It is in the interest of the pharmaceutical companies to reestablish a highly profitable market – one in which women would be kept on long-term therapy, regardless of their menopausal symptoms. The wider context of the debate over estrogen, including the role of the pharmaceutical companies, is presented in the next section, which examines the impact of this history on the relationships of the medical profession with the media, with government, with the pharmaceutical companies, and with women.

The impact of the debate

The media

Epstein argues that the press was slow to comment on the risks associated with DES and with the contraceptive pill (Epstein 1978: 225). However, as the different studies on estrogen therapy appeared in the *NEJM*, the media were quicker to report its iatrogenic properties and to comment on how widely it was used. A major controversy broke out in the *NEJM* when, to the anger of Inglefinger, a writer with the *Washington Post* reported an association between estrogen and breast cancer based on a leaked copy of the paper by Hoover *et al.* (1976a) before it appeared in the *NEJM* (Inglefinger 1976b: 897).

Throughout the material taken from the *NEJM* and *JAMA*, there are occasional references to the role of the media in the estrogen debate. A close, but uneasy, relationship prevailed between the medical profession and the press during the 1970s. In the Shattuck lecture, Inglefinger (1977), who was retiring as editor of the *NEJM*, claimed that press interest in medical matters was rare prior to 1960, but accelerated during the 1970s. As evidence, he compared the *New York Times* index for 1965 and 1975, and claimed that "the *Times* in 1975 carried about four times as much medically related news as it did a decade earlier" (Inglefinger 1977: 1261).

Inglefinger (1977) frankly admits that both journals fostered the interest of the press by a policy of press releases and advance copies of articles. On the other hand, he also castigates the press:

> Lay media, while relying on the reputation of the Journal, ignore the caveats and qualifications and translate the news for the public into accounts that are occasionally erroneous, and frequently unbalanced, and, even if accurate in text may appear under misleading banners.   (Inglefinger 1976a: 668)

There was some truth to these criticisms. The initial studies of the association between estrogen and endometrial cancer were poorly designed and their limitations were generally recognized by the research community. However, the media were not concerned with the niceties of epidemiological evidence; they attacked ERT with the same uncritical enthusiasm with which it had been originally promoted in women's magazines.

Whether one views the role of the press in positive or negative terms, the publicity had a major responsibility for the reduction in the use of estrogen after 1975. Although their circulation was high in comparison to other medical journals, the *NEJM* and *JAMA* each reached only approximately a third of the medical profession (Subcommittee on Health 1974). Media publicity served to carry the message of the researcher – that estrogen was potentially iatrogenic – into the wider medical community and to the lay public, including women taking estrogen.

Government response

As the agency with responsibility for drug safety, the FDA became involved in the debate soon after the publication of the initial studies implicating estrogen as a carcinogen. The FDA Commissioner, testifying before the Senate Health Sub-Committee in January, 1976, agreed that the evidence for the association seemed strong and promised a revision in the labeling of estrogen (*Washington Post* 1976). In October 1976, the FDA ruled that manufacturers should prepare a warning on the risks of estrogen for package insertion by the following year. There were precedents for the FDA action; a similar insert had been required for oral contraceptives since 1971 and was to be issued later for the IUD. As noted by the Agency itself, the insert had a marked impact on the market for estrogen: "It declined by 18 per cent from 1975–76 and by another 10 per cent from 1976 to 1977. . . . In 1977 approximately 5 per cent of women in the United States or 4.1 million were taking estrogen" (FDA Drug Bulletin 1979: 3). According to Jick *et al.* (1979), the incidence of endometrial cancer also fell over the same period.

The pharmaceutical companies launched an immediate counter-attack against this government action in cooperation with the clinicians. According to Johnson (1977), as the first studies on endometrial cancer appeared in the *NEJM*, Ayerst (the manufacturer of Premarin) sent out a circular advising clinicians that estrogen was safe. In the Shattuck lecture,

Inglefinger (1977) commented on the stream of articles supporting estrogen which appeared in the industry-controlled free medical press. The Pharmaceutical Manufacturers' Association took legal action against the FDA's regulation requiring the package insert. It argued that this was unconstitutional and that "patient information would reduce sales of estrogen drugs and, therefore, reduce profits" (Kasper 1978).

The manufacturers were joined in this suit by the American College of Obstetrics and Gynecology and had the formal support of the American Cancer Society and the American College of Internal Medicine (Epstein 1978; Kasper 1978). The College was concerned with the release of information to patients on their treatment, which in their view contravened the right of the profession to control access to medical knowledge. Furthermore, the FDA action was seen as government interference and, therefore, as a threat to professional autonomy. Material in the *NEJM* and *JAMA* suggests that the reaction in the profession was the expression of a more general sense of being persecuted by government and the press. For example, Inglefinger complained that it was "open season on doctors" (Inglefinger 1976a: 667); in *JAMA*, Landau argued that the FDA Commissioner had "officially expressed his distrust in the medical profession" (Landau 1979: 47).

Landau's hostility to the FDA was not universally shared. In an *NEJM* editorial reviewing FDA activity, Ryan (1977) agreed that "the package insert is clearly a challenge to the time-honored autonomy of the individual physician in determining what to disclose to a patient." But he continued by asking what alternatives were available when the FDA believed that "the present system is not working well, that there are excesses in prescribing practices of many drugs and that patients are not being adequately informed" (Ryan 1977: 1287). In Ryan's view, "those who would reject the FDA initiatives on the grounds that our present methods for assuring prescription safety are working well will have to come up with more convincing arguments" (Ryan 1977: 1288).

Ryan's reaction to the FDA regulation is more typical of the research than of the clinical communities within the medical profession. The prescription of estrogen in the late 1960s and early 1970s had been excessive given the lack of evidence on its safety or its efficacy. Researchers were not only aware of this, but they made it public; hence, the hostility of their clinical colleagues. Reading the reaction of clinicians to the debate over estrogen, it is clear that their objection was not to research being done, or even to the discussion of its results, so long as this took place within the boundaries of the profession. Publication in the *NEJM* had meant they were accessible to outsiders and to the media.

The medical community: researchers versus clinicians

The conflict generated a debate within the medical profession itself which is illustrated in an exchange of correspondence in the *NEJM*. A gynecologist's criticism of the *NEJM* for publishing the breast-cancer study by Hoover *et al.* (1976a) makes the point as seen by the clinician: "I criticize the *Journal* for releasing this information to the lay press and causing doubt, fear and anxiety among our patients before the facts are generally accepted by the majority of experts" (Baggs 1976: 898). The reply (Hoover *et al.* 1976b) not only justifies their own action, but states the countervailing values of the research as opposed to the clinical community. In response to the criticism that the *NEJM* should not have published the study, the letter reads:

> A scientific journal is precisely the place where responsible research should be presented so that criticism and suggestions can be elicited from other scientists so that research in these fields can move productively forward.
>
> (Hoover *et al.* 1976b: 1960)

The letter ends on the high note of a quotation from Jefferson:

> Dr. Baggs also believes that such scientific findings should not be available to the public. We do not agree, but would rather side with another person who has written letters on related issues. In 1820 Thomas Jefferson wrote, "I know no safe depository of the ultimate powers of society but the people themselves; and if we think them not enlightened enough to exercise their control with wholesome discretion, the remedy is not to take it from them, but to inform their discretion."
>
> (Hoover *et al.* 1976b: 1960)

The tension between the values of the physician as scientist and the physician as care-giver are invoked in this exchange. Yet there was also a difference in the real interests of the clinical and the research community as these were affected by government and media action over the estrogen debate.

The research community is dependent on government and the private foundations for funding. Estrogen acquired a highly visible profile as the result of the media publicity, the Senate hearings and the FDA ruling; that more money became available to researchers to look at the effects of estrogen and disease processes is evident from the increased volume of publication on the topic in the late 1970s and early 1980s. Yet seen from the clinician's point of view, the same publicity carried with it the economic risks of malpractice suits, plus the political costs of government interference in the practice of medicine. The conflict between the clinical and the research community is not simply a question of differences in economic and political interests. It brought into focus other issues which separate the two communities but which usually remain dormant. A discussion of these issues is necessary to understanding not only the conflict between clinicians and researchers, but the reasons why women were first given estrogen and why many clinicians continued to prescribe its use despite clear evidence of adverse side-effects.

In theory, both researchers and clinicians have the common goal of ''promoting the health of the people through the prevention and treatment of disease'' (Munson 1981). In practice, they do not necessarily agree over how this goal is to be achieved nor over what behavior on each other's part is appropriate to its implementation. Certainly, each had a different interpretation of their obligations as members of the medical community during the debate over estrogen therapy. Major differences are evident with respect to motivation, considerations of efficacy and safety, focus and training.

First, for the clinician, estrogen was a therapeutic response to the physiological inadequacy of the female body. It would be difficult to disentangle whether the definition of menopause as a deficiency condition preceded or was consequent on the development of replacement therapy, but according to the material appearing in *JAMA* between 1970 and 1974 the two had become inextricably linked. Discussing anaemia, Thomas (1981) suggests that to say someone is anaemic is to make:

> an appraising value judgement that views anaemic as bad (not merely a condition deviating from the known norm

expressed in statistical terms) which imposes an obligation on the physician to address the condition.

(Thomas 1981: 419)

By analogy, once menopause was defined as a deficiency condition, its treatment with estrogen was not only legitimate, but became an obligation.

In contrast to the clinicians, researchers became interested in estrogen because they saw it, not as a cure, but as a possible cause of illness. Prior research on the contraceptive pill and DES had already implicated the use of hormones as iatrogenic in both human and animal populations. In research terms, it was logical to investigate the role of estrogen. Furthermore, unlike those involved in the clinical trials of the 1960s who wanted to "cure" menopausal symptoms (cf. McKinlay and McKinlay 1973), this new group of researchers was preoccupied (as were the main funding agencies) with determining the causes of cancer or of coronary heart disease. If, as in the case of estrogen, they thought such a factor was uncovered, it was their obligation as medical scientists to report it.

Second, there was the balance between efficacy and safety. Whatever its other problems and associated risks, both physicians and their patients agreed that estrogen successfully managed the immediately apparent conditions of the menopause, the vasomotor symptoms and vaginal atrophy (although efficacy had *not* been clearly demonstrated in a well-designed trial (McKinlay and McKinlay 1973)). In this sense, estrogen was a highly satisfactory, albeit unevaluated, form of therapy. Furthermore, as was clear from the Kase (1974) editorial, many physicians saw themselves as meeting the need and demands for estrogen made by their female patients.

Third, there was the difference between the patient focus of the clinician and the population focus of the researcher. The risks of estrogen therapy were not at a level at which they could become apparent for the individual patient. Discussing the general problem of drug-induced illness Jick (1977) used estrogen as an example of a situation in which:

Adverse drug effects are unlikely to be discovered informally since the proportion of incident cases of the illness due to the drug is usually only a small fraction of total cases and no discernible epidemic occurs. (Jick 1977: 484)

Despite the overall number of patients receiving estrogen, few physicians would have seen many cases of endometrial cancer among the women for whom they prescribed the therapy. It was only when researchers, such as Weiss, Szekely, and Austin (1976), looked at the incidence of endometrial cancer within a much larger population that the increase could become apparent. Furthermore, the case-control retrospective method used in many of these studies involved starting from cases of the disease and looking back for prior estrogen use. Rather than dealing with the occasional woman with endometrial cancer (as would be the experience of a clinician) researchers started with an accumulated group of cases.

Fourth, there were differences in the training of clinician and researcher in terms of the ability to evaluate information. In the case of the estrogen debate, the situation facing the clinician was confusing. Evaluation of the early studies was not easy and led to argument even among researchers. Physicians were caught in a situation in which, on the one hand, the media were reporting that estrogen was iatrogenic and the FDA were insisting on package inserts. On the other hand, review articles in both *JAMA* and *NEJM* were relatively reassuring, while the manufacturers were swearing to them that estrogen was maligned. Placed in the middle of this argument, few clinicians had the training necessary to evaluate the information being made available to them by these different parties to the debate. Furthermore, they had to deal with the consequences of the controversy. Their treatment had been maligned as iatrogenic; more seriously, the debate's outcome threatened a number of fundamental principles in the physician–patient relationship.

Impact on the physician–patient relationship

As estrogen was among the top five prescription drugs in the United States, the suggestion that it might have carcinogenic properties had implications for the therapeutic content of many thousands of individual physician–patient dyads. The sharp decline in the prescription of estrogen after 1976 (FDA Drug Bulletin 1979) is indirect evidence of the impact of the estrogen debate at the physician–patient level. Other evidence lies in the criticisms of the publicity over estrogen on the grounds that it created fear and anxiety among patients (cf. Baggs 1976). An alternative explanation is that women had asked questions about estrogen and were angry about their treatment.

The debate over estrogen threatened the two principles which according to many clinicians and some philosophers of medicine (e.g. Ladd 1979) are the foundation of the physician–patient relationship. The first is that the physician always acts in the best interest of the patient and therefore must be trusted by the patient. Second, the physician's right to control the relationship is based on his or her exclusive possession of medical knowledge. The information about estrogen introduced the notion of iatrogenesis into the physician–patient relationship and was incompatible with the demand that the physician be trusted.

The combination of media activity and the FDA-required insert made information on estrogen directly available to the patient, thus breaking the physician's monopoly over the control of information. The type of knowledge was also a challenge to physician claims. As with the contraceptive pill and DES, the risks of estrogen therapy were no more apparent at the individual practitioner level than they were to the individual patient. On the other hand, once the level of risk was determined by researchers (whether for gall-bladder disease or endometrial cancer) it could be expressed in an odds ratio which would be understandable by anyone with sufficient mathematical ability or betting experience. Clinical experience and training were of little relevance.

The irony of the situation was that the patients actively implicated as users of estrogen were all women, usually in the pre- and post-menopausal age-group. According to one assistant FDA commissioner, they were also white and middle class: "The chronic users (of estrogen) tend to be middle class and upper income women, the kind of people who go to doctors. . . . It is an interesting example of the poor being spared" (FDA Consumer 1976: 5). In an earlier paper (Kaufert 1982) reference was made not only to the medicalization of the menopause, but to the medical stereotype of the menopausal patient–white, middle class, neurotic, physician-dependent. A physician affidavit submitted in support of the Pharmaceutical Manufacturers suit against the FDA argued that "it is hard to imagine a class of patients more susceptible to adverse psychological reaction than the menopausal female" (Kasper 1978).

Yet, once the estrogen was declared potentially iatrogenic, the old definitions of the patient role as essentially passive had to be discarded as no longer appropriate. As Weinstein argues (1980: 315), "the value attached to symptomatic improvement represents a personal judgement that will differ from patient to patient. Some patients may judge the benefits to outweigh the risks; others may not." In other words, only the patient could decide whether the control of her menopausal symptoms was worth the risks of therapy. In both journals, clinicians were repeatedly advised that "each woman be given as much information as possible about both the benefits and risk (estrogen therapy) and then, with her physician, reach an individualized decision about the use of estrogen" (Gastel, Cornoni-Huntley, and Brody 1980: 296).

The impact of the estrogen debate on physician–patient interaction patterns should not be exaggerated; the basic institutional structure and the attitudes which provide the context of that relationship were left unchanged (cf. Ketchum and Pierce 1981). On the other hand, the repeated advice to inform and consult with the patient, which appears in much of the *NEJM* and *JAMA* material, suggests that the estrogen debate promoted a move towards the liberalization of the physician-patient relationship. A more cynical interpretation might suggest other motives. Based on experience not only with estrogen, but with the pill and DES, the notion of the "passive," "compliant" patient was becoming a legal liability. In a climate of malpractice suits, it was becoming wiser to have a patient actively involved in the treatment decision when there was a risk of iatrogenesis.

The women's health movement

Since the people taking estrogen were women, the debate over its safety eventually involved the women's health movement. The movement had initially been preoccupied with issues of reproduction, such as the right to become or not become pregnant, the right to end pregnancy, the right to decide the place and context of birth. In the early years, menopausal women had tended to be neither the concern of, nor members in, the newly emergent feminist health groups. As women in the movement have grown older and as older women have entered it, there has been a growing interest in the menopause (e.g. "Menopause Collective" now forms part of the Boston Women's Health Collective). There are menopause support groups at women's health centers and an expanding literature presenting a feminist approach to menopause (cf. Kaufert 1982). As in the research community, alarm about the effects of the pill and DES led feminist health consumer advocates to turn their attention to the other use of hormones in estrogen therapy. ERT became another issue in the indictment of the use of hormones in the treatment of women by the medical profession. From a feminist perspective, the publicity over estrogen served to educate women and was used by the more polemically inclined as a warning to women on the consequences of passively accepting whatever they were told by their physicians.

The role of the women's health movement in relation to estrogen may become more central in the 1980s than it was in the 1970s. The earlier debate over estrogen proved that it was possible to reduce sales through a combination of media publicity and political action – the Senate and the FDA. Just as the Women's Health Network submitted a brief to the court in support of the FDA insert, similar actions may block the current moves to rehabilitate estrogen therapy and reestablish the market.

Conclusion

Our initial discussion depicted relationships among the major actors at the opening of the debate over ERT; we have also showed how these relationships changed as the debate progressed. The controversy was sparked by the activities of the research community, but would have remained confined to the medical press. It was because the media took up and publicized results in which estrogen was labeled as a carcinogen that the issue of ERT entered the public domain. One result was that the government came under pressure to regulate the pharmaceutical industry at least to the extent of requiring a package insert warning women of its dangers.

The FDA ruling provoked a strong reaction from both the pharmaceutical industry and the medical profession. The former saw it as interference in trade; the latter as interference

in their professional autonomy. The alliance of the two groups
was unsuccessful in blocking the FDA in the courts, but the
complete discrediting of ERT was prevented. Research showing
that estrogen, rather than being iatrogenic, may be beneficial to
women's health has been actively promoted and currently a
carefully orchestrated campaign is advocating estrogen as a
barrier against osteoporosis.

The debate over estrogen had major implications for the
physician–patient relationship. Clinicians objected to women
being given any information on their treatment (whether by the
media or the FDA) as it might destroy their trust in their physicians. At the same time, the medical journals were advising
change in this relationship. Physicians were told that estrogen
therapy was a case in which the tradition of the compliant
patient was inappropriate. Sharing therapeutic decision-
making with the patient was a counsel owing less to liberalism
than to the practice of defensive medicine.

Women are the final group of actors in this debate. Estrogen
was another item in a well-publicized series (the pill, DES,
medicalized childbirth, the high rate of hysterectomies) in
which medical care appeared to have acted in ways injurious to
women's health. Using these examples, the feminist health
movement argued that women must adopt a more aggressive,
activist stance in relation to their health care. Yet, regardless of
ideology, women continue to be dependent on the medical profession as providers of necessary care. It is for this reason that
it is important that we, as women, understand how medical
knowledge is produced and also the impact of health policy and
politics on its dissemination.

References

Antunes, C.M., Stolley, P.D., Rosenshein, N.B., Davies, J.L.,
    Tonascia, J.A., Brown, C., Burnett, L., Rutledge, A., Pokempner,
    M., and Garcia, R. (1979) Endometrial Cancer and Estrogen Use:
    Report of a Large Case-Control Study. *New England Journal of
    Medicine* 300 (1): 9–13.
Baggs, W.J. (1976) Publicity-seeking NEJM. *New England Journal of
    Medicine* 295 (16): 897–98.
Barrett-Connor, E., Brown, W.V., Turner, J., Austen, M., and Criqui,
    M.H. (1979) Heart Disease Risk Factors and Hormone Use in

Postmenopausal Women. *Journal of the American Medical Association* 241 (20): 2167–169.

Boston Collaborative Drug Surveillance Study (1974) Surgically Confirmed Gallbladder Disease, Venous Thromboembolism, and Breast Tumors in Relation to Postmenopausal Estrogen Therapy. *New England Journal of Medicine* 290 (1): 15–18.

Bradley, D.D., Wingerd, J., Petitti, D.B., Krauss, R.M., and Ramcharan, S. (1978) Serum High-Density Lipoprotein Cholesterol in Women Using Oral Contraceptives, Estrogens and Progestins. *New England Journal of Medicine* 299 (1): 17–20.

Bush, T., Cowen, L., Barrett-Connor, E., and Criqui, M. (1983) Estrogen Use and All Cause Mortality. *Journal of the American Medical Association* 249 (7): 903–06.

Epstein, S.S. (1978) *The Politics of Cancer.* San Francisco: Sierra Club Books.

FDA Consumer (1976) Women and Estrogens. *FDA Consumer* April: 4–8.

FDA Drug Bulletin (1979) Update on Estrogens and Uterine Cancer. *FDA Drug Bulletin* Feb.-March: 2–3.

Gastel, B., Cornoni-Huntley, J., and Brody, J.A. (1980) Pros and Cons of Estrogen-Replacement Therapy. *New England Journal of Medicine* 302 (5): 296.

Greenblatt, R.B. (1979) Estrogen Use and Endometrial Cancer. *New England Journal of Medicine* 300 (16): 921–22.

Herbst, A.L., Ulfelder, J., and Poskanzer, D.C. (1971) Adenocarcinoma of the Vagina: Association of Maternal Stilbestrol Therapy with Tumour Appearance in Young Women. *New England Journal of Medicine* 284: 878–81.

Hoover, R., Gray, L.A., Cole, P., and MacMahon, B. (1976a) Menopausal Estrogens and Breast Cancer. *New England Journal of Medicine* 295 (8): 401–05.

Hoover, R., Gray, L.A., Cole, P., and MacMahon, B. (1976b) Estrogens and Breast Cancer. *New England Journal of Medicine* 295 (22): 1960.

Horwitz, R.I. and Feinstein, A.R. (1978) Alternative Analytic Methods for Case-Control Studies of Estrogens and Endometrial Cancer. *New England Journal of Medicine* 299 (20): 1089–094.

Hulka, B.S. (1980) Effect of Exogenous Estrogen on Postmenopausal Women: The Epidemiologic Evidence. *Obstetrical and Gynecological Survey* 35 (6): 389–99.

Hulka, B.S., Kaufman, D.G., Fowler, W.C., Jr, Grimson, R.C., and Greenberg, B.G. (1980) Predominance of Early Endometrial Cancer after Long-term Estrogen Use. *Journal of the American Medical Association* 244 (21): 2419–422.

Inglefinger, F.J. (1976a) Misuse of Information Printed in the *Journal.*

New England Journal of Medicine 294 (12): 667–68.

—— (1976b) The Case of the Hoover Paper. *New England Journal of Medicine* 295 (16): 896–97.

—— (1977) Shattuck Lecture – The General Medical Journal: For Readers or Repositories? *New England Journal of Medicine* 296 (22): 1258–264.

Jick, H. (1977) The Discovery of Drug-Induced Illness. *New England Journal of Medicine* 296 (9): 481–85.

Jick, H., Dinan, B., and Rothman, K. (1978) Noncontraceptive Estrogens and Nonfatal Myocardial Infarction. *Journal of the American Medical Association* 239 (14): 1407–408.

Jick, H., Watkins, R.N., Hunter, J.R., Dinan, B.J., Madsen, B.S., Rothman, K.J., and Walker, A.M. (1979) Replacement Estrogens and Endometrial Cancer. *New England Journal of Medicine* 300 (5): 218–22.

Jick, H., Walker, A.M., Watkins, R.N., D'Wart, D.C., Hunter, J.R., Danford, A., Madsen, S., Dinan, B.J., and Rothman, K.J. (1980) Replacement Estrogens and Breast Cancer. *American Journal of Epidemiology* 112 (5): 586–94.

Johnson, A. (1977) The Risks of Sex Hormones as Drugs. *Women and Health* July-August.

Kase, N. (1974) Estrogens and the Menopause. *Journal of the American Medical Association* 227 (3): 318–19.

Kasper, A. (1978) Estrogens: Right-To-Know Scores One. *The Network News* Jan.

Kaufert, P.A. (1982) Myth and the Menopause. *Sociology of Health and Illness* 4 (2): 141–66.

Ketchum, S.A. and Pierce, C. (1981) Rights and Responsibilities. *The Journal of Medicine and Philosophy* 6: 271–80.

Ladd, J. (1979) Legalism and Medical Ethics. *The Journal of Medicine and Philosophy* 4: 70–80.

Landau, R.L. (1979) What You Should Know About Estrogens; Or the Perils of Pauline. *Journal of the American Medical Association* 241 (1): 47–51.

Lipsett, M.B. (1977) Estrogen Use and Cancer Risk. *Journal of the American Medical Association* 237 (11): 1112–115.

Mack, T.M., Henderson, B.E., Gerkins, V.R., Arthur, M., Baptista, J., and Pike, M.C. (1975) Reserpine and Breast Cancer in a Retirement Community. *New England Journal of Medicine* 292 (26): 1366–371.

Mack, T.M., Pike, M.C., Henderson, B.E., Pfeffer, R.I., Gerkins, V.R., Arthur, M., and Brown, S.E. (1976) Estrogens and Endometrial Cancer in a Retirement Community. *New England Journal of Medicine* 294 (23): 1262–267.

McKinlay, S.M. and McKinlay, J.M. (1973) Selected Studies of the Menopause. *Journal of Biosocial Science* 5: 533–54.

Meier, P. and Landau, R.L. (1980) Estrogen Replacement Therapy (editorial). *Journal of the American Medical Association* 243 (16): 1658–659.

Munson, R. (1981) Why Medicine Cannot Be a Science. *The Journal of Medicine and Philosophy* 6: 183–208.

Quigley, M.M. and Hammond, C.B. (1979) Estrogen-Replacement Therapy – Help or Hazard? *New England Journal of Medicine* 301 (12): 646–48.

Richardson, G. (1972) Endometrial Cancer as an Estrogen–Progesterone Target. *New England Journal of Medicine* 286 (12): 645–46.

Rosenberg, L., Armstrong, B., Phil, D., and Jick, H. (1976) Myocardial Infarction and Estrogen Therapy in Post-Menopausal Women. *New England Journal of Medicine* 294 (23): 1256–259.

Rosenberg, L., Slone, D., Shapiro, S., Kaufman, D., Stolley, P.D. and Miettinen, O.S. (1980) Noncontraceptive Estrogens and Myocardial Infarction in Young Women. *Journal of the American Medical Association* 244 (4): 339–42.

Ross, R.K., Paganini-Hill, A., Gerkins, V.R., Mack, T.M., Pfeffer, R., Arthur, M., and Henderson, B.E. (1980) A Case-Control Study of Menopausal Estrogen Therapy and Breast Cancer. *Journal of the American Medical Association* 243 (16): 1635–639.

Ryan, K. J. (1975) Cancer Risk and Estrogen Use in the Menopause. *New England Journal of Medicine* 293 (23): 1199–200.

—— (1977) The FDA and the Practice of Medicine. *New England Journal of Medicine* 297 (23): 1287–288.

Shapiro, S., Kaufman, D.W., Slone, D.S., Rosenberg, L., Miettinen, O.S., Stolley, P.D., Rosenshein, N.B., Watring, W.G., Leavitt, T., and Knapp, R.C. (1980) Recent and Past Use of Conjugated Estrogen in Relation to Adenocarcinoma of the Endometrium. *New England Journal of Medicine* 303 (9): 485–89.

Shoemaker, E.S., Forney, J.P., and MacDonald, P.C. (1977) Estrogen Treatment of Postmenopausal Women. *Journal of the American Medical Association* 238 (14): 1524–530.

Smith, D.C., Prentice, R., Thompson, D.J., and Herrmann, W.L. (1975) Association of Exogenous Estrogen and Endometrial Carcinoma. *New England Journal of Medicine* 293 (23): 1164–167.

Stavraky, K. and Emmons, S. (1974) Breast Cancer in Premenopausal and Postmenopausal Women. *Journal of the National Cancer Institute* 53 (3): 647–54.

Stern, M.P., Byron, W.B., Haskell, W.L., Farquhar, J.W., Wehrle, C.L., and Wood, P.D. (1976) Cardiovascular Risk and Use of Estrogen or Estrogen–Progestagen Combinations. *Journal of the American Medical Association* 235 (8): 811–15.

Studd, J.W.W. and Thom, M. (1979) Estrogen Use and Endometrial

Cancer. *New England Journal of Medicine* 300 (16): 923.

Subcommittee on Health, Committee on Labor and Public Welfare, United States Senate (1974) *Examination of the Pharmaceutical Industry, 1973-74.* Washington, DC: US Government Printing Office.

Thomas, J.E. (1981) Medicine and Sociology: A Parting of the Ways. *The Journal of Medicine and Philosophy* 6: 411-21.

Vessey, M.P. and Doll, R. (1968) Investigation of Relation Between Use of Oral Contraceptives and Thromboembolic Disease. *British Medical Journal* 2: 199-205.

Waldron, I. (1977) Increased Prescribing of Valium, Librium, and Other Drugs – An Example of the Influence of Economic and Social Factors on the Practice of Medicine. *International Journal of Health Sciences* 7 (1): 37-62.

Washington Post (1976) 15 Nov.: 3a.

Weinstein, M.C. (1980) Estrogen Use in Postmenopausal Women – Costs, Risks, and Benefits. *New England Journal of Medicine* 303 (6): 308-16.

Weiss, N.S. (1975) Risks and Benefits of Estrogen Use. *New England Journal of Medicine* 293 (23): 1200-201.

Weiss, N.S., Szekely, D.R., and Austin, F. (1976) Increasing Incidence of Endometrial Cancer in the US. *New England Journal of Medicine* 294: 1259-262.

Weiss, N.W., Szekely, D.R., English, D.R., and Schweid, A.I. (1979) Endometrial Cancer in Relation to Patterns of Menopausal Estrogen Use. *Journal of the American Medical Association* 242 (3): 261-64.

Weiss, N.S., Ure, C.L., Ballard, J.H., Williams, A.R., and Daling, J.R. (1980) Decreased Risk of Fractures of Hip and Lower Forearm with Postmenopausal Use of Estrogen. *New England Journal of Medicine* 303 (21): 1195-198.

WHO Scientific Group (1981) *Research on the Menopause.* Geneva: World Health Organisation.

Wilson, R. (1966) *Feminine Forever.* New York: M. Evans.

Ziel, H.K. and Finkle, W.D. (1975) Increased Risk of Endometrial Carcinoma Among Users of Conjugated Estrogens. *New England Journal of Medicine* 293 (23): 1167-170.

Six

Abortion in the 1980s: feminist morality and women's health[1]

Rosalind Pollack Petchesky

In the United States in the late 1970s and early 1980s, public policy regarding abortion and related reproductive health issues underwent a sharp reversal. A series of measures guided by a newly empowered conservatism, or "New Right," began to whittle away a mere decade of theoretically unrestricted legal abortion and a shorter period of government funding to provide abortions for poor women.

Although the 1973 Supreme Court ruling upholding a woman's constitutional right to decide, in consultation with her doctor, to terminate a pregnancy was affirmed by the court in 1983, it has been hedged around with numerous statutory, judicial, and administrative obstacles. In 1977 the United States Congress began to impose successively tighter restrictions on the payment of federal medicaid funds for abortion services; today such funds may be paid only in the tiny number of cases where a woman's life is endangered by a pregnancy. Congressional statutory amendments have also denied abortion reimbursement to federal civilian and military employees and their wives and dependents and refused funds to abortion-related research. Local and state laws began to require parental and spousal consent or notification before allowing abortions to be performed on unmarried minors or wives, and in the case of minors the Supreme Court has given conditional approval to such requirements. Meanwhile, the drive in Congress to pass some kind of constitutional amendment or statute that would declare the fetus a "person" and abortion "murder" (a "Human Life Amendment"), though foundering on internal divisions within the right, remains on the legislative agenda. Such a measure has the official backing of President Reagan, whose administration – particularly the conservatives and anti-abortionists appointed to positions of leadership in the Department of Health and Human Services – has meanwhile issued a series of regulations designed to further restrict availability of abortion services and the access of unmarried teenagers to birth control.

These shifts in United States public policy regarding abortion occur in a larger political and cultural context which has seen "right-to-life" ideology penetrate the thinking of policy-makers, judges, medical professionals, the popular media, and even some leftists and feminists. While so-called "elective" abortion remains legal in the United States, a scaffolding of renewed guilt and shame has been constructed around this fragile legality. Media stories and popular books proliferate representing women who get abortions as "ambivalent" and "agonized," or else as "selfish hedonists." Some feminists have become apologetic, retreating to the view that abortion is a "necessary evil" that "no one likes," with one prominent American liberal feminist comparing it to mastectomy. This is a far distance from the ethos surrounding the legalization of abortion a decade ago, when women jubilantly celebrated the end (we thought) of years of silent terror, morbidity and death, and sex ridden with shame. Even the Supreme Court justice who wrote the majority opinion in *Roe* v. *Wade* was quoted in the *New York Times* ten years later (17 January, 1983) as complaining, "People misunderstand. I am not for abortion. I hope my family never has to face such a decision."

The deeper causes of this turnaround, while both interesting and important, will receive only brief consideration here. My more immediate concern is to define the terms in which a strong defense of legal, funded, publicly supported abortion services should be made in this precarious period. In particular, I wish to examine the contradictory implications, from a feminist perspective, of regarding abortion as a "health issue" for women.

I shall argue that neither a "medical model" (supported by political liberals, family planners, and clinicians) nor a "moral model" (supported by "pro-lifers" but also by many "pro-choice" advocates of "freedom of conscience") adequately represents a feminist position on abortion. For feminists, access to safe abortion is an unmistakable condition of women's reproductive health, but also of their sexual freedom and their moral autonomy. A viable feminist politics of abortion for the 1980s has to encompass all these dimensions, as well as the tension between abortion as an individual right and as a social need (Petchesky 1980).

The "moralization" and "sexualization" of the abortion issue by the New Right must be understood as a reactionary response to feminist ideas, and particularly the idea that safe, legal abortion is a necessary (though not sufficient) condition of women's autonomy as moral and social beings and their sexual self-expression. But this refocusing of the political debate around abortion has simultaneously meant that the health dimensions of abortion – which family planners and clinicians in the past tended to emphasize almost to the exclusion of moral and sexual issues – have nearly gotten lost. Feminists since the days of illegality have opposed the idea that abortion, to be justified, has to be based on "therapeutic" criteria or "medical necessity," or any reason other than a woman's own judgment about whether or not she wished or was able to bear a child. Abortion has always been for feminists – and for most women – a decidedly moral and sexual question, and not only a matter of health. Since 1977, however, in the face of callous disregard of any health-related aspects of abortion by the Congress, the federal administration, and the United States Supreme Court, feminists have had to rethink the crucial links between abortion and women's health needs.

My purpose here is to analyze the contradictions inherent for feminist politics in the views and policies which define abortion rights in medical terms, particularly in light of the recent rightwing climate. First, I shall briefly trace the history of the medical model of abortion in the period prior to legalization and examine how that model became integrated in the thinking of policy-makers and the courts as the dominant justification for abortion. In this part of the analysis, my emphasis will be on how that model has been used to assure medical control over abortion services and in practice to exclude all but select women from access to them. This experience helps to explain feminist skepticism toward the "medical necessity" standard as one that confines women's reproductive control within narrow limits and vitiates the idea of reproductive freedom of any moral content. In a second section, I shall show why a feminist view of abortion must also take into account that the question of abortion is intimately connected to women's health. This reality comes home to us sharply in the Supreme Court's refusal to deal with the powerful medical testimony in the *McRae* case (where it approved the denial of federal medicaid funds for abortion to poor women); and in the actual consequences for poor women, young teenagers, women suffering from various chronic conditions, and others, of the loss of access to safe abortion.

In the face of this reality, I shall argue in favor of a "health model" of abortion rights rather than a "medical model"; one which posits the legitimacy of abortion not only in terms of women's need to control their bodies and sexual experience but also in terms of the basic need for decent health care made equally available to all people, regardless of class, race, gender, or age. And I shall attempt to distinguish this principle from one whose main end is professional autonomy for doctors. From a feminist perspective, there cannot and should not be a dichotomy between "health" and "morality."

The limits of "medical necessity" – *Roe* v. *Wade* and its legacy

The history of birth control and abortion politics throughout most of the twentieth century in America has been laced with a tension between the ideas and methods of popular organizers and mass movements on the one hand, and those of liberal reformers and sympathetic medical and legal professionals on the other. "Abortion on demand" and "a woman's right to control over her body" were never ideas that carried much weight in the family-planning conferences and American

Medical Association committees, in the legislative hearings and courtrooms where abortion policy, in fact, has been made. Yet those ideas have created important pressures on clinicians and policy-makers to find more "moderate" principles to accommodate women's demands. Public-health professionals and family-planning advocates, perceiving the strong resistance of state agencies and physicians to a feminist view of abortion, have opted – often out of sheer pragmatism – for an emphasis on the legitimacy of "therapeutic" abortion. This is the concept that the conditions justifying abortion are those that involve a woman's health, though this may be broadly defined to include a woman's mental or emotional health as well as fetal health. Those exclusively qualified to determine when such conditions or "medical indications" exist and to administer the procedures are certified physicians.

From a feminist perspective, the concept of "medical necessity," or "therapeutic abortions," implies that all non-medical abortions are "elective," meaning they are somehow frivolous, *merely* "personal," "unnecessary." This bifurcated view distorts reality, denying that familial, economic, and sexual conditions as well as physical health create genuine, pressing needs that justify abortion. It also reduces the meaning of "health," ignoring the extent to which medical problems themselves are related to social, economic, and family–sexual conditions. This point was eloquently advanced in Judge Dooling's comments in the *McRae* case on the health impact of the Hyde Amendment, when he argued that "poverty is itself, persistently, a medically relevant factor" (*McRae* v. *Harris* 1980: 689–90). On the other hand, it contains the old eugenic idea of childbearing as a "scientific" undertaking for which only certain women are "fit." Thus it can allow abortion in some cases because in those cases women are seen as too poor, too young, or too mentally or physically incompetent to bear children; or some fetuses as too defective to be born. Abortion and contraception become, in this framework, not a "right" of women to self-determination, but a *duty* (to the nation, the "race," the family, or even the self). In this way, therapeutic–eugenic discourse about fertility control, including abortion, allows the liberal state to accommodate without at the same time legitimating feminist demands.

A large part of the initiative in perpetuating the medical

model in abortion policy lies with the medical profession. The position of organized medicine with regard to abortion has historically, in the United States and elsewhere, been ridden with contradiction. On the one hand, the profession has never disguised its contempt for the practice; to this day, abortion is considered by many doctors as the boundary dividing professionals from charlatans and quacks. Historian James Mohr documents that it was primarily "regular" physicians, organized through the American Medical Association, who lobbied most forcefully for the criminalization of abortion in the nineteenth century; and that a large part of the drive behind this campaign was the desire to win a monopoly over health care, particularly obstetrics, from lay healers and midwives (Mohr 1978: 147–63). For all its disdain, however, the profession has never been successful in wiping out the practice of abortion (as opposed to quashing its legality and respectability), and so has been constantly preoccupied with the problem of how to control that practice, which persisted in spite of repression. In the long run, as with contraception, the medicalization of abortion has been a strategy to legitimate and contain its practice, in a cultural climate of moralistic repugnance and hostility that medical authorities themselves helped to create. A medical model of abortion has been the result of this professional need to assert control, in a social system in which health care is the monopoly of a hierarchically organized and proprietary medical establishment.[2] This is true *at the same time* as it is also undoubtedly true that the introduction of sanitary methods, antiseptics, and antibiotics in abortion procedures has saved women's lives.

Feminists have long raised vocal opposition to the distinction between "therapeutic" ("necessary") and "elective" ("unnecessary?") abortions. Radical and socialist feminists, working through organizations such as the Chicago Women's Liberation Union, NOW, Redstockings, and women's health activist groups, consciously rejected both the medical model of reproductive health and (though not always) populationist goals as the basis of birth control. In contrast to family planners and public-health practitioners, feminists put forward a libertarian view of "abortion on demand" as a necessary condition of women's right to control their bodies and pregnancy:

> All the excellent supporting reasons – improved health, lower birth and death rates, freer medical practice, the

separation of church and state, happier families, sexual privacy, lower welfare expenditures – are only embroidery on the basic fabric: *woman's right to limit her own reproduction*. It is this rationale that the new woman's movement has done so much to bring to the fore. Those who caution us to play down the women's-rights arguments are only trying to put off the inevitable day when the society must face and eradicate the misogynistic roots of the present situation. And anyone who has spoken publicly about abortion from the feminist point of view knows all too well that it is feminism – not abortion – that is the really disturbing idea.

(Cisler 1970: 276)

Feminists adamantly opposed "reform," which they contrasted to the more radical demand for repeal. They argued that any other position was steeped in medical and other conditions that denied women's capacity and right to make their own reproductive decisions. Medical and legalistic models of abortion, they pointed out, focused on "hardship" situations – rubella, rape, mental illness – and thus "always pictured women as victims . . . never as possible shapers of their own destinies" (Cisler 1970: 275). And these models implicitly suggested that women were incompetent to act as moral agents on their own behalf. Repeal, on the other hand, would simply abolish any restrictive, discriminatory conditions impeding abortion, so that medical authorities could no longer be used as moral gatekeepers. Legal abortions had always been possible in some states to save a woman's life or spare her "serious" health problems. But to obtain an abortion even under these requirements involved going through hospital committees and private networks that were penetrable only to privileged women. When the laws of some states underwent reform in the later 1960s, these restrictive conditions continued and, if anything, became more apparent under the rubric of (now legal) "therapeutic abortions." Physicians and hospital authorities in California and Colorado, for example, still imposed enormous red tape, requiring written consent from at least two physicians as well as the hospital committee, and insisting on inpatient (hence much costlier) procedures. Many hospitals – particularly the smaller ones – still feared the label "abortion mill," or had chiefs of service opposed to abortion, and thus refused to

perform any abortions, or imposed strict residency requirements. These restrictions effectively excluded poor women,
who lacked the personal connections to private doctors and the
funds necessary to obtain a safe hospital abortion (Callahan
1970: 137–42; Lader 1973: 22, 114).

During the New York State legal abortion campaign in the
late 1960s, radical feminists made clear the differences between
their approach, which emphasized concrete access to abortion
for all women, and that of more liberally oriented groups (such
as the National Association for Repeal of Abortion Laws, which
became the National Abortion Rights Action League, or
NARAL), which emphasized the legal "right to choose."
Feminists consistently opposed legislative proposals that
restricted legal abortion to "licensed physicians" and therapeutic criteria, insisting on the importance of paramedicals and
non-hierarchical forms of reproductive health care if all women
were to have access to services (Lader 1973: 130). This was a
practical way to criticize the elitism of the medical-care system
and the abstract idea of abortion as a "private matter" between
"a woman and her doctor." For the majority of women did not
and do not have access to a cozy, confidential relationship with
a private physician, traditionally the ticket to a safe abortion.
Thus the feminist position implicitly called for substantive
changes in the quality and conditions of reproductive health
care.

The philosophy of removing the state from abortion decisions altogether, of "repeal" pure and simple (still implied in
the slogan "get the State's laws off our bodies"), is at bottom
one of "laissez-faire." It contains an implicit presumption that
the "right to choose," or the relegation of abortion to the
"private sphere," will in itself guarantee that good, safe abortions will be provided. Many feminists have understood that
this is not a reasonable presumption; that the existing medical-
care system, like other capitalist markets, does not adequately
meet people's needs; that how and by whom abortions (or other
health services) are provided is a critical dimension of whether
real needs will be met.

This deeper understanding was often implicit in how radical
feminists conducted the abortion struggle, but it failed to be
translated either into a broadly articulated feminist discourse
or into public policy. Even in periods of heightened liberalism

and attention to social welfare, the feminist concept of abortion as rooted in women's right/need to control their bodies was never accorded legitimacy by the liberal state. Only four years after *Roe* v. *Wade*, in 1977, during the Congressional debates on the Hyde Amendment and when the rightwing, anti-feminist current was in full swing, not even the most liberal Congressmen were ready to stand up and defend a woman's fundamental right to decide about abortion *because* it is her body and she is the one who will bear the physical and social consequences of pregnancy and childbearing. Throughout the debates, those liberal senators who were most outspoken against the "right-to-life" proposals and in favor of retaining medicaid funding based their arguments on a strict notion of medical autonomy (see *Congressional Record* 1977: S11951–53).[3]

The decisions in *Roe* v. *Wade* and *Doe* v. *Bolton* were in fact very clear in stating that the "privacy right" involved in abortion decisions could not be taken as "absolute." In its most positive formulation, the Court held that "this right of privacy . . . is broad enough to encompass a woman's decision whether or not to terminate her pregnancy"; and went on to enumerate the serious health consequences that may result for women if this right is denied (including "a distressful life and future," "psychological harm," and harm to "mental and physical health"). However, it also concluded that the constitutional "right of privacy" does not entail "an unlimited right to do with one's body as one pleases," or "abortion on demand," and that the abortion decision may be limited by certain "important state interests in regulation" (*Roe* v. *Wade* 1973: 153). These "important and legitimate interests" of the state include that of "preserving and protecting the health of the pregnant woman," on the one hand, and "protecting the potentiality of human life," on the other. According to the Court's complicated formula – in actuality, the heart of *Roe* v. *Wade* – these two state interests are "separate and distinct," each becoming "compelling" at a different *stage* of pregnancy. Thus the Court implied that, during the first trimester, state regulation of abortion was unconstitutional altogether; during the second trimester, the state may intervene for reasons of "protecting the woman's health"; and in the final trimester, which the Court associated with fetal "viability," the state's "interest in potential life" could justify a complete *prohibition* of abortion "except when it is necessary to preserve the life or *health* of the mother" (*Roe* v. *Wade* 1973: 162–63).

May we nevertheless presume that women were being granted an unqualified "right to choose" abortion at least in the first stage of pregnancy? Here is how the Supreme Court clarified it in *Roe*:

> The decision vindicates *the right of the physician* to administer medical treatment *according to his professional judgment* up to the points where important state interests provide compelling justifications for intervention. Up to those points, the *abortion decision in all its aspects is inherently, and primarily, a medical decision, and basic responsibility for it must rest with the physician.* (*Roe* v. *Wade* 1973: 166)

As Kristin Glen remarks, the Court "was not upholding a woman's right to determine whether to bear a child, as abortion proponents and feminists had argued. Instead, it was upholding a *doctor's* right to make a medical decision!" (Glen 1978: 9). In a way, this was even clearer in *Doe* v. *Bolton*. There the Court's opinion appeared to reject the "medical model" by invalidating state statutory requirements that abortions be performed only in accredited hospitals, with the approval of the hospital staff abortion committee and two outside physicians. Although the Court was paring away some of the more cumbersome medical restrictions on abortion maintained by AMA policy and past medical practice, it did so explicitly on behalf of "*licensed physicians.*" (Nurses, counselors, paramedicals, and other potential providers were denied standing to sue in the case, since they "are in no position to render medical advice" (*Doe* v. *Bolton* 1973: 189). The bureaucratic restrictions were struck down by the Court because they were held to infringe on "*the woman's right to receive medical care in accordance with her licensed physician's best judgment and the physician's right to administer it,*" "*the physician's right to practice*" (*Doe* v. *Bolton* 1973: 189).

In other words, *Roe* v. *Wade* and *Doe* v. *Bolton* seem to have simply confirmed the model of abortion decisions being made within a private, confidential doctor–patient relationship – a model which already prevailed in clinical practice for some white middle-class women. But then, the Court in *Roe* and *Doe* was not saying anything about a woman's right to *have* this

kind of medical care. If anything, it was upholding the traditional professional autonomy of private-practicing physicians
over determinations of when (and for whom) medical care
is warranted – explicitly, then, fitting abortion within the
market-oriented medical paradigm. Moreover, it was reserving
the legitimacy of state interference with even this professional
autonomy, in the interests of ''protecting women's health'' or
''preserving potential life.''

Why, then, was the 1973 abortion decision so widely interpreted as a victory for women's individual right of privacy, and
the language about ''medical judgment'' and ''inherent difference'' from other ''privacy rights'' overlooked? We have to look
at the political and social context in which the decision was
rendered. The strength of the women's liberation movement
and the broad approval in the society and the culture for liberal
feminist ideas about equality and self-determination in 1973
meant that *Roe* would be interpreted by the lower courts and
policy-makers, as well as the general public, as giving women a
''fundamental right'' to abortion. But I would also argue that,
despite its limitations, *Roe* v. *Wade* did genuinely reflect this
liberal climate. It established the legitimacy of abortion, and
did so within a normative framework that emphasized the
priority of women's health, and ''health'' very broadly defined,
rather than abstract moralism or ''fetal rights.'' In this sense, it
was certainly progressive and its immediate impact was to
expand significantly women's real access to abortion.

In fact, the concept of ''medical necessity'' or ''protecting
women's health'' cuts in different ways. It may be interpreted
as, simply, whatever doctors decide is necessary; and this is the
outcome most frequently reinforced by the absence, in a hierarchical and private-enterprise medical system, of any socialized, uniform processes for determining standards of need and
care. However, it may also refer to such standards themselves,
their material content, as Judge Dooling did when he enumerated with great sympathy and detail the array of difficult
physical and psychological conditions that unwanted pregnancy may provoke. These two different criteria, *medical
authority* and *health needs*, may actually come into conflict, for example in the passage of ''conscience clause''
statutes which allow doctors to refuse to perform abortions on
grounds unrelated to women's health. Understood expansively,

however, "health reasons" for abortion may in fact provide the broadest practical basis for abortion services *within the United States health-care system as it is presently structured.* This is why the medical emphasis in *Roe* v. *Wade* may have been, at a particular moment, relatively progressive for women. In the broad language of the Court, the injuries to health that women suffer from being denied access to abortion may even include "a distressful life and future," and at *no* time during a pregnancy is the state justified in withholding legal abortion if such injuries to health could result.

While feminist thinking sees the "medical necessity" criterion as restrictive of women's rights in principle, increasingly since *Roe* v. *Wade* the opposite may be true in practice. That is, it has been a hard fight to get abortion recognized as a legitimate health concern at all, and this has powerful implications in terms of the dominant system of health-care administration and reimbursement in the United States. Within that system, only those conditions defined as "disease" usually receive insurance coverage, even though many nonpathological conditions (much of reproductive health and all preventive services) require the same costly medical facilities and personnel. If abortion were clearly understood as health-related, then it would be much more difficult politically to exclude it from medicaid coverage. (As we shall see below, the Supreme Court was able to rationalize denial of medicaid funding for abortion in 1980 only by choosing to ignore its own strong language about health consequences in 1973.)

The pressure that the existing health-care system exerts to define abortion in medical terms was spelled out in a memorandum by the late Frederick S. Jaffe, Director of Planned Parenthood's Center for Family Planning Program Development, shortly after *Roe* v. *Wade* (Jaffe 1974). Jaffe argued for the "need to develop rapidly a viable concept of 'medical necessity' or 'medical indications' for fertility control (and particularly abortion) – and that we have to find a way to have such a concept adopted by the medical profession and the insurance industry." The alternative, he warned, was that abortion would "be shut out of U.S. health financing mechanisms." Jaffe was aware of the problems in urging "medical indications" as the basis for abortion services for institutional and funding purposes. He acknowledged that it was "repugnant" to the idea of

women's "constitutional *right* to avoid involuntary pregnancy
. . . for her own reasons, without the need for any external justifications.'' But to define most abortions as ''elective'' (i.e. a
question of ''individual choice'')is *ipso facto* to disqualify them
''from public or private financing,'' thus to ''win the battle and
lose the war.'' The contradiction between abstract, formal
''right'', and practical access to services is structured into the
present system of health-care funding and delivery.

The connections between abortion and women's health

It is not only out of pragmatic concerns to accommodate the
dominant systems of reimbursement, however, that feminists
must reconsider the ''medical'' or ''health'' dimensions of
abortion. More importantly, abortion raises issues about the
very meaning of ''health'' and its pursuit in a decent society.
Once we discard the clearly unacceptable idea of ''medical
necessity'' as merely physicians' autonomy, with no reference
to socially defined standards of wellbeing, then health issues
become central to the morality of abortion, insofar as they com-
prise an essential part of the conditions that determine
women's need. For one thing, contrary to patriarchal ideologies
of motherhood as woman's ''natural'' condition, from the
standpoint of women's health, pregnancy and childbirth
involve a range of potential risks and disruptions to normal
physical and emotional functioning. This is true even under the
best of situations – when a woman's body is healthy and well
fed, her circumstances congenial, a child wanted.

Denying that abortion is in critical ways ''a health measure''
for women means on some level ignoring that ''control over
one's body'' has as much to do with health as it does with
sexuality. It also means ignoring that, in a class-divided
society, abortion, like health generally, is a class- as well as a
gender-related need. But it goes further than that, for if we
accept the dichotomization between ''health and wellbeing''
on the one hand and ''morality'' on the other, we are sub-
scribing unwittingly to the metaphysics of the anti-abortionists
and those who put women's health, and even their lives, on a
lower moral plane than a fetus' ''soul.'' The political crusade
of the so-called ''pro-life'' movement, based in conservative

religiosity and the Congressional "New Right," has succeeded in "remoralizing" abortion much as the moralistic medical profession did in the late nineteenth century. Under the influence of "right-to-life" ideology, the public-policy debate on abortion is cast in terms that completely separate the question of "morality" from questions about material need, including health. Feminists are caught between this surfeit of metaphysical and theological moralism, so removed from the real conditions that pregnant women have to deal with, and a long and sobering history of medically defined and controlled abortion practice, in which women's access to abortion is tied to medical approval and straitjacketed within narrow and arbitrary conceptions of "health" and "disease." The response should not be to replicate abstract moralism or least of all to abandon the conviction that abortion *is* a health need of women of the most vital and primary sort.

To speak of abortion as a purely "moral" issue, abstracted from the material – including the biomedical – conditions of reproduction as women experience them, is to dismiss what I believe are among the most powerful bases for arguing the morality of abortion. Even more is this the case when we consider the particular health problems involved in pregnancy and childbearing for particular groups of women – especially the poor and the very young – which the appeal to "moral right" glosses over rather than outlining. The *McRae* record enumerated the health risks of pregnancy – for women with phlebitis, varicose veins, diabetes, urinary infections, malnutrition, sicklecell anemia, emotional disorders, or even negative feelings about the pregnancy itself – in arresting detail, but particularly emphasizing the risks for teenagers (of prematurity, toxemia, low birth weight) and poor women (of malnutrition, anemia, mental anguish, and delayed abortions) (*McRae v. Harris* 1980: 678–86). These risks are starkly present under conditions of illegality, but they also exist when the absense of funding or accessible services makes abortion practically unavailable even where it is technically legal. And this was frequently the situation in the United States, especially for poor women and rural women, even in the years after abortion became a "constitutional right."

In reality, poor women and minority women have always gotten abortions, but they have done so under conditions that were, prior to 1973, frightening, unhygienic, and sometimes life-threatening. In the period before *Roe* v. *Wade*, the practical consequence of physicians' control over hospital abortions was the virtual exclusion of poor and minority women from "therapeutic" services. The main feature of the days of illegality, of course, was not the absence of abortions but rather their invisibility. In fact, abortions – hundreds of thousands of them a year – were performed in a class-divided system that relegated poor women to the dangerous and sordid conditions of "back-alley" abortionists while rich and middle-class women usually had access to safe, sanitary abortions in hospitals and private physicians' offices. Costs alone ($600–$800) would have prohibited most women from securing hospital abortions, even if restrictive medical rules and the elitist structure and biases of proprietary medicine had not. As a result, surveys done in the 1960s in New York City found that "four times" as many hospital abortions were done "on the private services as on the ward services," and that only a tiny number were done in the municipal hospitals that serviced primarily poor black and Puerto Rican women (Callahan 1970: 137–39). This is in sharp contrast to the much greater number of ward patients who were hospitalized during the 1960s for complications from illegal, out-of-hospital abortions (Cutright 1972: 400–93). Recorded deaths from illegal abortions (an inaccurate measure, since many deaths were probably unrecorded) were 320 in 1961. This figure declined steadily in the 1960s and dramatically after legalization (Jaffe, Lindheim, and Lee 1981: 22).

One of the major effects of both legalization and medicaid funding in the 1970s was to make abortion a "safe and legal" medical service that for the first time was available to poor women, who in the United States are disproportionately members of ethnic minorities. While black and hispanic women typically are somewhat older than white anglo women when they get their abortions, they are reportedly three times more likely to get abortions. Similarly, medicaid-eligible (low-income) women have an abortion rate that is three times higher than that of the white, unmarried, middle/working-class majority (*Safe and Legal* 1980: 30; Jaffe, Lindheim, and Lee 1981: 128). The percentage of all abortion recipients before the medicaid cutbacks who were either "black and other" (33 per cent) or medicaid patients (22 per cent nationally, 25 per cent in

New York State) substantially exceeded their proportion in the population at large (Henshaw *et al.* 1981: Table 10). Even if these differences are inflated (for example, by the likelihood of under-reporting of abortions among middle-class women in private, non-clinic settings), they still indicate an important shift from pre-legal days.

Legalization and increased availability of abortion services have also meant definite public-health benefits for poor and minority women. Maternal mortality in the United States has dropped sharply in the last two decades, and specifically since 1973 "abortion-related deaths have decreased by 73 per cent." Likewise, hospital data from New York City show that morbidity such as infections and uterine perforations caused by illegal abortions dropped substantially after legalization in 1970 (*Safe and Legal* 1980: 23; Cates 1982: 1586–587). Since poor and minority women are the main ones to suffer such deaths and morbidity, these declines are an important indicator that legalized abortion has meant better reproductive health for them in particular.[4]

Citing these figures underlines that class and race create very different conditions determining women's need for access to legal abortions, even though the need itself transcends class and race. For poor women, the need is obviously bound up with their basic health, even their life, given the reality of illegal abortions for the poor. If they are teenagers, their prospects if they bear a child and drop out of school are the lowest of any group in society; and there may well be no available or willing mother or grandmother or place in a child-care center (as child-care centers are rapidly shut down) to make dropping out avoidable. If they are older, the great likelihood is that they will be divorced or single mothers, supporting children on their own, on a wage that is below or near the minimum, or on welfare. Race–ethnicity compounds these realities: by 1980, 42 per cent of all black families in the United States were headed by women (as compared to 15 per cent of all white families), and nearly 50 per cent of these families were living below the poverty level (as compared to 33 per cent of white female-headed families) (Bureau of the Census 1981a: Table 5; 1981b: Table 21). Abortions in these cases, rather than a condition (necessary but not sufficient) of "self-improvement," may seem to be a condition of bare survival.

In such circumstances, it seems strained to speak of a "right to choose," when choice of any sort is hedged in on all sides by oppression. At the same time, the fact that abortion may be motivated by desperate circumstances does not make the denial of access to abortion services any less a denial of right. It is because of poor women's conditions and the pervasiveness of racism and class bias in American society that such women are in the apparently contradictory situation of being *both* three times more likely than other women to get abortions *and* much more likely to be denied access to abortions. For this is indeed the case. The years following *Roe* v. *Wade* gradually and painfully brought home the lesson that abstract legal guarantees of "a woman's right to choose" are a different matter from the actual delivery of the abortion services that women need, to *all* the women who need and want them. Most poor and minority people in the United States rely for their routine health care on the outpatient services of government (federal, county, municipal) hospitals and clinics. But even after abortion became legal throughout the United States and supposedly a "woman's right," surveys done by the Alan Guttmacher Institute and the Centers for Disease Control indicated that "eight out of 10 non-Catholic private hospitals," particularly in rural areas, provided *no* abortion services (Forrest, Tietze, and Sullivan 1978: 279).

Even those hospitals which do provide abortion services tend still to require costly inpatient procedures (although the vacuum-aspiration technique is decidedly cheaper and safer in early stages of pregnancy). They frequently fail to provide counseling or birth-control services and sustain costs ranging from one and a half to two times as high as those charged by private clinics. In fact, the total participation of United States hospitals in providing abortion services has *declined absolutely* since 1977 and relatively in the years between 1973 and 1977; whereas all of the growth in abortion-service providers must be attributed to freestanding abortion clinics, which provide three-fifths (6:10) of all the abortions in the United States (Forrest, Tietze, and Sullivan 1978: 276–79; Lindheim 1979: 283).

A major reason for the estrangement of mainstream health providers from the provision of abortion (Lindheim 1979: 289) has been found to be physicians' attitudes about abortion and the influence of attending physicians on hospitals' abortion practices. In two important articles, Constance Nathanson and

Marshall Becker analyze these attitudes and their impact on abortion availability, as revealed in their survey of all practicing obstetrician–gynecologists in the state of Maryland. (Maryland was one of the first states to legalize abortion in the late 1960s.) As Nathanson and Becker stress, "since no state has enacted legislation authorizing nonphysicians to perform abortions, *medical practitioners effectively control access to legal abortion services*" (1977: 158). This is true regarding Ob–Gyn practice in both private offices and hospitals. With respect to the latter, Nathanson and Becker found that the personal values and attitudes of staff obstetricians in the private, non-Catholic hospitals they surveyed were the main factor determining numbers of abortions performed in those hospitals; and that, where attending physicians were opposed to abortion psychologically or philosophically, their affiliated hospitals "were much less likely to perform abortions" – even when hospital policy favored providing abortion and contraceptive services (Nathanson and Becker 1980: 26, 30–1).[5]

Nathanson and Becker's survey of abortion performance in physicians' private practice found that, among the *providing* physicians (who are the majority), "close to 40 per cent . . . request women to obtain consent for the abortion from their husbands or parents," and "over half . . . report that they *do not accept Medicaid as payment for the abortion*," while fees average $250 for a first-trimester abortion and $300 for a later abortion. In other words, the abortion practices of providing physicians reflect a very pronounced upper-middle-class, patriarchal, and age bias. The physicians who have "liberal" values regarding the role of women in society and who are less likely to request parental or spousal consent are also those who refuse to treat medicaid patients (Nathanson and Becker 1980: 160–62). Thus an intimate doctor–patient relationship around abortion decisions is alive and well – for white middle-class ("older" or married) women. Conversely, the very structure of private, proprietary medical care continues to function as an exclusionary device to deny poor women access to abortion services and to supervise the access of dependent teenagers, according to traditional "family" norms.

Since the passage by Congress of the Hyde Amendment in the late 1970s, cutting off federal medicaid funds for abortion, *de facto* denial of access to abortions to poor women has become public policy. The virtual curtailment in most states following Hyde of publicly financed abortions aroused the apprehension of many feminists that poor women would be forced to bear unwanted children, to risk untold deaths and injuries from illegal abortions, or get unwanted sterilizations. Abortion cutbacks and rising sterilization of the poor are related aspects of an integrated federal family planning policy; for, at the same time as medicaid funds for abortion have been eliminated, the federal government continues to reimburse 90 per cent of the costs of tubal sterilization – thus making it a highly accessible "choice" (Ad Hoc Women's Studies Committee 1978; CARASA 1979: 51–2; Petchesky 1981b).[6]

While it is too soon to know the long-term impact of the loss of federal abortion funding, the immediate result of the Hyde Amendment was that an estimated 94 per cent of the medicaid-dependent women needing abortions continued to get them anyway (Cates 1981: 1109–112). The fact that the Hyde Amendment "did not deter the majority of low-income women from obtaining legal abortions" should not have surprised us; for it reflects two social realities that underlie abortion use and its restriction historically. First, since legal abortion services in the twentieth century were never available in practice to very many women outside the several states which continue to provide funding, the figure reflects the high concentration of medicaid abortion clients in those states; it is an artifact of the low availability of funded abortions even during the years since 1973 when abortion has been legal in the United States. Second, and more important, even in those states where medicaid funding has been cut off, "between 65 per cent and 80 per cent of medicaid-eligible women" estimated to want abortions managed to get them legally (and an undetermined additional number illegally). Sometimes this was because local providers continued to provide, despite loss of funding, under the pressure of popular demand. Elsewhere, however, poor women were undoubtedly borrowing from friends or relatives, depleting clothing or food money, relying on charity or clinic good will, travelling out of state and thus risking delay and medical complications: "Plenty of rent checks have gone unpaid, and plenty of food bills have been snipped in half, in order to pay for abortions – with disastrous results to poor women's health and that of their families" (Campbell 1981: 126).

158 Women, health, and healing

I cite these facts not to show that government funding is unnecessary, since its loss has brought poor women unaccountable distress. Rather the facts remind us of a lesson of history: that women will persist in getting abortions out of their own sense of need and right, even under substantial economic, legal, and medical obstacles. In the meantime, however, US government and medical policy favoring sterilization may yet result in a "trade-off" between abortion and sterilization for poor women; or between abortion and unwanted births.

Denying poor women access to abortion, thus forcing them to have children they do not want, and restricting their reproductive capacity through coercive measures such as sterilization abuse, would seem to be contradictory policies. Yet these contradictions are inherent in a society which has been geared historically to the need to control both its "relative surplus population" and the sexual and reproductive autonomy of women. While for historical and cultural reasons sterilization signifies the curtailment of fertility and sometimes even (symbolically) the suppression or punishment of sexuality, abortion signifies the opposite: women's determination to control the terms of sex and pregnancy as the need arises. At the moment, when neoconservatism and anti-feminism are the dominant political tendencies in the society, the denial of access to abortion is the most pressing threat to poor women as to others. Thus Campbell is partly correct when she says "the conservatives don't want women with insufficient funds – and that often means black women – to be in control of their bodies because that would put us in control of our lives. States will *still* pay for the births of unwanted children" (Campbell 1981: 87).

But this is only one dimension of the loss of reproductive control that poor women face. In certain locales – particularly where there are large concentrations of poor blacks, Puerto Ricans, Haitians, Chicanas, and Native Americans – it may be that a more serious problem regarding abortion is not its denial but its rude imposition. There is little concrete evidence to document this beyond the anecdotes of third world women from firsthand experience and of women who have worked in proprietary abortion clinics. According to such reports, poor women of ethnic minorities may find that a positive pregnancy test automatically results in abortion being pushed upon them in an all too eager manner; rather than being offered a "choice," they are presumed to be too poor, too young, or too multiparous to bear a child. This is a function not simply of the population-control mentality, although it is in part that, but also of economic interest that in some ways contradicts the traditional ideological and political opposition of many physicians to abortion. In profit-making abortion establishments, medicaid reimbursement operates as it does in many other aspects of a medical system based essentially on an unregulated private market, as an incentive to doctors to process as many abortion cases as possible.[7]

All these situations together make up a complicated reality: poor women, it would seem, often cannot get abortions when they want to; are sometimes pressured to get abortions when they do not want to; but most frequently seek and get abortions because they need to – necessity, not freedom, dictates "choice." All dimensions of this totality exist at the present time, and all are different in important ways from the reality of abortion for most middle-class women. Yet necessity is clearly a continuum that is relative to class circumstances, and the desire of a woman for control over her circumstances is not the monopoly of any one class. In his 1980 opinion ruling the Hyde Amendment unconstitutional (later overturned by the US Supreme Court in *Harris* v. *McRae*), Judge Dooling of the Federal District Court in New York presented this "doubled vision" of abortion: as a basic right "akin to a woman's right to be"; and as a health need that has special urgency for particular groups of women, such as the poor, the ailing, and the very young. The *McRae* record had determined that poor women were left with the unviable "choices" of going through with their unwanted or dangerous pregnancies, resorting to illegal or self-induced abortions, or seeking hard-to-find alternative services, all of which in turn may result in serious complications or risky delays. Dooling's summary of the record strongly emphasized the health risks involved in delay, particularly for poor women who are mainly dependent on large public or teaching hospitals and "as a class are not well served medically" (*McRae* v. *Harris* 1980: 660, 673). These risks include increased maternal mortality as well as morbidity and prolonged emotional stress.

Beyond just listing the risks, however, Dooling places them

in the context of an expanded concept of "health," one that is social and holistic. "Medical" indications, he suggests, cannot be separated from a wide spectrum of conditions including psychological and emotional factors, age, family situation, the woman's attitude toward the pregnancy, her general health and nutritional level, and poverty itself, which "takes its toll on pregnant women's general health and in the heightening of the health risks of pregnancy." "The unwanted pregnancy," Dooling asserts, *"[never occurs] as an abstraction or in isolation from the woman's total life circumstance."* The Hyde Amendment, he concludes, discriminates against poor women, subordinating their health needs to survival of the fetus:

> The relevance of the woman's poverty is that medicaid is her health care reliance, and when she is excluded from receiving under medicaid the therapeutic abortion that is to her a medical necessity, there can be no assurance that she will receive the medically necessary abortion elsewhere. She is effectively denied assurance of *a basic necessity of life.*
> (*McRae* v. *Harris* 1980: 668–69, 737)

But the Supreme Court in *McRae* saw it differently, rejecting both of Dooling's fundamental principles: that a woman's health must take priority over fetal survival, and that health care must be considered "a basic necessity of life." We need to look at the Court's reasoning with regard to each of these principles and to review the political reasons why their rejection is coupled.

Harris v. *McRae* strikes two blows at once. It is an attack on the idea of women's right to abortion as so fundamental that no woman (however poor) should be denied it; and an attack on the idea of decent health care as a basic human need which society should meet regardless of people's ability to pay. No matter how one reads it, and in spite of all the loopholes left in *Roe* v. *Wade*, it is difficult to reconcile the position the Court took in 1980 with its opinion in 1973. There, it will be remembered, a distinction was drawn between the early stages of pregnancy and the point of "viability": during the period before that point, the *only* "compelling interest" the state might justifiably claim for interfering in the abortion decision was to "protect the woman's health"; after that point, it might claim a "legitimate interest" in preserving the "potentiality of human life" –

except when abortion "is necessary to preserve the life *or health* of the mother"! In *Harris* v. *McRae*, the "viability" distinction gets dropped, the exception to protect women's health gets dropped, and the Court upholds the Hyde Amendment's curtailment of federally funded abortions at *any* stage of pregnancy for *any* reason other than to save a woman's life (*Harris* v. *McRae* 1981).

There was, of course, a technical difference between *Roe* and *Harris*, in that the former involved lifting a criminal prohibition whereas the latter involves the denial of federal funding under medicaid. The only way the Court could consider this difference important was by flatly denying Judge Dooling's reasoning: that abortion services are fundamental to women's health; that health care is itself "a basic necessity of life"; and that, for poor women, medicaid funding "is [their] health care reliance." Its decision to uphold the constitutionality of Hyde rests on the distinction between a "governmental obstacle" or "unduly burdensome interference," on the one hand (e.g. criminal penalties), and governmental subsidization, on the other. Acknowledging the fact that the Hyde Amendment curtails payment for *medically necessary* abortions, and that access to such abortions at *all* stages of pregnancy is undoubtedly protected by "the constitutional liberty identified in *Wade*," the Court nevertheless held that even in the case of "medically necessary" procedures a "constitutional right" docs not entitle anyone to the material means needed to exercise that right in practice:

> it simply does not follow that a woman's freedom of choice carries with it a constitutional entitlement to the financial resources to avail herself of the full range of protected choices. The reason why was explained in *Maher*: although government may not place obstacles in the path of a woman's exercise of her freedom of choice, it need not remove those not of its own creation. Indigency falls in the latter category. (*Harris* v. *McRae* 1981: 316)

In a period of political conservatism and attacks on the very principle of social welfare, medical rationales for abortion, rather than being used as an exclusionary and credentialling device, are simply discarded. The message of the Supreme Court in *Harris* v. *McRae* is that abortion is no longer a matter of *public* concern, a *social* question, at all, but to be tossed by the state back into the private market. But the political implications of this message go much deeper, echoing both the anti-feminist ("moral") and the anti-social welfare ("economic") themes of neoconservative and New Right doctrine. In the context of economic and fiscal crisis, military buildup, and environmental and business deregulation, the restriction of medicaid abortions – among the first in a series of escalating cutbacks in social services that began even before the Reagan government – has played an important role. Focused on an area of human activity that appears to be the most deeply associated with a "private," "personal" realm, and affecting the most vulnerable, least powerful group in society (poor young women, many of them members of racial–ethnic minorities), the policy curtailing medicaid abortions has provided a politically acceptable wedge for the agenda of "reprivatization" to be applied on a larger scale. In *Harris* v. *McRae*, the Supreme Court is saying that the state is under no constitutional obligation to provide benefits necessary to make good the social welfare rights it has itself bestowed (or to redress the social evils it has not itself created). The tacit assumption is that those benefits must therefore come from the private sector if they are to come at all (Petchesky 1981a: 209).

But the attack on federal abortion funding – which was an attack on the idea of abortion as a health issue for women – did more than provide a precedent for social-welfare cutbacks; it also resonated a compelling "moral" argument. Women who seek abortions and public support for them are accused of "selfishness" and "hedonism," a theme which is extended to welfare clients, food-stamp recipients, legal-services clients, and all those dependent on social-welfare programs to survive – who happen to be predominantly women and their children (Ehrenreich and Stallard 1982). Abortion is "evil" not only because it represents women who "get away" with something, who get a "free ride." Medicaid funding for abortions gives poor women a "license" for illicit sex (as bad as illicit babies). They don't have to "pay" for their sins, they get something (sex) for nothing, courtesy of taxpayers. That, far more than the killing of fetuses, makes not only conservative politicians but many working-class and middle-class people angry. In this way, the campaign against abortion funding – and abortion generally –

exploited both the "taxpayer revolt" mentality and the rightward-drifting sexual morality in order to propagate an ethic of self-denial and female subordination, in a period of capitalist retrenchment and patriarchal revival.

Besides poor women, teenagers make up the other constituency whose basic health and wellbeing benefited most from expanded access to abortion services in the 1970s. In the case of teenagers too, however, the specific health benefits of abortion availability, remarked so eloquently by Judge Dooling, have disappeared from view for the Supreme Court and the Reagan administration. Family-planning researchers have presented ample evidence that the impact of early childbearing on teenagers' lives and futures is frequently catastrophic, resulting in losses of social development, educational attainment, and work experience from which they "never catch up" (Moore and Waite 1977: 220–25; Mott and Maxwell 1981: 287). Moreover, public-health data show that maternal mortality risks are seven times greater for women of all ages from childbirth than they are from abortion, when abortion is conducted early, under safe and sanitary conditions (Cates *et al.* 1982: 192). Finally, it is clear that, whatever health risks – both physical and emotional – are presented by abortion, they increase substantially as a result of delay; and it is teenagers who, because of both cultural inhibitions and institutional barriers, are most likely to delay getting an abortion in a situation of unwanted pregnancy. One of the main causes of such delay is the fear that clinic personnel will inform parents. Yet the New Right, the Reagan administration, and the courts now endorse policies that require such informing, through parental notification and consent laws regarding abortion.

In its recent decisions on this matter, the Supreme Court has upheld statutes requiring a physician to notify "if possible" a minor's parents prior to performing an abortion on her, if she is "living with and dependent on her parents" and is not found by the court to be "mature" (*Bellotti* v. *Baird* 1979; *HL* v. *Matheson* 1981). In a complete departure from the principle of "privacy of choice" enunciated in *Roe* v. *Wade*, the Court in *HL* v. *Matheson* suggested that certain categories of women, such as "immature" minors, may lack the "capacity" for choice, especially in matters involving "moral and religious" concerns. In the face of this "moral" argument, the Court's own strong recognition of the medical and psychological deficits of early childbearing eight years earlier in *Roe* v. *Wade* seems to have been cast aside.

But the Court does not simply ignore the health issue; rather it turns it upside down, stressing now the "potentially traumatic and permanent (medical, emotional, and psychological) consequences" of abortion for teenage women. This "medical" argument, which implies that abortion is more dangerous to young women's health than is childbearing, is in diametric opposition to medical fact, as well as to the reasoning in *Roe* v. *Wade*. In a statement that left some of its own brethren as well as the medical profession stunned, the Court's majority declared in *Matheson*: "If the pregnant girl elects to carry her child to term, the *medical* decisions to be made entail few – perhaps none – of the potentially grave emotional and psychological consequences of the decision to abort" (*HL* v. *Matheson* 1981: 1173).

The Supreme Court's concern with the "emotional and psychological consequences" of abortion, and its unfounded assumption that childbearing for a young teenager involves no such problems, rest on deeply misogynist and biological views about pregnancy and "woman's nature." Behind the belief that a teenage girl could be too young or immature to understand the implications of abortion but mature enough to bear a child is the ancient patriarchal idea of childbearing as woman's "natural" biological function, whatever her age or situation; and abortion as a violation of her "nature." Obviously this idea is in tension with the dominant liberal notion of a few years ago (embodied in the federal government's Adolescent Pregnancy Prevention program) that teenage pregnancies were an "epidemic" and must be halted through direct public intervention. The Court's position in *Matheson* both echoes and reinforces the increasing cult of maternity found in mass media, the press, and neoconservative state policies to encourage childbearing and adoption programs rather than abortion for pregnant teenagers. And in this sense it has turned dramatically from the basic impetus of *Roe* v. *Wade*, acting once again as a barometer of rightward political trends.

In a decision that surprised both feminists and anti-abortionists, the Supreme Court in June of 1983 seemed to revert from its rightward course and to affirm its more liberal position in *Roe* v. *Wade*. The problem was that it did so in terms that reinvoked the restrictive as well as the expansive aspects of *Roe*, including its deference to medical authority. The case challenged the constitutionality of an Akron, Ohio ordinance (a model of "local legislation" for the anti-abortion movement) intended to curtail women's access to abortion. This ordinance (and many similar ones throughout the country) required a twenty-four-hour waiting period after a woman signed a consent form and hospitalization for all second-trimester abortions (thus doubling their cost and increasing the likelihood that women would have to travel to procure services). Most insidiously, it required physicians to read their abortion patients an "informed consent" form telling them "that the unborn child is a human life from the moment of conception" and describing "in detail the anatomical and physiological characteristics of the particular unborn child at the gestational point of development at which time the abortion is to be performed" (Greenhouse 1982: A12; *Akron Center for Reproductive Health* v. *City of Akron* 1983).

In its majority opinion, the Court strongly rejected all parts of the Akron ordinance as unconstitutional and inconsistent with *Roe* v. *Wade*. Emphasizing both the "right of privacy" and current medical standards of women's health, it found the delay and hospitalization requirements unnecessarily burdensome and costly, given "present medical knowledge" and the safety of second-trimester abortions using outpatient evacuation procedures. It identified the so-called informed-consent provision as one "designed not to inform the woman's consent but to persuade her to withhold it altogether." Yet, in regard to all these issues, medical criteria and medical authority were the cutting edge of the decision. What the court was really objecting to, in response to extensive *amicus* briefs by several major medical organizations, was less the intrusion by the state on the woman's abortion decision than its intrusion on the physician's autonomy (Greenhouse 1983: B10–11). This reality presents a dilemma to feminists who seek to expand the meaning of "abortion rights," for it is surely commendable that the medical profession in the United States has finally mobilized in support of "pro-choice" forces. Yet the privatized medical definition of abortion is a limiting one for women: the *Akron* decision easily accommodates the conservative sexual and welfare policy that monitors teenagers' abortion access and curtails funding for poor women.[8]

Beyond the medical and the moral models

Is there a way of understanding the health aspects of abortion, given their devaluation by the Supreme Court, that is broader and more connected to the whole of women's reproductive needs than the medical paradigm as it has been traditionally interpreted and practiced? If anything, *Harris* v. *McRae* teaches us, in a negative way, the critical importance of reintegrating abortion within a larger public-health framework, understood from a perspective that sees abortion as a social and health need – a "basic necessity of life" – that must be met through a public commitment of resources. But *HL* v. *Matheson* reminds us that "health needs" may also be used paternalistically, as a pretext to "protect" women from "danger," in the process denying that the abortion decision is not only a matter of health but one of women's moral and sexual integrity. The "danger" from which parental notification and consent requirements and their sponsors claim to protect young women is ostensibly that of abortion itself, but one suspects that it is something different. For the thinking underlying such provisions is that the threat of parental involvement will itself operate to deter young women from sexual activity in the first place; the "danger" is sex.

Confronting the reality of "squeal" rules regarding abortion and birth control,[9] or the prospect of a "Human Life Amendment," brings home as nothing else can the inadequacy of a "health" framework to address the full meaning of abortion in women's lives. Abortion is not analogous to tuberculosis inoculations, and certainly not to mastectomies. As I have written elsewhere, "abortion has to do with the possibility for women, especially young women, to be sexual beings, in a context where birth control alternatives arc inadequate and heterosexual relations often undependable" (Petchesky 1981a: 210). But while we appear to have moved out of the framework of "health" and into that of individual "morality," the truth is that the moral model cannot articulate the abortion question for feminists any better than the medical model. Control over one's own body – including, for women, control over whether, when, and in what circumstances they shall bear children – is not just a libertarian "right," i.e. a private space in which I am free to maneuver so long as I do no one else any harm. It is, rather, a positive and necessary enabling condition for full human participation in social and communal life. It, too, is a social need and has social prerequisites.

As we have seen, even during the halcyon days of legal, funded, and presumably unrestricted abortions, medical control over reproductive health services determined in practice the extent of the "personal right" to choose abortion, especially for poor women. Within the context of the capitalist state and privatized medicine, social and medical services become mechanisms for reproducing the dominant social divisions rather than facilitating personal autonomy; "basic needs," including health, assume different meanings and different standards for different groups, depending on the structural divisions in health facilities and the social values of providers. Thus there is a fundamental problem in conceptualizing abortion, or any other socially determined need, within the framework of "individual (moral) rights," insofar as that framework does not, nor can it ever, confront the institutional bases and power structures that control quality of and access to abortion services for most women. "Individual rights" in American constitutional law, as the Supreme Court has insisted on reminding us, guarantee only that the state will erect no "obstacles," no roadblocks, in our path – for example, will not arrest us on the way to the doctor's office or shut down the (free market) abortion clinics. They do not assure us of money to pay for the abortions or that the state's own public hospitals will provide them, or provide them in a decent and humane setting, or even that the private clinics will be protected by the state from vandals, arsonists, and exploitive hucksters.

Clearly, then, we have to address the concrete conditions which make abortion a socially defined need and not just an abstract moral right if we are going to transform not only the laws but the social structures which keep that need from being met. A rigid dichotomization between a "medical model" of abortion and a "moral model," between "medical procedures" and "political acts" (Willis 1981), gets in the way of dealing directly with these conditions, which are pervasively medical conditions; the "moral model," in other words, simply turns the medical model upside down. The abortion experience of the past 100 years confirms that realizing the right to abortion requires transforming privatized, class-divided medicine. This would mean, not that health needs become the only legitimate ground for abortion, but that they are one essential ground, and that medical personnel who fail to provide essential services should be publicly called to account.

The Jaffe memorandum quoted earlier begins to suggest, though very cautiously, that the alternative to twisting abortion into the narrow, restrictive framework of "medical necessity" and pathology is to broaden the dominant meanings of the "medical" (and consequently the standards of reimbursement) to include *all* aspects of health – preventive, reproductive, and socioeconomic as well as remedial. (This expansive approach to a concept of reproductive health would of course affect public and private financing of not only abortion but contraception, pregnancy, and prenatal and child care.) But to say this is to invite a thorough transformation not only of the ideology and methods of the medical-care system (in US capitalist society) but of its hierarchical structure as well. If "health needs" are not only those which will save an individual from death or disease (although they are importantly these) but also needs which refer to an individual's basic wellbeing, then they are the province not only of professional experts but of both individual "consumers" and social organizations designed to "enforce more uniform – and more liberalized – standards of practice throughout the country." Jaffe's concept of a *social* approach to reproductive health care which respects both "medical knowledge" and "individuals' life choices" has never been applied in American society as a whole, but it remains a necessary precondition to the realization of the "right" to abortion for all women, including the poorest and the youngest.

To achieve this requires not only a socialist transformation of the health-care system, its standards of care, and its methods of distribution, but a new definition of the very meaning of "health," a feminist definition. Returning to the social-contextual concept of Judge Dooling in *McRae*, we might posit that sexual self-expression is itself a human need so allied to a person's physical and emotional wellbeing as to constitute an aspect of her "health," in the largest sense. This is really not a radical or a new idea at all, but it too is surely an important dimension of a feminist perspective on abortion – and on health. Moreover, the principle of control over one's body must also be incorporated into an expanded concept of "health needs," since if things can be done to my body and its essential processes over which I have no control (for example, forced pregnancy) this impairs my ability to function as a fully responsible – i.e. healthy – human being. A position that links abortion to justice is one in which health needs are viewed on a continuum with social, economic, and sexual needs; and needs are understood as the measure of rights.

Notes

1 Sections of this chapter have been adapted from my book (Petchesky 1984).
2 Not until 1967 did the AMA come out with its first official position on abortion since 1871. At that time it essentially confirmed its longstanding policy of opposition, but embedded it within more explicit medical criteria which somewhat expanded the range of exceptions. These would now include cases where there was *"documented medical evidence"* of a threat not only to the life but to the *health* of the mother; where the child "may be born with incapacitating physical deformity or mental deficiency"; where "forcible rape or incest may constitute a threat to the mental or physical health of the patient" (rape or incest in themselves, note, were insufficient grounds); and where two outside physicians, "chosen because of their recognized professional competence," have concurred in writing and the procedure is performed in an accredited hospital. See *Roe* v. *Wade* 1973: 143.
3 The debates are also summarized in an appendix in *McRae* v. *Harris* 1980: 645, 787–95. Senator Brooke, who had introduced an amendment which would have attached the phrase "where medically necessary" to the provisions, clarified the concept thus: "the only alternative was to allow the doctors to make the decisions that only they were qualified to make, and that [the principle of 'medical necessity'] would leave the medical decisions where they so clearly belonged . . . [he] made clear that the doctor would have to make a medical determination, however, and not take the word of the pregnant woman." Brooke's position, considered the most liberal in the Congress at the time, is immediately recognizable as the official AMA policy since 1967 on abortion. Likewise, other liberal

senators, such as Javits, Bayh, and Kennedy, declared their support
for federal funding for abortion where *doctors* determine there are
"sound medical reasons" (Javits), "in cases of genuine medical
necessity" (Kennedy), but decidedly not (the senators were anxious
to stress) for "abortion on demand," or "as a matter of family
planning or for emotional or social convenience." But the seeds for
this apparent retreat had already been sown in *Roe* v. *Wade* itself,
which maintained a footing in the respectable fortress of "medical
necessity."

4 *Vital Statistics of the United States* (Department of Health,
Education, and Welfare 1978: "Mortality," 2, 1970–78) shows a
drop in the maternal mortality rate (per 100,000 live births) from
21.5 in 1970 to 9.6 in 1978. *Monthly Vital Statistics Report* (Department
of Health, Education, and Welfare 1979: Annual Summary for
the US, 1979, Table 9) shows a drop in maternal deaths from abortion-related
causes from 128 in 1970 to 16 in 1978. Although the
DHHS estimated a rise again to 60 in 1979 with the defunding of
medicaid abortions, this did not occur, as I shall explain below.

5 While the Nathanson and Becker studies unfortunately exclude
public hospitals, there has been no known case of a public hospital
attempting to compel a staff physician to perform an abortion
(although other forms of surgery are not generally considered a
matter of "personal choice" or "conscience" for the resident or
attending physician on service wards). It seems reasonable to
assume that, in public hospitals as well, doctors' attitudes have a
decisive impact on the level of abortion services provided.

6 A recent report from the Population Information Program, The
Johns Hopkins University, concludes that "at present the odds on
reversing female sterilization are not good," and that the claimed
60 per cent success rate in reversals applies only to highly specialized,
skilled surgeons, operating "on good candidates," at very high
cost. See Reversing Female Sterilization 1980: C–97.

7 Evidence of coercive or overly zealous abortion practices in clinics
servicing largely poor and third world women comes from interviews
with women who have worked as counselors in such clinics
and have observed firsthand the "medicaid-mill" syndrome there.

8 The majority in *Akron* rejected the provision of the ordinance
requiring the "informed written consent" of a parent or guardian of
a minor woman under the age of 15 seeking an abortion, because it
did not make an exception for "mature" minors. This is consistent
with the Court's position in *Bellotti* v. *Baird.*

9 A measure to require physicians and family planners to notify
parents when minors are given birth control was passed by the
Reagan administration in early 1983 as a regulation attached to
Title X of the Social Security Act. It became known among its

opponents – who registered their opposition through tens of thousands of letters, newspaper editorials, and public testimony – as the "squeal rule" (see Kenney, Forrest, and Torres 1982). At this writing, the rule has been successfully blocked in the federal courts.

References

Ad Hoc Women's Studies Committee Against Sterilization Abuse (1978) *Workbook on Sterilization and Sterilization Abuse.* Bronxville, NY: Sarah Lawrence College.

Akron Center for Reproductive Health v. *City of Akron* (1983) 103 S. Ct 2481, 76L. Ed. 2d 687.

Bellotti v. *Baird* (1979) 443 US 622.

Bureau of the Census (1981a) *Household and Family Characteristics: March 1980.* Current Population Reports, Series P–20, no. 366 (Sept.).

—— (1981b) *Money Income and Poverty Status of Families and Persons in the United States: 1980.* Current Population Reports, Series P–60, no. 127 (Aug.).

Callahan, D. (1970) *Abortion: Law, Choice and Morality.* New York: Macmillan Press.

Campbell, B.M. (1981) Abortion: The New Facts of Life. *Essence:* 86–7, 126–310.

CARASA (Committee for Abortion Rights and Against Sterilization Abuse) (1979) *Women Under Attack: Abortion, Sterilization Abuse, and Reproductive Freedom.* New York.

Cates, W. (1981) The Hyde Amendment in Action. *Journal of the American Medical Association* 19: 1109–112.

—— (1982) Legal Abortion: The Public Health Record. *Science* 215: 1586–590.

Cates, W., Smith, J.C., Rochat, R.W., and Grimes, D.A. (1982) Mortality from Abortion and Childbirth: Are the Statistics Biased? *Journal of the American Medical Association* 248: 192–96.

Cisler, L. (1970) Unfinished Business: Birth Control and Women's Liberation. In R. Morgan (ed.) *Sisterhood is Powerful.* New York: Vintage Books.

Congressional Record 123 (1977) 95th Congress., 1st Sess.

Cutright, P. (1972) Illegitimacy in the United States: 1920–1968. In C.P. Westoff and R. Parke, Jr (eds) *Demographic and Social Aspects of Population Growth.* Washington, DC: US Government Printing Office.

Department of Health, Education, and Welfare (1978) *Vital Statistics of the United States.* Hyattsville, MD: National Center for Health Statistics.

172   *Women, health, and healing*

—— (1979) Monthly Vital Statistics Report. Hyattsville, MD: National Center for Health Statistics.

Doe v. *Bolton* (1973) 410 US 179.

Ehrenreich, B. and Stallard, K. (1982) The Nouveau Poor. *MS.* 11: 217–24.

Forrest, J., Tietze, C., and Sullivan, E. (1978) Abortion in the United States, 1976–1977. *Family Planning Perspectives* 10: 271–79.

Glen, K.B. (1978) Abortion in the Courts: A Laywoman's Guide to the New Disaster Area. *Feminist Studies* 4: 1–26.

Greenhouse, L. (1982) Medical Groups Opposing Curbs in Abortion Law. *New York Times* 31 Aug.: A1, A12.

—— (1983) Court Reaffirms Right to Abortion and Bars Variety of Local Curbs. *New York Times* 16 June: A1, B10–11.

Harris v. *McRae* (1981) 448 US 297, 100 S. Ct 2671.

Henshaw, S., Forrest, J.D., Sullivan, E., and Tietze, C. (1981) Abortion in the United States, 1978–1979. *Family Planning Perspectives* 13: 6–18.

HL v. *Matheson* (1981) 450 US 398, 101 S. Ct 1164.

Jaffe, F.S. (1974) Memorandum to Harriet Pilpel *et al.*, 4 Jan. New York: Center for Family Planning Program Development, Planned Parenthood–World Population. Unpublished.

Jaffe, F.S., Lindheim, B.L., and Lee, P.R. (1981) *Abortion Politics: Private Morality and Public Policy.* New York: McGraw-Hill.

Kenney, A.M., Forrest, J.D., and Torres, A. (1982) Storm over Washington: The Parental Notification Proposal. *Family Planning Perspectives* 14: 185–97.

Lader, L. (1973) *Abortion II: Making the Revolution.* Boston: Beacon Press.

Lindheim, B.L. (1979) Services, Policies and Costs in US Abortion Facilities. *Family Planning Perspectives* 11: 283–89.

McRae v. *Harris* (1980) 491 F. Supp. 630.

Mohr, J.C. (1978) *Abortion in America.* New York: Oxford University Press.

Moore, K.A. and Waite, L.J. (1977) Early Childbearing and Educational Attainment. *Family Planning Perspectives* 9: 220–25.

Mott, L. and Maxwell, N.L. (1981) School-Age Mothers: 1968 and 1979. *Family Planning Perspectives* 13: 287–92.

Nathanson, C.A. and Becker, M.H. (1977) The Influence of Physicians' Attitudes on Abortion Performance, Patient Management and Professional Fees. *Family Planning Perspectives* 9: 158–63.

Nathanson, C.A. and Becker, M.H. (1980) Obstetricians' Attitudes and Hospital Abortion Services. *Family Planning Perspectives* 12: 26–32.

Petchesky, R.P. (1980) Reproductive Freedom: Beyond ''A Woman's

Right to Choose." In C.R. Stimpson and E.S. Person (eds) *Women: Sex and Sexuality*. Chicago: University of Chicago Press.

—— (1981a) Antiabortion, Antifeminism, and the Rise of the New Right. *Feminist Studies* 7: 206–46.

—— (1981b) "Reproductive Choice" in the Contemporary United States: A Social Analysis of Female Sterilization. In K.L. Michaelson (ed.) *And The Poor Get Children: Radical Perspectives on Population Dynamics*. New York: Monthly Review Press.

—— (1984) *Abortion and Woman's Choice: The State, Sexuality and Reproductive Freedom*. Boston: Northeastern University Press.

Reversing Female Sterilization (1980) *Population Reports* 13. Series C, no. 8. Baltimore, MD: The Johns Hopkins University Press.

Roe v. Wade (1973) 410 US 142.

Safe and Legal: Ten Years' Experience with Legal Abortion in New York State (1980) New York: Alan Guttmacher Institute.

Willis, E. (1981) *Beginning To See the Light*. New York: Knopf.

Acknowledgements

Special thanks go to Rhonda Copelon and Meredith Tax for reading and critiquing earlier versions of this chapter; and to Rhonda Copelon, Hal Benenson, and my father, Simon Pollack MD, for providing me with helpful sources.

Seven

Struggle between providers and recipients: the case of birth practices

Shelly Romalis

Maternity care – high technology versus primary prevention – what implications would these have for Canadian health policy? This was the issue which was raised in a struggle which occurred over the plan to regionalize obstetrical services in Toronto in 1980. This struggle in microcosm illustrates how the contending forces of consumers concerned with primary prevention are polarized against health-care providers in the area of obstetrical services. An analysis of this conflict reveals some fundamental strains in the relationship between patients and doctors, consumer advocates and politicians, seekers and providers of health care. This chapter presents an analysis of that case history, suggests historical and social reasons for the emergence of such a conflict, examines it in the context of other consumer birth struggles and looks at some larger implications for women's health-care delivery.

Background of the struggle in Toronto

Regionalization of obstetrical services is an attempt by health providers to organize and consolidate maternity care (see Shearer 1977; Sugarman 1979). Because of the tremendous proliferation of technology used in childbirth, great advances in neonatal care, and a lower birthrate which has reduced the need for maternity facilities, it has been necessary to coordinate efforts and avoid duplication of services, the aim being to reduce health-care costs. Varieties of regionalization systems have been established in a number of states and cities in the United States and Canada. All regionalization plans try to locate the high-risk mother and baby during pregnancy by using some kind of risk-scoring system, in order to refer them to appropriately staffed and equipped hospitals.

An important aspect of regionalization involves the classification of hospitals into three levels. Level I (primary care) hospitals are small and primarily for uncomplicated low-risk patients. Since these units tend to duplicate services of larger hospitals, they are frequently closed unless serving remote areas. Level II (intermediate care) hospitals handle from 1,000 to 2,000 births per year, have laboratory and testing facilities, and are capable of managing some high-risk patients. Level III (tertiary care) hospitals are teaching and research centers, do a large number of births per year, and are geared to handle more complicated deliveries and care of high-risk newborns. As well, these hospitals have to provide services to low-risk patients in order to gain revenues for managing some higher-risk births (from Sugarman 1979: 111, Figure I). Referral and transport from outlying areas to ·Level III hospitals equipped with neonatal intensive-care units is another aspect of regionalized care. A third type of program that some regionalization systems offer is a perinatal network system which has centralized computer terminals for early detection of a high-risk mother, referring her to appropriate units and personnel.

Critics of regionalization systems argue (e.g. Shearer 1977; Sugarman 1979) that while it is necessary to establish new administrative structures to coordinate increasingly complex maternity services, certain types of regionalization plans might cause problems for the normal or low-risk mother and baby who constitute over 85 per cent of all maternity cases. The closing of smaller units means in practice that the funds for maternity care will be concentrated in the larger, more highly technologized hospitals. As a result, there will be an increase in testing facilities, special staffing, more focus on high risk and pathology, leading to increasingly more and more intervention and surgical birthing. This involves less a reduction of expenditures than a reallocation of monies into high-risk care (Shearer 1977: 144). It is claimed that women are forced to travel farther to obtain still more costly births (whether covered by a medical plan or paid for privately), as well as being subject to the more alienating, impersonal care associated with large-scale hospitals. Another problem associated with having a "normal" birth in a hospital geared to high-risk delivery is that the so-called normal birth is managed as if it were high risk – the "just-in-case" approach.

A related concern is that the normal hospital nurseries will be increasingly converted into more profitable neonatal intensive-care units. In order to support the newborn with severe problems, infants with mild respiratory problems or jaundice will have to be referred to the units. A more serious criticism is that the hospital will establish alternative in-hospital-birthing facilities precisely to attract customers for their high-risk units (Shearer 1980). In Britain, admission to special-care baby units corresponds with the availability of places and the accessibility of the unit, rather than with the perinatal mortality rate or with percentage of low-birthweight babies in that region (Richards 1980).

One question asked, then, is what is the cost in terms of mortality and morbidity of high-risk treatment for all maternity cases? Another question is whether regionalization will be an effective way of reducing the number of babies at risk? Two major risk problems – low birthweight and prematurity – are associated with prenatal problems: adolescent pregnancy, nutritional deficiencies, smoking, drug and alcohol addiction (Comstock *et al.* 1971; Niswander and Gordon 1972; Green 1974; Wynn and Wynn 1979). While a good risk-scoring system might locate some of these potential risk cases, it is argued that the very women who might be at highest risk will not be consulting a physician early enough in pregnancy to get the benefit of such a system. It has been shown in Finland, France, and Sweden, for example, that a more effective means of attacking low birthweight and prematurity problems would be to establish outreach programs concerned with primary prevention rather than focusing on high-risk care after birth (Wynn and Wynn 1979). To summarize, then, the general objection to obstetrical regionalization is the investment of massive funds into high-risk management while ignoring the efficacy of primary prevention. It was over this issue that the Toronto providers and consumers came to battle.

The Toronto struggle: events and protagonists[1]

In 1977, the Hospital Council of Metropolitan Toronto and the University Teaching Hospital Association established a joint committee (HCMT–UTHA) to study the causes and prevention of high-risk pregnancy with the goal of decreasing perinatal mortality and morbidity in Toronto.[2] The committee was chaired by a Toronto hospital trustee (also the president of a software research company), and consisted of six physicians, the executive director of a hospital, and one public-health nurse, who was invited to be the ''consumer representative.'' The nurse, a maternal and child health consultant for the Toronto Board of Health, was the only woman on the committee, except for the hospital executive director, a nun. The committee met for a year, and during that time worked out a proposal for a Toronto regionalization system. It recommended that (1) a perinatal network be established, and that all women be computer-scored for risk level; (2) Toronto hospitals be graded into three categories; (3) a new neonatal intensive-care unit be set up at a major downtown tertiary hospital and that another expand its facilities. The $6 million budget for creating (not maintaining) this administrative structure and newborn units allocated only about 1 per cent for primary preventative services.

The public-health nurse, aware of the burgeoning literature on primary prevention and the critiques of regionalization plans, had been increasingly uneasy with the committee's proposal. She objected to the blind acceptance that regionalization plans are effective, to the use of an American city (Cleveland) as a model, rather than a European one, to the lack of evaluation of different perspectives, and to the complete disregard of primary prevention. When discussing her objection with the senior medical officer at the Board of Health (her supervisor), she was told to cooperate with the committee and not to "make waves." After much discussion, and with support from colleagues on the Board of Health, she dissociated herself from the committee's report and wrote and submitted a minority report (Hamilton 1979). Her objection was not to regionalization *per se*, but to the infusion of money into an elaborate computerized perinatal network that would be physician-managed and -controlled. She claimed that since regionalization proposed for Toronto would focus on the growth of high-risk centers, the smaller hospitals, outreach, and preventative programs would be neglected. In addition, she argued, the existing facilities for neonatal care in Toronto were sufficient, given the present and proposed birthrate. The establishment of an entirely new unit would simply duplicate services and increase costs.

Her alternative plan proposed a more cost-efficient approach ($1 million, as opposed to $6 million) to reducing mortality and morbidity in Toronto. The primary-prevention approach would allocate the money to establish large-scale education programs regarding drugs, nutrition, and the ill effects of diagnostic procedures. Government would subsidize prenatal classes and genetic counseling. She encouraged the use of models from such countries as Holland and Sweden that have effective regionalization systems incorporating solid preventive care, rather than from the United States where infant death rates are high. Her case that primary prevention is effective in reducing babies at risk was clear and well documented.

When the public-health nurse submitted her minority report to the Toronto Board of Health, the Senior Medical Officer refused to release it. The nurse then resigned from her position and presented it directly to the Board, which in turn set up its own task force. At the same time, the presentation of the minority report became a citywide issue. The media picked up the story, and radio, television, and newspaper interviews reported the controversy. The nurse asked the public to become involved through a letter-writing campaign to the Ontario Minister of Health. A public forum was organized at a large auditorium in Toronto for April 1980, called *Childbirth in the 80s: High Technology Health Care Under Fire*. Invited panelists included two representatives of the high-risk side: the chairman of the HCMT–UTHA Committee on High-Risk Pregnancy and the director of perinatal medicine at a large Toronto children's hospital, and two representatives of the prevention side: a family physician and myself, an anthropologist–childbirth educator.

The auditorium was packed with an overflow crowd of an estimated five hundred, representing both sides of the issue. A contingent of mothers of damaged babies sat together wearing white flowers. Prevention advocates suspected that the mothers' group was organized by the high-risk advocates to demonstrate that their concerns were also motherhood- and consumer-oriented. After the panelists' presentations, there was open emotional discussion. The high-risk advocates accused the prevention advocates of ignoring the needs of babies, of being too romantic, and of trying to hold back progress. The prevention advocates claimed that high-risk care only benefited the medical hierarchies.

The issue remained in the public consciousness for a number of weeks afterward. A noted *Toronto Star* columnist who attended the forum wrote an impassioned account of the debate supporting the "prevention" side.

For the most part, however, the high-risk argument was given more play in the media. Frequent items would appear in two of the major Toronto newspapers quoting doctors and hospital personnel who were predicting potential tragedies if neonatal care facilities were not increased.

In the view of the prevention advocates, this was the result of pressure from powerful medical antagonists. The task force that had been set up by the Toronto Board of Health met from February to May 1980, evaluated all the reports, and did a comprehensive study of the literature on both sides. They developed a plan for a rational regional program that could effectively combine and reconcile all concerns stressing the importance of allocating funds to preventative care (Toronto Department of Public Health 1980). The report was submitted to the Provincial Minister of Health for consideration.

The Minister seemed well disposed towards the consumer-prevention concerns. He arranged a trip to Europe during the summer of 1980 to examine for himself various obstetrical systems, including that of Holland. After this visit, he met with consumer representatives, told them he was convinced of the value of primary prevention, and promised a report by the fall of 1980.

Denouement

This report came in the form of a speech in February 1981, which was delivered at the downtown tertiary hospital selected for the establishment of the new high-risk neonatal unit. Acknowledging the contribution of the various committees, the Minister described the proposed five-year perinatal care policy in Ontario. He took care to say that prevention and treatment were both to be incorporated. "Prevention" was to be handled by local health units and public education efforts. The latter would involve programs to improve nutrition and childbirth education. There would be regional perinatal planning committees acting as coordinating bodies which would have consumer input (Timbrell 1981).

But the real emphasis of the proposal and specific plans for implementation seemed to stress treatment rather than prevention. The major portion of the funding was to be used for staff training in obstetrical facilities, the building of transfer networks and the upgrading and additions of new hospital units for neonatal care. A new neonatal care unit was to be built at one large tertiary Toronto hospital and the existing unit in another was to be expanded. There would, as well, be two more hospital units added as the need was determined.

Consumer advocates found the speech keenly disappointing. Although lip-service was again given to the importance of prevention, the funding was earmarked almost entirely for high-risk neonatal care. They also harbored suspicions that the Minister was yielding to pre-election pressures and political expedience, and that he had simply waited for the hullabaloo to die down and for the troublemakers to run out of steam, in order to finish what the high-risk committee had originally proposed.

The Assistant to the Minister of Health, however, holds a contrasting view of what has happened (interview, 23 September, 1982). He sees the government proposals as expressing a genuine compromise and credits consumer activism with having a real impact on health-care change. The plans for the elaborate computerized perinatal network proposed by the HCMT–UTHA committee were, in fact, cancelled – not only, he claimed, because of the costs and difficulty of administration, but also because of objections raised regarding the possible invasion of privacy with ready access to records. He claimed, as well, that primary prevention was actually being reflected in new health unit budgets. Although the revised plans involved a grading of hospitals within the province into three levels, there was no intention to close smaller units, which was one of the major worries of the prevention advocates.

Consumers who worked hard during this controversy, gathering data on preventative systems, attending endless meetings with representatives of government, organizing public campaigns to bring the issues to the public, perceive few tangible gains. There has been no written communication from the Ministry regarding the new regionalization plans and no meetings were arranged in order to advise consumer advocates about the implementation. Several of the most active consumers have expressed resignation and cynicism regarding their impact on health-care policy and have withdrawn from public into more private interests.

The Toronto struggle in context

What occurred in Toronto reflects broad tendencies in the history of western medicine and of recent consumer movements which have come in conflict with established medicine since the early 1960s. Contentions over birth practices have frequently been at the center of this conflict. In order to understand more fully the case described above, particularly as it reflects some fundamental themes in the struggles between providers and recipients, a brief review of cultural–historical themes will be useful.

Since medicine's establishment as a new science in the late nineteenth century, it has influenced not only our biological, but our moral selves. In western society, professional practitioners have been trained to seek single causes for disease within the individual rather than in the physical or political environment. The medical profession's control over the selection, education, and certification of physicians, together with the massive research investment in developing new technologies, have led to incredibly specialized training and practice. One consequence of the extension of medical technology and expertise has been to broaden the definition of illness to include deviant and socially problematic behavior such as criminality, homosexuality, drug and alcohol addiction (Conrad and Schneider 1980) as well as the medicalization of such normal biological events as pregnancy and childbirth, aging and death. Doctors, legitimized by science, have become our moral arbiters. They have the right to decide who is really ill and who is simply misbehaving, and who should have access to drugs and treatment. Their unique status and role allows them entry into the most private reaches of our bodies and minds. As the only figures who can legally dispense chemical cures and arrange for surgery, they possess considerable power.

The profession of medicine has not been without its critics in other centuries but contemporary questioning of medicine can be traced to the 1960s. The cost of health care had become increasingly burdensome with no clear evidence that the system was working effectively. While new sophisticated diagnostic treatment procedures were developed, major causes of death like heart disease and cancer were increasing. At the same time that studies were revealing that some procedures (e.g. X-ray) were not only of doubtful benefit, but were actually creating iatrogenic illness, the impact on disease of such factors as environment, diet, and stress was becoming clearer.[3]

In Canada, as in most advanced western societies, the emphasis is on curative rather than preventive care. There is a bureaucratized health system, emphasizing specialization and technology, which is run as a costly, profitable enterprise. While the Canadian experience parallels that of other advanced societies in the decline of traditional diseases, and the emergence of new ones, the dominance of the medical profession, and the general expropriation of health by the medical model, there are distinguishing features. The development of medicine in Canada is marked by a strong professional elitism (which contrasts with the more egalitarian roots of United States medical institutions) and a long struggle toward the establishment of government health insurance (Torrance 1981: 9–28).[4]

Following fifty years of public debate, medical-profession resistance, and political struggles, by the late 1960s all provinces provided schemes for universal patient coverage (Taylor 1980: 189). In Canada today, there is no problem of access to medical care as all provinces have prepaid plans which cover costs of physicians (general practitioners as well as specialists), in-hospital treatment and a wide variety of outpatient services.

The coverage is portable within Canada and to some extent outside the country as well (Bennett and Krasny 1981: 43–4).

Unlike the system in the United States where the patient is directly billed by the physician, in Canada virtually all physicians send their billings to their provincial health insurance scheme which is financially supported by varying and complex types of cost-sharing – a mixture of federal and provincial monies gained from taxes and health premiums. A small percentage of physicians bill above the provincial fee schedule allowance for office visits and some have "opted out" of the public-health scheme entirely, asking their patients to pay directly for treatment, with reimbursement to be sent directly to the patient. Patients, of course, have the option of not using a physician who charges above the fee schedule.[5]

The Canadian program resembles the British National Health Service in its ideology of universal coverage. However, as a typical Canadian hybrid which incorporates elements of British and American societies, the Canadian scheme resembles the American system in that the patient is free to go to the doctor of choice and to switch at will, regardless of geographical boundaries or other limitations within a province. In Britain one registers with a local clinic and if one does not relocate residentially, one can only with great bureaucratic difficulty obtain permission to attend another clinic. As well, under the National Health Service a general practitioner does not have hospital privileges and can neither admit nor follow through a patient. The specialist "takes over" the patient in hospital and the general practitioner frequently is not even consulted. In Canada all doctors have hospital privileges so that more consulting follow-up attention in hospital is possible, although in-hospital care tends to be specialist-dominated.

Birth as a consumer issue

The mistrust of medical invasiveness in North America has given rise to a consumer movement which aims at demedicalizing, demystifying, and humanizing health care. Holistic health advocates reject technological medicine with its single-cause etiology in favor of a more balanced view of the individual within his/her social and physical environment. Holism

promotes the integration of the mind and body, primary prevention rather than acute care, and self-help in order to decrease
dependence on professional practitioners.[6]

The emergence of a consumer-health movement, along with
the women's movement in the 1970s, has had important implications for women's health. As major users of medical care,
women are particularly affected by the impact of the professionalization of medicine and have been at the forefront of
demanding changes in health-care delivery (Ruzek 1979). The
women's movement has been especially concerned with the
difficulties created by the gynecological–obstetrical relationship, with birth control, abortion, childbirth, and menopause:
all events coopted by medicine (Kaiser and Kaiser 1974; Ruzek
1979; Scully 1980).

Consumer trends in obstetrical care have emphasized a rejection of the medical model which perceives and treats birth as
an illness. In both the United States and Canada obstetrical
services are offered mainly by male physicians trained in conventional medical schools to conform to medical models. The
evolution of male-dominated obstetrics in the west can be traced
through a number of centuries of struggle between female midwives and male doctors. Since the late nineteenth century,
however, male practitioners have successfully wrested control
from female midwives in both England and North America,
although for different reasons and at different paces (see
accounts by Oakley 1976; Donnison 1977; Donegan 1978;
Ehrenreich and English 1978; Wertz and Wertz 1979; Romalis
1981a). The new science of obstetrics gained momentum in the
United States around 1900, promising that not only would
babies and mothers be saved from the "intuition" of the lay
midwife and its probably fatal consequences, but that birth
could be less painful as well. The move to hospitals in North
America during the early twentieth century was welcomed by
middle- and upper-class women after the incidence of childbirth (puerperal) fever was reduced subsequent to the discovery
of asepsis (Wertz 1980: 155–59). Hospital rooms were made
comfortable, even elegant for women, providing a brief respite
from domestic responsibilities. The attention made women
feel special and nurtured. Even in Victorian society it had been
more prestigious for middle-class women to have a male attendant (despite modesty problems). Home birth with a midwife

fast became the method for the hapless poor.

By 1914 many women were demanding the revolutionary new "twilight sleep" (a combination of morphine and scopolamine), which promised that even if a woman felt pain she would not remember it. The method was particularly recommended for middle-class women who were thought to be more sensitive to pain than those of the lower classes. Ironically, this new anesthesia was resisted by doctors who were concerned about its possible dangers. Women accused doctors of not wanting to use it because it was too time-consuming. It became a public and media issue with women being encouraged to fight for their rights to have twilight-sleep deliveries. A National Twilight Sleep Association was even formed by society women joined by feminists (Leavitt 1980: 153; Wertz 1980: 159). By 1915 many doctors became convinced that they could manage births more easily when women were under this kind of anesthesia. One physician thus sang its praises in a medical journal, "You are 'boss,'" and "I am never harassed by relatives who want me to tell them things" (Leavitt 1980: 159).[7] For women the issue of control was central with regard to twilight sleep. Although they lost actual control during their deliveries, they perceived themselves as having increased control over the kind of delivery they would choose to have. Although twilight sleep was used in some places until the 1960s, its use declined considerably by the 1940s because of increased understanding of morphine's dangers. By the 1930s, however, "safe" anesthetized birthing was the progressive way (mainly with Demerol), and the "modern" package began to include shaving and enemas, episiotomies and Cesareans. Ironically, the very power that women were seeking in pain-free labors had actually played into the hands of the medical practitioners and to the model which defined birth as a medical event (Leavitt 1980: 161–64).

The needs and ideologies of highly trained, pathologically oriented practitioners have shaped all aspects of contemporary pregnancy and birth. Modern hospital obstetrical practices have included invasive diagnostic procedures, induction and acceleration of labor, reliance on drugs for pain, routine electronic fetal monitoring, dramatically increasing Cesarean-section rates, and separation of mother and baby after the birth. Each of these practices has been shown to be problematic, if not dangerous (see e.g. Haire 1972; Shaw 1974; Arms 1975; Chard and Richards 1977; Banta and Thacker 1979; Holmes, Hoskins, and Gross 1980). The medical assumption is that all babies' chances for survival and optimal health will be improved by intervention. However, despite great advances in labor-management technology, North American fetal mortality rates have remained behind those of other industrialized countries. Although there is the cultural belief that more exacting or simply more technology is responsible for a decline in morbidity and mortality rates, this relationship has been questioned (Illich 1976; McKeown 1976). As Jordan reminds us, a culture has a heavy investment in the technical and moral superiority of its own system of health care which makes it difficult to accept the validity of any other mode (1978: 2–4). Proponents of the medical model refuse to acknowledge that advances in science may have a magical and mythical component, and may not necessarily be responsible for a healthier population. In this view machines and chemicals, rather than social and environmental conditions, may be credited for positive benefits to health. An integral belief in our culture is that medicine is purely a science and that medical services are simply commodities, but medicine is as full of fads and fancies as any other cultural system, and involves a set of entrenched social relationships supporting its ideology (Ehrenreich 1978).

In this technological era women have come to believe that having a baby is a complicated and dangerous affair, that all kinds of physical and emotional problems can arise, often at the eleventh hour, making prediction impossible. It is therefore necessary to have a highly trained expert on hand to locate and manage these problems when they occur. Use of an obstetrician, then, is the only solution if one wants a pregnancy with the best possible outcome. Although most doctor–patient relationships are asymmetrical, regardless of what or who is being treated, women patients have special problems. Even when the doctor and patient are class and intellectual equals, when the woman is educated and articulate, when doctors and patients share values and agree on goals and treatment, sexual politics are in play. The perception of women in our culture cannot help but be extended into the medico-social relationship. The consequences for women of the transplanting of these ideological components into the healing relationship is that they are given more drugs and are subject to more untested procedures and surgery (Corea 1977: 90–1).

Dependence on the doctor's knowledge rather than that of other women is encouraged. In fact, the information that women share with each other regarding pregnancy and birth is actually seen by some as damaging. In 1957, one eminent obstetrician wrote: "Do not hesitate to bring your physician any question that may be bothering you. Above all, ask *him* your questions, *not* your friends at the bridge table" (Eastman 1957: 45–66). Although this book appeared twenty-five years ago, this view which discounts women's culture is not infrequently expressed by obstetricians today, albeit in more sophisticated terms (see, for example, Bourne 1975: 6–8).

Convincing a woman that she will be unable to cope with labor and birth without anesthesia also perpetuates dependence. Although the doctor is not mischievously motivated to undermine a woman's faith in herself, rarely does she get the kind of encouragement she needs to cope with labor without medication. The doctor rarely, if ever, has had the opportunity to observe nonmedicated births, since the hospital in which he or she did his or her internship or residency was most likely a large teaching institution in which almost all births are medically managed (Carver 1981). When a mishap occurs, it is seen as a failure of technology or, more likely, lack of quick enough intervention, rather than the possible result of it. The doctor's decisions, then, are based on his or her training, experience, and perceptions of women, in addition to what Freidson calls the "clinical mind" (1973: 158–84). It is the daily observation and face-to-face contact with patients that influence the physician's behavior, rather than the findings of studies in journals. He or she must respond to his particular work context, hospital colleagues, and pressure from more powerful doctors in the hospital hierarchy. The clinical mind and social factors shape not only the doctor's behavior towards women but that of women towards themselves. They lose confidence and accept medical definitions when they hear, "Very rarely does anyone not need anesthetic," or "Why are you being a martyr?" Most women, then, are fully socialized by the end of their pregnancies not to expect, or at least not to count on, a problem-free labor. They expect to cede control and have someone there to take care of them.

The critics and alternatives

Although the majority of women in North America accept medical childbirth as the best solution for themselves and their babies, critiques and challenges to it have begun to develop a broader base. During the past ten years Canadian women have been exposed to a new consciousness about childbirth, as it has become quite common for popular women's magazines or newspapers to publish articles critical of contemporary hospital birthing practices. Moreover, books have appeared geared to consumer strategies (for example, *The Rights of the Pregnant Parent* (Elkins 1976)). Distrust of doctors appears to be growing and the once untouched culture hero appears to stand on a slightly lower pedestal. Pregnant women are attending child-birth-education classes in greater numbers and enter the birth situation with some idea of what to expect. Increasing numbers of women, then, who become consumers of obstetrical care are questioning medical childbirth, trying to make informed decisions, and seeking alternatives which are seen as ''prevention''-oriented.[8]

The situation in Canada is similar to that of the United States. Toronto has much in common with large cities like Boston where there is a concentration of medical schools, research facilities, and teaching hospitals. There is a tendency, however, for innovations to be incorporated at a much slower rate, due to the differences in the two health-care systems and the forces discussed in this chapter which influence consumer activism. Although there are a number of birth coalitions and childbirth-education organizations in different cities in Canada, no national coordination exists. The alternative birth movement is therefore fragmented and regionalized with individuals working within their own provinces or cities to promote change.

There are a number of alternatives to conventional birthing that have arisen in the past five to ten years which have become incorporated into middle-class birth culture in parts of the United States and Canada. I will discuss five of these (natural childbirth, Leboyer gentle birthing, in-hospital birth centers, home births, out-of-hospital centers) as they particularly relate to the Canadian situation. It will be useful to explore the way they highlight the conflicts between primary-prevention advocates and medical caregivers and thus provide a larger framework for understanding the Toronto high-risk prevention controversy.

Natural childbirth

The natural childbirth movement in North America is about forty years old, becoming more widespread during the past ten years.[9] Physicians' responses to different types of natural (prepared) childbirth have been mixed. Conflicts frequently arise between doctors and patients when a woman wants a nonmedicated birth. The concept seems to run counter to everything a doctor knows or has seen regarding potential pathology and problems, and a woman's ability to cope with labor. If a woman is seriously motivated, it places a strain on the conventional doctor–patient relationship. Doctors are taken aback by expressions of doubts about their expertise (Romalis 1981b). The special relationship between husband and wife planning a nonmedicated birth also confounds the doctor. He sees this as interfering with his own special communication with the woman and altering the more traditional (if tacit) agreement between doctor and husband to "take care of the little woman" (Romalis 1981). The response on the part of the doctor is therefore defensiveness, annoyance, and impatience, resulting not infrequently in belittlement of the woman and her (feminized) husband. Moreover, if the obstetric relationship is very strained, more actively aggressive responses may emerge like "the works" (e.g. induction, sections) for the "know-it-alls," serving as reminder of "who is boss."[10]

The North American natural-childbirth movement has been criticized as being particularly suited to white, middle-class, Judeo-Christian nuclear families (Wertz and Wertz 1979: 185–95) who accept traditional gender roles, as it encourages the dependence of women on men, as well as the continuing domination of the medical practitioner. However, much other criticism of the natural childbirth movement comes from the institutional forces of medicine who favor high-risk care. This view claims that childbirth educators, whatever technique they teach, frequently underplay the painfulness of labor and communicate a sense of failure to women who opt for medication.

Whereas at first only doctors were saying this, I and other teachers now consistently hear it among women after their first births, especially if they have taken medication. The response of the childbirth educator to criticism has been to bend over backwards to encourage women not to be martyrs, to make compromises, to take medication when needed or if seen as necessary by their doctors. The teachers are concerned not to lose the ground that they have gained in reforming medical opinions and hospital practices. The message in most childbirth-education classes, then, is that the doctor should be considered the ultimate authority because of his expertise. As Rothman has argued, the prepared-childbirth movement (she refers to Lamaze in particular) is one in which patients are socialized to accept the medical model (1981). Doctors can thus send patients without worry to childbirth-education classes, since they encourage, for the most part, cooperation with the rules.

Most doctors in Toronto are not really supportive of non-medicated births (regardless of testimony to the contrary) for a variety of reasons – they do not think it works, they do not believe that women should do without something that diminishes pain, they believe modern anesthetics are virtually risk-free, or they want to have optimal control over the birth. Most women, therefore, do not have nonmedicated births. Confidence becomes eroded during pregnancy when one is warned about the problems that might occur that will make interference necessary. When labor is not "progressing" the merry-go-round is set in motion: Oxitocin, fetal monitors, anesthesia, episiotomy, perhaps a Cesarean. Some kind of intervention is almost always "necessary" (even if only mechanical induction – breaking the membranes), or at least it is rationalized as necessary in retrospect. The "final say" clause in the doctor–patient contract is negotiated relatively early in the pregnancy relationship. "You can have your baby any way you like as long as you understand that I must step in when safety of you and the baby is involved." The doctor has the ultimate weapon – the safety of your baby – and anything can be done with this consideration in mind. What is not communicated (or even recognized), however, is that safety is an extremely amorphous notion and might involve more guesswork and judgment than science.

Since childbirth classes are so commonly attended in middle-class circles, no real selection of motivated participants occurs. Doctors refer patients who share their own medical models, frequently directing them to compliant birth teachers. Even if attendance in a birth class raises doubts about the medical model, or at minimum illuminates the difference between medical and nonmedical perceptions, very little can be done to alter practice. Once one has agreed to have a particular doctor manage the birth, the patient understands that the doctor is to make the "important" decisions, and that these are not negotiable, since they are necessary for a "safe" outcome. "Meaningful experiences" are mocked and trivialized next to the overwhelming importance of this goal (with which no responsible person could disagree).

While childbirth education was well established in large United States cities by mid-1960s it was much slower to gain wide Canadian acceptance. In the early 1970s Toronto was still relatively dormant in this regard except for the Childbirth Education Association, which offered classes to women who were aggressive enough to seek them out. In 1974 a small group of women, mainly American, decided to attack the conservative birth system head on, by becoming certified Lamaze teachers (by the American Society for Psychoprophylaxis in Obstetrics). As no training organization existed locally they went to Buffalo for a course and ultimately became certified by the American organization based in Washington, DC. The new teachers were the catalyst for real change. At the time they challenged conventional wisdom and medical authorities in birthing, and were seen as quite a radical consumer interest group. The Childbirth Education Association had receded quietly into the background. But by 1979 a reversal had occurred. The small activist Lamaze group became a larger multileveled organization, with United States links, running its own training programs, concerned with professionalism, teaching classes within hospitals and distancing itself from the more problematic political issues such as home birth and out-of-hospital birthing centers. A more politicized Childbirth Education Association reemerged in the last few years as the greater challenge to the medical model, supporting the current movement to establish an out-of-hospital birth center.

Leboyer, gentle birthing, and bonding

This new era of childbearing focuses pointedly on the child who is the center of the family, the reason for it all. There is an implicit value that each child's health is to be optimal – at the cost of the mother's, if necessary. In *Birth Without Violence*, Dr Frederick Leboyer painted a graphic picture of his view of the baby's prebirth environment, as it struggles to be liberated from the mother. As unpleasant as labor is for the mother, for the baby it is seen as an assault, "the prison has gone berserk, demanding its prisoner's death" (1975: 26). The mother is the enemy, the monster in Leboyer's telling of the baby's view, who is both holding the baby back and pushing it out. To make this horrible experience tolerable, various postbirth ministrations can be performed. A warm water bath and baby massage can help ease the shock, but the expert once again has to be called upon to show mothers the way. "How many mothers briskly pat their babies! Or shake them, while believing that they're rocking and caressing them. . . . How many preoccupied by their own emotions actually threaten to smother their children!" (Leboyer 1975). Although Leboyer assures us that, in most cases, women know naturally what to do, the entire tone of the book tells us otherwise. Leboyer himself took to wearing a clerical-type collar in various newspaper photos and television appearances, and interviewers treated him with reverence. Early doctor response to the poetic translation of the French book was mainly amusement and dismissal. In the United States and Canada the Leboyer technique, however, was being requested by parents and soon became part of some doctors' delivery-room repertoire. Although the bath was often seen as disruptive of normal routine, dimming the lights, baby massage, and delayed cutting of the cord were widely practiced. Doctors could be seen as progressive while not altering their dominant role. Studies of the Leboyer technique showed no significant differences in the baby's behavioral responses when compared with those having normal gentle births (Nelson *et al.* 1979). Although the Leboyer ritual lost its appeal in Toronto a few years after the publication of the book, it raised consciousnesses of both medical personnel and parents regarding the incorporation of more humane handling of the newborn.

The care given to the newborn began to include a concern

with mother–infant bonding, which became a consumer issue in Canada after the publication of Klaus and Kennell's 1976 *Maternal and Infant Bonding*. The authors emphasized the importance of mother–baby attachment right after birth for later emotional development. Bonding theory, which has become incorporated into many hospital routines, has been questioned not only for its methodological problems but for its political implications. Consumer involvement with mother–child bonding has somewhat deflected concern from issues of labor medication, medical control, and its consequences for the baby and mother. In his discussion of bonding theory, Arney (1980) claims that the uncritical acceptance of bonding and the lack of methodological evaluation of it can be explained by its socially useful role. Although challenges to hospital practice have been occurring for about forty years, the medical profession has been resistant to change. Bonding theory seemed to provide some sort of "scientific" evidence which appealed to medical personnel to rationalize changing old practices. With the pressure for demedicalizing and humanizing of birth practices on one hand, and the doctors' increasing concern for safety and belief in technology on the other, we have a potentially unresolvable problem. By focusing, then, on mother–child attachment and the potential pathology that deprivation can cause, the conflict can be diverted to other grounds. In Arney's words: "As pregnancy became natural once again, . . . it was essential that there be new 'diseases' for the doctor to 'treat,' potentially pathological processes in which she or he could intervene" (1980: 561). We have here yet another extension of the medical model: defining family roles and expectations and serving to protect hallowed institutions. The mother is retained as the central figure in the child's life, not only with regard to bonding, but to continually interact with her baby in order for its normal development to proceed. What better rationale for full-time motherhood and preventing women from working or from being serious contenders for career advancement. At the very least, one will feel guilty for making the nonmothering choice. Despite recent attempts to speak about "parenting" rather than mothering, it is questionable whether there have been any real changes in the fundamental view that women, and not men, are the "natural" baby tenders. Bonding theory fits well with the anti-feminist backlash among the general public, tied in with the damaging consequences of women's involvement outside the home which leads to "latch key" children and child neglect, while the mothers are out satisfying their "selfish" personal needs to compete with men in the job market.

The in-hospital alternative

In both Canada and the United States in-hospital birth rooms and centers have been attempts on the part of hospitals and medical personnel to respond to consumer demands for alternative births and to counter the growing interest in home births. Rooms in several Toronto hospitals have been set aside for quieter, less harried birthing and to provide a more pleasant physical alternative to the stark labor rooms in most hospitals. The more humane context might indeed have some effect on the comfort of the laboring woman, but offers no change in the decision-making policy around the birth. Because the birthing rooms are close to the conventional delivery rooms equipped for surgery, transfer to delivery rooms seems all too easy. Not only are machines accessible – just down the hall – but the dominance of medical views of birth will frequently lead to medical solutions. In one major Toronto teaching hospital, the so-called "birthing rooms" are a few selected labor rooms. According to the nursing supervisor, they are "underused," since less than 1 per cent of mothers request them. This "evidence" that the rooms are unnecessary tells us more about how the doctors view them than the patients. Doctors' attitudes are all-important for the reasons mentioned earlier. When the doctor is reluctant, drags his feet, or does not heartily encourage innovative practices, most patients hesitate to take the initiative. Why add another complication to the already confusing process? In this way, innovations are trivialized. The same hospital with underused birthing rooms tried to introduce a birth chair for a year before giving it to another hospital in the city. Some obstetricians explained that the chair was not requested because women were more comfortable in a prone position. Women claimed, however, that this particular chair, a beige plastic affair looking like something out of an astronaut's space capsule, was uncomfortable. But the patients' rejection of the chair was simply seen as more evidence that chairs are unnecessary. There are countless such examples of efforts made to alter practices. As long as the institution and its personnel define birth as an illness and make decisions accordingly, many consumers see real change within the hospital as impossible.

Home birth

The home-birth movement has epitomized consumer rejection of the modern birth context. Many people are beginning to despair of changes in the system and are deciding on a more radical alternative as an expression of their disenchantment with health-care institutions. Home-birth women or couples seek a more relaxed environment; they want to choose their own attendants, to have friends and family around, to avoid excessive intervention, to labor in their own style, using whatever position is comfortable. Each of these options is reasonable and safe for the low-risk woman (Mehl 1977). In fact, the home has been clearly demonstrated by controlled study to be as safe for birthing, if not safer, when selectively used, than is a hospital (cf. Kitzinger and Davis 1978). In Holland, where half the births still occur at home with midwives in attendance, the mortality rate is much lower than in North America, where the whole process is controlled and the woman has access to and uses all the benefits of technological medicine (Kloosterman 1978, 1982). When necessary, a Dutch woman will be referred by a midwife either to a hospital or to a clinic. Even in a maternity hospital (much unlike our own) over two-thirds of the women had neither episiotomies or perineal tearing (Jordan 1978: 64). Despite the growing evidence from academic researchers, physicians, and data from other countries, as well as consumer advocates, that home birth is a safe and viable alternative to expensive hospital birth, official medicine intensely stigmatizes home birthing and sees it as a retrogressive movement. Indeed, the concern about and fear of home births almost reaches phobic proportions among doctors, who claim they are risky and foolhardy. The death rate is said to be much higher than that of hospital births (Aubrey 1977a) and that it is "unrealistic, irresponsible, and incredibly selfish" for a couple to demand a home delivery (Inquiry 1974). One popular physician with a regular column in one of Toronto's major newspapers wrote, "I am in full agreement with proponents who insist that a woman having a normal delivery is not sick and need not be placed in a disease-oriented environment," and then went on in the same column "Perhaps advocates of home births have never seen a near disaster. I have. No doctor, midwife or fortune teller can predict with certainty which births will go well, which will be high risk. Every birth has the potential for disaster" (Seiden 1983). A physician trained to see birth as a life-threatening, medical event, no matter how "progressive," cannot understand why parents would take such a chance with the life of their child.

In Canada, home births are not illegal (except in Alberta), but the Provincial Colleges of Physicians and Surgeons have the power to withdraw licensing from physicians who perform them, although this has not yet happened in Ontario. It is difficult to obtain figures, but relatively few births are done at home and only a handful of doctors will attend them. Even those who advocate the concept of home birth are concerned about the adverse publicity and pressure from colleagues. Medicine seems to have gone on the offensive, seeking out those doctors and midwives who attend home births. In the past year, several instances have come to the public's attention (via newspaper articles) of doctors and midwives (unlicensed) who have attended some births, have had complications, which sometimes resulted in the baby's death, and were brought up on charges of negligence (see *Toronto Star* 1983 – a Halifax case of midwives). The informal controls, warnings about dire consequences, as well as the threat of formal legal strictures, serve to prevent a more broadly based home-birth movement in Canada. Moreover, the provincial funding of obstetrical care makes it possible for all consumers to have access to free hospital and doctor care during pregnancy and birth. Consequently, home birth might be more expensive for the consumer if she were to engage the services of a midwife in addition to a doctor. If practiced on a large scale by those able to afford the option, it would withdraw business from hospitals, which are already suffering from the decline in birth rates. It is in the vested interests of the medical profession and the hospitals, therefore, to perpetuate "safety" concerns.

While the home-birth movement expresses some of our

culture's noblest humanitarian aspirations, it can be criticized for being a middle-class, educated solution to technological overkill. Very much a self-help trend, it is an opting out of, rather than an attempt to change, the present structure of maternity care. Paradoxically, it constitutes both a radical political statement and an extreme privatization of health care. Since it is unlikely that we will shift away from a hospital-based to a home-based birthing system, the home-birth movement functions more as a reminder that the system needs change and that a range of options should be available. It also underscores the real polarity between those who see birth as a natural process, a collaborative family-based event, and those who see it as high-risk, requiring medical control at every stage. These two orientations are so very different and have such dramatically different consequences that one wonders if they can ever be reconciled.

The out-of-hospital birth center

The option of an out-of-hospital maternity center to provide a compromise between home and hospital may be a way to integrate the trend towards self-help and demedicalization of birth with a more active political approach to change. There are about a hundred freestanding centers in the United States, most of which are run by nurse–midwives; and at the time of this writing, none in Canada. The best-known freestanding birth center is the Childbearing Center of the Maternity Center Association, New York City. In operation since 1975, its goal is to be an extension of the home, rather than a mini-hospital. The birth team consists of nurse–midwives, pediatricians, public-health nurses, and support persons who do a careful screening of applicants, providing comprehensive prenatal care. The center has emergency back-up equipment, is within a short drive to the nearest back-up hospital, is less costly than the hospital, and has an excellent safety record. The Childbearing Center, however, had major difficulties becoming established, meeting resistance from the medical establishment, the New York City Health Department, and funding agencies. Having overcome its initial problems and in operation for over nine years now, it is continually scrutinized by the Department of

Health, and by obstetricians and gynecologists who see its existence as threatening (Lubic 1981).

In a freestanding birth center, the consumer is truly seen as an integral member of the birth team, capable of understanding the consequences of various options and helping to make decisions about her health. This notion runs counter to the orientation of high-risk professional care, and is very different from that of an in-hospital birth center.

The position of the American College of Obstetricians and Gynecologists regarding out-of-hospital birth centers has been negative. It is argued that their case loads are too small and experiments too short-lived to evaluate, and that even truly low-risk cases may develop life-threatening problems. They are not seen as being much more cost-effective than early hospital discharge or use of nurse–midwives in hospital, and the savings "can never justify even a single maternal death or mentally retarded child, which the in-hospital setting may have prevented" (Aubrey 1977b).[11]

Movements to establish out-of-hospital centers in Canada have thus far failed. There had been an attempt to create an out-of-hospital birth center in Vancouver, BC several years ago, which was refused funding from the federal government. In Toronto, a birth-center committee has been meeting since 1979 and has the support of a large number of professionals throughout the city (although not surprisingly only a few obstetricians will associate their names with it). The goal of the committee is to set up a small freestanding center near a major downtown hospital, much on the model of the Maternity Center Association in New York City. An elaborate proposal for funds was submitted to the federal government in July, 1983 and was almost immediately rejected. The reasons given ranged from the high cost of bottom-up funding, to unnecessary budgetary details (e.g. toy box and cable television), and lack of adequate evaluation procedures of both research and service. It seemed clear to those involved that the brusque nature of the rejection indicated the center had low priority for funding. The committee is now attempting different strategies, including a research design which will involve randomized sampling, an appeal to the Ontario provincial government for money, and a search for private-foundation funding. As in all of the other alternatives discussed it is clear that there is an unequal burden of proof on any approach which diverges from conventional medicine.

Providers versus recipients: a discussion

In the United States, the direct consumer costs for health care are astronomical and although insurance plans help to defray some of these, there is a severe problem of unequal access. A routine pregnancy and hospital birth can impose a heavy expense on a couple. Resentments at "inadequate" care are more easily bred and are fertile ground for medical consumer movements and for alternatives to the high cost of health care to find support, whether the alternatives are business ventures in a free-enterprise system or a result of the idealism of health advocates. In Britain, the long history of minimal intervention in obstetrical care laid the groundwork for greater resistance to its relatively recent increase. During the past ten years in Britain, the medicalization of childbirth has become common, and most births are in hospital. There is, however, much vociferous reaction to this trend, not only from consumer groups, but from medical professionals. Radical midwives, well-known academics and obstetricians are objecting to the doubtful benefits and increasing risks of technology (Chalmers and Richards 1977; Chalmers 1978; Oakley 1980). There is, at the same time, increasing dissatisfaction with the National Health Service, with more patients seeking private-practitioner care, resulting in a growing polarization of interests.

Due to the existence of a publicly funded health-care system in Canada, medical treatment is available to all without the burdensome financial consequences that exist in the United States nor the limitations of bureaucracy as in Britain. The consumer does not feel directly the financial burden of a medical in-hospital birth, which is still costly to the public economy. Consequently the movement for out-of-hospital birth centers or home births have not had this additional important economic incentive. Without the direct monetary link between the patient and health-care personnel the consumer is unaware of the cost of various tests, examinations, and services and therefore is less likely to seek cheaper alternatives or to organize collectively to create cheaper options. Furthermore, since the consumer does not feel the direct costs, tests and procedures are more easily carried out by medical authorities without consulting the patient, which increases the amount of control within medical hands and perpetuates the continuation of high-risk medicine.

This is not to say that there have not been tensions between doctors and patients over financial issues. Indeed, recent conflicts between doctors' desires to increase their incomes and government's desire to keep health-care cost down have been very public. Although doctors in Canada are likely to make less than their counterparts in the United States, their incomes are still far above many other professional wage earners'. Doctors' anger at the provincial and federal governments for failing to offer them sufficient compensation for services has alienated the Canadian medical consumer. However, as in Britain, the Canadian consumer movement has been more concerned with the quality of the experience and with the medical consequences than with the need to escape the clutches of a free-enterprise medical system which charges what the traffic will bear. Given the present economics of Canadian health care, the creation of consumer alternatives would be high-cost considerations, both for consumers and for government. Since hospitals in the Province of Ontario, for example, are funded to maintain a constant number of maternity beds, there is heavy pressure from the hospitals to prevent government from reducing or reallocating the funding. The establishment of small out-of-hospital units also runs counter to the present trend towards the centralization of maternity services.

Obstetrical care, in sum, is seen by the public as reasonably good and equitable, at least in ideology if not in practice, in that everyone has access to it. As well, there have been humane modifications within hospital maternity units and (at least) lip-service given to the importance of primary prevention, satisfying most users of the maternity care system.[12] Those who are still pushing for change are generally defined as "fringe" radicals who never will be quite satisfied.

The regionalization controversy gives rise to different interpretations of the impact of consumer action on health policy. There is, however, general agreement that the controversy served to raise the public awareness regarding these different perspective. Many users of the maternity system had never before considered the pros and cons of these issues, and were now becoming more aware not only of childbirth politics, but of the politics of health-care funding. One might suggest that, for the first time at least in this area of the country, there was something resembling a "consumer movement" in health care.

What can we predict, then, in terms of real structural change in Canadian obstetrical care? Perhaps the increasing recognition of different perspectives will reduce the chances for accommodation and compromise within established institutions. As doctors increasingly see intervention, surgical delivery, and intensive-care units as the only means to improve perinatal outcome, and as consumers reject the technological "solutions" and their growing negative consequences for people, there will be larger gaps between providers and recipients. This might eventually force the hand of Canadian federal and provincial governments to create, or to allow the creation of, real alternatives, or provide the impetus for consumer groups to create alternatives on their own. A rational birth system that will truly lower mortality rates, as well as provide humane care, must encourage all kinds of options for both low- and high-risk mothers. What is called for, therefore, is human flexibility rather than the machinelike rigidity that so often accompanies technological change.

Notes

1 As an anthropologist–childbirth educator in Toronto, I have been studying childbirth for the past seven years. This chapter is largely based on data from participant observation in Toronto hospitals and at home births; interviews with pregnant women and their partners, with doctors, and with childbirth educators, as well as with health activists and politicians in Ontario. My sources for the case study are mainly unpublished documents, interviews, and fieldwork notes.

2 Definitions of the perinatal mortality vary. Some sources define it as the death of fetuses of any age gestation to seven days of life; others, as the sum of deaths of fetuses and infants weighing 1,000 grams or over that occur between twenty-eight weeks of gestation and four weeks of age. Mortality figures (calculated on the basis of per 1,000 births) must therefore be seen as very rough indicators and in relative terms. The Report of the Task Force on High Risk

Pregnancy by the City of Toronto Department of Public Health, 26 May, 1980, gathered these figures from different sources: For 1977, Canada, 13.8; Sweden, 9.4; Holland, 12.5; United States, 20.7. The Ontario perinatal mortality rate was 13.8.

3 Critics of capitalist health-care systems have focused on several basic issues. Political economists view the problem as rooted in the unequal access to and inadequate distribution of health-care resources as well as the vested interests of the medical profession, which a public national health system could correct. Other radical critics are more troubled with the nature and quality of the services themselves. The "cultural critique" charges that professionalism, racism, and sexism are endemic in existing medical services, and questions whether we want more of a bad thing (Ehrenreich 1978). Whether focusing on the inaccessibility of medical services or on the nature of the services themselves, there is agreement that medicine as practiced in North America is overspecialized, and more responsive to the needs of the market than to those of people. Specialization and technology have come to dominate humanity in a way which can endanger our health and wellbeing.

4 The elitist nature in Canada was characterized by earlier and more successful medical licensing laws and greater control over medical education than that existing in the United States. Medical schools were affiliated with universities which served to elevate standards and reduce the numbers of marginal practitioners (Torrance 1981: 14–15).

5 This had been a very hot political issue in Ontario in 1982 when the doctors had organized to pressure the government to raise fee schedule reimbursement and actually withdrew services. A federal health bill introduced in December, 1983 and passed into law in April, 1984 prohibits extra billing by doctors, thus attempting to insure universal coverage. Various provinces have threatened to get around this by charging family tax supplements or simply absorbing the penalties (one dollar withheld from grants to provinces for every one charged to patients) in order to avoid confrontation with physicians. In any case, fee schedules will be much higher to compensate doctors for their losses of income. Bennett and Krasny argue that physicians can augment their incomes by manipulating the volume of cases (i.e. number of follow-up visits) or type of service to patient. Fee schedules thus do not, in fact, keep down health-care costs (1981: 52).

6 Critics of the holistic health movement claim that while holism places disease within the larger social and political context, the individual is still seen as responsible for his or her illness, and

prevention and treatment of it through appropriate diet and exercise. It is argued as well that rather than demedicalize and decrease dependence, holism (or "healthism", in Crawford's term (1980)) tends to be a cultish replacement of old gurus with new ones, and offers more the illusion than the reality of change. Moreover, the effect is to privatize and individualize the problem of health care which deflects our energies from structural change (Berliner and Salmon 1980; Crawford 1980).

7 It is interesting to note that one of the benefits claimed for epidural anesthesia (the most current form of regional anesthesia with the least number of known consequences) is that "relatives are placated." This appears in a well-known obstetrical textbook, Oxorn and Foote, *Human Labor and Birth* (1975: 390). The increase in the number of older women having first babies (30 and over) results in some paradoxes. Their higher education (many delayed having a baby for career reasons) exposes them in greater numbers to instruction in "how to do it," as well as to critical books on childbirth. Yet their age places them in a more vulnerable position in the medical context. They are considered higher risk and are more likely to be subjects for diagnostic procedures like ultrasound and amniocentesis. They are also more subject to psychological manipulation by the "expert" because they will probably only have one, maximum two, children, giving each birth a special importance. If they have been socialized into the medical model (as indeed we all have been) any new found skepticism is overridden by the desire to have everything go all right.

8 Figures collected from sixteen agencies in the metropolitan Toronto area show that in 1981, 9,138 mothers (the great majority primiparas) attended childbirth classes. This is an approximate 20 per cent increase over figures in the mid-1970s (personal communication from Margaret McGovern, executive director of Prenatal and Parenthood Educational Service, Metropolitan Toronto).

9 Grantly Dick Read, a British physician, published a book in the early 1940s called *Childbirth Without Fear: The Principles and Practices of Childbirth* (1944), which communicated a new philosophy of birthing. Read claimed that fear and anxiety were culturally conditioned states and were at the basis of labor pain. If a woman could conquer her fear by gaining knowledge of the labor process and by using relaxation, a painless birth was possible. The Read method had a number of proponents in the United States in the 1940s, but it was French obstetrician Fernand Lamaze's psychoprophylactic techniques that proved most useful in the modern hospital setting. With a set of breathing and concentration techniques, and a partner–coach (which in the United States was the husband), a woman could experience a pain-free labor,

204 Women, health, and healing

eliminating or minimizing the need for drugs. The support person who could block interference from intrusive, if well-meaning, hospital personnel was deemed vital, particularly in the North American hospital, an alienating environment that potentially could intensify anxiety and pain.

10 I am not implying that there is a conscious response on the part of the doctor to teach the woman a lesson. It is more a case of the dynamics in the doctor–patient relationship, which gradually lead to tests being done for the "patient's own good." When questioned by the newly assertive woman patient, the resentful doctor orders more tests and procedures to confirm the need for the first, etc. Ruzek says that some doctors attribute their patients' assertiveness directly to the Women's Movement and find these "new patients" difficult. Other doctors credit themselves for initiating changes rather than attributing them to the demands of patients, and in this way maintain control (1979: 219–20).

11 In a more recent statement (1981), the present President of American College of Obstetrics and Gynecology (ACOG) has apparently been more open to the option of an out-of-hospital birth center (personal communication, Karen Walker, Childbirth Education Association, Toronto).

12 The system seems to have a remarkable ability for accommodation. In Toronto, when complaints about the growing Cesarean-section rate were arising, a task force was set up, sections were monitored in the major hospitals, and the rate decreased. Several hospitals have established in-hospital rooms, which appeased consumers. More training for nurses in techniques of childbirth education is encouraged, either by having educators give classes in hospitals, or by having hospitals set up their own classes.

References

Arms, S. (1975) *Immaculate Deception. A New Look at Women and Childbirth in America.* Boston: Houghton Mifflin.

Arney, W.R. (1980) Maternal-Infant Bonding: The Politics of Falling in Love with Your Child. *Feminist Studies* 6 (3, Fall): 547–69.

Aubrey, R. (1977a) The American College of Obstetricians and Gynecologists Standards for Safe Childbearing. In L. Stewart and D. Stewart (eds) *21st Century Obstetrics Now!*, 1, second edition. Marble Hill, MO: NAPSAC.

—— (1977b) Position Paper on Out-of-Hospital Maternity Care (ACOG, District II, adopted January). In L. Stewart and D. Stewart (eds) *21st Century Obstetrics Now!*, 1, second edition. Marble Hill, MO: NAPSAC.

Banta, D. and Thacker, S. (1979) *Costs and Benefits of Electronic Fetal Monitoring: A Review of the Literature.* Research Report Series. US Department of Health, Education, and Welfare, Public Health Service, Office of Health Research, Statistics and Technology National Center for Health Service Research, DHEW Publication No. (PHS) 79-3245, April.

Bennett, J.E. and Krasny, J. (1981) Health Care in Canada. In D. Coburn, C. D'Arcy, P. New, and G. Torrance (eds) *Health and Canadian Society.* Toronto: Fitzhenry & Whiteside.

Berliner, H.S. and Salmon, J.W. (1980) The Holistic Alternative to Scientific Medicine: History and Analysis. *International Journal of Health Services* 10(1): 133–47.

Bourne, G. (1975) *Pregnancy.* London: Pan Books.

Carver, C. (1981) The Deliverers: A Woman Doctor's Reflections on Medical Socialization. In S. Romalis (ed.) *Childbirth: Alternatives to Medical Control.* Austin, TX: University of Texas Press.

Chalmers, I. (1978) Implications of the Current Debate on Obstetrical Practices. In S. Kitzinger and J. Davis (eds) *Place of Birth.* London: Oxford University Press.

Chalmers, I. and Richards, M. (1977) Intervention and Causal Interference in Obstetric Practice. In T.M. Chard and M. Richards (eds) *Benefits and Hazards of the New Obstetrics.* London: Heinemann.

Chard, T. and Richards, M. (eds) (1977) *Benefits and Hazards of the New Obstetrics.* London: Heinemann.

Comstock, G., Shah, F., Meyer, M., and Abbey, H. (1971) Low Birth Weight and Neonatal Morbidity Rate Related to Maternal Smoking and Socioeconomic Status. *American Journal of Obstetrics and Gynecology* 3: 53.

Conrad, P. and Schneider, J. (1980) *Deviance and Medicalization: From Badness to Sickness.* St Louis, Toronto, London: C.V. Mosby.

Corea, G. (1977) *The Hidden Malpractice: How American Medicine Mistreats Women.* New York: Jove Publication.

Crawford, R. (1980) Healthism and the Medicalization of Everyday Life. *International Journal of Health Services* 10: 365–88.

Donegan, J.B. (1978) *Women and Men Midwives: Medicine, Morality and Misogyny in Early America.* Westport, CT, London: Greenwood Press.

Donnison, J. (1977) *Midwives and Medical Men.* London: Heinemann.

Eastman, N.J. (1957) *Expectant Motherhood*, third edition. Boston: Little Brown.

Ehrenreich, B. and English, D. (1978) *For Her Own Good: 150 Years of Experts' Advice to Women.* New York: Anchor Press, Doubleday.

Ehrenreich, J. (1978) Introduction. In J. Ehrenreich (ed.) *The Cultural*

Crisis of Modern Medicine. New York, London: Monthly Review Press.

Elkins, V.H. (1976) *The Rights of the Pregnant Parent.* Ottawa: Waxwing Productions; New York: Two Continents.

Freidson, E. (1973) *The Profession of Medicine.* New York: Dodd, Mead.

Green, J. (1974) Infants of Alcoholic Mothers. *American Journal of Obstetrics and Gynecology* 118: 713.

Haire, D. (1972) *The Cultural Warping of Childbirth.* Milwaukee: International Childbirth Education Association.

Hamilton, D. (1979) *A Minority Report,* as a member of the HCMT–UTHA Joint Committee on High Risk Pregnancy, 6 April, Toronto, Canada.

HCMT–UTHA (1978) Report of the HCMT–UTHA Joint Committee on High Risk Pregnancy Study, Phase I, November, Toronto, Canada.

Holmes, H.B., Hoskins, B., and Gross, M. (eds) (1980) *Birth Control and Controlling Birth: Woman Centered Perspectives.* Clifton, NJ: The Humana Press.

Illich, I. (1976) *Medical Nemesis.* New York: Pantheon.

Inquiry (1974) *Canadian Doctor,* February, Westmount, Quebec.

Jordan, B. (1978) *Birth in Four Cultures. A Cross-Cultural Investigation of Childbirth in Yucatan, Holland, Sweden, and the United States.* Montreal: Eden Press.

Kaiser, B. and Kaiser, I. (1974) The Challenge of the Woman's Movement to American Gynecology. *American Journal of Obstetrics and Gynecology* 120 (5): 652–65.

Kitzinger, S. and Davis, J. (eds) (1978) *The Place of Birth.* New York, London, Toronto: Oxford University Press.

Klaus, M. and Kennell, J.H. (1976) *Maternal and Infant Bonding: The Impact of Early Separation or Loss on Family Development.* St Louis, MO: C.V. Mosby.

Kloosterman, G.L. (1978) The Dutch System of Home Births. In S. Kitzinger and J. Davis (eds) *The Place of Birth.* New York, London, Toronto: Oxford University Press.

—— (1982) The Universal Aspects of Childbirth: Human Birth as a Socio-psychosomatic Paradigm. *Journal of Psychosomatic Obstetrics and Gynecology* 1 (1, May): 35–41.

Leavitt, J.W. (1980) Birthing and Anesthesia: The Debate over Twilight Sleep. *Signs* 6 (1, Autumn): 147–64.

Leboyer, F. (1975) *Birth without Violence.* New York: Knopf.

Lubic, R.W. (1981) Alternative Maternity Care: Resistance and Change. In S. Romalis (ed.) *Childbirth: Alternatives to Medical Control.* Austin, TX: University of Texas Press.

McKeown, T. (1976) *The Modern Rise of Population*. London: Edward Arnold.

Mehl, L.E. (1977) Options in Maternity Care. *Journal of Women and Health* 2 (2, Sept.-Oct.): 29–42.

Nelson, N., Enkin, M., Sigal, S., and Bennet, K. (1979) A Prospective, Randomized Clinical Trial of the Leboyer Approach to Childbirth. McMaster University, Hamilton, Ontario, February.

Niswander, K. and Gordon, A. (1972) *Women and their Pregnancies*. The Collaborative Perinatal Study of the National Institute of Neurological Diseases and Strokes. New York: W.B. Saunders.

Oakley, A. (1976) Wisewoman and Medicine Man: Changes in the Management of Childbirth. In J. Mitchell and A. Oakley (eds) *The Rights and Wrongs of Women*. Harmondsworth: Penguin Books.

—— (1980) *Women Confined: Towards a Sociology of Childbirth*. New York: Schocken Books.

Oxorn, H. and Foote, W. (1975) *Human Labor and Birth*, third edition. New York: Appleton Century Crofts.

Read, G.D. (1944) *Childbirth Without Fear: The Principles and Practices of Natural Childbirth*. New York: Harper & Brothers.

Richards, M.P.M. (1980) Is Neonatal Special Care Overused? *Birth and Family Journal* 7 (4, Winter): 225–33.

Romalis, C. (1981) Taking Care of the Little Woman: Father–Physician Relations during Pregnancy and Childbirth. In S. Romalis (ed.) *Childbirth: Alternatives to Medical Control*. Austin, TX: University of Texas Press.

Romalis, S. (1981a) Overview. In S. Romalis (ed.) *Childbirth: Alternatives to Medical Control*. Austin, TX: University of Texas Press.

—— (1981b) Natural Childbirth and the Reluctant Physician. In S. Romalis (ed.) *Childbirth: Alternatives to Medical Control*. Austin, TX: University of Texas Press.

Rothman, B.K. (1981) Awake and Aware, or False Consciousness: The Cooptation of Childbirth Reform in America. In S. Romalis (ed.) *Childbirth: Alternatives to Medical Control*. Austin, TX: University of Texas Press.

Ruzek, S.B. (1979) *The Women's Health Movement: Feminist Alternatives to Medical Control*. New York: Praeger.

Scully, D. (1980) *Men Who Control Women's Health: The Miseducation of Obstetrician–Gynecologists*. Boston: Houghton Mifflin.

Seiden, H. (1983) Your Baby Deserves the Safety of a Hospital Birth. *Toronto Star*, 17 Feb.

Shaw, N.S. (1974) *Forced Labor: Maternity Care in the United States*. New York: Pergamon Press.

Shearer, M. (1977) The Effects of Regionalization of Perinatal Care on

Hospital Services for Normal Childbirth. *Birth and the Family Journal* 4 (4, Winter): 139–51.
—— (1980) The Economics of Intensive Care for the Full-Term Newborn. *Birth and the Family Journal* 7 (4, Winter): 234–41.
Sugarman, M. (1979) Towards Really Improving the Outcome of Pregnancy: What You Can Do. *Birth and the Family Journal* 6 (2, Summer): 109–18.
Taylor, M. (1980) The Canadian Health Insurance Program. In C. Meilicke and J. Storch (eds) *Perspectives on Canadian Health and Social Services Policy: History and Emerging Trends.* Ann Arbor: Ann Arbor Health Administration Press.
Timbrell, D. (1981) Perinatal Policy Announcement. Mount Sinai Hospital, 19 Feb.
Toronto Department of Public Health (1980) *Report of the Task Force on High-Risk Pregnancy,* 26 May.
Toronto Star (1983) Charged Midwives Cheered On. 11 Feb.
Torrance, G. (1981) Socio-Historical Overview: The Development of the Canadian Health System. In D. Coburn, C. D'Arcy, P. New, and G. Torrance (eds) *Health and Canadian Society.* Toronto: Fitzhenry & Whiteside.
Wertz, D.C. (1980) Man Midwifery and the Rise of Technology: The Problems and Proposals for Resolution. In H. Holmes, B. Hoskins, and M. Gross (eds) *Birth Control and Controlling Birth.* Clifton, NJ: The Humana Press.
Wertz, R.W. and Wertz, D.C. (1979) *Lying In: A History of Childbirth in America.* New York: Schocken Books.
Wynn, M. and Wynn, A. (1979) *Prevention of Handicap and the Health of Women.* London: Routledge & Kegan Paul.

Acknowledgements

I want to thank numerous colleagues in the Childbirth Education Association of Toronto and the Lamaze Association of Ontario for sharing views and ideas, and Doreen Hamilton, Karen Walker, Elaine Carty, and Coleman Romalis for their special help. The editorial judgment of Ellen Lewin and Virginia Olesen was invaluable throughout the writing and revisions of this chapter, and I very much appreciate it.

Eight

Women and sports: reflections on health and policy

Mary Boutilier and
Lucinda SanGiovanni

During the past decade in the United States women's participation in physical exercise and in organized sport has increased dramatically. The changing patterns of participation to be discussed in this chapter have emerged partly as a result of the parallel growth of two social movements, the emergent mid-century emphasis on physical fitness which has affected nearly all segments of the population, and feminism, which has encouraged women to explore domains of activity beyond the boundaries of traditional sex roles.

This chapter will examine several implications of these recent developments. First, we review changing patterns of women's increased sports participation and how that has been reflected in policy. Then we examine biophysical considerations in exercise and fitness with attention to some selected health problems. Consideration of psychosocial issues then leads to policy implications and the potential impact on women's health.

Sport, recreation, and fitness

In this chapter we differentiate sport from physical exercise and recreation. Although everyday usage often refers to sports, games, fitness, exercise, and recreation without differentiation, clear distinctions among the concepts of sport, recreation, exercise, and fitness will facilitate this discussion.

Sport refers to human activity that meets three essential conditions (Coakley 1982: 5–12). First, it must involve the use of relatively complex physical skills or strenuous physical exertion. Second, sport is characterized by competition that occurs under formal and organized conditions – that is, it is a competitive activity that is institutionalized. Third, intrinsic and extrinsic rewards characterize sport, engendering dual motives among participants.

Recreation, by contrast, is more closely related to play. The playlike themes of voluntariness, minimal and emergent structure, spontaneity, expressivity, and intrinsic motivation mark recreation. Unlike play, however, which some have conceptualized as unrelated to the demands of everyday life, recreation is frequently a reaction to our daily lives (Huizinga 1950; Stone 1955). "We engage in recreation for refreshment or release; it is a 're-creation' of the individual often necessitated by the demands of everyday life" (Coakley 1982: 13).

We conceptualize exercise as a particular form of physical activity and use this term to refer to "reasonably *vigorous* or continuous physical activity" (Johnson *et al.* 1975: 1; italics in original). Physical fitness is defined as the ability to engage in fairly vigorous physical activities and includes those qualities believed essential to a person's health and general wellbeing. Generally, there are four dimensions that are essential to physical fitness: circularespiratory capacity, muscular endurance, strength, and flexibility (Johnson *et al.* 1975: 25–30).

Changing patterns of female participation

Starting in the 1960s, more women began participating in a greater number and range of sports in more social settings than ever before. The past two decades have witnessed a virtual flood of new sports opportunities and an enormous growth in the number of women and girls willing to seize them. The sports explosion for women has dramatically affected the educational arena, the amateur community sport and recreation scene, and the professional sport workplace. Each of these settings has witnessed an increase in number of participants, the opening of sports previously unavailable to women, a greater allocation of social resources to women's sports, and increased financial rewards for the women who play them.

Today in high-school and college athletic programs, approximately one in three varsity athletes is a female. The number of girls in interscholastic sports programs has increased by 600 per cent since 1970. However, numbers alone do not tell the whole story. During the past ten years the diversity of athletic opportunities for high-school girls has changed. As late as 1971 nearly 50 per cent of all female athletes were engaged in a single sport, basketball. But by 1977 basketball, though still growing in actual numbers of participants, accounted for only 25 per cent of all female athletic participation. During these years other team sports such as volleyball, softball, and field hockey, and the individual sports of golf and cross-country, experienced the most rapid growth in the nation's high schools. Along with the growth in the numbers and types of sports in the high schools came the greater expenditure of tax dollars on girls' sports programs. For example, in 1972, 46 per cent of the high schools had spent 9 per cent or less of their school athletic budget for girls, but by 1978, 77 per cent of the schools were allocating 30 per cent or more to girls' programs (Staffo 1978: 3).

A similar pattern emerges from the data on female intercollegiate activity. From 1973 to 1978 the number of women competing in intercollegiate sports doubled so that women now account for 30 per cent of all college athletes (West 1979: 1). By 1980 over seven hundred colleges and universities offered some form of athletic scholarship for women and most had broadened the range of sports for which scholarships were available. Collegiate budgeting for women's athletics for travel, recruitment, equipment, personnel, facilities, and the like also had increased dramatically. Figures for intramural activities and extension of scholastic and collegiate physical education programs for females point to similar expansion.

Women also participate increasingly in community recreation. In 1978 25 per cent of the runners in the United States were women (Boutilier and SanGiovanni 1983: 38). As an index of this, one manufacturer of running shoes designed for women reported a 63 per cent increase in sales in a one-year period. In another sport, tennis, six and one-half million females now compete for playing times on the nation's tennis courts. As women have come to participate more often, they have increasingly demanded quality equipment designed for females, adequate officiating, longer schedules, more practice times and better-groomed fields and courts, as well as facilities for the newer team sports of crew, rugby, and soccer.

These patterns are duplicated at the professional level. Women today earn money and, in some cases, very lucrative livings from "playing" sports. Women professional tennis players have led the way in this regard. Starting with equal prize monies at the United States Open in 1975, the earnings of women tennis players have sky-rocketed in the last decade. As late as 1970 Margaret Court could win the Grand Slam of tennis and still earn less than $15,000 for the year. Today women participate in single tournaments with prize monies in excess of $100,000. A similar pattern arose in golf, the other major women's professional sport, which by 1978 included four women whose earnings exeeded $100,000 a year. Other professional tours are not as financially successful for women as tennis and golf, but being paid for competing has become a fact in bowling, basketball, boxing, horse and car racing, racketball, surfing, volleyball, track and field, and softball. Along with these changes, corporate America saw the sport world and market open to women. Demand for and endorsement of sporting equipment as well as other products, and the coverage of women's professional sports, have all signalled the arrival of occupational and monetary rewards previously unknown to the woman athlete.

Policy and participation: a dialectic

As a social institution, sport has been highly resistant to change, in part because it serves as a mechanism in the societal division of labor and in part because of negative interpretations of the consequences of sport for women. People in the medical field worried about biological and physiological damage.

Psychoanalysts warned about "loss of femininity," the emergence of psychic stress, and emotional breakdown. Public figures predicted threats to morality, family, and nationhood if women were to take to the playing fields and sports arenas of the republic.

In spite of these concerns the changes which have just been documented finally found the attention of policy-makers and made their way into legislation. In 1972 Title IX of the Higher Education Act prohibited sex discrimination in educational institutions receiving federal funds. Thus Title IX made a public commitment to change sports arrangements in educational institutions.[1] This was not accomplished without controversy. While the topic of sexual discrimination generally addressed by the Act was a "highly emotional one and the issues involved go to the root of societal sex roles, on which most of the male members of Congress remain extremely traditional in outlook," the provisions for athletics brought to the surface "expressions of the personal value systems of the members of Congress" and produced extensive debate (Fishel and Pottker 1977: 132). It seemed that provisions for equal pay for equal work for male and female teachers, elimination of sex-biased career and achievement counseling, and acceptance of sex-blind admissions criteria could be endorsed more easily by Congress and the larger society than equality in athletic facilities and programs.

The history of Title IX reveals a variety of consequences, both anticipated and unforeseen. Most of these are beyond the scope of our effort here, but three will be noted: first, educational opportunities for female athletes increased, particularly in higher education where scholarships became more available. Second, there was a dramatic increase in opportunities for female sports at all levels of education. Varsity athletics, intramural competitions, coed gym classes, and new sports for females were but a few of the consequences of Title IX. Third and rather ironically, the most measurable effect of Title IX was that the substantial increase in women's collegiate sports has meant more employment opportunities for *white males*. By 1979 "at the head-coach level the men's positions are up 137 percent, while women's have *decreased* 20 percent" (Parkhouse 1980: 44; italics in original). A similar employment pattern was found among black men and women (Anderson 1977).

Women's fitness: biophysical considerations

Despite the recent rise of sports medicine as an accepted spe-
cialty within the medical profession and related research into
the health consequences of athletics, little direct investigation
has focused on the biophysical or biosocial issues of women in
sports (Wyrick 1974). Some extensively quoted studies have
compared elite male and female athletes, but this focus seriously
limits the generalizability of the findings (Wilmore 1974;
Harris 1979).

The few studies done on non-elite female athletes generally
have centered on biological and physiological aspects, i.e.
endocrinology, pulmonary physiology, neuromuscular characteristics, menstruation and pregnancy, body composition, and
VO_2 max. capacity. The question of biology has always been
central to the issue of women's involvement in play and sport
because, first, their assumed biological differences and limitations relative to men had been and still are used as rational-
izations for excluding women from sport, and second, very
little has been known about the realities of women's biology as
it relates to physical activity.

Studies show that there are very few significant inhibitions to
women's general participation, thus dispelling most of the
more outlandish myths about the physical abilities of women
(Harris 1973; Wilmore 1974; Ryan 1975; Adrian and Brame
1977; Hudson 1978). Nevertheless, it would be a mistake to
conclude that this issue has been settled once and for all in
favor of a "nurture" as opposed to a "nature" explanation
of women's degree and type of athletic participation and
achievement.

This precautionary statement does not alter the fact that the
asking of the question rises out of an underlying philosophical
position. The very question posed, how and why it is asked, and
the conclusions drawn from the answer require critical evaluation. We do not wish to imply that investigations into the
biological differences between the sexes and their consequences for women's sports are not appropriate and important.
However, much of this research, in our opinion, is grounded
in unconscious and unexamined sexist assumptions. For
example, studies of women's biological proficiency at tasks
requiring strength, speed, and endurance (attributes that favor

male biology) are not complemented by equally enthusiastic studies of male proficiency at tasks requiring balance, dexterity, and flexibility. Thus women typically are measured against male standards in sports that are structured to favor precisely those characteristics grounded in men's biology. The implication is that male performance is the bench-mark against which females should be judged without a complementary attention to the deficiencies of male performance and effort to encourage their improvement in areas where females excel. For example, a recent study reported the efforts of a motor-development program to *reduce* ''feminine game choices'' among boys (Marlowe *et al.* 1978). The underlying bias in this and other research is clear: females can and should be encouraged to throw farther, run faster, jump higher, and endure longer but males should avoid the movement vocabulary and games choices associated with ''feminine'' play and athletic activity.

Only recently have biophysical scientists begun to turn specific attention to females and to establish research institutes to study the woman in sports, not as a ''truncated male,'' but as a sportswoman with her own strengths and problems (Weiss 1969: 219). However, bias even exists in sports medicine:

A more subtle bias in my approach to sports medicine is my view of the active, fit person as ''normal.'' If you stop to think about it, traditional medicine is so focused on the ''*sick*'' that it regards ''non-sick'' as the norm. But non-sick is not the same as healthy, and physicians can make mistakes in judging athletes by the standards they use for the typical American whose pulse is a ''normal'' 80 beats/minute. I once examined one of our outstanding local woman runners and was delighted with my findings. Pulse 45 at rest, 10 per cent body fat content, a strong heartbeat with audible murmur, a high voltage EKG with changes indicative of a powerful left ventricle. No matter that she hadn't had a menstrual period for two years; she didn't wish to get pregnant anyway. The next day this fine athlete had another physical for her job. The examining physician was shocked at so many ''abnormal'' findings and referred the now-alarmed runner back to me for diagnosis and treatment. The diagnosis, of course, was ''super-fit syndrome'' and no treatment was indicated.   (Ullyot 1981: 51)

This sensitive disclosure of the competing and conflicting medical models of the healthy female adult illustrates our earlier point about the value biases that silently shape "expert opinion." We wonder, none the less, if it would be better to make the cessation of menstruation problematic, a question to investigate, rather than to assume as the above quote implies that it is only an issue if one's goal is reproduction.

While much remains to be known about the precise effects of sport and training on the female body, the evidence posits the following propositions: (1) level of physical fitness is more important than gender in determining the effects of exercise; women and men have similar responses to exercise regimens; (2) there are more differences within the sexes than between them in response to strenuous exercise; that is, female and male athletes are more similar to one another than they are to non-athletic members within their own sexes; (3) "The best available evidence suggests that the responses to exercise for both sexes are overwhelmingly positive in both physiological and psychological ways" (Harris 1979: 45).

A review of the literature on the effects of exercise and recreation on physical and psychosocial wellbeing suggests that females may benefit at all stages of the life cycle. For example, research indicates that play and recreation during childhood contribute to an awareness of the physical world and enhance the ability to manipulate and control one's surroundings (Havighurst 1971: 12–13). The now-classic studies of children's play by Piaget (1965) underscore the importance of play in developing moral judgments and in learning to acquire a sense of social expectations that will facilitate future role-playing and group memberships.

As children grow and begin to experience social life outside the family context, in the school and the peer group, we also note the beneficial consequences of participation in play and exercise. An innovative approach to elementary-school physical education programs (Owens 1976) revealed that gym classes, if properly restructured, could enhance children's fitness and motor-skill level as well as provide a stronger sense of bodily awareness and an improved self-concept. In terms of academic achievement by children, some evidence suggests that learning abilities themselves are partially rooted in and related to the development of basic motor skills (Kephart 1960).

In adulthood, there is considerable support for the encouragement of informed leisure choices. Leisure has the potential to give individuals a chance to explore their individual and social identities (Kenniston 1965; Martin 1967). It can also function as a means to expand social participation and enlarge the circle of one's social interaction (Burch 1969).

At a later stage of life, the effects of exercise on the elderly are evident in their improved fitness level. Exercise by the elderly is related to increased muscle stamina, improved physical functioning and reaction time; it can delay or retard age-related changes in the musculoskeletal, respiratory, cardiovascular, and central nervous systems (Harris 1976). In terms of life-style and self-image, the elderly who exercise are more productive at work, more active and relaxed, have better self-concepts and lower levels of psychological tension (Harris 1976).

These suggestive findings hold considerable promise for women, at all stages of the life cycle, who wish to improve their fitness levels and psychosocial life experiences. They are especially important findings for the large majority of female citizens who, for a variety of reasons, are excluded from or who exempt themselves from participation in organized sport. Since an overwhelming percentage of the female population (and the male population as well) will find recreation, exercise, and leisure their main vehicles for the pursuit of physical activity, these and other findings could result in a call for development of policies on exercise and recreation. Such policies would involve this large group of women in their local communities, in schools, in the workplace, and in the leisure and retirement communities that are becoming increasingly popular among elderly Americans.

Selected health problems

While the initial research findings on the benefits of sport and exercise for women are encouraging, we wish to highlight some of the more specific health-related issues surrounding women's pursuits in sports. We are clearly in uncharted waters here; a few issues have already begun to surface, for example the use of steroids and other drugs by elite female athletes (Gilbert 1980; Shuer 1982) and the tensions surrounding the sex testing of female Olympic competitors (Gerber *et al.* 1974; Kaplan 1979; Boutilier and SanGiovanni 1983), but other biophysical problems have barely been identified and work on them is still highly exploratory.

One question arising in the study of physically active women centers on the effects for reproductive functioning. Over the past decade researchers have noted a new menstrual pattern emerging in women who engage in strenuous athletic training. Estimates are that approximately 15 to 20 per cent of these athletes at some time experience "secondary amenorrhea" or the cessation of menses (Harris 1979: 44). The scientific community has offered several tentative hypotheses to explain this phenomenon, ranging from biological variables such as alteration in body fat or changes in hormonal balance to psychological factors such as how individual athletes respond to both physical and emotional stress, but no explanation has yet proved fully satisfying (Harris 1979: 44).

A related concern focuses on the possible effects of strenuous exercise on the menarche. As with the issue of secondary amenorrhea, a few empirical patterns have appeared, such as the delay of menarche among some girls who engage in strenuous competition. However, little agreement exists about the causes of this phenomenon since a variety of menstrual patterns have been described for female athletes, thus making it difficult to reach conclusions about the specific effects of exercise (Harris 1979). Future research on these patterns might well consider the culturally and socially constructed meanings of and responses to menarche and menstruation that women bring to their physiological functioning.

The issue of remaining active during pregnancy has been discussed extensively. Physicians do not agree about the advice given to pregnant women, but the virtual prohibition of all exercise for these women has rapidly diminished over the past decade, particularly when physicians take into account both the stage of pregnancy and the nature of the proposed exercise (Harris 1979; Schneider 1980).

The extensive attention given to reproductive functioning should not rule out a consideration of women outside the reproductive years. For instance, we need to know a great deal more about the effects of physical activity on very young girls. As they are encouraged to pursue exercise and athletic training at earlier ages, longitudinal studies are needed which would monitor biophysical effects over the life-course. At the later stages of the life cycle questions arise concerning the ways in which physical activity may influence the nature of and reaction to menopause. Beyond this, further work needs to be done on other health problems that face older women. At the later stages of life, the effects of exercise on the elderly are evident in their improved fitness level. Regular exercise has the potential to delay or prevent osteoporosis, and may therefore be appropriately encouraged for older women (Harris 1979).

More generally, research is needed which focuses on females throughout their life-course, rather than being centered, as is often the case in the sport sciences, solely on adolescents and younger adults. Such research should also consider how the effects of athletic activities on women may be shaped by their other social characteristics; their race, ethnicity, religion, marital status, economic class, sexual orientation, and other life-style variables all may alter the impact of sports participation on women.

The issue of obesity has been one that is closely implicated in the rapid expansion of women's involvement with such activities as exercising, aerobic conditioning, body-building, running, and other recreational pursuits. Many women appear to be involved in these activities for the instrumental purpose of losing weight or remaining at desired weight. However, increasing debate over the alleged dangers of obesity has begun to appear in the scientific literature (Lewin 1981). At the same time, some critics are challenging the validity of the "desired" weights that guided physicians and insurance companies for over twenty years, suggesting that those figures may be perhaps 15 pounds too low, due to biases in the sampling process that produced the charts.

Depending on which criteria are used, as many as 50 per cent of the adult women in the United States are considered seriously overweight. This figure does not include the greater number of women who are not clinically overweight but whose lives "are a continuous cycle of self-denial and self-hatred" as they strive to attain an almost impossible body ideal espoused by the fashion industry, the drug industry, the fitness industry, and others who clearly benefit from the business of inches and pounds (Romano 1980: 22). The emergence of "health fetishism" is another example of our failure to question conventional "truths" about women's bodies. While not denying the validity of the concern over the possible negative consequences of obesity, we should remember that definitions of desirable weight and ideal body types are culturally constructed. Some observers have raised the possibility that women's exaggerated concern with weight and their striving to be thin, hard, strong, and lean is an emulation of the male physique founded on a latent but correct assessment of male status and privilege (Millman 1980; Romano 1980: 23).

Indeed, there has been much more attention paid to the health risks of obesity while many of the risks associated with extreme leanness are still unrecognized (Lewin 1981). The tentative relation between young girls' obsessive concern with thinness and the cultural image of femininity that dominates mass media and advertising messages has begun to be explored in efforts to understand the disorders of bulimia and anorexia (Combs 1982). That these disorders are more prevalent among young women and rarely seen in men suggests the larger sociocultural forces at work in generating these disorders.

While the study of the relation between eating disorders and athletics has barely begun, some impressionistic evidence points to an increase of these disorders among female athletes in sports like gymnastics and figure skating which stress physical appearance as much as skill (Combs 1982: 12). Other studies reveal that bulimia may also be emerging as a problem in team sports as well as in individual ones (Combs 1982: 13) and that the dedication to rigorous training of some bulimic and anorexic athletes may be tied to their desire to lose weight.

Sports participation: psychological issues

A growing body of research, conducted by sports psychologists and physical educators, scrutinizes the question of the supposed contradiction between femininity and athleticism in part as a response to the simplistic presentation of this issue in the mass media. Other questions follow: how do people perceive and respond to the female athlete? How does participation influence the athlete's self-perception, self-esteem, sexual identity, and self-image?

As the results of empirical psychological research appeared, it became apparent that in most cases the assumed negative consequences were either clearly inaccurate, exaggerated, or speculative. Apart from differences in height and weight, female athletes did not differ physically from their non-athletic peers (Wyrick 1974; Snyder and Kivlin 1975). Pursuing the possibility that the issue might be one of subjective experience of her body rather than its objective comparison with her non-athletic counterparts, some researchers found that female athletes have more positive feelings toward their bodies than do non-athletes. The same relationship held crossculturally in a study of Australian and Indian athletes and non-athletes (Snyder and Kivlin 1975). This work suggests that, as is true for male athletes, positive body images were correlated with self-esteem and self-concept and were negatively correlated with anxiety and insecurity (Secord and Jourard 1953; Zion 1965).

Other researchers have inquired into the possible effects of different types of athletic experience on female personality. They hypothesized that the social acceptability attached to certain types of involvement might affect women's psychological profile. Thus some sports were identified as socially unacceptable for women, typically where women used physical force to overpower or subdue opponents, or used strength as a means of victory and had bodily contact during competition, as in softball and team contact sports (Metheny 1965).

Participants in such sports, it was hypothesized, would be subjected to negative, stigmatizing responses from others. Some found that a sample of the adult population did generate what might be termed a desirability index of sports for women in line with the earlier 1965 categorization (Snyder, Kivlin, and Spreitzer 1975). However, other work throws doubt on the equation that "unfeminine" sport participation leads to anxiety and conflict over femininity and social acceptability (Kingsley, Foster, and Seibert 1977). In a later study utilizing a larger sample, these same scholars found the popular stereotypes were *not* shared by samples of college students including both athletes and non-athletes.

Other psychological studies have addressed the question of how female athletic involvement affects self-esteem, self-image, and self-actualization. A variety of preliminary studies suggest that there is a positive correlation between athletic participation and these psychological variables (Harris 1973;

Snyder and Kivlin 1975; Snyder and Spreitzer 1976). Women who are active in sports "tend to demonstrate more positive attitudes toward themselves and life" and report higher levels of positive responses to questions of being in good spirits, of satisfaction with and happiness in life (Snyder, Kivlin, and Spreitzer 1975: 206).

The research of some sports psychologists finds that female athletes exhibit a tendency to be more autonomous, creative, and independent than their male counterparts (Ogilvie and Tutko 1971). While it remains to be determined if these and similar findings are due to self-selection or are the result of participation and competition, they do parallel the studies of male athletes, which have consistently shown that physical activity and fitness tend to promote psychological wellbeing (Snyder and Spreitzer 1978). Other research has found that self-confidence and self-identity were enhanced if girls began their sports activities early, especially during adolescence (Vincent quoted in Rohrbaugh 1979: 41). Work aimed at assessing factors of self-actualization indicates that athletic participation has positive psychological effects for women: "the female athletes were more self-actualized – surer of themselves, their world and of their ability to relate meaningfully to that world" (Rohrbaugh 1979: 41).

Sociological issues

While supporters of women's sports might understandably be pleased with the directions of these findings, it is necessary nevertheless to be aware of the underlying assumptions that generate some of these psychological inquiries. Much of the psychological debate still centers on whether females can be athletic *and* feminine. While some researchers in psychology and physical education gave legitimacy to this issue by pursuing it in their research, others sought to discover how women "resolved" this assumed conflict. Indeed, an entire theory called "apologetics" has been offered as an explanation of how the presumed cognitive dissonance, that is conflict between the roles of athlete and woman, was experienced and reduced (Felshin 1974; Del Rey 1978).[2] Classified as phenomenological indicators of "apologetics" were behaviors including exaggerated use of feminine accoutrements such as make-up, denial that women take sports seriously, assertions that sports are merely casual forms of sociability, pursuit of more socially acceptable individual sports such as tennis, affirmation of feminine values of beauty and grace as justifications for playing sports, and adherence to a conservative view of women's roles.

This issue creates important conceptual and methodological difficulties. At the conceptual level the approach to conflict leaves the two roles – woman and sports participant – unexamined, vague, and amorphous. Each of these roles has clusters of expectations that link the role incumbent to many other roles, yet these investigations fail to specify the complex relational axes along which conflict may emerge. Roles take shape and are activated in specific social contexts; thus a sportswoman may perceive her body as acceptable in athletic contests, but not in social settings (Mathes 1979: 68). Her presumed dilemmas may take differing forms in the clubhouse, the locker-room, the trainer's office, or at post-game socials. Role-conflict research has failed to adequately consider these contextual influences.

Further, the type and level of women's sports involvement have been conceptualized too narrowly. The classification of individual versus team involvement, for example, leaves many dimensions unexamined. The nature of potential conflicts may also differ depending on whether one is a novice athlete or a veteran, a "star" player or a bench-warmer, an intramural or a varsity player, an amateur or a professional, to mention a few factors apt to be relevant.

Women also bring to sports not only their gender but other social memberships as well, such as age, race and ethnicity, social class, sexual preference, marital status, and the like. Each of these social locations influences how a woman is oriented toward sport *and* how she defines herself as a woman. For example, team-sport participants are more likely to come from lower social classes than individual-sport participants (Greendorfer 1983: 129–30). In light of findings that traditional, conservative images of women's roles in society are more usually found among lower-class women (Yorburg 1974), we must ask, for instance, whether expressed conservative attitudes of softball players towards women's roles results from the perceived conflict generated by their sport selection or from the antecedent variable of social class. With respect to age, research shows that persons in adolescence and young adulthood are more likely than mature adults to emphasize and exhibit sex-role differences (Maccoby and Jacklin 1974; Birrell 1983). Perhaps, then, it is the stage of the life-cycle that generates role-conflict problems, rather than sports participation itself.

Thus whether a woman is rich or poor, black or white, young or old, lesbian or heterosexual, or resides in an urban or rural environment may affect the type and amount of conflict she may encounter in relation to sports participation. Studies of women and sports, then, need to be grounded more firmly in a recognition of the social heterogeneity of women, their locations in different parts of the social structure, their participation in different subcultures and their enactment of different roles – all of which may affect the multiple ways in which role-conflict may be perceived. And above all, studies must attend to what women themselves report about the meaning of sports, athletics, and exercise in their own experience.

The very suggestion of "apologetics" as a means to resolve role-conflict raises questions about the interpretation of attitudes and behaviors as apologies in the first place. Merely because some women choose to play socially acceptable sports, espouse traditional views of women's roles, or wear jewelry does not necessarily mean that these behaviors constitute "apologetics." Instead of assuming meanings, research should be designed to elicit from respondents the meanings they assign their own behavior, leading to the construction of theories grounded adequately in the reality being explored (Glaser and Strauss 1967; SanGiovanni 1978).

Sport and the social actor

Women's greatest access to sport has come precisely during the period when the dimensions of sport were assuming the shape of the modern nation-state. The very conditions of modern sport have *structurally eliminated* those aspects of sport which most closely would have resembled and approximated the "feminine" experience of the world (Bernard 1981). Thus women entered sport at the very time when the character of the activity itself was most alien to their experiential world as *women*. Equality of opportunity to participate in games that increasingly exclude the traits traditionally accepted as "feminine," that is, spiritual, general, emotional, egalitarian, qualitative, and unrecorded, produces a unique problem for the woman athlete. She seeks entrance into an institution that increasingly negates many of the characteristics traditionally associated with her gender identity. As she encounters this social barrier, she is simultaneously involved in the quest for other social roles peculiar to the modern state. Sport thus becomes both a "training" ground for the acquisition of the "right values" and an arena to test out the new identities and traits the modern nation-state expects of her.

Systematic research has just begun to pursue the connection between sport and other sectors of life. Some early findings suggest that having participated in sports might help explain why certain women become active politically and others do not (Kelly and Boutilier 1978: 273–75). One study which looked at twenty-five women who, by 1970, had reached top management positions in American corporations, found that every one of them had participated in sports, usually team sports, as youngsters (Henning and Jardim 1978: 111). The following is a list of what male executives reported about the value of having played team sports and how this experience is linked to the training required of new corporate "recruits" of either sex:

It was boys only; team work; hard work; preparation and practice, practice, practice; if you were knocked down, you had to get up again; it gave you a sense of belonging, of being part of something bigger than yourself; you learned that a team needs a leader because motivation or lack of it depends on the coach; you learned fast that some people were better than others – but you had to have eleven; competition, you had to win; cooperation to get a job done; . . . losing, what it felt like to lose; that you win some, you lose some; . . . that you didn't get anywhere without planning and you had to have alternative plans; once you knew the rules you could bend them – and you could influence the referee.

(Henning and Jardim 1978: 42)

Henning and Jardim point to the dilemma women face as they move into the world of men. Because the version of men's world expressed in organized team sports is usually unknown to them, they enter at a disadvantage and must run farther and faster merely to catch up. Males by contrast usually bring fifteen years of sports experience to their corporate "team." The isomorphic relationship between sports and corporate America is so complete that an inevitable policy recommendation for women who wish to join would seem to be: start early, play hard, join the team and compete.

Such a policy, namely to encourage women to engage in sports for the purposes of learning competitive behaviors which can be transferred to the corporate world, must of course be viewed with some reservation. It is one thing to establish that with proper diet, training, facilities, and coaching females *can* play baseball, football, or ice hockey; it is another thing to argue that they *should* play these sports given their attendant emphasis on male-centered biological, psychological, and social preferences. Until recently, women were excluded from many spheres of social life (wars, competitive jobs, as well as sports) because of presumed biological limits that said "we couldn't do it." The use of biological criteria as the sole basis of recommendations for future sports participation for women is subject to the same limitations as earlier work which suggested excluding women from sports on these grounds. These approaches fail to consider the meaning and context of sports or their links to particular behavior patterns.

To the extent that girls and women have not fully joined or been incorporated into the dominant culture of sport, they can use their "otherness" as a wedge to insist upon reevaluation of this institution. However, since the official policy aim has been equality of opportunity, the time for such a critical assessment may be running out. Girls and women flushed with the "victories" of Title IX and their new athletic selves may fail to realize the costs of such pursuits. To get into the game, to measure oneself against the winner and the record-holder, to play with the same rigor, abandon, and goals may be to endanger some of the qualities by which females have differentiated themselves and to which value is finally being attached.

Sex differences in games and sports for children have been documented (Lever 1976). Sport and games have been closely associated with a range of developmental processes from mastery and control competence (Renshon 1974) to cognitive development (Piaget 1965) and even to moral development (Kohlberg 1976). Feminist scholars have just begun the task of jettisoning the masculine bias implicit in most of this developmental literature and questioning the conclusion that "the male model is the better one since it fits the requirement of modern corporate success" (Gilligan 1982: 10). It may indeed better fit the requirements for modern corporate success but the question is whether this *is* success; whether the costs of such success are too high; and whether other models of success and development (cognitive, psychological, and moral) might not be found through a serious consideration of the world girls and women inhabit and the games and sports they play. The first concerted effort to isolate a female's moral development from the "known standard" has revealed "two modes of judging, two different constructions of the moral domain – one traditionally associated with masculinity and the public world of social power, the other with femininity and the privacy of domestic interchange" (Gilligan 1982: 69). Since the implications of this morality initially suggest a vision which includes as a vital element an ethic of care, women and men might and should be careful not to unknowingly endorse policies which undermine this difference.

As some women have entered corporate life, their tendency to embrace the cultural values and structural forms of their male counterparts has gained the label "corporate feminism" (Gordon 1983). This emergent mix of corporate values and "equal rights" for women is evident in the popular books, magazines and articles, seminars, workshops, and conferences which teach women how to succeed in business. Women are being encouraged to abandon their traditional gender socialization, with its emphasis on nurturance, cooperation, subordination of the self, expressivity, and the like to accept the masculine ethos of "managerial man" with its stress on control, competition, self-interest, rationality, and power (Kanter 1977).

While many factors have contributed to the emergence of corporate feminism, we wish to stress only one here: namely, a failure on the part of many women to grasp a basic sociological insight about the power of social structures and institutional forces to shape people's values and behaviors. Specifically, the goals, roles, rules, and relationships that make up the culture and social organization of corporate systems are firmly established mechanisms through which all corporate thought and action *must* occur. This is true for the men and it is no less true for the women who would join the corporation. The mere presence of greater numbers of females in previously all-male groups, organizations, and institutions will not alter the nature and dynamics of these social units unless and until there is a change in these units' goals, structural forms, and social processes. Obviously, the warning serves to remind women of the problems of unthinking entrance into male sports even as anticipatory socialization for their future in the corporation (Boutilier and SanGiovanni 1983).

Policy implications for women's health

To address policy issues which arise from an analysis of women's participation in exercise and sport necessitates recognition that formal implementation of major advances such as Title IX also rest on informal articulation of societal values and gender stratification. Very much like other advanced legislation, such as the rights to unionize or to vote or the Civil Rights Act of 1964, Title IX, as a legal and political step, cannot alone assure equity, though it constitutes an impetus for change. Public policy is also made and implemented by unseen persons both in the formal legal structures and elsewhere. For instance, ''public officials'' involved with the execution of Title IX have often been male athletic administrators whose interests and networks were oriented to already established male sports.

Quite apart from the legislative agenda which may follow Title IX, however, is the important reality of women's increased participation both in competitive sports and in personal physical exercise. The involvement has had – and will have – policy implications in that it presents new health issues and challenges traditional understandings of women's physical potential.

Although the state of our knowledge about the impact of exercise and sports participation for women's physical health and psychosocial wellbeing is preliminary, initial research findings do suggest that we can expect sports to have positive consequences for women's general health. To the degree that this is true, we wish to explore here some of the possible health issues embedded in the dynamics of increasing female involvement in exercise and sport.

One issue of concern centers on ways in which male and female standards of health may take shape in the future. At present, national trends indicate that women exceed men in frequency of visits to physicians, greater use of prescription drugs, higher rates of hospital admissions, and greater utilization of psychiatric resources and services (Nathanson 1977; Mechanic 1978; Verbrugge 1980). To the extent that exercise and sport, when properly pursued, enhance bodily functioning, reduce the negative consequences of illness and injury, improve one's physical ability to respond to medical and surgical intervention, and strengthen the psychological sense of wellbeing that good health implies, we would expect that physically active and fit women would make different, if indeed not lowered, use of health services than they presently do. Specifically, we would predict that physically active women would have less need for physicians' services, drugs, and other health resources to deal effectively with many of the physical challenges that present themselves during menstruation, pregnancy and childbirth, postpartum, and menopause (Johnson *et al.* 1975).

Beyond the benefits for reproductive health, exercise and sport by women could reduce some of the specific health problems facing elderly women who make up a substantial majority of health consumers at this stage of the life-cycle. There is considerable evidence that regular exercise can prevent or delay cardiovascular degeneration, osteoporosis, and senescence, all common disorders associated with aging (Johnson *et al.* 1975).

It would be naive to believe that increased participation in sport and exercise would not create potential problems for girls and women. As we mentioned earlier, there is some evidence that indicates that for some women strenuous exercise and sports training can result in changes in bodily functioning whose potential dangers must be carefully investigated. Some women may also sabotage the intentions of exercise and sport and use them as a a way of limiting their bodily weight and self-presentation that can result in severe and fatal eating disorders. There are other potential dangers that, while not as dramatic and serious as bulimia and anorexia nervosa, should be monitored. Women who exercise and engage in sport may be vulnerable to physical and mental problems that result from inadequate diet and nutritional advice, improper training regimens, poorly designed equipment and clothing, and improper diagnostic and treatment modalities. These can be addressed only if we treat seriously the physically active and athletic woman as we create those resources that she needs to pursue such activities. We need to find out much more about how exercise and sport affect women's bodies and not assume, as is often the case, that what works for physically active men will suffice for women. This implies that health-care practitioners, nutritionists, coaches and athletic trainers, gym teachers, equipment manufacturers, and others must reevaluate their understandings of women's bodies and psychosocial selves as they become more active physically.

Exercise and sport, by enhancing women's physical and psychosocial wellbeing, may function to challenge conventional medical definitions of what constitutes the healthy female person. The sexist underpinnings of the medical and health professions, and their consequences for the female patient, have already been addressed by feminists (Lennane and Lennane 1973; Lorber 1975). But the emergence of the physically active woman presents an opportunity for members of the health professions to rethink conventionally accepted definitions of and responses to women's reproductive functioning. For example, the appearance of secondary amenorrhea among some athletes who engage in strenuous physical exercise raises important research questions about its subjective meanings, its effects on overall health, and specific reproductive dynamics. It further suggests that "regular" or monthly menstruation may not be the only normal pattern. Additional questions which challenge conventional beliefs about pregnancy, menopause, and old age may emerge from observations of physically active women who may experience less pathology in association with adult development than has come to be seen as usual.

A related issue arises in considering women's vulnerability to crime and the levels of fear which victimization engenders in women. Studies have shown that women, when comparing themselves to "the average man and the average woman," perceive themselves to be weaker and slower than both men and other women (Riger 1981: 58). Since perceptions of physical competence are an important predictor of levels of fear, it may be important to raise women's level of perceived physical competence to give them a greater sense of security.

Though it must be clearly recognized that the fundamental causes of public, violent criminal activity directed toward women in America are complex and are deeply rooted in both gender meanings and social issues, nevertheless it appears that policy connections between enhanced opportunities in women's sports and fitness activity may lead to diminution of a sense of vulnerability. Thus women's sports may not be merely a matter of individual physical health, but can be viewed as contributing to mental health in helping women to cope with stressful conditions.

In summation, we are suggesting that the emergence of a new type of woman, who is increasing her level of physical fitness through exercise and sport, should become the focus of serious study by health professionals. Obviously, the most likely place to begin such research, as is presently being done, is with elite female athletes who represent the extreme case of the physically fit and athletic female. However, this should only be the beginning; we need to extend our research to the larger segment of the female population whose activity levels are more attuned to the leisure and recreational pursuits of everyday life. Since females differ considerably among themselves both in the meanings they bring to their physicality and in their understandings of themselves as women, research should be sensitive to these differences as they occur within subgroups differing as to age, race and ethnicity, social class, life-style choices, and the like. Most importantly, none of this research can be meaningful until and unless it is grounded in non-sexist conceptual and methodological strategies. Research of this type should generate informed policy, expanding women's access to sports and exercise, and thereby enhancing their health.

Notes

1 The Civil Rights Act of 1964 and Equal Pay Act of 1967 had significant effects on women's social roles; however, neither was directed at athletics *per se*. In being adopted by Congress, although it was

not ratified, the Equal Rights Amendment may have been symbolically more important. For real impact on the sexual division of labor
in sport no legislation compares with the Higher Education Act of
1972 with its Title IX provision. The Act represented a public solution to women's problems in this area, a move which confirmed
feminist criticisms that women's problems were not amenable to
individualized formulas but, rather, merited public attention.
2 The phenomenon of "apologetics" received one of its most thorough
and earliest treatments by Jan Felshin (1974). Her use of the term
became the focus of a great deal of scholarly debate.

References

Adrian, M. and Brame, J. (eds) (1977) National Association of Girls'
and Women's Sports. *Research Reports*, 3. Washington, DC: Amer-
ican Alliance for Health, Physical Education, and Recreation.
Anderson, A. (1977) *Status of Minority Women in the Association of
Intercollegiate Athletics for Women*. Unpublished Master's thesis,
Temple University.
Bernard, J. (1981) *The Female World*. New York: The Free Press.
Birrell, S. (1983) The Psychological Dimensions of Female Sport Par-
ticipation. In M. Boutilier and L. SanGiovanni (eds) *The Sporting
Woman*. Illinois: Human Kinetics Publishers.
Boutilier, M. and SanGiovanni, L. (eds) (1983) *The Sporting Woman*.
Illinois: Human Kinetics Publishers.
Burch, W. (1969) The Social Circles of Leisure: Competing Explana-
tions. *Journal of Leisure Research* 1: 125–47.
Coakley, J. (1982) *Sport in Society*. St Louis: C.V. Mosby.
Combs, M.R. (1982) By Food Possessed. *Women's Sports* Feb.: 12–17.
Del Rey, P. (1978) Apologetics and Androgyny: The Past and the
Future. *Frontiers: A Journal of Women's Studies* 3: 8–10.
Felshin, J. (1974) The Social View. In E. Gerber, J. Felshin, P. Berlin,
and W. Wyrick (eds) *The American Woman in Sport*. Reading, MA:
Addison-Wesley.
Fishel, A. and Pottker, J. (1977) *National Politics and Sex Discrimina-
tion in Education*. Lexington, MA: D.C. Heath.
Gerber, E., Felshin, J., Berlin, P., and Wyrick, W. (eds) (1974) *The
American Woman in Sport*. Reading, MA: Addison-Wesley.
Gilbert, D. (1980) *The Miracle Machine*. New York: Coward, McCann
& Geoghagan.
Gilligan, C. (1982) *In a Different Voice*. Cambridge, MA: Harvard
University Press.

Glaser, B.G. and Strauss, A.L. (1967) *Discovery of Grounded Theory*. Chicago: Aldine.

Gordon, S. (1983) The New Corporate Feminism. *The Nation*, Feb.: 129ff.

Greendorfer, S. (1983) Shaping the Female Athlete: The Impact of the Family. In M. Boutilier and L. SanGiovanni (eds) *The Sporting Woman*. Illinois: Human Kinetics Publishers.

Harris, D.V. (1973) *Involvement in Sport*. Philadelphia: Lea & Febiger.

—— (1975) Research Studies on the Female Athlete: Psychosocial Considerations. *Journal of Physical Education and Recreation* 46: 32–6.

—— (1979) Update: Women's Sports Medicine. *Women's Sports* Feb.: 43–5.

Harris, R.H. (1976) Leisure Time and Exercise Activities for the Elderly. In T. Craig (ed.) *The Humanistic and Mental Health Aspects of Sports, Exercise and Recreation*. Chicago: American Medical Association.

Havighurst, R. (1971) The Nature and Values of Meaningful Free Activity. In M. Kaplan and R. Bosserman (eds) *Technology, Human Values and Leisure*. New York: Abingdon Press.

Henning, M. and Jardim, A. (1978) *The Managerial Woman*. New York: Simon & Schuster.

Hudson, J. (1978) Physical Parameters Used for Female Exclusion from Law Enforcement and Athletics. In C.A. Oglesby (ed.) *Women and Sport: From Myth to Reality*. Philadelphia: Lea & Febiger.

Huizinga, J. (1950) *Homo Ludens*. Boston: Beacon Press

Johnson, P.B., Updyke, W.F., Schaefer, M., and Stolberg, D.C. (1975) *Sport, Exercise and You*. New York: Holt Rinehart & Winston.

Kanter, R. (1977) *Men and Women of the Corporation*. New York: Basic Books.

Kaplan, J. (1979) *Woman and Sport*. New York: Viking Press.

Kelly, R. and Boutilier, M. (1978) *The Making of Political Women*. Chicago: Nelson-Hall.

Kenniston, K. (1965) *The Uncommitted*. New York: Harcourt, Brace & World.

Kephart, N.C. (1960) *The Slow Learner in the Classroom*. Ohio: Charles E. Merrill.

Kingsley, J., Foster, F.L., and Seibert, M.E. (1977) Social Acceptance of Female Athletes by College Women. *Research Quarterly* 48: 727–33.

Kohlberg, L. (1976) Moral Stages and Moralization: The Cognitive–Developmental Approach. In T. Lickona (ed.) *Moral Development and Behavior: Theory, Research and Social Issues*. New York: Holt, Rinehart & Winston.

Lennane, K. and Lennane, R. (1973) Alleged Psychogenic Disorders in Women – A Possible Manifestation of Sexual Prejudice. *New England Journal of Medicine* 288: 288–92.

Lever, J. (1976) Sex Differences in the Games Children Play. *Social Problems* 23: 478–87.

Lewin, R. (1981) Overblown Reports Distort Obesity Risks. *Science* 211: 258.

Lorber, J. (1975) Women and Medical Sociology: Invisible Professionals and Ubiquitous Patients. In M. Millman and R.M. Kanter (eds) *Another Voice*. New York: Anchor Books.

Maccoby, E. and Jacklin, C. (1974) *The Psychology of Sex Differences*. California: Stanford University Press.

Marlowe, M., Algozzine, B., Zerch, H.A., and Welch, P.D. (1978) The Game Analysis Intervention as a Method of Decreasing Feminine Play Patterns of Emotionally Disturbed Boys. *Research Quarterly* 49: 484–90.

Martin, P. (1967) Work, Leisure and Identity in Adolescence and Adulthood. In *Leisure and Mental Health*. Washington, DC: American Psychiatric Association.

Mathes, S. (1979) Body Image and Sex Stereotyping. In C. Oglesby (ed.) *Women and Sport: From Myth to Reality*. Philadelphia: Lea & Febiger.

Mechanic, D. (1978) Sex, Illness, Illness Behavior and the Use of the Health Services. *Social Science and Medicine* 12b: 207–14.

Metheny, E. (1965) *Connotations of Movement in Sport and Dance*. Dubuque: Wm C. Brown.

Millman, M. (1980) *Such a Pretty Face: Being Fat in America*. New York: W.W. Norton.

Nathanson, C. (1977) Sex, Illness and Medical Care: A Review of Data, Theory and Method. *Social Science and Medicine* 11: 13–25.

Ogilvie, R. and Tutko, T. (1971) Sport: If You Want To Build Character, Try Something Else. *Psychology Today* 5: 61–3.

Owens, M. (1976) Every Child a Winner. In T. Craig (ed.) *The Humanistic and Mental Health Aspects of Sports, Exercise and Recreation*. Chicago: American Medical Association.

Parkhouse, B. (1980) Strides. *Women's Sports* Feb.: 44.

Piaget, J. (1965) *The Moral Judgment of the Child (1932)*. New York: The Free Press.

Renshon, S. (1974) *Psychological Needs and Political Behavior*. New York: The Free Press.

Riger, S. (1981) On Women. In D.A. Lewis (ed.) *Reactions to Crime*. Beverly Hills: Sage Publications.

Rohrbaugh, J.B. (1979) Femininity on the Line. *Psychology Today* 8: 30–42.

Romano, D.L. (1980) Eating Our Hearts Out. *Mother Jones* June: 20–3.

Ryan, J. (1975) Gynecological Considerations. *Journal of Physical Education and Recreation* 46: 40.

SanGiovanni, L. (1978) *Ex-Nuns: A Study of Emergent Role Passage.* New Jersey: Ablex.

Schneider, I. (1980) Pregnant Pause. *Women's Sports* July: 17.

Secord, P. and Jourard, S. (1953) The Appraisal of Body-Cathexis: Body-Cathexis and the Self. *Journal of Consulting Psychology* 12: 343–47.

Shuer, M. (1982) Steroids. *Women's Sports* April: 17–23.

Snyder, E.E. and Kivlin, J.E. (1975) Women Athletes and Aspects of Psychological Well-Being and Body Image. *Research Quarterly* 46: 191–99.

Snyder, E.E., Kivlin, J.E., and Spreitzer, E. (1975) The Female Athlete: An Analysis of Objective and Subjective Role Conflict. In D. Landers (ed.) *Psychology of Sport and Motor Behavior.* University Park: Pennsylvania State University Press.

Snyder, E.E. and Spreitzer, E. (1976) Correlates of Sport Participation Among Adolescent Girls. *Research Quarterly* 47: 804–09.

Snyder, E.E. and Spreitzer, E. (1978) *Social Aspects of Sport.* Englewood Cliffs, NJ: Prentice-Hall.

Staffo, D. (1978) Survey Report Action in New York State to Provide Athletic Opportunities to Girls. *AAHPER Update* Dec.: 1.

Stone, G. (1955) American Sports-Play and Dis-Play. *Chicago Review* 9: 83–100.

Ullyot, J. (1981) Housecalls. *Women's Sports* March: 51.

Verbrugge, L. (1980) Sex Differences in Complaints and Diagnoses. *Journal of Behavioral Medicine* 3: 327–55.

Weiss, P. (1969) *Sport: A Philosophy Inquiry.* Carbondale, IL: Southern Illinois University Press.

West, P. (1979) Massive Lobbying Campaign Seeks To Gut Title IX. *National NOW Times* 12: 13.

Wilmore, J. (ed.) (1974) Research Methodology in the Sociology of Sport. *Exercise and Sport Sciences Review*, 2. New York: Academic Press.

Wyrick, W. (1974) Biophysical Perspective. In E. Gerber, J. Felshin, P. Berlin, and W. Wyrick (eds) *The American Woman in Sport.* Reading, MA: Addison-Wesley.

Yorburg, B. (1974) *Sexual Identity: Sex Roles and Social Change.* New York: Wiley.

Zion, L. (1965) Body Concept as it Relates to Self-Concept. *Research Quarterly* 36: 490–95.

Nine

Women and the National Health Service: the carers and the careless

Lesley Doyal

Introduction

There can be little doubt that the creation of the National Health Service (NHS) in 1948 brought considerable benefits to the majority of the British people. Both primary care (from a general practitioner) and hospital treatment were made available free at source to all those in need, with the cost being met by a combination of general taxation, national insurance contributions, and charges for certain items such as dentures and spectacles. By this means, access to services was made more equal and many were freed from the burden of anxiety over the cost of medical care. As we shall see, women in particular benefited from the new system both because of their special health needs connected with fertility and reproduction, and because many of them had only had limited access to medical care in the past. However, these gains have been relatively limited, and the health service has a long way to go to meet all women's needs – whether as users of health care or as health workers.

It is clear that the NHS offered women much greater access to medical care than they had in the past (Townsend and Davidson 1982). No distinction was made by sex or marital status, and services were available to all. As a result, there is evidence of a marked rise in minor gynecological surgery in the period immediately after the service was set up, as the chronic conditions that had ailed so many women at last received attention.[1] Others obtained spectacles and false teeth for the first time, since they no longer had to be purchased entirely out of the family budget. As the health service expanded it also became an important new source of jobs for women. The NHS is now the largest single employer of women in the country and about 75 per cent of its employees are female.

It would seem, then, that British women should be well satisfied with the National Health Service, which has met many of their needs both as consumers of health care and increasingly as workers. Indeed the significance of the service for women is witnessed by the central role they are now playing in campaigns to defend it. But if we look more closely it becomes apparent that the success of the NHS in meeting women's needs has been only partial. In the final analysis it has failed to live up to its potential for improving women's health or for providing equal opportunities in the workplace. Indeed it has, in many ways, facilitated the development of *new* sources of control over women (Smart and Smart 1978; Doyal 1979b; Hutter and Williams 1981). Not surprisingly, then, a feminist critique of the NHS is now emerging, so that women are concerned at one and the same time with the defense of the NHS and also with the formulation of proposals for qualitative changes in its organization and control. The reasons for this apparent paradox are explored in more detail in the remaining sections of this chapter.

Women, inequalities, and the NHS

At first sight, the benefits received by women from the NHS appear to have been very great. To begin with the most obvious indicator of health, it is well known that the average woman can now expect to live about six years longer than her male counterpart (Governmental Statistical Service 1981). However, it can be misleading to treat men and women as homogeneous groups in this way. There are also marked differences in mortality rates *within* gender groups – differences relating to marital status, to region of residence, to race and especially to social class. We will examine the impact of race and class in particular on female patterns of morbidity and mortality and also on women's use of services. An understanding of these processes is important because it shows that for women as for men the undoubted benefits of the NHS have been mediated by the basic inequalities that still characterize British society. Furthermore, it highlights the continuing importance of wider social and economic factors (income, work, and housing in particular) on the determination of human health and illness.

The avowed intention of the architects of the NHS was to set up a system that gave everyone in the population equal access to *medical care*, their aim being to "divorce the care of health from questions of personal means or other factors irrelevant to it." It was assumed that this would equalize the *health* of different groups. But almost from its inception it became clear that like other parts of the welfare state, the NHS was not being used equally by all social groups. This impression was reinforced in the mid-1960s when it became apparent that the gap between the standards of health of different social classes remained wide (Townsend and Davidson 1982: 51–64). Thus there began a continuing debate about the extent of social-class differences in the utilization of services, about the reasons for these differences, and about their impact (if any) on patterns of health and illness.

Class effects

One of the first detailed studies claimed on the basis of evidence already available that "higher income groups know how to make better use of the service: they tend to receive more specialist attention: occupy more of the beds in better equipped and staffed hospitals" (Titmuss 1968). Later studies confirmed this view and a wide range of corroborating evidence was gathered together in an official government report *Inequalities in Health* published in 1980 (Townsend and Davidson 1982).[2] In what follows, we will provide a brief summary of this evidence as it relates to women. However, it is important to note that most discussions of the relationship between class and health have tended to concentrate on men and any attempt to correct this bias has to contend with the fact that women are considerably less visible than men in routine statistics on health, illness, and medical care (Oakley and Oakley 1979; Macfarlane 1980).

We begin by looking at the most comprehensive (though also the crudest) data on the health of women in different social classes. These are the mortality statistics recorded in the Registrar General's Decennial Supplement (1978).[3] As we have already seen, male mortality exceeds female mortality at all ages. Indeed, on the basis of evidence drawn from the early 1970s, the ratio of male to female deaths is about 2:1 *within* each social class. In social class I (professional and managerial) the death rate for men aged 15–64 is 3.98 per 1,000, while for women it was only 2.15. But the comparable figures for social class V (unskilled) are 9.88 and 5.31, showing not only a marked difference between the sexes but also a steep social class gradient. Thus women in different social classes have continued to have very different mortality rates. Indeed this social class gradient sometimes crosses gender boundaries so that *women* in social classes IV and V have higher rates of mortality than *men* in social class I.

Among partly skilled and unskilled women aged 15–64, there is markedly higher mortality from infectious and parasitic diseases, circulatory and respiratory diseases, and diseases of the genito-urinary system. These women also suffer slightly more deaths from congenital abnormalities, diseases of the blood, endocrine and nutritional diseases, and diseases of the digestive system. The position is reversed only in the case of mental disorders, diseases of the nervous system, malignant neoplasms,[4] and accidents, poisonings, and violence, where there is a higher rate of mortality among women in social classes I and II. Finally, it is worth pointing out that although maternal mortality fell by more than a third during the 1960s, the rate among women in social class V is still nearly double that of social classes I and II (Townsend and Davidson 1982: 70).

Before proceeding further, we should note the limitations of mortality rates as a source of information on married women. In British official statistics, single women are assigned to a social class on the basis of their own occupation but married women are often classified only according to that of their present (or even former) husband. For the 1970–72 Decennial Supplement, married women were originally classified by both their husband's occupation and their own (where applicable) but most of the subsequent tables present information by husband's social class only. More detailed analysis does suggest that class differences in female mortality show much the same pattern whether they are classified according to the woman's own occupation or that of her husband (Macfarlane 1980: 11). However, lack of information about women's own occupations is important because without it we cannot *explain* these class differences as fully as possible.

British epidemiologists have traditionally used statistics on married women to differentiate between occupational and "way of life" factors in the causation of *male* mortality. That is to say, they have assumed that the excess of male over married female mortality in a given social class represents that proportion of mortality that is work-related. However, this practice has recently come under strong criticism on two grounds (Registrar General's Decennial Supplement 1978). First it is argued that women themselves will often be harmed by their own work (both inside the home and outside it) and second both husband and wife may harm each other through the toxic substances to which they are exposed at work.[5] If women's own jobs are not recorded then no assessment can be made of the independent effects of such occupational hazards, either on the women themselves or on their families.

Class differentials are also apparent in patterns of female morbidity – in the incidence of sickness and ill health suffered by women. It is of course somewhat paradoxical that despite their greater life-expectancy, women do report more sickness than men and make more visits to their doctors (Macfarlane 1980). But again these sex differences have to be looked at very carefully because they mask the very different experiences of women in different social classes. If we take the rates of self-reported sickness from the *General Household Survey 1976* (Office of Population Censuses and Surveys 1979) we find that the rate of "limiting long-standing illness" was 257 per 1,000 women in social class V compared with only 81 per 1,000 professional women – a ratio of more than 3:1.[6] Less dramatically but still meaningfully, 103 per 1,000 women in the unskilled manual group reported restricted activity (or acute illness) in the previous period compared with only 89 in the professional group – a ratio of 1.2:1. In an examination of male morbidity rates these figures are usually augmented by data on absence from work through sickness which show a very marked class differential.[7] The comparable data for women are very limited in their coverage since they apply only to those women in paid employment paying a full national insurance contribution. Yet they do suggest a very similar class distribution to that found among men.

Thus the creation of the NHS has not equalized the life-chances of British women, nor their standards of health. The reasons for this are complex and stem in large part from continuing inequalities in living and working conditions. But they are also related to the fact that the NHS has not equalized women's access to medical care. While women as a group make greater overall use of the health service than men (due mainly to their reproductive potential and greater longevity) there are still very marked class differences in utilization of general-practitioner services, of inpatient and outpatient hospital facilities and of preventive services.

Information on the use of general practitioner (GP) services is not routinely collected and again the best source of data is probably the *General Household Survey (GHS)*. *GHS* figures show that both the number of women consulting a doctor and the average number of consultations for each individual tend to increase with falling social class (Townsend and Davidson 1982: 77). This is not, of course, surprising given the much higher rates of mortality and morbidity we have already identified in social classes IV and V. In order to see whether women in different social classes are getting a "fair share" of resources we therefore need to measure utilization in a more sophisticated way, comparing consultation rates not simply on the basis of numbers in the population, but according to the *need* for care (Le Grand 1978). One recent study attempted to do this with *GHS* data, dividing the number of GP consultations in each social class by the number of days of restricted activity, each in a two-week reference period (Brotherston 1976). Measured in this way, the use/need ratios clearly declined, going down the social scale from women in socioeconomic group I with a ratio of 0.23 to those in socioeconomic group V with a figure of 0.19. Thus the simple statement that the poor use services "more" is reversed when usage alone is corrected for need. It is clear that women in the semi-skilled and unskilled groups make relatively *less* use of GP services than other groups when their higher rates of sickness are taken into account.

However, even these relatively sophisticated measures of use and need are still only partial in that they do not take into account the quality of care provided. The technical standard of care is difficult to assess but there is evidence that compared with their colleagues in more affluent areas, GPs in working-class districts tend to have fewer facilities for diagnosis and treatment (Cartwright and Marshall 1963; Tudor Hart 1971; Noyce, Snaith, and Trickey 1974; Backett 1977).

Moreover, the quality of the personal relationships that are so important in health care also seem to vary between social classes. Several studies have shown that middle-class patients (both male and female) tend to have longer consultations with more extensive discussion of their problems than their working-class counterparts. One study also found that middle-class patients got more out of the consultation time in terms of information communicated and questions answered (Cartwright and O'Brien 1976). Although working-class patients had usually been registered with their GP longer, doctors tended to know more about their middle-class patients and were more likely to visit them in hospital (Cartwright 1964). Surveys suggest that these variations in the subjective experience of health care are even more important to women than to men (Cartwright and Anderson 1981: 164). Part of the reason for this is that women are more likely to visit their doctors when they are not ''sick,'' as when they are seeking advice about contraception or when they need reassurance in a state of depression or anxiety. They appear to bring different expectations to the medical encounter and working-class women in particular may find that their need for communication and for information will not be met.

If we turn to the use made by women of hospital services, we face the problem that no statistics are collected on either inpatient or outpatient services by social class. Questions about attendance at hospitals are asked in the *GHS* but given the size of the sample, the resulting figures for inpatient admissions are too small to be of any value. *GHS* figures for outpatient attendance are obviously higher but since 1972 they have not been analyzed by social class. The only figures that do give clues about social class differentials come from the Hospital Inpatient Enquiry (HIPE) for England and Wales *before* 1963 and the Scottish Hospital Inpatient Enquiry (SHIPE). Both suggest that the use of hospital beds rises with declining social class for both sexes (Townsend and Davidson 1982: 80), but there is no clear evidence about whether this greater use is commensurate with the much higher levels of working-class need (Le Grand 1978). We have very little evidence concerning class differences in the technical quality of hospital treatment. However, some studies have indicated differences in the more personal aspects of care, similar to those identified in general practice (Cartwright 1964; Howlett and Ashley 1972).

In general, then, we can see that women's access to medical care has not been equalized by the introduction of the NHS. But one of the main advantages of the NHS for women *as a group* was their improved access to preventive services and to techniques of fertility control in particular. We therefore need to determine how far these services have been made equally available to all. Again this task poses considerable methodological problems, since no regular statistics are collected on the utilization of preventive services. However, there is now a growing volume of research in this area, most of it suggesting that women in social classes IV and V make markedly less use of most of these services than those higher up the occupational hierarchy (Townsend and Davidson 1982: 81–3).

We look first at the use of cervical screening, an important service that has been of genuine value in identifying potential cancers in women and in preventing their further development (Saffron 1983). It is clear that the wives of manual workers are much less likely to obtain cervical smears than their middle-class counterparts. One study undertaken in Manchester in 1968 found that while women from social class I constituted only 2.6 per cent of the local population they accounted for 7.7 per cent of the smears done in the area. Social class IV and V women on the other hand were 33 per cent of the population but obtained only 15 per cent of the smears (Wakefield 1972). This class differential in the utilization of cervical cytology is highlighted when seen against the background of class differentials in death from cervical cancer. The standardized mortality ratio (SMR)[8] for deaths from cervical cancer in 1970–72 was 42 for women in social class I compared with 140 in social class IV and

161 in social class V (Registrar General's Decennial Supplement 1978). This makes cancer of the cervix one of the most class-linked of all female cancers, yet those women most at risk are still the least likely to obtain smear tests.

If we look at the area of control over fertility there again appears to be a marked class differential in use of services. Recent studies have shown a clear class gradient with middle-class mothers being more likely to attend a family-planning clinic or discuss birth control with their GP (Cartwright 1970; Bone 1973). Not surprisingly, perhaps, there is also evidence of a higher proportion of unwanted pregnancies among working-class women. In the case of abortion, there is very little evidence of the class origin of the women using such services. However, we do know that the NHS does not meet current needs and that the women with fewest resources are most likely to lose out. Most importantly, the NHS now performs less than 50 per cent of all abortions carried out in the UK, the rest being performed within what is called the "charity sector." These providers are not profit-making but charge a "reasonable" sum for their services (currently about £120). Thus for many women, the ability to obtain an abortion (especially a quick and easy one) may still depend on whether or not they have the means to pay.

This point is highlighted by the fact that the standard of abortions performed (as measured by subsequent mortality and morbidity rates) is considerably better in the charity sector than the NHS, thus bestowing an even greater benefit on those who can pay (Brewer 1977). The main reasons for this are thought to be the low priority given to abortions in NHS resource allocation, and the relatively longer time women have to wait for NHS abortions. It is also significant that NHS abortions are more likely to involve a general anesthetic and an overnight stay in a hospital, thus rendering them potentially more hazardous and stressful (Hindell and Graham 1974). Finally, there is a very marked regional inequality in access to abortion, a situation that arises from the so-called "conscience clause" that allows NHS staff with religious or moral objections not to carry out abortions. In 1974, for example, of women having abortions, 91 per cent of those resident in Newcastle had the operation in NHS premises in their own region compared with 75 per cent of Bristol women, 25 per cent of those in Leeds and only 12 per cent of those in Birmingham. Thus women are still being denied NHS abortions not on medical or social grounds but because they live in an area where medical personnel refuse to perform them. Only those women with enough resources will be able to circumvent this problem, possibly by travelling to another area to obtain an NHS abortion or, more likely, by paying for the service.

There has been considerable concern about women's access to sterilization on the NHS. As with abortion and contraception, sterilization continues to be an issue where women's rights and ability to choose are not always taken seriously. There is, however, something of a reversal in class patterns of use in that child-less (often middle-class) women frequently have difficulties *obtaining* sterilization on the NHS while those (usually black and/or working-class) women defined by doctors as "ignorant" or "feckless" will often be *persuaded* to do so. This probably occurs most frequently in connection with abortion. The Lane Committee Report on the Abortion Act drew attention to the fact that some abortions are only granted *subject* to sterilization, and that the two procedures are often carried out simultaneously (Lane Committee 1974). Thus in 1973, 10.8 per cent of all abortions but 20.6 per cent of NHS abortions in England and Wales were accompanied by sterilization. It appears, moreover, that the highest rate of sterilization and abortion combined occurs in those areas where abortions themselves are hardest to obtain. In 1973, as many as 35 per cent of NHS abortions performed on women resident in the Birmingham region (a notoriously diffi-cult place to get an abortion) were accompanied by sterilization. Thus poor women who cannot "opt out" of the NHS are more likely to be coerced into a sterilization they would not have freely chosen, while those with more resources can pay to obtain the treatment they would prefer.

The race factor

We have discussed the considerable class differences that still exist in the utilization of medical care and in the quality of the care received. In recent years it has increasingly been argued that these class differences are exacerbated by racial factors, leading to a situation of double discrimination for many of the most deprived women in the British population. Claims of this kind are extremely difficult to substantiate in any quantitative way. British official statistics do not include any racial break-down and we have to rely on more anecdotal evidence (Runnymede Trust and Radical Statistics Race Group 1980). However, it is clear that most black women are to be found at the bottom end of the occupational hierarchy and this inevitably affects their health. Although some ethnic groups have a higher incidence of particular health problems (sickle-cell anemia among blacks being a case in point) patterns of morbidity and mortality among black women are broadly similar to those of other women in social classes IV and V, reflecting their low income and unhealthy living and working conditions.[9]

So far as use of the health service is concerned, we know that *overall* (and contrary to popular belief) black women in the British population receive less medical care than whites, largely because of demographic differences between the two groups (Runnymede Trust and Radical Statistics Race Group 1980). The black population is a much younger one and its somewhat greater use of maternity services is more than com-pensated for by the low numbers of black people over the age of 65. At the same time, there is growing evidence that black women, like white women in the same socioeconomic group, suffer from the lack of effective services in the deprived inner-city areas where most of them are concentrated (Wandsworth and East Merton Health District 1979; Brent Community Health Council 1981).

However, black women also have to bear the added burden of the racial discrimination that still permeates many aspects of the functioning of the NHS (Homans and Satow 1981, 1982). In some cases this is manifested by a lack of concern by health workers for the needs, desires, and life-style of the patient, or even a straightforward attack on values and practices perceived to be alien. This can be a particular problem when the patient's native language is not English, and Asian women receiving obstetric care have often suffered in this way (Henley 1979; Baxter 1980; Homans 1980). But it can also amount to a more institutional form of racism as recent developments affecting women in particular have shown.

Over the last few years, the use of the injectable contraceptive

Depo-Provera has gradually increased in Britain (Rakusen 1981). The drug is now banned in the USA and there is considerable controversy about its effects on women's health.[10] It can certainly produce "menstrual chaos." Some studies (U S Food and Drug Administration 1983) have suggested that it may also lead to an increase in uterine cancer; it may be transmitted through breast-milk and affect the infant; and finally there are fears that it may cause infertility. Not surprisingly then, there have been protests about the disproportionate use of this drug on poor working-class women and on black women, particularly when it is dispensed *without their informed consent*. One recent estimate suggested that about half the relevant prescriptions written were for black women, presumably reflecting a belief in the ignorance and unreliability of the women concerned and in the need to reduce the black birthrate (Brent Community Health Council 1981: 22).

As British immigration laws have been tightened up, NHS doctors (and others) have increasingly been involved in examinations that can be both physically and psychologically damaging to women. These are performed not for medical but for purely administrative purposes. In 1978, it was revealed that medical practitioners were performing vaginal examinations on women coming to Britain from Asia as the fiancées of men already in the country. The declared aim was to determine whether or not they were "bona fide virgins." As one young Asian girl described it: "He was wearing rubber gloves and took some medicine out of a tube and put it on some cotton and inserted it into me. He said there was no need to get shy" (Manchester Law Centre 1982: 52). It was further revealed in February 1979 that medical referees in India and Pakistan were subjecting applicants for entry to Britain to X-ray examinations. The results were then used to estimate age in order to confirm or disprove the identity claimed by the potential migrant (Manchester Law Centre 1982: 52). As a result of the public outcry that followed these revelations, both virginity tests and the administrative use of X-rays have apparently ceased. However, the links between the health service and immigration control continue and female dependents of those already in Britain are major targets.

In October 1982 new health regulations were introduced which undermined what *had* been a fundamental principle of the NHS that health care should be available to all and should be free at the point of treatment. Under this new scheme the sick will first have to prove that they are "ordinarily resident" in the UK before being entitled to free treatment. These proposals were implemented against widespread opposition from health trade unions, community health councils, and organizations representing the rights of black people and immigrants to Britain. It is generally agreed that the administrative cost of implementing them will be greater than any money saved by refusing treatment,[11] and that they will entail a much closer surveillance on the black population. This is because in practice it will not be white people who are called upon to prove their eligibility but those who look "different" and/or speak a foreign language. Although most black people in Britain will remain eligible for free treatment, there can be no doubt that these regulations will heighten the racist attitudes already present in the NHS and may well deter people from going for treatment. In its submission to the Home Affairs Committee, the West Midlands Regional Health Authority pointed out that this is likely to affect women in particular, since the regulations might:

> discourage from attending those very women from ethnic minority groups who might most benefit from NHS services. Where such women have no knowledge of English and where it may be difficult to provide adequate interpreters there are already sufficient disincentives to such women attending without adding further obstacles and fears.
>
> (Manchester Law Centre 1982: 11)

Women, medicine, and social control

Our previous discussion has shown that all women have not benefited equally from the NHS: class and race continue to exert a strong influence both on their health and on their utilization of medical services. But of course British society is also differentiated on the basis of gender, and women *as a group* continue to experience discrimination and disadvantage (Whitelegg *et al.* 1982). That is, women tend to be seen as inferior to men – whatever their social and economic status – and this general denigration of women has been reflected in the functioning of the health service. As feminists have been concerned to point out, many of the gains women have made in *access* to medical care have been accompanied by a growth in the degree of control doctors are able to exert over fundamental aspects of their lives (Leeson and Gray 1978; Smart and Smart 1978; Hutter and Williams 1981; Roberts 1981; Doyal and Elston 1983).

This point is particularly clear in the case of medical control over reproductive technology. Perfectly healthy women are still dependent on doctors for information, advice, and sometimes even physical access to contraception (Aitken-Swan 1977; Roberts 1981: 1–17). And as we have seen, abortion in particular remains firmly in medical hands (Macintyre 1977). But doctors increasingly control not just the means to *prevent* pregnancy but also the conditions under which women give birth. While medical intervention has played some part in improving rates of infant and maternal mortality, its importance has often been greatly overestimated. In fact, there is a growing belief that the medicalization of childbirth in Britain now goes beyond what is necessary or desirable (Chard and Richards 1977; Kitzinger and Davis 1978; Oakley 1980). Throughout the postwar period there has been a marked trend towards hospital deliveries and the percentage of home births declined from 33 per cent in 1961 to only 2.5 per cent in 1976 (Doyal and Elston 1983). Not surprisingly, this has been accompanied by a growing medical domination of pregnancy and childbirth. Women have complained about the unnecessary and demeaning rituals involved in such births (the shaving of pubic hair and the use of enemas for instance) as well as the pervasive use of anesthetics and analgesics, the denial to women of the right to choose the position in which they will deliver, and the inflexible routines of many postnatal wards (Oakley 1981; Graham and Oakley 1981).

In particular there has been growing criticism (some of it from within the medical profession) of an increase in the "active management of labor" (Chard and Richards 1977). This involves the use of artificial means to start labor before it would have occurred naturally and usually necessitates electronic monitoring during labor. These procedures do, in themselves, appear to be associated with more Cesarean sections and forceps deliveries, a higher incidence of pre-term babies and increased rates of neonatal jaundice. Opponents have argued that while they are obviously of value in *some instances* their routine use (40 per cent of all births were induced in 1974) can be distressing and possibly damaging to both mother and baby (Chalmers and Richards 1977). Thus attempts by administrators to cut the costs of maternity services and to increase bureaucratic efficiency and the desire of doctors to develop more sophisticated technology have often been allowed to override the interests of mothers and babies. Indeed there is a real sense in which doctors whose job satisfaction often lies in high technology intervention have been able to appropriate much of the satisfaction of childbirth from the woman concerned (Doyal 1979b; Oakley 1980).

We have seen that as users women have little say in the running of the NHS and that this affects the nature of the services they receive. Just as importantly the majority of health workers who are women have very little control over their own working conditions. The implications of this are examined in the next section.

Women working for the health service

About 75 per cent of NHS workers are women but they are not evenly distributed among the various occupational groups.[12] Both within the NHS itself and within each category of work, women are mostly to be found in those positions that are lowest in status and reward. Thus NHS work is predominantly women's work, but it is, in the main, controlled by men in the persons of doctors and senior administrators.

First, we have to consider the huge number of women employed as ''ancillary workers'' who occupy the lowest echelons of the health labor force.[13] About one-third of all hospital workers (some 240,000 people) fall into this category and about 75 per cent of these are women, the majority working part-time. We know very little indeed about this group of workers since not much information is collected about their characteristics or circumstances (Doyal 1979a). However, it is clear that ancillary jobs are markedly sex-differentiated, with men doing portering and maintenance jobs while women are involved in catering and domestic work.[14] As a group these workers are particularly badly paid with few opportunities for advancement. Since most women work part-time in the jobs with fewest responsibilities, there is also a marked sex differential in earnings.

It is clear, then, that the NHS discriminates against many women workers in the same way that it disadvantages many women patients. A relatively low-cost and labor-intensive service is maintained by the part-time employment of large numbers of working-class women who would otherwise find it difficult to get jobs. But closer examination reveals that divisions of race and nationality are also very evident in the health labor force. Black and overseas-born women make a major contribution to the running of the NHS in many parts of the country, with their participation being greatest in nursing and ancillary work (Doyal, Hunt, and Mellor 1981).[15] The little evidence we have suggests that a great many unskilled health workers are foreign women, many of them black. One of the few government reports to examine this group of workers suggested that in 1971 about 14 per cent of male and 21 per cent of female ancillary workers were born abroad. However, these workers are concentrated in particular geographical areas, and one study of a London general hospital found that as many as 78 per cent of all ancillary workers were born outside Britain (Doyal, Hunt, and Mellor 1981). Moreover in some sectors of the hospital, this percentage was even higher with 84 per cent of domestic workers and 82 per cent of catering workers (most of them women) being born overseas (Doyal, Hunt, and Mellor 1981). Again, then, these women provide an important source of cheap labor while themselves suffering the deprivation of work in a low-paid, low-prestige sector, and the double discrimination of being both a woman and black and/or overseas-born.

A large number of women from overseas are also to be found in nursing. In 1977 12 per cent of all student and pupil nurses and pupil midwives in the NHS came from abroad, 66 per cent of them from the New Commonwealth[16] and 22 per cent from Ireland. However, there are marked discrepancies in the distribution of these overseas nursing students between regional health authorities and different types of hospitals. In 1977, foreign student nurses accounted for about 17 per cent of the total in England and Wales but only about 4 per cent of those in the prestigious London teaching hospitals. Similarly, overseas students are disproportionately concentrated in the relatively unpopular psychiatric and geriatric hospitals. They have therefore been of particular value in caring for the growing number of old and chronically sick that British nurses are often less willing to look after. It is for this reason that many overseas nurses have been recruited *directly* into psychiatric hospitals, despite the fact that any qualification they obtain may be of very little value in their own countries. Overseas nurses are also more frequently found on courses leading to a state enrolled nurse (SEN) certification, a qualification which is generally regarded as inferior to the state registered nurse (SRN) and carries no automatic international recognition (Walsh 1979).

There is a widespread belief that these trainee nurses return home after gaining their qualifications, thus providing a form of British aid to the Third World. But what little evidence we have suggests that this is by no means the case. If anything, the NHS appears to be more reliant on overseas nurses in *qualified* positions than on those in training. No national statistics are available but the previously mentioned survey of a London general hospital found that a staggering 81 per cent of the qualified nursing workforce was born overseas (Doyal, Hunt, and Mellor 1981). While this pattern would certainly not be repeated throughout the country it does give some indication of the importance of overseas nurses in running the NHS.

This raises the question of why women from overseas have continued to be used as an important source of labor in the health sector in particular. After the influx of overseas workers in the immediate postwar period, successive British immigration policies were designed to prevent the entry of more people from overseas, particularly from Asia and the Caribbean (Moore and Wallace 1975). However, the NHS has always been treated as a "special case" in such legislation. Qualified doctors and nurses were among the few categories of workers entitled to receive an employment voucher under the 1962 Commonwealth Immigration Act, and special arrangements continue to be made for student nurses to come to Britain for training. We can see some of the reasons for this officially sanctioned reliance on overseas workers if we look at the particular case of nursing.

The status of nursing as an occupation is somewhat

anomalous. It is relatively high in the hospital hierarchy of prestige and skill, yet it often involves unsocial hours, disagreeable working conditions, and low pay. When these are combined with the very repressive controls still placed on student nurses, and the continuing demand for unquestioning compliance with authority, it is perhaps not surprising that British-born women have become increasingly less willing to train except in the more prestigious nursing schools. As a result, the NHS has been forced throughout its history to recruit students from overseas, and particularly from former British colonies (Doyal, Hunt, and Mellor 1981). The recession has now reduced this need, and recruitment from abroad has fallen, but overseas nurses still provide a very important source of cheap labor while in training, as well as a permanent reserve of skilled workers once they have qualified. It is important to stress also that in the past they have been particularly "valued" for their relative compliance and passivity (though this is now changing). Their isolated situation in a strange country has made them especially vulnerable and in some cases their own socialization may have encouraged a greater degree of obedience and acceptance of authority than would be found in British women of the same age. But above all, the continuation of their status as overseas students is always dependent on their satisfactory performance in whatever tasks are allotted to them, while after qualification they must obtain a job in order to remain in this country. They are therefore under considerable pressure to accept long hours, low pay, and difficult working conditions that may well be compounded by racist attitudes from other staff or patients (Hicks 1982).

There are now about 400,000 nurses in the NHS of whom about 90 per cent are women. Historically, the nursing profession has been unique in having women dominant in both junior and senior positions, but this has not always brought the advantages that might have been expected. In the first place nurses have usually been thought of as the "handmaidens" of doctors, with "femininity" built into the very definition of what it is to be a nurse (Ehrenreich and English 1978; Gamarnikow 1978; Davies 1981; Salvage 1982). As a result, nurses have always been closely controlled by doctors both at an interprofessional level and also in their everyday practice. They have been trained to obey their superiors unquestioningly and to dedicate themselves to their patients and their "calling," a vocational ethos that has traditionally encouraged them to accept low pay and difficult working conditions.

In recent years the situation of many nurses has changed dramatically. A growing number now work part-time. In 1975 some 62 per cent of staff nurses, 45 per cent of state enrolled nurses, 57 per cent of nursing assistants and 74 per cent of nursing auxiliaries were not full-time employees, and as in other sectors of the health labor force, this has put them at a considerable disadvantage in career and promotion prospects. In particular it has facilitated the growing power and prestige of that 10 per cent of nurses who are male. About 25 per cent of senior nursing posts (above staff nurse level) are now occupied by men, yet they provide only about 5 per cent of untrained auxiliary nurses. Much of this can be traced to an underlying belief that men are more competent in "tough" managerial positions and conversely that women's talents are best used in "caring." However, it is also a reflection of the real obstacles facing married women taking on full-time jobs in the absence of effective child-care arrangements. The end result is that women have not been the main beneficiaries of recent developments in nursing in the NHS. They have not received a representative number of senior administrative jobs, yet it is still difficult for them to achieve promotion in clinical posts or to use their clinical skills effectively in independent practice. Thus there are growing signs of a rising male elite in the traditionally female nursing profession (Austin 1977; Carpenter 1977).

Women doctors are, of course, the elite of female health workers, having gained entry to a high-status, highly paid profession. Moreover, they are unlikely to have achieved this position without the advantage of a middle-class background. However, they still face many of the problems common to their sex, and can in no sense be said to enjoy opportunities equal to those of their male colleagues (Elston 1977b). In 1978 nearly 25 per cent of all doctors on the Medical Register were women and there are now about 17,000 women in British medicine. Quotas on female entry to medical schools have gradually been abolished, and in 1982 the proportion of female medical students had risen to about 45 per cent. It seems certain, then, that in future a higher percentage of qualified doctors will be women.

Yet it is unlikely that a proportional increase of this kind will, in itself, remove existing patterns of discrimination. The problems faced by women doctors are evident from their distribution within the profession (Beaumont 1975; Bewley and Bewley 1975). First, they are unevenly divided among the three broad categories of medical practice. Women provide about 55 per cent of doctors in community health services (child health, family-planning clinics, school health services, and the administration of community medicine) but only about 17 per cent of GPs and 20 per cent of hospital doctors. This distribution is significant because studies of medical students' career preferences show that community-health posts are unpopular. It is regarded as a less "scientific," low-status field, is usually less well paid and provides fewer opportunities than other specialties for private practice. Within hospital medicine itself there are various grades of physicians and here again there is a marked degree of segregation by sex with women being greatly underrepresented in the more senior posts.

There is also a striking variation in the proportion of women consultants found in different hospital specialties. Child psychiatry, mental handicap, anesthetics, and pediatrics, for instance, could all be described as relatively "feminine" spe cialties with more than 15 per cent of the consultants being female. In more "masculine" specialties such as general surgery on the other hand, only 0.7 per cent of consultants are women, and even in general medicine the percentage is as low as 3.7. Again it is notable that by and large men predominate in those specialties that are regarded as the most prestigious, powerful, and professionally lucrative (Elston 1977a). No figures are available on the racial distribution of female doctors. However, observation suggests that the relatively few women physicians from overseas working in the NHS are doubly disadvantaged. Both their sex and their race are likely to limit their chances of obtaining a satisfactory training post or of progressing up to consultant status.[17]

Women fight back[18]

We have seen that the early promise of the NHS for women has not been fulfilled. Real gains have been made, but often at considerable cost and many needs remain unmet. A great deal of NHS care is provided by women for women yet it still remains firmly under male control. With the development of the contemporary women's movement in the late 1960s the male domination of medical care became an important focus for political action. This feminist critique of the NHS has continued into the 1980s, and women are now fighting both to maintain current levels of resources in the health sector, and also to make it more responsive to their real needs as users and workers.

The earliest of the modern feminist health campaigns were concerned primarily with medical sexism. Women began to discuss their experiences of health care, to identify the particular forms of sexism encountered in medical practice, and to formulate strategies for their elimination (MacKeith 1978; Phillips and Rakusen 1978; Elston 1981). The emphasis was on women taking care of themselves and each other; challenging the policies and priorities of the NHS itself was not seen as a major priority. However, in recent years, wider economic and political developments have highlighted the fact that strategies of this kind can provide only a partial solution to the health problems facing British women. This has prompted new ways of thinking about women's health needs and a reorientation of political practice. In particular it has led women to a much greater awareness of the class and racial differences in their experiences of health care, and also to a recognition of the need to go beyond medical care itself to identify – and ultimately to change – those aspects of society that make women ill.

The single most important factor responsible for these developments was the attack on the welfare state begun under Labour but greatly accelerated by the Conservative administration elected in 1979. As the resources available to the NHS were reduced, the service could no longer be taken for granted, and its role in meeting some of the women's most basic health needs has been thrown into sharp relief. In particular, the problems suffered by the most needy have become glaringly obvious as services are cut back in already deprived areas and the economic recession makes it more difficult for people to obtain the basic necessities for a healthy life.

Women have been affected even more than men by the

deterioration of the NHS. As we have seen, their utilization of most services is greater than that of men, and the community services used mostly by women and children have frequently been major targets for "economies." Since women provide the majority of health workers, they have also been disproportionately affected by reductions in staffing levels and deteriorating conditions, especially at the lowest levels of the workforce. Finally, since women are usually held responsible for those people whom the NHS will not look after, the decrease in the number of hospital beds has led to a greater burden of invisible labor for women in the home. For all these reasons women have been profoundly affected by the reduction in NHS resources and this has led to shifts in the practical politics of the women's health movement.

Most importantly, the campaign has broadened into attempts to save hospitals, jobs, and services and to oppose the move towards the privatization of medical care. Inevitably this has involved women not just as users of medical services but also as health workers. Women working for the NHS are now questioning the vocational ethos that has underlain so much low-paid health work. They have joined trade unions in ever-increasing numbers, playing a major part in the health workers' strike of 1982, and have also formed new groups based on their position in the medical hierarchy. Feminist nurses, midwives, health visitors, medical students, and doctors have all begun to organize. They are fighting both sexual and racial discrimination in the workplace and have joined with women's health groups and trade unions in an effort to resist the reductions in staffing and hospital closures now being imposed on the NHS.

Thus women have been active participants in the defense of the NHS and their growing recognition of the inequalities generated by race and class has led to the forging of important links between feminist health and wider political campaigns. Not surprisingly, however, the qualified nature of women's support for the health service, *in its present form*, has sometimes led them to be critical of the orthodox defensive strategies of the male-dominated trade unions. Indeed the experience of recent years strongly suggests the need for the continuing participation of an autonomous women's health movement if current campaigns are to go beyond a defense of what already exists toward a critical reevaluation of some of the basic beliefs and practices of western scientific medicine.

In its early stages the feminist critique of the NHS concentrated on the treatment women received at the hands of doctors, and the genesis of health problems themselves was given little attention. In the last few years, however, attention has gradually begun to shift towards an understanding of what it is that makes women sick. Thus feminists have begun to examine the illness and disabilities that bring women into the medical-care system and to explore the ways in which these problems can be explained by particular aspects of women's lives. In theoretical terms this has meant the beginnings of a socialist feminist epidemiology and in more practical terms it has led to campaigns to improve the living and working conditions of women. But above all it has meant a recognition that the National Health Service is in reality a National Sickness Service. It provides a certain level of medical care for women, but plays only a very small part in the active promotion of their health (Doyal 1979b).

Traditional accounts of women's health problems usually focus on their reproductive role. While their biological capacity for pregnancy and childbirth is obviously of considerable significance, it is by no means the only factor influencing women's health. Feminists have therefore begun to stress the social and economic aspects of women's role by examining the impact of both domestic labor and wage labor on women's health. In the case of domestic labor they have emphasized the importance of the physical condition of the workplace – the home. Dampness, for instance, a growing problem in Britain as the housing stock deteriorates, is a significant cause of respiratory illness (Bedale and Fletcher 1982), while women are especially susceptible to home accidents (Eddy 1972). Insights of this kind have led women into campaigns for better housing conditions and improved social security benefits. Domestic violence can also be a serious hazard to women's health and feminists have set up refuges for women threatened in this way, as well as campaigning for appropriate legal reforms (Dobash and Dobash 1980; Binney 1981; Wilson 1983).

There is also growing concern about the most common occupational disease of domestic labor – depression. Recent research in south London has borne out the fact that working-class mothers who stay at home with small children are more likely to suffer from depression than other groups in the population (Brown and Harris 1978; Davies and Roche 1980). Responses to this situation have included the development of new types of feminist organization as well as various forms of feminist psychotherapy in which the aim is not merely to help women adjust to their gender (and of course race and class) roles but rather to enable them to understand the nature of their situation in more realistic ways – and thereby to change it (Ernst and Goodison 1981; Eichenbaum and Orbach 1982).

Despite the recession, women are still in paid employment in unprecedented numbers. Although they are not usually employed in the traditionally dangerous industries such as mining, there is growing evidence that as well as being exposed to the more common hazards of factory production, they also face particular hazards of their own. Secretaries and clerical workers are at risk from toxic chemicals, and the stress produced by noise and bad lighting. They also face the growing health risks generated by the new technology, including headaches and eyestrain from the use of video display units (VDU) (Craig 1981; Huws 1982). Hotel and catering workers are put at risk by the antiquated conditions in many kitchens and laundries, while hairdressers may be harmed by sprays, dyes, and detergents. Ironically, female health workers are themselves a high-risk group, with many of them being exposed to hazards such as infection and radiation, and to toxic chemicals such as formaldehyde or the cytotoxic drugs used to treat cancer (Lunn 1976). Nurses also suffer frequently from accidents while moving patients, often without the necessary help or equipment (Nurses Action Group 1981). Finally many health workers (like other women workers) are exposed to reproductive hazards that can threaten their fertility or damage their unborn children. Women working in operating theaters, for instance, are at risk from leakage of anesthetic gases and have higher miscarriage rates than workers elsewhere in the hospital.

Growing evidence of the health hazards of waged work has meant that feminists have increasingly been involved in health and safety issues.[19] But again cooperation with trade unions has

not always been easy. British trade unions, with few exceptions, have tended to give health and safety issues a low priority
and their efforts have usually been concerned with male
hazards. As a result, specifically feminist campaigns continue
to be essential if the health of those women most at risk is to be
protected.

Conclusion

The NHS has greatly improved women's access to medical care,
removing many of the deprivations of the past. But many of
women's needs both as users and as providers of health services
remain unmet. The capacity of the NHS to benefit women has
been limited in fundamental ways and in order to understand
these limitations we need to place the NHS in its broader social
context.

At its inception the NHS was hailed as a "socialist island."
As part of the first "welfare state" in a non-communist country
it was said to herald the dawn of a new "affluent society" in
which the class divisions of the past would disappear. But these
hopes were soon dashed. The British health service certainly
provided a more humane and effective method of organizing
health care than a system based on private practice, but this
does not make it in any real sense a "socialist" service. It made
no decisive break with the past and its original structure
reflected the class and sex divisions inherent in British society
(Doyal 1979b). Power remained firmly in the hands of middle-
and upper-class males and as a result the service has continued
to reflect their interests and priorities. Similarly, the arrival of
large numbers of immigrants during the postwar period had no
impact on the distribution of power within the NHS, and the
racial divisions in British society are now reflected in the provision of services.

This method of organizing health care has had significant
effects on all women. Their lack of power in the NHS and in the
wider society has meant that their needs have often been given
insufficient attention by the controllers of medical resources. It
has disadvantaged in particular those working-class and/or
black women whose needs are greatest but who have fewer

resources with which to manipulate the system. Furthermore, the NHS has not given equal job opportunities to men and women, or to women from different socioeconomic and racial backgrounds. Most women therefore continue to be concentrated in low-paid, low-status jobs.

These divisions now appear to be widening and there is little chance of improvement in the near future. The current Conservative administration is committed to a narrowing of the NHS accompanied by an expansion of the private sector. This reduction in standards and services will naturally have the greatest impact on those women who are poorest and least able to fend for themselves. At the same time, jobs will continue to be cut back and it seems likely that, in the unskilled sector at least, those from overseas may suffer even more heavily than indigenous workers. The entry of unskilled workers into Britain has already been stopped with the general tightening up of immigration controls. At the same time, overseas workers already in Britain are finding it harder to get NHS jobs as the recession makes them more attractive to unemployed British people. This is limiting the range of jobs available to overseas women in particular, and contributing to the already high rate of unemployment in immigrant communities. The trend, then, is towards a reinforcement of racial, sexual, and class divisions, with those most in need missing out not only on services but also on employment opportunities in the health sector.

We have noted that the NHS has made little impact on those causes of ill-health that lie in women's situation in the wider society. It is increasingly clear that most sexual, racial, and class variations in patterns of health and illness are neither "natural" nor the outcome of inequalities in access to medical care. Rather they reflect differences in living and working conditions and in the social distribution of income and wealth. Again, these differentials are widening as monetarist economic policies emphasize the gap between rich and poor and between working and non-working groups in the population. The authors of *Inequalities in Health* concluded their report by emphasizing that an effective national health service will not be achieved without an effective education system, a properly funded housing program, and comprehensive employment and anti-poverty strategies (Townsend and Davidson 1982). Thus women's health will not improve while the current "retreat from welfare" continues. But even more fundamentally, the true potential of the NHS for women (and for men) will not be achieved unless it is reorganized as part of a much wider restructuring of British society, a restructuring that begins to break down the privileges of class, sex, and race in order to meet the needs and desires of the majority of the population.

Notes

1 We have little information with which to compare use of GP services before and after the NHS. However, it is interesting to note that contrary to what might have been expected, the increase in female use of services after 1948 was apparently *less* than the increase in male use (Walters 1980: 110).
2 In 1977 a working party was set up by the then Labour government to examine existing evidence of inequalities in health and medical care. Its ensuing report *Inequalities in Health* (1980), also known as the Black Report after its chairman Sir Douglas Black, proved unacceptable to the then Conservative Secretary of State for Social Services, Patrick Jenkin. The report was given only very limited publicity and circulation but nevertheless received enormous public attention. It was later published in an amended version by Penguin and it is to this edition that we shall refer (Townsend and Davidson 1982).
3 The Registrar General's Decennial Supplement is a report on the relationship between occupation and mortality produced every ten years. The most recent (series DS No. 1) refers to the period 1970–72.
4 It is important to note, however, that some female cancers have a marked social-class gradient in the other direction, cervical cancer in particular (Robinson 1981).
5 Recent examples of the impact of male work hazards on women in the home have come from the asbestos industry and also from the current debate on the epidemiology of cancer. In the latter case, it is argued that much cervical cancer may be caused by the woman's exposure during intercourse to toxic substances picked up by her partner at work (Robinson 1981).
6 The *General Household Survey* is a sample survey carried out annually by the Government Statistical Service on a representative group of households. It covers a wide range of topics including use of the NHS, and experiences of ill-health.

7 Sickness-absence statistics are collected by the Department of Health and Social Security and include only those people actually in receipt of sickness benefit.

8 The standardized mortality ratio is the percentage ratio of the number of deaths observed in a specific group studied to the number that would be expected from the age-specific death rates for the total population. The "norm" is 100 and the SMRs show the distribution of different social groups around this figure.

9 It is difficult to compare mortality rates between the black and white British populations, because the black population is much younger and may also represent the outcome of selective migration by the healthiest people. It is also difficult to generalize since there are some differences between more affluent Asian groups and the poorer Asian and West Indian populations (Runnymede Trust and Radical Statistics Race Group 1980). In general, however, when we talk about the "black" population here, we are referring to people of Afro-Caribbean or Asian descent, though many of the comments also apply to other ethnic minorities in Britain, Turks or Cypriots for example.

10 As of June 1983, Depo-Provera has been licensed for long-term use by the British regulatory body, the Commission for the Safety of Medicines.

11 It was found in March 1983, some six months after the regulations were introduced, that only a handful of patients had been found ineligible for treatment. The Royal Free Hospital, an 840-bed hospital in north London had raised only £167 in payment and the Royal Liverpool Hospital only £71. Thus there is no evidence of the widespread foreign exploitation said to have existed, and the cost of the scheme far outweighs its financial benefits (*Observer*, 27 March, 1983).

12 There has been very little analysis of the overall position of women health workers. One of the best sources of information on the role of women workers in the NHS comes from an unpublished report prepared by Mary Ann Elston for the Equal Opportunities Commission (1977a).

13 "Ancillary work" is a term used to define unskilled or semi-skilled work in the NHS. It does *not* include what are often referred to as "para-medical" jobs or "professions supplementary to medicine," such as physiotherapy, occupational therapy, and radiography. All these are of course also jobs done predominantly by women.

14 Though men are employed in certain catering jobs, with southern European cooks being especially common.

15 A detailed report *Migrant Workers in the National Health Service*

prepared for the Social Science Research Council by Lesley Doyal, Frances Gee, Geoff Hunt, Jenny Mellor, and Imogen Pennell is available from the authors at the Sociology Department, Polytechnic of North London, Highbury Grove, London N5. ·A summary is contained in Doyal, Hunt, and Mellor (1981).

16   "New Commonwealth" refers to all Commonwealth countries except the "Old Commonwealth," Australia, New Zealand, and Canada.

17   We have only discussed the role of women as paid workers here, but of course it is unpaid women *at home* who are taking care of the increasing numbers of people for whom the NHS will not take responsibility (Taylor 1979; Stacey 1982; Graham this volume (Chapter 2)).

18   The ideas in this section are developed in more detail in Doyal (1983).

19   Women and Work Hazards can be contacted at 9 Poland Street, London W1V 3DG.

References

Aitken-Swan, J. (1977) *Fertility Control and the Medical Profession.* London: Croom Helm.

Austin, R. (1977) Sex and Gender in the Future of Nursing: 1 and 2. *Nursing Times* 2 Aug. and 1 Sept.

Backett, M. (1977) Health Services. In F. Williams (ed.) *Why the Poor Pay More.* London: National Consumer Council.

Baxter, C. (1980) Communication Difficulties Between the Staff and Asian Women in the Ante-natal Clinic of North Manchester General Hospital. Unpublished paper. Health Education Unit, Manchester Area Health Authority.

Beaumont, B. (1975) Training and Careers of Women Doctors in the Thames Regions. *British Medical Journal* 21 Jan: 191–93.

Bedale, C. and Fletcher, T. (1982) A Damp Site Worse. *Times Health Supplement* 12 Feb.

Bewley, B.R. and Bewley, T.H. (1975) Hospital Doctors' Career Structure and the Misuse of Medical Womanpower. *Lancet* 2: 270–72.

Binney, V. (1981) Domestic Violence: Battered Women in Britain in the 1970's. In Cambridge Women's Studies Group *Women in Society.* London: Virago.

Bone, M. (1973) *Family Planning Services in England and Wales.* London: HMSO.

Brent Community Health Council (1981) *Black People and the National Health Service*. London.

Brewer, C. (1977) Abortion 2. The Risk. *New Society* 10 Feb.

Brotherston, J. (1976) Inequality: Is It Inevitable? In C. Carter and J. Peel (eds) *Equalities and Inequalities in Health*. London: Academic Press.

Brown, G.W. and Harris, T. (1978) *Social Origins of Depression: A Study of Psychiatric Disorder in Women*. London: Tavistock Publications.

Carpenter, M. (1977) The New Managerialism and Professionalism in Nursing. In M. Stacey, M. Reid, C. Heath, and R. Dingwall (eds) *Health and the Division of Labour*. London: Croom Helm.

Cartwright, A. (1964) *Human Relations and Hospital Care*. London: Routledge & Kegan Paul.

—— (1970) *Parents and Family Planning Services*. London: Routledge & Kegan Paul.

Cartwright, A. and Anderson, R. (1981) *General Practice Revisited*. London and New York: Tavistock Publications.

Cartwright, A. and Marshall, R. (1963) General Practice in 1963: Its Conditions, Contents and Satisfactions. *Medical Care* 3 (2): 69–87.

Cartwright, A. and O'Brien, M. (1976) Social Class Variations in Health Care and in General Practice Consultations. In M. Stacey (ed.) *The Sociology of the NHS*. Sociological Review Monograph 22. University of Keele.

Chalmers, I. and Richards, M. (1977) Intervention and Causal Inference in Obstetric Practice. In T. Chard and M. Richards (eds) *Benefits and Hazards of the New Obstetrics*. London: SIM with Heinemann Medical.

Chard, T. and Richards, M. (eds)(1977) *Benefits and Hazards of the New Obstetrics*. London: SIM with Heinemann Medical.

Craig, M. (1981) *The Office Workers' Survival Handbook*. London: British Society for Social Responsibility in Science.

Davies, C. (ed.) (1981) *Rewriting Nursing History*. London: Croom Helm.

Davies, C. and Roche, S. (1980) The Place of Methodology: A Critique of Brown and Harris. *Sociological Review* 28 (3).

Dobash, R.E. and Dobash, R.P. (1980) *Violence Against Wives. A Case Against the Patriarchy*. New York: Free Press.

Doyal, L. (1979a) A Matter of Life and Death: Medicine, Health and Statistics. In J. Irvine, I. Miles, and J. Evans (eds) *Demystifying Social Statistics*. London: Pluto Press.

—— (with Pennell, I.) (1979b) *The Political Economy of Health*. London: Pluto Press.

—— (1983) Women, Health and the Sexual Division of Labor: A Case Study of the Women's Health Movement in Britain. *Critical Social Policy* 7: 21–33, and *International Journal of Health Services* 13 (3): 373–87.

Doyal, L. and Elston, M.A. (1983) Unit 14 *Medicine and Health* Course U221, The Changing Experience of Women. Milton Keynes: Open University.

Doyal, L., Hunt, G., and Mellor, J. (1981) Your Life in their Hands: Migrant Workers in the National Health Service. *Critical Social Policy* 1 (2): 54–71.

Eddy, T.P. (1972) Deaths from Domestic Falls and Fractures. *British Journal of Preventive and Social Medicine* 26: 173–79.

Ehrenreich, B. and English, D. (1978) *Witches, Midwives and Nurses.* London: Readers & Writers Publishing Cooperative.

Eichenbaum, L. and Orbach, S. (1982) *Inside Out, Outside In.* Harmondsworth: Penguin Books.

Elston, M.A. (1977a) Women, Equal Opportunity and the NHS. Unpublished draft prepared for the Equal Opportunities Commission as evidence to the Royal Commission on the NHS.

—— (1977b) Women Doctors: Whose Problem? In M. Stacey, M. Reid, C. Heath, and R. Dingwall (eds) *Health and the Division of Labour.* London: Croom Helm.

—— (1981) Medicine as Old Husbands' Tales: The Impact of Feminism. In D. Spender (ed.) *Men's Studies Modified.* London: Pergamon Press.

Ernst, S. and Goodison, L. (1981) *In Our Own Hands, A Book of Self-Help Therapy.* London: Women's Press.

Gamarnikow, E. (1978) Sexual Division of Labour: The Case of Nursing. In A. Kuhn and A.M. Wolpe (eds) *Feminism and Materialism.* London: Routledge & Kegan Paul.

Government Statistical Service (1981) *Social Trends No. 12.* London: HMSO.

Graham, H. and Oakley, A. (1981) Competing Ideologies of Reproduction: Medical and Maternal Perspectives on Pregnancy. In H. Roberts (ed.) *Women, Health and Reproduction.* London: Routledge & Kegan Paul.

Henley, A. (1979) *Asian Patients in Hospital and at Home.* King Edward's Hospital Fund.

Hicks, C. (1982) Racism in Nursing. *Nursing Times* 5 May and 12 May.

Hindell, K. and Graham, H. (eds) (1974) *Outpatient Abortion.* London: Pregnancy Advisory Service.

Homans, H. (1980) Pregnant in Britain: A Sociological Approach to

Asian and British Women's Experiences. Unpublished PhD thesis, University of Warwick.

Homans, H. and Satow, A. (1981 and 1982) Community Nursing in a Multi-Racial Society. *Journal of Community Nursing* Oct., Nov., Dec. 1981 and Jan., Feb. 1982.

Howlett, A. and Ashley, J. (1972) Selective Care. *New Society* 2 (Nov.): 270.

Hutter, B. and Williams, G. (1981) *Controlling Women: The Normal and the Deviant.* London: Croom Helm.

Huws, U. (1982) *A Woman's Guide to the New Technology.* London: Pluto Press.

Kitzinger, S. and Davis, J. (1978) *The Place of Birth.* London: Oxford Medical Publications.

Lane Committee (1974) *Report of the Committee on the Working of the Abortion Act 1967.* London: HMSO.

Leeson, J. and Gray, J. (1978) *Women and Medicine.* London and New York: Tavistock Publications.

Le Grand, J. (1978) The Distribution of Public Expenditure: The Case of Health Care. *Economica* 45 (178): 125–42.

Lunn, J.A. (1976) *The Health of Staff in Hospitals.* London: Heinemann.

Macfarlane, A. (1980) Women and Health: Official Statistics on Women and Aspects of Health and Illness. Paper prepared for SSRC/EOC Seminar on Women in Government Statistics.

Macintyre, S. (1977) *Single and Pregnant.* London: Croom Helm.

MacKeith, N. (1978) *The New Women's Self-Health Handbook.* London: Virago.

Manchester Law Centre (1982) *From Ill Treatment to No Treatment.*

Moore, R. and Wallace, T. (1975) *Slamming the Door.* Oxford: Martin Robertson.

Noyce, J., Snaith, A.H., and Trickey, A.J. (1974) Regional Variations in the Allocation of Financial Resources to the Community Health Services. *Lancet* 1: 554–57.

Nurses Action Group (1981) The Backbone of the Service. *Nursing Mirror* 29 Jan.

Oakley, A. (1980) *Women Confined: Towards a Sociology of Child-birth.* Oxford: Martin Robertson.

—– (1981) *From Here to Maternity: Becoming a Mother.* Harmondsworth: Penguin Books.

Oakley, A. and Oakley, R. (1979) Sexism in Official Statistics. In J. Irvine, I. Miles, and J. Evans (eds) *Demystifying Social Statistics.* London: Pluto Press.

Office of Population Censuses and Surveys (1979) *General Household Survey 1976*. London: HMSO.

Phillips, A. and Rakusen, J. (1978) *Boston Women's Health Collective. Our Bodies Ourselves: A Health Book by and for Women.* Harmondsworth: Penguin Books.

Rakusen, J. (1981) Depo Provera: The Extent of the Problem. A Case Study in the Politics of Birth Control. In H. Roberts (ed.) *Women, Health and Reproduction*. London: Routledge & Kegan Paul.

Registrar General's Decennial Supplement (1978) *Occupational Mortality 1970-72*. OPCS Series DS no. 1.

Roberts, H. (ed.) (1981) *Women, Health and Reproduction*. London: Routledge & Kegan Paul.

Robinson, J. (1981) Cervical Cancer: A Feminist Critique. *Times Health Supplement* 27 Nov.

Runnymede Trust and Radical Statistics Race Group (1980) *Britain's Black Population*. London: Heinemann.

Saffron, L. (1983) Cervical Cancer. *Spare Rib* 129.

Salvage, J. (1982) Images of Nursing. *The Health Services* 10 Sept.

Smart, B. and Smart, C. (1978) *Women, Sexuality and Social Control.* London: Routledge & Kegan Paul.

Stacey, M. (1982) Who Are the Health Workers? Patients and Other Unpaid Workers in Health Care. Paper presented at the World Congress of Sociology, Mexico, Aug.

Taylor, J. (1979) Hidden Labour and the NHS. In P. Atkinson, R. Dingwall, and A. Murcott (eds) *Prospects for the National Health*. London: Croom Helm.

Titmuss, R.M. (1968) *Commitment to Welfare*. London: Allen & Unwin.

Townsend, P. and Davidson, N. (1982) *Inequalities in Health*. Harmondsworth: Penguin Books.

Tudor Hart, J. (1971) The Inverse Care Law. *Lancet* 1: 405-12.

US Food and Drug Administration (1983) Depo Provera, Public Board Inquiry. Official Transcript of Proceedings, vol. 2, 11 Jan.

Wakefield, J. (1972) *Seek Wisely to Prevent*. London: HMSO.

Walsh, S. (1979) *Overseas Nurses*. London: Channel (Centre of Help and Education for Newcomers to Nursing Education).

Walters, V. (1980) *Class, Inequality and Health Care*. London: Croom Helm.

Wandsworth and East Merton Health District (1979) *Ethnic Minorities and the Health Service*. A report produced by Wandsworth and East Merton Health District.

Whitelegg, E., Arnot, M., Bartels, E., Beechey, V., Birke, L., Himmelweit, S., Leonard, D., Ruehl, S., and Speakman, M.A.

(1982) *The Changing Experience of Women.* London: Martin Robertson and the Open University.

Wilson, E. (1983) *What Should Be Done About Violence Against Women?* Harmondsworth: Penguin Books.

Ten

Women and health: the United States and the United Kingdom compared

Margaret Stacey

"The manner in which a society handles the crucial matters of birth and death and of sickness and health not only reflect, but reinforce, the major institutions and values of that society" (Stacey with Homans 1978). The same could be said about the way a society treats women. When we consider both together, and our topic is women and health, much may be revealed about a society. This chapter compares the United States and the United Kingdom and shows how in their treatment of women, health, illness, and suffering, and particularly of women's health, illness, and suffering, the two countries have much in common, but also some crucial differences.

Underlying themes

Individualism, capitalism, and collectivism

England emerged gradually from feudalism without the bloody revolutions experienced on the continent; the United States was founded by people escaping from European societies. It is a nation in which individualism and equality are highly elaborated (de Tocqueville 1956; Dumont 1970). Modern Britain, on the other hand, arose through a series of transformations of the feudal past. Like the United States it is by now highly individualistic; the development of individualism and of citizenship was important for the rise of the English bourgeoisie and the development of capitalism (Weber 1930; Marshall 1963; Nisbet 1967; Perkin 1969; Briggs 1983; for a discussion of the meanings of individualism and the history of the idea in England and the United States see Lukes 1973; for a discussion in relation to women see Stacey and Price 1981, ch. 4). Industrial capitalism developed in Britain but has reached its most powerful flowering in the United States; nor has individualism in England ever quite reached the rugged quality it has in the United States. Furthermore, a distinction might be made, for example, between the assertion of individuality and respect for the individual, the former being stressed in the United States and the latter in Britain. In addition, the welfare state has earlier origins in Britain than in the United States; in Britain it can better be dated from Elizabeth I, during whose reign the foundations of the Poor Law which survived into the twentieth century were laid, than from the reforms of the nineteenth century or of the period after World War II.

These differences are reflected in the organization of the two systems of government, their judiciaries, and the uses that individual citizens make of them. The federal system in the United States with its many varied states contrasts with the unitary British system, which has only weak delegation to regions and a constantly increasing central government control of local government.

Divisions of class and color

Both societies share the experience of being divided along lines of class and color-caste. The contemporary British class system derives from the earlier structure of feudal estates, modified by the rise of capitalism, and subsequently modified again by the intervention of the welfare state. While these developments introduced some egalitarian elements, British society remains markedly class-divided. In the United States, on the other hand, the firm commitment to the ideal of equality of opportunity has often obscured Americans' ability to recognize the pervasiveness of major class divisions. It is noteworthy that American stratification theories in the 1950s found the need to point out the existence of major class divisions to their readers, presumably catching up with the disillusionment prompted by the experience of the Great Depression. Class divisions in America, as Sennett and Cobb (1977: 12–16, 18–19) make plain, are, and are perceived as, very different from those in Europe (Marwick 1982; Robinson 1983).

Though the United States from its earliest days was a society composed of numerous ethnic groups, some of whom were people of color, many whites believed that these people served, but did not truly belong in, the society. Indeed, some analysts could characterize divisions among the races on the basis of color as constituting caste as well as class systems in the United States (Davis, Gardner, and Gardner 1965). In the civil rights movement of the 1960s black Americans and their liberal white allies attempted to alter the consciousness of the American people in a direction which would emphasize the common membership and common humanity of the former slaves' descendants.

Britain is also a color-caste society. For many years, however, the issue was not on the doorstep of the British people but in the imperial territories. That is to say, the colonial peoples were seen as black, conquered, inferior, backward, the object of missionary activity abroad and charitable collections at home. Only in the post-imperial phase after World War II when non-white immigrants diffused widely in Britain's major cities were the color-caste lines drawn within the home territories themselves. Many still think of the children of that postwar migration, the second generation of black British, as outsiders, "immigrants," experiencing a shock when such "immigrants" speak with home-grown Birmingham, Cockney, or Yorkshire accents.

British governmental policy has been discriminatory against these members of the new Commonwealth and their British descendants. Further, both the British and the US health systems fail to provide equally for black and white women.

Universalism versus selectivity

In Britain after World War II, the principle of universalism was established, that is to say the notion that all citizens were equally entitled to minimum welfare benefits (see e.g. Jones, Brown, and Bradshaw 1978). This universalism derives in part from administration by a centralized and centralizing government and in part from a strong socialist working-class movement. Gill (n.d.) has argued that the presence of a socialist trade union movement in Britain played an important part in the establishment of the welfare state and the nationalized health service. There is no doubt that the detail of the health service as established in 1948 was strongly influenced by the egalitarian and socialist ideas of the Labour Party in power at the time. Nevertheless, it has to be said that the plans were laid by professionals and the dream of a state health service began among doctors in the second half of the nineteenth century (Abel-Smith 1964). Gill attributes the absence of a socialist working-class movement in the United States to the crushing of early trade unions and indicates that otherwise health for profit would have been more bridled in the United States. It is, however, also important to remember that in Britain the limited-liability companies and the trade unions succeeded the corporations and guilds of the medieval period. They emerged out of struggle, first of the bourgeoisie with the aristocracy and second of the workers with the employers. In one sense they were continuing a collective tradition of a kind which never existed in the United States. The collectivist tradition remains, although under strong attack by the present government, which, while challenging universalism and encouraging selectivity, is at the same time actively strengthening central government control (see also Kaim-Caudle 1973; Gough 1979; Pinker 1979; Coughlin 1980; Lee and Raban 1983).

Even with the present move in Britain to greater individualism and privatization a British visitor observes health care being bought and sold as a commodity in the United States in blatant ways and on a scale which are not seen in Britain. Money is made out of illness and fear more openly and to a greater degree than in Britain. However, the present British government policy is rapidly opening up more possibilities for treating health care as a commodity rather than a service. Abuses are arising which require lay and professional vigilance and have (perhaps paradoxically) called forth intervention from the Department of Health. The great majority of the British medical profession continue opposed to such moves, notwithstanding the political conservatism of most.

Male domination

In both the United States and the United Kingdom the public domain, that is the world of industry, the market place, the state, has historically been and continues to be, notwithstanding contemporary changes, dominated by men. In both countries the ideology of domesticity, so strongly established in the nineteenth century, still survives, and women, even though so many now are in paid employment and taking part in public affairs, are held primarily responsible for the organization of and work in the private or domestic domain of the home (Stacey and Price 1981; Randall 1982). On both sides of the Atlantic women experience the two forms of male control: of the public domain and of the patriarchal family. Although women are not without influence in either place, the political and economic organization of both countries has largely been created and sustained by men. Differences in these institutions are the subject of the next section.

Differences in political and economic organization

Alternative welfare state models

The major variations in politics, government, and economics are also associated with major variations in the administration of health and welfare regulations. All British citizens are entitled to unemployment and sickness benefits according to standardized scales and subject only to previous qualifying payments of insurance contributions. The state administers these standardized benefits. When first instituted they were paid on a flat rate; nowadays they are income-related. Since they were designed for conditions of full employment, their fate under a policy of high unemployment remains to be seen. All the elderly (women at 60 and men at 65) who are retired from work are entitled to a state pension. While some also have work-related pensions in addition, none can fall below the state minimum. In contrast, in the United States there is a wide range of insurance and welfare entitlement systems and the concept of benefit as of right appears not to have been established nationwide. Thus, while the formal concept of entitlement may be articulated similarly in the United States and in the United Kingdom, it is not well understood in the United States, where it refers only to particular sections of the population, not to all (Estes 1979; Bucher 1983). Entitlement in the United States must be specifically earned or accumulated and is not associated with rights of citizenship as it is in Britain.

EOC and EEOC compared

Meehan (1983) contrasts the British Equal Opportunities Commission (EOC) with the Equal Employment Opportunities Commission (EEOC) of the United States, pointing to differences in the power of litigation. On the one hand, the EEOC was granted the power to litigate in 1972 and has tended to use it with some vigor. By comparison, the British EOC, which lacks this power, appears laggardly, using persuasion rather than legal powers or sanctions, attempting to "raise the consciousness" of government departments and agencies as to their duties under the Sex Discrimination and Equal Opportunities Acts. This contrasts strongly with the more aggressive and topic-oriented manner of the US EEOC.

In the United States the looser system of political parties, the greater equality between executive and legislative branches, and the importance of the civil rights constituency in recent presidential elections all make it easier for women to organize lobbies than is the case in Britain.

Meehan also stresses the permanence of the British civil service compared with the politicized US administration. However, from the outset the EEOC unlike the EOC has worked through women's groups. The British civil service is familiar with working through established groups but slow to recognize newer groups. Moreover, equal-opportunities interests are less clearly defined at the grass-roots level than in the United States. Therefore British politicians take less account of women's groups (see also Robarts with Cooke and Ball 1981: 42).

Health-care delivery in Britain and the United States

Flowing from differences in entitlement are major variations in the mode of health-care delivery[1]. In Britain the pattern is set by the National Health Service, which is freely available to all at the point of delivery. The major funding of the health service comes out of general taxation to which all contribute depending on their income, wealth, and purchases. While part-payments are made by about half the population for medicaments on prescription, and for dentures and spectacles, there is no form of fee for service or pre-payment by individuals. Furthermore, the elderly, children, pregnant women, and certain categories of the chronically ill or disabled are exempt from all or most payments. The system is uniform throughout the country in principle and central government policy and conscious administrative efforts are made to overcome regional variations in the provisions available. Nevertheless, in some areas important to women – most notably abortion – conscience clauses available to providers may lead to variations in the availability of services (see Doyal Chapter 9).

The introduction of National Health Insurance in 1911 led to an improvement of the working conditions and occupational status of general practitioners (Parry and Parry 1976; Honigsbaum 1979). The National Health Service, which succeeded it in 1948, embracing hospital doctors as well as general practitioners, provided hospitals with large capital resources and doctors with an insured clientele. For these reasons and because they appreciate treating patients exclusively on the merits of their condition British doctors are committed to the NHS. At the same time, although doctors have recently protested cuts in the service, they are also keen to preserve and use their freedom to practice privately, a right which was ensured from the inception of the NHS. Most recently, this interest in private medicine, with active government encouragement, has been reflected both in the rapid growth of private insurance schemes and in the rate of construction of private hospitals (both often financed with US capital). Thus, at the same time that all United Kingdom citizens still receive necessary medical treatment free at the point of delivery, government policy appears to be moving to a more selective mode, unknown in Britain since the establishment of the NHS.

These arrangements contrast strongly with those in the

United States, where the majority of the organized medical profession have long opposed both national insurance and taxation-based services. Health-care delivery in the United States is characterized by great variability both in quality and in mode. Insurance-based, fee-for-service medicine prevails and varies in quantity and quality even more markedly than in Britain. At the same time, health maintenance organizations (HMOs) utilize a prepayment system and somewhat resemble the system in the United Kingdom. However, HMOs do not provide universal coverage and have been criticized by Marmor (1978) for their failure to meet the needs of the poor through Medicaid. In a different area, federal programs like Medicare and Medicaid have succeeded in providing health care to many who were formerly denied it, but still have never constituted anything as broad as the services which the universal British system has made the right of every citizen. Furthermore, the inflation of fees and the costs of medicaments have generated anxieties about cost containment, leading to erosion of the limited service provided. Estes (1979), for example, has reported that the elderly have had to pay more for treatment in the wake of Medicaid.

These variations mean that while the best of US medicine may be superior in many ways (mainly technologically) to the average treatment available in the United Kingdom, the service available to the poor in the United States tends to be a good deal worse. For example, it is likely under present conditions that an impoverished black woman in the United Kingdom would stand a better chance of receiving adequate treatment than in the United States. However, some of these differences may now be eroding. We do not yet know enough, for instance, about the way the British health regulations of October 1982 will work out in practice except to say that "they will entail a much closer surveillance of the black population" (Doyal Chapter 9).

The differences outlined between the practice of medicine in Britain and in the United States lead us back to the recurrent theme of individualism versus centralism. In the American case, the high standard associated with medicine at its best derives in part from the absence of centralization and the concomitant freedom to experiment which this implies. For many years, federal funds have been available for many different kinds of clinical research facilities, and the variety of these settings has diversified the conditions under which new ideas are tested. In Britain, on the other hand, centralization has fostered uniformity. Phillips and Rakusen (1978), for example, editing Boston Women's Health Book Collective (1971) for a UK audience suggest that it is only in general practice in Britain that anything comparable to the American freedom to experiment exists, as British GPs are not state employees but hire out their services to the state. While the number of radical experiments attempted in Britain is quite limited (for one example, see Gardner 1981) NHS consultants can and do introduce new techniques sometimes in ways which embarrass both the government and the health service (Council for Science and Society 1983).

Domestic and public domains

Two worlds of work for women

In the United States just as in the United Kingdom women work in two distinct but overlapping arenas: paid employment (in the public domain) and the home (the domestic or private domain). To distinguish these simply as women's parts in production and reproduction is to miss a great deal. Women are engaged in service and productive work both in the public domain, where most paid work is carried out, and in the domestic domain, where work is typically unwaged. Nor is reproduction solely a private matter as women work to maintain and service the labor force in both domestic and public domains.

Women's domestic work obviously varies depending upon the kind of household they live in. Those rearing young children or caring for dependent or disabled people clearly have a greater workload than lone householders or childless women. Unsupported mothers and single women caring for elderly parents are among those with most domestic work and household responsibility. Domestic work has certain peculiarities. It is an open-ended commitment which is done not under contract but for 'love'; it is not a matter of wages but of duty (cf. Finch and Groves 1983).

With regard to paid employment we know that the pattern of change as it affects women has been roughly the same in both

Britain and the United States during this century, although there have been some differences in timing British women have a longer history of participation in the paid labor force although the increase in the number of women involved in paid employment since the turn of the century has been greater in the United States (Hakim 1979). Women typically begin paid employment when they complete their education, withdraw to the domestic arena while rearing children, and return to paid work as the children grow older. This bimodal work profile emerged more quickly in the United States, where it was well entrenched by 1950, than it did in the United Kingdom, where it was not apparent until 1961.

Hakim (1979) suggests for Britain, as Oppenheimer (1970) does for the United States, that the *de jure* and *de facto* barriers to married women doing paid work were dropped because of a shortage of single women to supply female-dominated occupations. Push factors, such as those mentioned by Brody (1981: 473), namely rising divorce rates, fewer children, labor-saving devices, inflation, and the desire for a higher standard of living, have also played their part. Nevertheless, those push factors would not have brought women into paid employment in the absence of the needs of industrial and commercial employers for labor and their readiness, in the absence of other options, to accept married women in these roles.

Despite these changes, in both the United States and the United Kingdom, the work profiles of women and men continue to differ markedly. More men are employed than women and their work profiles show fewer interruptions. Nor has the increase in the numbers of women in paid work modified the pattern of sex segregation which prevails in both countries. Occupational segregation falls into two types. The first, horizontal segregation, occurs when different kinds of work are allocated to women and men. In contrast, vertical segregation applies when women and men both participate in the same field of work but where women are disproportionately concentrated in the lower grades and men in the higher, whether these are defined in terms of skill, responsibility, prestige, or financial reward (Hakim 1979). These two types of sex segregation are logically separate although they may occur together. It is important to distinguish them in any analysis of the social relations of occupations and, as we shall see shortly, both forms may appear in health occupations.

A comparison of changes in sex segregation undertaken by Hakim (1979), including an update of Oppenheimer's (1970) work, suggests that the more rapid increase in women's participation in the labor force in the United States has been accompanied by a greater reduction of sex segregation. But sex segregation remains and Hakim's (1979) analysis suggests that its nature is similar in the two countries. (The data are computed slightly differently but broad comparability can be achieved.) In the United States, clerical workers, sales and service workers, and domestic workers include high proportions of women. The British data show a high concentration of women in clerical work, shop work, semiskilled and unskilled manual work. Within those last two categories women are disproportionately likely to work in food processing and in service occupations such as hairdressing and domestic work. Nursing is another typically female occupation. In both countries the data show clear evidence of vertical segregation: there are proportionately more women in the less skilled and less prestigious jobs and fewer in those jobs which carry some degree of work autonomy and managerial authority. In Britain, as in the United States, the proportion of women in professional work shows an overall decline since World War II. Furthermore, in both Britain and America, conventionally male occupations continue to be resistant to women's entry, while conventionally female occupations are becoming more open to male entry (Gross 1968, for the United States see Hakim 1979). The implications of these changes for the health-care division of labor will be discussed later in this chapter.

In both countries not only do women work at different jobs, they also share the experience of being less well paid than men. The pace of change differs however. Comparing equal-opportunity policies in the United Kingdom and the United States, Elizabeth Meehan argues that "in terms of political discourse and action, women's rights have been taken more seriously in the United States than in Britain . . . [but] paradoxically, at the material level of pay, Britain appears to be in advance of the US" (1983: 170). In Britain women's pay relative to men's improved from 1970 reaching 75.5 per cent in 1975 but falling back to 73.5 per cent by 1980. In the United States the gap has widened from just above 60 per cent in 1963 to just below. However this is not a simple failure of the equal-pay arrangements: in part at least it reflects the greater United States success in getting more women in new jobs since the Civil Rights Act and Executive Orders. New entrants push down average earnings overall (Meehan 1983; for further detail on the United States see Kahn and Grune 1982; Norgren 1982; Stoper 1982).

The households women live in

In both Britain and the United States the household is an arena in which women spend much of their personal and work lives. Thus its form, size, and relationship with the family and kin are crucial for women's health. Family size on both sides of the Atlantic has declined in recent years and at the same time longevity has increased. Along with the effects of divorce and death these trends mean that the nuclear-family household is an increasingly shortlived social unit. Economic and social circumstances force some, as they always have, into alternative household formations. In addition, people are increasingly choosing alternative household structures. This has included a growth in single-person households and those headed by single women.

Households headed by lone mothers have increased in Britain from 7.1 per cent of families with dependent children in 1971–73 to 10.1 per cent in 1978–80. In the same period the number of lone fathers rose from 1.2 per cent to 1.4 per cent (Office of Population Censuses and Surveys 1980: Table 2. 4). Similar trends appear in the United States. Women family householders with no spouse present and with one or more children under 18 constituted 18 per cent of all American families in 1981 (US Bureau of the Census 1982–83: Table 73). This meant that of US children under 18, 1.9 per cent were living with their father only and 18.1 per cent with their mother only at the time of the survey (US Bureau of the Census 1982–83: Table 76). Given that the number of elderly people has increased and the number of children born has decreased, there are fewer children and fewer productive workers to care for more elderly people. Most of the carers, whether daughters or others, are women. Brody (1981), discussing the question in the United States, has called these people the "women in the middle." The trend in both countries now is that aging children increasingly care for ever more aged parents. Since there are so many more elderly women than men, the problems of the elderly, in terms of both the givers and recipients of care, are to a large extent problems of women. Old women's problems differ in some important ways from those of old men as Evers (1981a, 1981b, and this volume Chapter 4) reminds us. Old women in both countries are much more likely to live alone (US Bureau of the Census 1982–83; UK Central Statistical Office 1983). There are other clear similarities between the two countries in their elderly populations, but as I indicate later in this chapter they have each developed widely differing solutions to similar problems.

Women, health, and women's movements in Britain and the United States

On both sides of the Atlantic women's concerns with health have a long history. Throughout the twentieth century, the British women's movements were active in agitation over maternal and child health, although, as Palmer (1983) has shown, the concerns of working-class movements such as the Women's Cooperative Guild were sometimes at variance with those of the middle-class movements. In the interwar period, however, the women's movement in Britain did not challenge the value of medicine and medical care; they wanted it available (cf. Ehrenreich 1978). Women were highly conscious of excessive morbidity among mothers, especially in the working class, to which inadequate attention was paid. Few women at that time (except those who wrote in *Time and Tide*) challenged the domestic division of labor or related the "double burden" of working wives and mothers to health issues (Palmer 1983).

The postwar period saw an expansion of women's health activities in Britain, particularly in relation to the improvement of maternity services. Well ahead of the most recent feminist movement, women joined together to form AIMS, the Association for the Improvement of the Maternity Services. Around 1950, the Association for the Welfare of Children in Hospital (AWCH) was formed in Wales and almost simultaneously, Mother Care for Children in Hospital in England, later to become the National Association for the Welfare of Children in Hospital (NAWCH).[2]

British women, like American women, have been concerned to control their own fertility. Following the work of socialist and feminist women such as Stella Browne, Dora Russell, and Janet Chance in the 1920s (Doyal with Pennell 1979), a British feminist pressure group began in 1936 to work to extend the availability of legal abortions (Randall 1982). When Doyal (1982) writes that the British women's health movement can be divided into three stages, she is speaking only of the health movement associated with latter-day feminism, what Randall (1982) calls "second wave feminism."[3] Doyal argues that the first phase of the women's health movement in Britain closely mirrored that in the United States in that its primary concern was women as health consumers. Its goals were to challenge doctors' control over reproductive technology, to claim women's right to control their own bodies, and to develop self-help groups and feminist education. In the United States this phase was characterized by the establishment of women's alternative clinics, a less frequent phenomenon in the United Kingdom because of the health service free at the point of delivery. This led, in the second phase, to British feminist concern with defending the NHS against attacks from the government at the same time that criticisms of its failures with regard to women continue. The third phase Doyal identifies is characterized by attempts to develop a socialist feminist epidemiology which would lead to "the understanding of women's sickness and health in the context of the patriarchal and capitalist nature of society." American feminists have also made efforts in this direction, as for example in the work of Marieskind (1975, 1980).

Sex segregation in health care

The vertical and horizontal divisions which constitute occupational segregation were identified earlier. These divisions are also found in health services on both sides of the Atlantic. The health-care division of labor is dominated by the medical profession, itself predominantly male. Doyal (Chapter 9) has reminded us that in 1978 nearly 25 per cent of all doctors on the British Medical Register were women, a proportion which has since risen as increasing numbers of women medical students qualify. Women students now constitute half of medical undergraduates. Quotas, long imposed upon British women wishing to enter medical school, have now been abolished. Marieskind (1980) reports a lower figure for the United States where 25 or 30 per cent of US medical students are women.

In both countries, medical school staffs, as all elite medical groups, remain predominately male, particularly in the higher-status grades. UK women share the problems which Marieskind reports for US medicine. In both countries, women are disproportionately represented in some specialities and under-represented in others. Doyal (Chapter 9) lists child and adolescent psychiatry, mental handicap, anesthetics, radiotherapy, and medical microbiology as the top "feminine" specialities in the United Kingdom, while for the United States, Marieskind (1980: 132) shows that pediatrics is the most popular choice for women physicians. (It is sixth in the British list. However, we must remember that in Britain GPs or Clinical Medical Officers, the latter predominantly women, do much of what US pediatricians do (Stacey and Davies 1983).) Pediatrics is followed by psychiatry, anesthesiology, radiology, and obstetrics and gynecology. In the United Kingdom obstetrics and gynecology is neither among the most "feminine" or most "masculine" of specialities. Traumatic and orthopedic surgery appear to be viewed as most "masculine"; indeed in the United Kingdom, as in the United States, most forms of surgery are dominated by men.

Allowing for differences in the organization of specialities it does seem that there are considerable similarities between the two countries. First, women are found disproportionately in the "opportunity specialities," i.e. the less popular fields where they find it easier to get appointments and promotion. Second, women, encouraged by their male partners, tend to select specialities which both partners feel the woman can combine harmoniously with her domestic duties, including childrearing.

Similarities also characterize the situation of other health workers in the two countries. The evidence from both sides of the Atlantic shows that the great majority of workers in health services are women. The data also show that they are to be found more often in the lowly paid posts. Furthermore, even where they are in higher posts they earn less overall than their male counterparts (Marieskind 1980; Doyal Chapter 9). On the other hand, the disappearance and reappearance of midwives in the United States contrasts with their continued presence in the United Kingdom as an independent and licensed profession distinct from nurses. Their *de facto* status has, however, been diminished by the transfer of births to hospital and obstetricians' active management of labor (see Arney 1982 for US).

The development and present situation of the nursing profession in the two countries is particularly enlightening. It not only illustrates similarities derived from the activity of nursing as caring women's work, common to both sides of the Atlantic, but at the same time reveals important differences based on the relative individualism of the United States and centralism of the United Kingdom. In both countries nurses were established as handmaidens to doctors, but their struggle for independence and autonomy has taken somewhat different routes. In an historical analysis of the regulation of nursing work in the two countries, Celia Davies (1982) shows how underlying similarities are masked by differences of strategy and tactics. She concludes that, despite differences in nursing practice and the regulation of nursing work, nurses have no real functional autonomy in either country. The forms of the health-care systems, their organized sites, and modes of practice have all contributed to these differences. These can at least in part be explained, Davies argues, by the underlying differences between the two countries, between the more market-oriented and individualistic United States of America compared with the more interventionist, collectivist, and centralist United Kingdom.

Early American nurses trained in hospital but did not practice there. They did private work, public-health work, and nurse education, selling their labor in the market place in common with others. The great depression of the interwar years interrupted this pattern. Trained nurses returned to the hospital and issues about work regulation arose. These were not seriously addressed until after World War II when a variety of solutions was attempted, including modifying the head nurse role and concentrating on bedside nursing for the trained.

The British history contrasts with that of the United States, as Davies shows, because of a long history of nursing the poor in hospital, financed both by charity and by public funds. Hospital work was always "a key site of practice" (1982: 151). The past and present financial difficulties in Britain have led to a continued reliance on student and pupil nurses for ward work leading to problems in nurse education of the worker–learner (Fretwell 1983). The attempted British solution has been to develop a managerial structure which has not only left the ward problem unresolved but, Davies argues, has reaffirmed the pattern of work regulation. It has, however, introduced nurses to the decision-making structure at all levels in the NHS.

British nursing outside hospital never experienced the transformation that occurred with the development of public-health nursing in the United States.[4] The local government framework in England, while allowing for some variation, has never incorporated anything like the demonstration project and program so commonly found in public-health nursing in the thirties in the United States. In Britain, more centralist and interventionist, the emphasis has been on health-care delivery, aiming for universal coverage and minimum standards, in contrast with the greater US stress on demonstration and improvement. As Davies points out, value choices are involved "between maxima and minima, welfare 'floors' versus exemplary 'ceilings,' standard provision versus variable, sometimes innovatory ones" (1982: 153). These variations affect nurses as they affect other workers through different welfare provisions and different collective goals. It is in this context, Davies argues, that the contrast between hierarchical and managerial goals of the British nurses and the development of new forms of nurse education and practice in the United States can be understood.

What Davies does not draw out is the common womanhood of the majority of US and UK nurses. The subservient role in relation to the dominant and male-dominated medical profession which they both experience is not just the subordination of nurses to doctors but was, and continues to be, part of the general subordination of women to men. Gamarnikow (1978) has shown the historical origins well, arguing that what Florence Nightingale did in her nursing reforms was to recreate the Victorian bourgeois family, casting the doctor in the role of the husband–father, the nurse in that of the wife–mother, and the patient in that of the child.

On neither side of the Atlantic, least of all the United States, do nurses nowadays see themselves as handmaidens of doctors. Nevertheless, on both sides of the Atlantic, they have failed to achieve functional autonomy overall, despite pockets of autonomy associated with special expertise, especially in the United States. This failure is associated not only with doctor domination but also with male domination. In addition it is important to draw attention to the consequence in Britain of the policy of managerialism. The job descriptions for nurse managers were written in such a way that they evoked the notion of a man. Drawn from a relatively small number of male nurses, mostly in psychiatric nursing, and paradoxically generally less well educated than most women nurses, a disproportionately large number of men were appointed to the new managerial posts (Austin 1977; Carpenter 1979; Hardy 1983; Nuttall 1983). This sad quirk of "equal opportunities" is leading to vertical segregation in what, so far as nursing physical illness was concerned, was once an all-woman and woman-managed occupation.

The unpaid work of women

As we have already noted, women on both sides of the Atlantic do a great deal of unpaid work. Indeed, there is a lot to be said for the view that women's domestic labor is a cause of their depressed public-domain earnings. The narrow view whereby for "work" we read "paid work" has not helped our understanding of these phenomena. Waldo has demonstrated that our concept of work has led us not to include in "work" those activities which maintain our most private or our most public relations (1979: 381). Despite recent efforts, our explanations of the division of labor in the public domain, the world of industry, state, and the market place, remain sharply divided from our explanations of unpaid work in the home (Stacey 1981). Indeed when Hakim (1979) indicates that women's "work profile" is broken, what she means is not that her *work* profile but her *paid work* profile is interrupted by childrearing, undeniably a form of work. This failure to think of paid and unpaid health work as part and parcel of the same activity leads to the denigration of unpaid health work on both sides of the Atlantic.

It is clear that health care in the United States and the United Kingdom depends very heavily upon the unpaid work of women. As more women are involved in the paid-labor market the responsibility becomes harder to bear. Brody (1981) has shown that American women accept responsibility for the care of their elderly relatives, although some of the elderly are themselves less enthusiastic about relying on kin.

One consequence of these narrow definitions is that we do not unite the bodies of knowledge we have about paid and unpaid work. Nor do there seem to be many studies of the health consequences for women of carrying the "double burden" of simultaneously working in the domestic and the public domains. For example, a considerable body of research now shows that being a "captive" wife or mother has deleterious health consequences (cf. Brown and Harris 1978). We do not usually think of death or damage in childbirth as being an occupational hazard, yet it can be productive to consider it in this light. In both Britain and the United States the hazards have been much reduced over the last fifty years. Oakley (1980, 1981) has demonstrated that the loss of a place in the public domain paradoxically constitutes childbirth as bereavement; the first-time mother finds that she must part with many valued activities when she begins to care for her child. What does it do to a woman's physical health to have two full-time jobs, one paid and one unpaid, and to have little leisure beyond these jobs? We know that adding a paid job can improve her mental health and some research indicates that women's health behavior differs according to their marital status (Nathanson 1975, 1977). While marriage appears to be good for a man's health it seems to be less beneficial for a woman's (Gove 1972, 1973; Gove and Tudor 1973; Bernard 1975; Oakley 1980). Further, while there is little systematic evidence (despite numerous pontifications) about the possible occupational hazards of housework and of housework combined with paid work, the extent to which women undertake part-time rather than full-time work when their children are young at least suggests that many of them, in essence, conclude that they cannot manage two full-time jobs. The health implications of caring for others in the household is coming to be better recognized (Gove 1984 a, b) but the (apparently endless) debate on "fixed role" versus "nurturant role" does not address the issue of the double burden sufficiently directly, nor the relatively subservient role experienced by most women. Graham (1984) has begun to explore how women's dual position in household and workplace affects their health, but evidence remains insufficient for clarity (Rice, Hing, and Kovar 1983). The paradox of their greater longevity remains (Nathanson 1975; Marcus, Seeman, and Telesky 1984).

Socialized childcare facilities would go a long way to help women resolve this problem as would the provision of socialized laundry and cooking facilities. However, neither in Britain nor in the United States does one hear the demands for childcare or housekeeping facilities discussed in terms of health policy, or in terms of the improvement in women's health which might be expected to follow from them. There is no doubt that women in the United States benefit from privately provided amenities such as laundries and restaurants more than their British counterparts simply because they enjoy a generally higher standard of living. This, however, only applies to the better off. The poor in the United States and Britain lack access to such facilities. Thus in both countries, women in less privileged social classes and women of color experience the double burden more intensely in many ways than those in higher social classes (but see Smith 1974). In seems likely that in both countries women's health is affected by their life chances and achievable standard of life as is the health of their menfolk and their children (for the UK see Townsend and Davidson 1982; Graham 1984).

Consequences for the women's movements

American women, Randall (1982: 117) argues, have been more fortunate than British in those policy areas affected by the ideological commitment of the United States to equality of opportunity, education, pay, and employment. They have been less fortunate when policy has been influenced by the widespread mistrust of direct state intervention and expenditure.

She argues, for example, that birth-control policy has been more oppressive in the States than in Britain both because of mistrust of state intervention and because of decentralization. The federal Comstock Law of 1873 prohibited the importation, interstate transportation, or spread of information about contraceptive devices and prompted similar laws in about half the states. Many still restricted the distribution and display of contraceptives as late as 1968. In 1965 the Supreme Court ruled on the grounds of a married couple's right to privacy that they had right of choice, but this was not extended to unmarried couples until 1972. In addition, she goes on, the federal government has been unwilling to provide family planning as a public service except, since the mid-sixties, for the very poor.

In Britain the sheath and the diaphragm were in production in the 1880s, but the government did not permit dissemination of information through public health authorities until 1930 when they accepted that birth-control information should be provided to married women on specific medical grounds. Not until 1948 could the information be made available to all married women. Since 1967 birth-control advice has been publicly available to anyone in need, and, if necessary, free. It is now available on the NHS.

Abortion was illegal in nineteenth-century Britain; by 1900 most state legislatures in the United States had banned abortion. Although in Britain it was illegal, by the end of the nineteenth century doctors regularly performed abortions when a woman's life was in danger, a procedure which was recognized in legislation in 1929. Abortion was thus legally available to those who could afford the fees. In 1938 legal abortions were also permitted to safeguard a woman's physical or mental health. A feminist pressure group first formed in 1936 worked to increase the grounds for legal abortion and later to make abortion available on the National Health Service. They succeeded by 1967. In Britain, therefore, "second wave feminism had to defend, not to win abortion law reform" (Randall 1982: 111).

In the United States, on the other hand, the abortion laws were not generally liberalized until the 1960s and this was not condoned by the Supreme Court until 1973 (see Petchesky Chapter 6). As Randall points out, it is partly the U S political system itself which has made abortion law reform difficult (1982: 116). The 1967 Act in Britain was well ahead of public opinion, a possibility deriving from the mode of election and accountability of the House of Commons, notwithstanding its heavy male domination. Nevertheless, despite sharper recent polarization in the United States than in the United Kingdom between those feminists who wished the law totally repealed and the well-organized anti-abortionists, the reforms ultimately went further in the US system.

However, in neither country has legislation or judicial ruling been made in response to women's requests or in women's interests. In Britain and in the United States in the 1930s policies of the eugenicists concerned with the maintenance of the white upper and middle classes and worried about the "prolific breeding" of the lower classes did much to publicize and popularize "family planning." The banning of abortion in the United States at the turn of the century was partly the result of medical pressure when doctors were anxious to discredit "unqualified" practitioners.

Right and left in feminism

The stronger socialist tradition of the United Kingdom has had important implications for the women's movement. Although Marieskind (1975) has argued that there is a move to socialism in the US women's health movement, the UK movement, while less widespread among the population at large, is more deeply imbued with socialist ideas. This is partly because socialist ideas have permeated British society more widely than in America, where individualistic ideas continue to prevail. Demands for women's rights are salient for any American when expressed in terms of an inalienable right to life, liberty, and the pursuit of happiness, slogans which have no counterpart in British ideology.

The same trends have also had consequences in analyses of the division of labor in health care. Apart from Navarro (1976), American analysts have not systematically addressed gender as well as class differences (Olesen 1980). At the same time, U S research on women's health issues in general tends to neglect the importance of class and ethnicity. The notion of hidden labor or unpaid health work (see Graham Chapter 2) is also less well developed and less well integrated in American sociological thinking.

While US publications such as those produced by Health PAC have drawn attention to variations in the distribution of health by social class (Ehrenreich and Ehrenreich 1970; Ehrenreich 1978), I have not been able to trace any U S document as prestigious as that of the Black Report on inequalities in health. Headed by the then President of the Royal College of Physicians and composed of two senior physicians and two social scientists, the committee produced a report which exposed the continuing class difference in health and in life and death chances in the United Kingdom. These class variations are shared by men and women alike. But the Black Report does not systematically examine gender differences.

Consequences for health policies

These differing approaches, the collectivist and the individualist, affect many health policy matters. Two which bear particularly on women, policies which relate to the welfare of the elderly and to preventive health care, may serve as illustrations.

Following in the tradition of the written constitution, when American citizens decide to take collective welfare action, they are perhaps more likely than the British, who have no written constitution, to make overt and principled statements of their intentions. The objectives of the Older Americans Act of 1965 as set out in Title I is without parallel in Britain, where above and beyond the minimum state pension there is no consistent or nationwide policy for the elderly. Some British personnel struggling to understand what they should provide and how they might do it envy this. Yet when we come to read Estes' (1979) study of policy and service provision for the aged we learn that deeds have not followed words and many problems remain, often much like those in Britain. In Britain as the United States, "Politics, economics, and social structure have far more to do with the role and the status of the aged than does the ageing process and its effects on the individual" (Estes 1979: 221).

Nevertheless, the attempts to solve the problems differ and one must agree with Estes (1979: 222) that there is a greater willingness for direct government intervention in the United Kingdom than the United States and possibly less opportunity in the United Kingdom for special interests to sway policy decisions. The United Kingdom centralization does mean, however, that governments must be persuaded to act, to make mandatory arrangements for local authorities to deliver the goods. In the area of the elderly in the United Kingdom the vast array of standards and modes of provision indicates the lack of a unified government policy. The amounts of sheltered housing available vary from place to place as do policies and the standards of health care, its type and locale. Policies for the elderly gravely affect women on both sides of the Atlantic, since they are the majority of the elderly (cf. Peace 1981).

Similar contrasts emerge in the history of maternal and child health. In the United States the inclination to rely on private arrangements contrasts with nationwide pregnancy- and child-surveillance schemes in the United Kingdom where all women and children regardless of their socioeconomic background have routine checks and immunizations free at the point of delivery. The same disinclination to direct universal provision seen in the administration of the Older Americans Act is also demonstrated by the fate of the Sheppard–Towner Act intended to make available universal maternal preventive services (Rothman 1981) and of child health policies under Medicaid (Foltz 1982).

Differences in political structures require reformers to use different strategies in each of our countries. For abortion law reform the target for pressure in the United Kingdom is Parliament; in the United States it may be the state legislature, the Congress, or the courts (Randall 1982: 178). In the United Kingdom for reforms related to childbirth as much as reforms related to abortion, central government is the target, but pressure can also be exerted on the medical profession through the centrally organized Royal College of Obstetricians and Gynaecologists. Within central government requests for childbirth reforms will be directed towards policymakers in the DHSS, the medical people who advise them, and parliamentary committees concerned with value for money in public expenditure. In the United States there is much greater chance for experimentation and the pressure is upon local health-care providers in particular facilities.

A principal advantage of the British system is that so long as women's health problems are recognized the best available methods can be prescribed for any woman no matter who or what she is or what her financial means. On the other hand, the disadvantage of the British system is that if women's problems are not acknowledged it is much harder to find a way out: there is little or no space for the US style demonstration project.

As we have seen, in Britain as in the United States, women's health problems have in the past been defined by a male-dominated medical profession. Thus a series of government committees, first Cranbrook (Ministry of Health 1959) and then Peel (DHSS 1970) decided that childbirth would be better located in hospital. These committees did not include representatives of the women childbearers; they were mostly composed of medical men, with a token midwife. Nor did they include any social scientists. The medical men who proposed this major change of locale were making social decisions without social research and well outside their competence, for birth is a social event. Births were transferred to hospitals. The confidence of general practitioners to attend deliveries was destroyed by the hospital consultants.

The move to hospital deliveries took place earlier in the United States. Indeed, British obstetricians were greatly influenced by American teaching and practices. One policy debate the author had with a leading British professor of obstetrics in the early 1970s concluded with his saying when all other arguments had deserted him, "Well, they do it in America" (cf. Arney 1982).

At the same time there is nowadays a much greater range of birthing arrangements available in the United States than in the United Kingdom, enabling the informed to make better choices, so long as they can acquire the right "ticket" for access to the facilities they prefer (see Romalis Chapter 7, on the options in Canada). There has been some effort to make hospitalized birth facilities more homelike in the United Kingdom, but this seems to be done more in the United States. Decorating a labor room to make it look like a home does not of course make it home: the totality of social relationships remains quite different. Nevertheless, as Ruzek (1978) has pointed out, US physicians are now more willing to make deliveries in these "alternative" birth facilities than to do home deliveries. There is greater likelihood that cosmetic arrangements will be made to please customers where there is patient choice and medical facilities depend upon attracting custom to make a profit and meet expenses. There are no such pressures in the NHS although there are those doctors who dissent from the way birth arrangements have been altered in the last fifteen years. They and the women who also have reservations, such as those organized in AIMS, have to work through the channels already indicated.

Again, while women benefit in Britain when the centralized services work well and in their interests, the availability of a service free at the point of delivery has made it less easy to run women's health groups. It requires a great deal of alienation before women are going to pay, even cost only, for a medical service they can get free, and have already paid for through their taxes. Patients are prepared to put up with a certain amount of discomfort in an as-of-right free service. As Doyal (1983) has pointed out, the one really successful women's clinic is the Women's Therapy Centre, providing a service which is in any case hard for either sex to get under the NHS. Other services exist in areas where NHS provision is patchy (for example because of conscience clauses) in pregnancy advice and abortion provision. Women's health centers and clinics in the United States, on the other hand, can charge a modest fee, provide a service by women and for women, and benefit their clients on two counts: first, the service is to be preferred to the conventional male-dominated provision as it restores some command of their bodies to the women, and second, it is probably cheaper or at least no more expensive than conventional medicine.

Ruzek sums up the American side of this story well. She argues that obstetricians and gynecologists have responded to challenge from the women's movement about birth styles "partly in order to keep control of their clientele" (1978: 336). Obstetrics and gynecology are big business and women's alternative services are seen as a real economic threat to medical hegemony and are therefore fought vigorously by the medical establishment. Providing "consumer-oriented services" is seen as one way to attract customers in a competitive market place. At the same time, home-style birth programs may cost more than conventional obstetric services, perhaps a third as much again, without counting the physician's fee (Ruzek 1978: 348). Continued competition is upheld by the judiciary as, for example, in the important Tallahassee case, in which the medical establishment's right to maintain a monopoly of care and to exclude alternative practice was held to be against "the public interest" (Ruzek 1980).

Conclusion

This chapter has explored the world of women and health in the United States and the United Kingdom. We have seen time and again how similar are women's problems in both countries derived from their common situation in patriarchal and capitalist societies. At the same time we have learned that the men who took command in former days of our several public domains used their power differently. They created different institutions of government, their practice of medicine has varied in ways partly, but not entirely, explicable by the economic and governmental ethos of each. We see that in both countries government is attempting not only to reverse hard-won welfare rights but to undermine gains women have made in recent years. Essentially we have learned how much we have in common in our struggle for health and a healthy life, how in both our countries women carry the burdens of oppression unequally, and how each can learn from the other about the pitfalls, when applied in the other's country, of what seem splendid answers in their country of origin. Processes of attack and protest must differ because of our differing legislative and judicial systems. Foci for pressure also differ because of the widely differing potentials and constraints of our health-care systems. We understand better that what is the solution for one would at best be inappropriate, at worst disastrous, for the other. Our mutual understanding can help to give us insight into ways of forwarding our common struggle.

Notes

1   Bunker (1970) contrasts the very different organization of health care in the United States and the United Kingdom and notes the far higher rates of surgery in the United States; while he thinks this may in part be cultural he attributes at least some of the difference to the contrasting payments system (fee-for-services versus salary) and the GP screening system. Stimson (1977) points out that the British GP is introducing the notion of the social into medicine in ways which are specific to Britain because of the NHS structure.
2   These associations were formed when the works of John Bowlby were much in vogue: some of the mothers were concerned simply

about the hazards of separation, for themselves as well as their children; others used the Bowlby argument as a lever to persuade hospitals to open their doors. Not acting as feminists either in AIMS, AWCH, or NAWCH, but as mothers on behalf of their own and their children's health, these women gained experience of public life. Some later moved towards "second wave" feminism; others are now staunch defenders of the conventional nuclear family and exhibit deference to the medical profession in the sense that they challenge modes of health-care delivery but not medical knowledge itself.

3 The quotation marks indicate that in my view what I prefer to call "latter-day feminism" is something more like the fourth rather than the second wave, if one can indeed reasonably render the women's movement discontinuous. As Dale Spender (1983) quoting Mary Stott says: "There's always been a woman's movement this century."

4 The term "public health" is used somewhat differently on the two sides of the Atlantic, particularly with regard to the roles of doctors and nurses. Public health in Britain derives from the public-health movement of the nineteenth century. The term is used for activities undertaken by local government, with the permission of, or at the requirement of, central government, including clean water and food, refuse disposal, the control of infectious disease, and health education, especially of mothers. These activities until 1974 were under the control of Medical Officers of Health. Public health in Britain does not include medical or nursing treatment. In the United States, on the other hand, this may be included; thus the public-health nurses referred to here may undertake preventive medicine, health education but also treatment. "Public health" is also used more widely in the United States to include environmental health matters, as well as birth control, unemployment, poverty, and so forth (Jaco 1979: 5). In other cases (e.g. Beauchamp 1979), a public-health approach is contrasted with a market-mechanism one, and also reactive curative medicine is contrasted with preventive medicine. The market control of the former is seen to inhibit the development of the latter. But note: the British public-health movement developed during the heyday of British capitalism.

References

Abel-Smith, B. (1964) *The Hospitals*. London: Heinemann.

Arney, W.R. (1982) *Power and the Profession of Obstetrics*. Chicago and London: University of Chicago Press.

Austin, R. (1977) Sex and Gender in the Future of Nursing, 1 & 2, *Nursing Times*, 25 August and 1 September.

Bernard, J.S. (1975) *Women, Wives and Mothers*. Chicago: Aldine.

Beauchamp, D.E. (1979) Public Health as Social Justice. In E.G. Jaco (ed.) *Patients, Physicians and Illness*. New York: Free Press; London: Collier Macmillan.

Boston Women's Health Book Collective (1971) *Our Bodies Ourselves*. New York: Simon & Schuster.

Briggs, A. (1983) *A Social History of England*. New York: Charles Scribner's Sons. London: Weidenfeld & Nicolson.

Brody, E.M. (1981) "Women in the Middle" and Family Help to Older People. *The Gerontologist* 21: 5.

Brown, G.W. and Harris, T. (1978) *Social Origins of Depression: A Study of Psychiatric Disorder in Women*. London: Tavistock Publications.

Bucher, R. (1983) Personal communication.

Bunker, J.P. (1970) Surgical Manpower: A Comparison of Operations and Surgeons in the U S and in England & Wales. *The New England Journal of Medicine* 282 (3): 135.

Carpenter, M. (1979) The New Managerialism and Professionalism in Nursing. In M. Stacey, M. Reid, C. Heath, and R. Dingwall (eds) *Health and the Division of Labour*. London: Croom Helm.

Coughlin, R.M. (1980) *Ideology, Public Opinion and Welfare Policy. Attitudes Toward Taxes and Spending in Industrialized Societies*. Berkeley: Institute of International Studies, University of California.

Council for Science and Society (1983) *Expensive Medical Techniques*, Report of the Working Party. London.

Davies, C. (1982) The Regulation of Nursing Work: An Historical Comparison of Britain and the USA. In J. Roth (ed.) *Research in the Sociology of Health Care*, vol. 2. Greenwich, CT: JAI Press, pp. 121–60.

Davis, A., Gardner, B.B., and Gardner, M.R. (1965) *Deep South: A Social Anthropological Study of Caste and Class*. Chicago: University of Chicago Press.

DHSS (1970) *Domiciliary Midwifery and Maternity Bed Needs*, Peel Report. London: HMSO.

Doyal, L. (1983) Women, Health and the Sexual Division of Labour: A Case Study of the Women's Health Movement in Britain. *Critical Social Policy* 7 (Summer): 21–33.

Doyal, L. with Pennell, I. (1979) *The Political Economy of Health*. London: Pluto Press.

Dumont, L. (1970) *Homo Hierarchicus: The Caste System and Its Implications*. Chicago: University of Chicago Press.

Ehrenreich, B. and Ehrenreich, J. (1970) *The American Health Empire:*

Power, Profits and Politics. New York: Random House.

Ehrenreich, J. (ed.) (1978) *The Cultural Crisis of Modern Medicine*. New York, London: Monthly Review Press.

Estes, C. (1979) *The Aging Enterprise: A Critical Examination of Social Policies and Services for the Aged*. San Francisco, London: Jossey-Bass.

Evers, H. (1981a) The Creation of Patient Carers in Geriatric Wards: Aspects of Policy and Practice. *Social Science and Medicine* 15A: 581–88.

—— (1981b) Care or Custody? The Experiences of Women Patients in Long-Stay Geriatric Wards. In B. Hutter and G. Williams (eds) *Controlling Women: The Normal and the Deviant*. London: Croom Helm.

Finch, J. and Groves, D. (eds) (1983) *A Labour of Love: Women, Work and Caring*. London, Boston, Melbourne, and Henley: Routledge & Kegan Paul.

Foltz, A. (1982) *An Ounce of Prevention: Child Health Policies under Medicaid*. Cambridge, MA: MIT Press.

Fretwell, J.E. (1983) *Ward Teaching and Learning: Sister and the Learning Environment*. London: Royal College of Nursing.

Gamarnikow, E. (1978) Sexual Divisions of Labour: The Case of Nursing. In A. Kuhn and A-M. Wolpe (eds) *Feminism and Materialism*. London: Routledge & Kegan Paul.

Gardner, K. (1981) Well Woman Clinics: A Positive Approach. In H. Roberts (ed.) *Women, Health and Reproduction*. London: Routledge & Kegan Paul.

Gill, D. (n.d.) The British and American Medical Care Systems: Contrasts and Comparisons. Paper presented to Second Conference on the Clinical Application of the Social Sciences to Health, University of Missouri-Columbia. Mimeographed.

Gough, I. (1979) *The Political Economy of the Welfare State*. London: Macmillan.

Gove, W.R. (1972) The Relationships Between Sex Roles, Marital Status and Mental Illness. *Social Forces* 51: 34.

—— (1973) Sex, Marital Status and Mortality. *American Journal of Sociology* 79: 45.

—— (1984a) Gender Differences in Mental and Physical Illness: The Effects of Fixed Roles and Nurturant Roles. *Social Science and Medicine* 19: 84.

—— (1984b) Author's Reply: On Understanding Illness, Illness Behavior and Reading What Has Been Written: A Reply to Marcus, Seeman and Telesky. *Social Science and Medicine* 19: 88–91.

Gove, W.R. and Tudor, J. (1973) Adult Sex Roles and Mental Illness. *American Journal of Sociology* 78: 812.

Graham, H. (1984) *Women, Health and the Family*. Brighton:

Wheatsheaf, distributed by Harvester Press.

Gross, E. (1968) Plus ca change . . .? The Sexual Structure of Occupations Over Time. *Social Problems* 16 (Fall): 198–208.

Hakim, C. (1979) *Occupational Segregation: A Comparative Study of the Degree and Pattern of the Differentiation Between Men and Women's Work in Britain, the United States and Other Countries.* Research Paper No. 9. London: Department of Employment.

Hardy, L. (1983) The Emergency of Nursing Leaders – A Case in Spite of, Not Because of. *Nursing Times* (Occasional Papers), 12 Jan.

Honigsbaum, F. (1979) *The Division in British Medicine.* London: Kogan Page.

Jaco, E. Gartley (1979) (ed.) *Patients, Physicians, and Illness: A Source Book in Behavioral Science and Health,* 3rd edition. New York: Free Press; London: Collier Macmillan.

Jones, K., Brown, J., and Bradshaw, J. (1978) *Issues in Social Policy.* London, Henley, and Boston: Routledge & Kegan Paul.

Kahn, W. and Grune, J.A. (1982) Pay Equity: Beyond Equal Pay for Equal Work. In E. Boneparth (ed.) *Women, Power and Policy.* New York and Oxford: Pergamon.

Kaim-Caudle, P.R. (1973) *Comparative Social Policy and Social Security: A Ten-country Study.* London: Martin Robinson.

Lee, P. and Raban, C. (1983) Welfare and Ideology. In M. Loney, D. Boswell, and J. Clarke (eds) *Social Policy and Social Welfare.* Milton Keynes: Open University Press.

Lukes, S. (1973) *Individualism.* Oxford: Basil Blackwell.

Marcus, A.C., Seeman, T.S., and Telesky C.W. (1984) Comments: Teetering on the Horns of a Dilemma: Professor Gove's Latest Paper on Sex Differences in Illness Behavior. *Social Science and Medicine* 19: 84–8.

Marieskind, H. (1975) The Women's Health Movement. *International Journal of Health Services* 5 (2): 217.

—— (1980) *Women in the Health System.* St Louis, MO: C.V. Mosby.

Marmor, T.R. (1978) Innovation and the Health Sector: Notes on the U S. Mimeographed W2B/OECD Conference, Berlin, 13–16 June.

Marshall, T.H. (1963) Citizenship and Social Class. In *Sociology at the Crossroads.* London: Heinemann.

Marwick, A. (1982) *Class, Image and Reality in Britain, France and the USA Since 1930.* London: Fontana/Collins.

Meehan, E. (1983) Equal Opportunity Policies: Some Implications for Women of Contrasts Between Enforcement Bodies in Britain and the USA. In J. Lewis (ed.) *Women's Welfare: Women's Rights.* London: Croom Helm.

Ministry of Health (1959) *Report of the Maternity Services Committee* (Cranbrook Report). London: HMSO.

Nathanson, C.A. (1975) Illness and the Feminine Role: A Theoretical Review. *Social Science and Medicine* 9: 57.

—— (1977) Sex, Illness, and Medical Care. A Review of Data, Theory, and Method. *Social Science and Medicine* 11: 13.

Navarro, V. (1976) *Medicine under Capitalism*, New York: Prodist.

Nisbet, R.A. (1967) *The Sociological Tradition.* Heinemann: London.

Norgren, J. (1982) In Search of a National Child-Care Policy: Background and Prospects. In E. Boneparth (ed.) *Women, Power and Policy.* New York and Oxford: Pergamon.

Nuttall, P.D. (1983) British Nursing – Beginning of a Power Struggle. *Nursing Outlook* 31: 3.

Oakley, A. (1980) *Women Confined: Towards a Sociology of Childbirth.* London: Martin Robertson.

—— (1981) *From Here to Maternity: Becoming a Mother.* Harmondsworth: Penguin.

Office of Population Censuses and Surveys, Social Survey Division (1980) *General Household Survey.* London: HMSO.

Olesen, V. (1980) Gender and Medicine: A Critique of Contemporary Medical Sociology in the U S, Plenary address to the Medical Sociology Group of The British Sociological Association, Warwick. Mimeographed.

Oppenheimer, V.K. (1970) *The Female Labor Force in the United States.* Berkeley: Institute of International Studies, University of California.

Palmer, D. (1983) Women and Health Between the Two World Wars. PhD thesis in preparation, University of Warwick.

Parry, N. and Parry, J. (1976) *The Rise of the Medical Profession.* London: Croom Helm.

Peace, S. (1981) *An International Perspective on the Status of Older Women.* Washington, DC: International Federation of Aging.

Perkin, H. (1969) *The Origins of Modern English Society.* London and Henley: Routledge & Kegan Paul.

Phillips, A. and Rakusen, J. (eds) (1978) *Our Bodies Ourselves: A Health Book By and For Women.* Harmondsworth: Penguin. British edition of the Boston Women's Health Book Collective of the same title.

Pinker, R. (1979) *The Idea of the Welfare State.* London: Heinemann.

Randall, V. (1982) *Women and Politics.* London: St Martin.

Rice, D., Hing, E., and Kovar, M.G. (1983) Sex Differences in Disease Risk. In E.B. Gold (ed.) *The Changing Risk of Disease in Women.* Lexington, MA: The Collamore Press, pp. 1–24.

Robarts, S. with Cooke, A. and Ball, E. (1981) *Positive Action for Women: The Next Step.* London: National Council for Civil Liberties.

Robinson, R.V. (1983) Explaining Perceptions of Class and Racial

Inequality in England and the United States of America. *The British Journal of Sociology* 34 (3) Sept.: 344.

Rothman, S.M. (1981) Women's Clinics or Doctors' Offices: The Sheppard–Towner Act and the Promotion of Preventive Health Care. In J. Rothman and S. Wheeler (eds) *Social History and Social Policy*. New York: Academic Press.

Ruzek, S.B. (1978) *The Women's Health Movement: Feminist Alternatives to Medical Control*. New York: Praeger.

—— (1980) Medical Response to Women's Health Activities: Conflict, Accommodation and Cooptation. In J. Roth (ed.) *Research in the Sociology of Health Care*, vol. 1, *Professional Control of Health Services and Challenges to Such Control*. Greenwich, CT: JAI Press.

Sennett, R. and Cobb, J. (1977) *The Hidden Injuries of Class*. Cambridge: Cambridge University Press.

Smith, D. (1974) Women, the Family and Corporate Capitalism. In M. Stephensen (ed.) *Women in Canada*. Toronto: New Press.

Spender, D. (1983) *There's Always Been a Woman's Movement This Century*. London: Pandora Press (Routledge & Kegan Paul).

Stacey, M. (1981) The Division of Labour Revisited or Overcoming the Two Adams. In P. Abrams, R. Deem, J. Finch, and P. Rock (eds) *Practice and Progress: British Sociology 1950–1980*. London: Allen & Unwin.

Stacey, M. and Davies, C. (1983) *The Division of Labour in Child Health Care*. Final Report to the SSRC. Mimeo: The University of Warwick.

Stacey, M. with Homans, H. (1978) The Sociology of Health and Illness: Its Present State, Future Prospects and Potential for Health Research. *Sociology* 12 (2) May: 281.

Stacey, M. and Price, M. (1981) *Women, Power and Politics*. London and New York: Tavistock Publications.

Stimson, G.V. (1977) Social Care and the Role of the General Practitioner. *Social Science and Medicine* 11: 485.

Stoper, E. (1982) Alternative Work Patterns and the Double Life. In E. Boneparth (ed.) *Women, Power and Policy*. New York and Oxford: Pergamon.

Tocqueville, A. de (1956) *Democracy in America*. New York: New American Library.

Townsend, P. and Davidson, N. (1982) *Inequalities in Health: The Black Report* (DHSS 1980). Harmondsworth: Penguin.

UK Central Statistical Office (1983) *Social Trends* 13. London: HMSO.

United Nations (1980) *Demographic Year Book*. New York: United Nations Publishing Service.

US Bureau of the Census (1982-83) *Statistical Abstract of the United States*. Washington, DC: US Dept of Commerce.

Waldo, C. (1979) The Hidden Work of Everyday Life. In S. Wallman (ed.) *Social Anthropology of Work*. New York, Academic Press.

Weber, M. (1930) *The Protestant Ethic and the Spirit of Capitalism*. London: Allen & Unwin.

Acknowledgements

Many people's ideas have contributed to this chapter. I would particularly like to thank Celia Davies, Helen Evers, Jennifer Lorch, and the editors, Ellen Lewin and Virginia Olesen, for their contributions.

Name index

Abel-Smith, B. 273
Abrams, M. 87, 88
Abrams, P. 44
Adams, M. 36
Adrian, M. 214
Aitken-Swan, J. 249
Anderson, A. 213
Anderson, D. 102
Anderson, R. 242
Antunes, C.M. 117
Arms, S. 3, 186
Arney, W.R. 193, 285, 294
Arnold, E. 68
Ashley, J. 243
Atkinson, P. 4, 7
Aubrey, R. 195, 198
Austin, D.R. 114, 117, 130
Austin, R. 254, 287

Backett, M. 242
Baggs, W.J. 127, 130
Ball, E. 275
Banta, D. 186
Barrett-Connor, E. 119
Barron, I. 65

Bart, P. 3
Barth, F. 8
Baxter, C. 246
Bayh, Sen. 170
Beauchamp, D.E. 297
Beaumont, B. 255
Becker, M.H. 155–56, 170
Bedale, C. 258
Bell, C. 54
Bennett, J.E. 183, 202
Berger, P. 8
Berk, S.F. 4
Berliner, H.S. 203
Bernard, J. 14, 224, 298
Best, F. 57
Bewley, B.R. and T.H. 255
Bingham, E. 54
Binney, V. 258
Birke, L. 68
Birrell, S. 224
Black, Sir D. 262
Blaxter, M. 7, 34
Blumer, H. 80
Bologh, R.W. 19
Bond, M. 99, 101

Bone, M. 244
Boneparth, E. 15
Bonnerjea, L. 96, 101, 103
Bourne, G. 187
Boutilier, M. 212, 218, 225, 228; on sports 11–12, 15, 209–35
Bowen, D.D. 59
Bowlby, J. 296–97
Bowling, A. 100
Bradley, D.D. 119
Bradshaw, J. 273
Brame, J. 214
Braverman, H. 65
Brewer, C. 244
Bridbord, K. 53
Briggs, A. 271
Brion, M. 90
Brody, E.M. 109, 279, 281, 288
Brooke, Sen. 169
Brotherston, J. 241
Brown, G.W. 259, 288
Brown, J. 273
Browne, S. 283
Bruegel, I. 33
Bucher, R. 275
Bunker, J.P. 296
Burch, W. 217
Burghes, L. 37
Burling, R. 80
Bush, T. 123

Callahan, D. 146, 153
Campbell, B.M. 157–58
Campbell, J. 48
Campbell, M. 3
Carden, M.L. 17
Carpenter, E. 41
Carpenter, M. 254, 287
Cartwright, A. 100, 107, 242–44
Carver, C. 187
Castleman, M. 3
Cates, W. 154, 157
Chalmers, I. 199, 250
Chance, J. 283
Chard, T. 186, 249
Charles, N. 37
Chesler, P. 2
Cisler, L. 145
Clelland, V. 3
Coakley, J. 210
Cobb, J. 272
Cockburn, C. 41
Cohen, B.G.F. 69
Combs, M.R. 220
Comstock, G. 176

Conrad, P. 182
Cooke, A. 275
Coote, A. 42
Corea, G. 187
Cornoni-Huntley, J. 121, 132
Coughlin, R.M. 273
Coussins, J. 42
Craig, D. 8
Craig, M. 259
Cralley, L.V. 53
Crawford, R. 203
Crompton, R. 66
Cumming, E. 92
Curnow, R. 65
Cutright, P. 153

Dahl, T. 35
David, M. 42
Davidson, N. 289
Davies, C. 253, 259, 284, 285–86
Davies, J. 249
Davies, M. 56, 78
Davin, A. 42
Davis, A. 272
Davis, A.Y. 4
Davis, J. 195
DelRay, P. 222
Delamont, S. 31
Delphy, C. 107
DeWinter, A. 71
Dick-Read, G. 203
Dinan, B. 119
Dingwall, R. 8
Dobach, R.E. and R.P 41, 258
Doll, R. 116
Donegan, J.B. 184
Donnison, J. 29, 184
Dooling, Judge 143, 149, 159–60, 163, 168
Doyal, L. 45, 237, 249, 250, 251–53, 258, 260, 263, 264, 283, 295; on National Health Service 13, 15, 236–69
Driscoll, J.W. 58
Dubos, R. 43
Dumont, L. 271
Durie, A. 101

Eastman, N.J. 187
Eddy, T.P. 258
Edmonds, B.C. 14, 16
Ehrenreich, B. 2, 29, 162, 184, 253, 291
Ehrenreich, J. 186, 202, 282, 291
Eichenbaum, L. 259

Elkins, V.H. 188
Elshtain, J.B. 32
Elston, M.A. 249, 254, 255, 256, 263
Emmons, S. 119
English, D. 2, 29, 184, 253
Epstein, C.F. 55
Epstein, S.S. 124, 126
Ermish, J. 88
Ernst, S. 259
Estes, C.L. 14, 16, 275, 277, 292
Evers, H. 104, 105, 109, 282; on elderly
    frail women 13, 16, 18, 86–112

Fairhurst, E. 86
Farber, D.J. 65
Faulkner, W. 68
Feinleib, M. 59, 79
Feinstein, A.R. 117, 118
Feldberg, R.L. 68–9, 70, 72
Felshin, J. 222, 232
Finch, J. 4, 36, 42–3, 101, 104, 278
Finkle, W.D. 117, 118, 120
Firth, R. 63
Fishel, A. 213
Fletcher, T. 258
Fogarty, M.P. 54
Foltz, A. 293
Foote, W. 203
Foreman, A. 32
Forge, A. 63
Forney, J.P. 121, 122
Forrest, J. 155, 171
Foster, F.L. 221
Frankfort, E. 2
Freidson, E. 8, 27, 30–2, 187
French, J. 53
French, L. 108
Fretwell, J.E. 286

Gamarnikow, E. 26, 36, 253, 286
Gardner, A.W. 53
Gardner, B.B. 272
Gardner, K. 278
Gardner, M.R. 272
Gastel, B. 121, 132
Gavron, H. 36
Gee, F. 263
Geertz, C. 8
Gelb, J. 17, 20
Gerber, E. 4, 218
Gilbert, D. 217
Gill, D. 273
Gilligan, C. 227
Giuliano, V.E. 65
Glaser, B.G. 224

Glazer-Malbin, N. 20
Glen, K.B. 148
Glenn, E.N. 68–9, 70
Goldfield, R.J. 67
Goodison, L. 259
Gordon, A. 176
Gordon, L. 3
Gordon, S. 227
Gough, I. 273
Gove, W.R. 288
Graham, H. 36, 38–40, 43–4, 103, 244,
    249, 264, 288, 289, 291; on hidden
    carers 4, 13, 16, 25–52
Gray, J. 28, 249
Green, J. 176
Greenblatt, R.B. 121
Greendorfer, S. 223
Greenhouse, L. 165
Gross, E. 280
Gross, M. 186
Groves, D. 4, 36, 42–3, 101, 104, 278
Grune, J.A. 281
Guettel, C. 17

Haber, A. 18
Haire, D. 186
Haire, E. 3
Hakim, C. 279–80, 287
Hamilton, D. 178
Hammond, C.B. 120
Hardy, L. 287
Harman, C. 58
Harris, D.V. 214, 216–19, 221
Harris, M. 80
Harris, T. 259, 288
Hartmann, H. 33, 78
Havighurst, R. 216
Haw, M.A. 54
Hayes-Bautista, D. 7
Hayler, B. 4
Haynes, S.B. 59, 79
Hearn, J. 26
Heighton, R.H. Jr and C. 14
Helman, C.G. 7
Henifin, M.S. 72
Henley, A. 246
Henning, M. 225
Henry, W. 92
Henshaw, S. 154
Herbert, G. 34
Herbst, ɔ L. 116
Hewitt, N. 102
Hindell, K. 244
Hing, E. 289
Hoffman, L.W. 79

Holmes, H.B. 186
Homans, H. 27, 246, 270
Honigsbaum, F. 276
Hoos, I.R. 66, 67, 68
Hoover, R. 114, 118, 124, 127
Hope, E. 71
Horwitz, R. I. 117, 118
Hoskins, B. 186
Howlett, A. 243
Hubert, J. 63
Hudson, J. 214
Hughes, M. 35-6
Huizinga, J. 210
Hulka, B.S. 118, 120, 122
Hult, M. 57, 66, 67
Hunt, A. 89, 90, 100, 108
Hunt, G. 251-53, 263
Hunt, V.R. 54, 79
Hunter, D. 53
Hutter, B. 237, 249
Huws, U. 259

Illich, I. 186
Inglefinger, F.J. 124, 126
Isaacs, B. 100

Jacklin, C. 224
Jaco, E.G. 297
Jacobson, B. 40
Jaffe, F.S. 150, 153, 168
Jardim, A. 225
Javits, Sen. 170
Jefferson, T. 127
Jenkin, P. 42, 262
Jerrome, D. 88
Jick, H. 118, 119, 120, 125, 129
Johnson, A. 125
Johnson, P.B. 210, 229
Jones, G. 66
Jones, K. 273
Jordan, B. 9, 186, 195
Joshi, H. 88
Jourard, S. 221

Kahn, W. 281
Kaim-Caudle, P.R. 273
Kaiser, B. and J. 184
Kanter, R.M. 73, 80, 227
Kaplan, J. 218
Kaplan, R. 227
Kase, N. 116, 129
Kasper, A. 126, 131
Katsuranis, M.E. 3, 61
Kaufert, P.A. 131, 133; on estrogen-replacement therapy 12, 15, 113-38

Kelly, R. 225
Kelman, S. 7
Kennedy, M. 71
Kennedy, Sen. 170
Kennell, J.H. 193
Kenney, A.M. 171
Kenniston, K. 217
Kephart, N.C. 216
Kerr, N. 37
Ketchum, S.A. 132
Kichs, C. 253
Kingsley, J. 221
Kitzinger, S. 195, 249
Kivlin, J.E. 221, 222
Klaus, M. 193
Kleiber, N. 9
Kloosterman, G.L. 195
Kohlberg, L. 227
Komarovsky, M. 63
Kovar, M.G. 289
Krasney, J. 183, 202
Kundsin, R.S. 55

Ladd, J. 131
Lader, L. 146
Lamaze, F. 190, 191, 203
Land, H. 36-8, 42
Landau, R.L. 118, 121, 122, 126
Landy, D. 7
Leach, E.R. 8
Leavitt, J.W. 185
Leboyer, F. 192
Lee, P. 153, 273
Leeson, J. 28, 249
LeGrand, J. 241, 243
Leira, A. 55
Lemkau, J.P. 54, 59
Lennane, K. and R. 230
Lessor, R. 76
Lever, J. 226
Levine, S. 74
Levitt, J. 28
Lewin, E. 3, 9; on clerical work 11-12, 15, 53-85; on theory 1-24
Lewin, R. 219, 220
Lewis, G.L. 7
Lewis, J. 38, 42
Liff, S. 36
Light, L. 9
Lightup, R. 86
Lindheim, B.L. 153, 155
Lipman-Blumen, J. 14
Lipsett, M.B. 121
Litman, T. 32, 40
Litwak, E. 25

Locker, D. 8
Lopata, H.4
Lopate, C. 3, 55
Lorber, J. 230
Lubic, R.W. 198
Luckman, T. 8
Luker, K. 3
Lukes, S. 271
Lunn, J.A. 259

McCartney, L.D. 69, 72
Maccoby, E. 224
MacDonald, P.C. 121, 122
Macfarlane, A. 239-40
MacGovern, M. 203
McIntosh, M. 30-2
Macintyre, S. 5, 249
Mack, T.M. 117, 118
MacKee, L. 39
MacKeith, N. 256
McKeown, T. 186
McKinlay S.M. 114, 129; on estrogen-
  replacement therapy 12, 15, 113-38
McKinlay, J. 8, 114, 129
McNally, F. 68
McNally, J. 36
Mandelbaum, D.R. 55
Marcus, A.C. 289
Marieskind, H. 283-84, 285, 291
Marlowe, M. 215
Marmor, T.R. 277
Marshall, R. 242
Marshall, T.H. 271
Martin, P. 217
Marwick, A. 272
Mathes, S. 223
Maxwell, N.L. 163
Mechanic, D. 229
Meehan, E. 275, 280-81
Mehl, L.E. 195
Meier, P. 118, 121, 122
Mellor, J. 251-53, 263
Menzies, H. 58
Metheny, E. 221
Miller, J. 59, 70
Millman, M. 220
Minc, A. 66
Mohr, J.C. 144
Moore, K.A. 163
Moore, R. 252
Morgall, J. 58, 64, 65, 66, 67
Mortimer, J. 108
Moss, C.E. 58
Mott, L. 163
Munson, R. 128

Murphree, M. 65, 68
Murray, W.E. 58

Nakamura, R.T. 14
Nathanson, C. 79, 155-56, 170, 229,
  288, 289
Navarro, V. 28, 291
Nelson, C. 9
Nelson, N. 192
Neville, Y. 100
Nightingale, F. 286
Nisbet, R.A. 271
Nissel, M. 96, 101, 103
Niswander, K. 176
Nora, S. 66
Norgren, J. 281
Norman, A. 108
Noyce, J. 242
Nussbaum, K. 70
Nuttall, P.D. 287
Nye, F.I. 79

Oakley, A. 29, 36, 184, 199, 239, 249,
  250, 288
O'Brien, M. 107, 242
Ogilvie, R. 222
Olesen, V. 3, 9, 61, 291; on clerical
  work 11-12, 15, 53-85; on theory
  1-24
Olson, M. 71
Oppenheimer, V.K. 59, 279-80
Orbach, S. 259
Oren, L. 37
Owens, M. 216
Oxorn, H. 203

Paller, M.L. 17, 20
Palmer, D. 282
Parker, R. 42, 103
Parkhouse, B. 213
Parr, W.H. 58
Parry, N. and J. 276
Paterson, E. 7, 34
Peace, S. 109, 293
Pearce, D. 77
Pennell, I. 263, 283
Perkin, H. 271
Petchesky, R. 54, 79, 141, 162, 166,
  169; on abortion 11-12, 15, 17,
  139-73
Phillips, A. 256, 278
Phillipson, C. 86, 109
Piaget, J. 216, 227
Pierce, C. 132
Pike, K. 80

Pill, R. 7
Pinker, R. 273
Pitt, B. 108
Poskanzer, D.C. 116
Pottker, J. 213
Price, M. 32, 271

Quigley, M.M. 120

Raban, C. 273
Rabinow, P. 8
Rakusen, J. 247, 256, 278
Randall, V. 274, 283, 289, 290, 293
Rapoport, R. 36, 54
Rapoport, R.M. 36
Reagan, R. 140, 163
Rees-Davies, W. 45-6
Reid, S. 66
Rein, M. 14, 16
Renshon, S. 227
Rice, D. 54, 80, 289
Richards, M. 186, 249, 250
Richardson, G. 115
Riger, S. 231
Rivlin, A. 14
Robarts, S. 275
Roberts, H. 249
Robinson, D. 8
Robinson, J. 262
Robinson, R.V. 273
Roche, S. 259
Rohrbaugh, J.B. 222
Romalis, C. 189
Romalis, S. 184, 189; on birth practices 11-12, 174-208
Romano, D.L. 219, 220
Rose, H. 27
Rosenberg, L. 119
Ross, R.K. 118
Rossiter, C. 101
Rotella, E.J. 78
Rothman, B.K. 190
Rothman, K. 119
Rothman, S.M. 293
Rowbotham, S. 32, 38
Rowlings, C. 87
Rowntree, B.S. 34
Rubin, L.B. 63
Rumberger, R.W. 57
Russell, D. 283
Ruzek, S.B. 3-4, 9-10, 18, 184, 204, 294, 295
Ryan, J. 214
Ryan, K.J. 120, 126
Rytina, N.F. 57

Saffron, L. 243
Salmon, J.W. 203
Salvage, J. 253
SanGiovanni, L. 212, 218, 224, 228; on sports 11-12, 15, 209-35
Satow, A. 246
Scambler, A. 8
Scambler, G. 8
Schneider, I. 218
Schneider, J. 182
Schuman, L. 108
Scotch, N. 74
Scott, R.A. 16
Scully, D. 3, 184
Seaman, B. 2-3
Secord, P. 221
Seeman, T.S. 289
Seibert, M.E. 221
Seiden, H. 196
Seldon, A. 46
Sennett, R. 272
Shannon, C. 33
Shapiro, S. 118
Shaw, J. 42
Shaw, N.S. 3, 186
Shearer, M. 175, 176
Sheldon, J.H. 89
Shimmin, S. 36
Shoemaker, E.S. 121, 122
Shore, A. 16
Shryrock, R.G. 20
Shuer, M. 217
Simon, H.A. 61
Sims, M. 4
Sleigh, J.M. 66, 67
Smallwood, S. 14
Smart, B. and C. 237, 249
Smith, D. 289
Smith, D.C. 117, 120
Smith, M.J. 69
Snaith, A.H. 242
Snare, A. 35
Snyder, E.E. 221, 222
Spender, D. 297
Spreitzer, E. 221, 222
Spring Rice, M. 34-5
Stacey, M. 4-5, 27-8, 32, 264, 270-71, 284; on comparison of UK and USA health systems 270-303
Staffo, D. 211
Stallard, K. 162
Stammerjohn, L.W. 69
Stavraky, K. 119
Stellman, J. 72
Stern, B. 57

Stern, M.P. 119
Stimson, G.V. 296
Stone, G. 210
Stoper, E. 281
Stott, M. 297
Stott, N.C.H. 7
Strauss, A.L. 224
Studd, M.P. 121
Sugarman, M. 175
Sullivan, E. 155
Sullivan, W.M. 8
Szekely, D.R. 114, 117, 130

Taylor, J. 101, 264
Taylor, M. 182
Telesky, C.W. 289
Thacker, S. 186
Thom, M. 121
Thomas, G. 33
Thomas, J.E. 128-29
Tietze, C. 155
Timbrell, D. 180
Tinker, A. 90
Titmuss, R.M. 27, 29, 238
Tocqueville, A. de 271
Torrance, G. 182, 202
Torres, A. 171
Townsend, P. 34, 103, 107, 109,
    237-39, 241, 243, 261-62, 289
Trickey, A.J. 242
Truman, D.J. 78
Tudor Hart, J. 242
Tudor, J. 288
Tutko, T. 222

Uhlig, R. 65
Ulfelder, J. 116
Ullyot, J. 215
Ungerson, C. 4, 101

Verbrugge, L. 79, 229
Versluysen, M. 29, 34
Vessey, M.P. 116

Vincent, M. 222
Voysey, M. 38

Waite, L.J. 163
Wakefield, J. 243
Waldron, I. 54, 114
Walker, A. 97, 99, 101, 102, 109
Walker, K. 204
Wallace, T. 252
Walsh, S. 252
Walshok, M.L. 55, 78
Walters, V. 262
Ward, S. 88
Weber, M. 271
Wedderburn, D. 103
Weinstein, M.C. 120, 132
Weiss, J. 15
Weiss, N.S. 114, 117, 118, 120, 122,
    130
Weiss, P. 215
Weldon, F. 34
Wertz, D.C. 184, 185, 189
Wertz, R.W. 184, 189
West, C. 9
West, P. 211
Whitelegg, E. 248
Wicks, M. 101
Wilkin, D. 101
Willcocks, D. 104
Williams, G. 237, 249
Willis, E. 167
Wilmore, J. 214
Wilson, E. 32, 258
Wilson, H. 34
Wilson, R. 115
Wright, F. 101
Wright, M.J. 54
Wynn, M. and A. 176-77
Wyrick, W. 214, 221

Yorburgh, B. 223

Ziel, H.K. 117, 118, 120
Zion, L. 221
Zola, I.K. 8, 41
Zuboff, S. 69, 70

Subject index

abortion: and class and race 151, 153–56, 158; costs of 139, 150–51, 153, 156–58, 161–62, 167; legislation 4–5, 139–73 *passim*, 283, 290–91, 293; mortality 153–54, 163, 170; in United Kingdom 244, 276

abortion and feminist morality (USA) 4–6, 10, 12, 17, 139–73; beyond medical and moral issues 166–69; 'medical necessity', limits of 142–51; and women's health 151–66

access: to contraception 244, 249; to hospitals 242–43; to National Health Service 236–38, 242–43, 260; to preventive care 243–44, 262

active initiators, elderly as 91–4, 97–8, 106

advancement, occupational 68

age: and sport 216–18, 222, 224–27; *see also* elderly

alcohol 39

alternative birth practices 188–99; centers, out-of-hospital 197–99; home deliveries 195–97, 199, 249; hospital birthing rooms 194–95;

Leboyer method 192–94; natural childbirth 189–91

ambiguity and health, clerical workers 72–8

American Medical Association and abortion 144, 148, 169

anesthesia and childbirth *see* birth, drugs

anorexia and sport 220

anthropology 8

'apologetics' and role conflict 222–24

arthritis 90

associations for women's health 282–83

atherosclerotic disease 121

beliefs, health, transmission of 34

biophysical considerations and sport 214–17

birth: centers *see* alternative; Cesarian 185, 204, 249; and class 185, 188, 191, 197; comparison, UK and USA 285, 294–95; costs of 176, 182–83, 199–200, 202; and drugs 184–90 *passim*, 203–04; in hospitals 175–76, 194–95, 204, 249, 285, 294–95; and

mortality 176, 178, 195, 201, 239;
risks of 176–80, 200; and technology
249–50
birth practices in Canada, struggle 5–6,
11–12, 174–208; background
175–77; consumer activism 183–87,
193, 195, 200–01, 204; in context
181–83; critics 188–89; events
177–81; providers v. recipients
199–201; *see also* alternative
Black Report (UK, 1980) 262, 292
body image and sport 221
breast: cancer 2, 118–19, 124, 127;
–feeding 38–9, 44
British Provident Association (BUPA)
47
budgeting *see* costs
bulimia and sport 220

Canada *see* birth practices
cancer: breast 2, 118–19, 124, 127;
cervical 143–44, 262; and class 247,
262; and DES 116, 124; and
estrogen-replacement therapy 115,
117–19, 121, 124, 130–31; mortality
243–44; uterine 247
capitalism 270–71
cardiovascular disease 116, 122–23
carers, hidden (UK) 4, 6, 13, 16–17,
25–32, 257, 264, 278, 281, 287–89;
and legislation 42–3; medical
sociology and social policy 27–33;
mothers' and daughters' perceptions
95–9; in old age *see* passive
responders; policy and 27–33, 42–8,
99–103; providers, negotiators, and
mediators 26, 34–41
centers for childbirth, out-of-hospital
197–99, 204
centralism 277–78
cervical cancer 143–44, 262; screening
for 243–44, 262
Cesarians, rate of 185, 204, 249
change *see* technology
changing patterns, women and sport
210–12
childbirth *see* birth; birth practices;
reproductive system
children: care facilities 289; health of
44, 282–83, 293, 297; rearing 35–9,
44–5; and sport 216, 218, 222,
226–27; *see also* birth; mothers;
teenagers
class, social 5, 7; and abortion 151,
152–56, 158; and cancer 247, 262;

and childbirth 185, 188, 191, 197;
comparison, UK and USA 271–72,
277, 289; consciousness, lack of 80;
and elderly, care of 91, 107; and
estrogen-replacement therapy 131;
and mortality 239–40; and National
Health Service 238–45, 247; and
sport 223
clerical work (USA) 11–12, 16–17,
53–85, 280; ambiguity and health
72–8; development of 56–7; and
health 57–8, 72–8; new approach
60–3; social relationships 70–2; and
stress 54, 58–60, 69, 71, 73, 76–7,
80; technological change *see*
computers
collectivism 270–71, 292
color *see* race
community care: for elderly woman
99–103, 106; and women doctors
255; *see also* carers, hidden
community recreation 211
comparison, health care in UK and
USA 6, 13–14, 270–303; domestic
and public domain 278–82; political
and economic organization,
different 274–78; themes,
underlying 270–74; women's
movements 282–95
competitive behavior and sport 225–26
computers and clerical workers 64–78,
259; ambiguity and health 72–8; and
health 58–9, 72–8; and social
relations 70–2
conflicts and hidden carers 97
consumer activism and childbirth 180–
81, 183–87, 193, 195, 200–01, 204
contraception 143, 150, 170, 289–90;
access to 244, 249; legislation
289–90; pill 116, 121, 124, 129, 133;
risks of 3, 116, 121, 246–47, 263;
sterilization 157, 170, 245; and
teenagers 166, 170–71
control: by women, of childbirth 185,
187; *see also* men
coping strategies 39–41, 231
coronary health disease 59, 119
corporations, women in, and sport
225–28
cost-benefit approach to estrogen-
replacement therapy 120–21
costs: of health care 276–77; of
sterilization 157, 170; of welfare
state 42–3; *see also* abortion; birth
Counter Information Services 46–7

Cranbrook Report (UK, 1959) 294

daughters, perspectives on support relationship 96–9
debate on estrogen-replacement therapy 115–16, 124–32; government response 125–27; and media 124–25; and medical community 127–30; and physician-patient relationship 130–32; and women's health movement 132–33
deficiency condition, menopause seen as 128–29
Depo-Provera 247, 263
depression and mothers 258
DES 129, 133; and cancer 116, 124
'deskilling' of clerical work 68–9
diet 37; breast-feeding 38–9, 44; disorders and sport 220, 230
'disengagement' *see* passive respondents
division of labor *see* sexual
doctors *see* physicians
Doe versus Bolton and abortion 147–48
domestic tasks *see* household work
drugs: adverse effects of *see* contraception, estrogen-replacement; and childbirth 184–85, 187, 189–90, 203–04; companies 125–26, 131; negative imagery of women in advertisements for 2–3; psychotropic 3, 39
'dual-career' families 54
dying spouse, caring for 100–01

eating *see* diet
education: about childbirth 176, 178, 188–91, 197, 203; level of clerical workers 57, 59
elderly, care for 2, 6, 13, 16–18, 86–112, 278, 281–82, 292–93; and class 91, 107; demographic issue 87–90; institutional care 90, 103–06, 252; isolation of 87–9, 91, 108; and National Health Service 47; numbers of 87; policies about 99–106; and sport 217, 219; subjective assessments 90–9, 106; White Paper on 43–4, 99
'elective' abortion 143–44, 151
elitism, physicians' 182, 202
'emic' approach 60, 80
employer, unsympathetic 63
employment: opportunities and new technology 66–7, 77; *see also* clerical workers; workers; health; working women

endometrial cancer 117–19, 121, 124, 130–31
'engagement' *see* active initiators
Equal Employment Opportunities Commission (USA) 275–78
Equal Opportunities Commission (UK) 34–5, 44, 96, 101, 109, 275–78
estrogen-replacement therapy (USA) 6, 12, 15, 113–38; and class 131; clinical response and rehabilitation of 120–22; debate on *see* debate; diseases and 115, 117–19, 121–24, 130–31; research on 114–20
eugenics 143, 291
'extrinsic' work-related factors in health of clerical workers 61–2

family: allowance 42; care for elderly 85, 91, *see also* carers, hidden, elderly; composition of 42, 281; as primary unit 31; *see also* children; married women; mothers
fees *see* costs
femininity: of doctors' specialties 255; and sport 220–21, 223
feminists 1–24 *passim*; comparison UK and USA 282–95; critique of National Health Service 237, 256–58; morality *see* abortion; Marxist 30, 32–3; and psychotherapy 259
feminization of institutions for elderly 90, 103–04
'fetishism, health' 219
finance *see* costs
Finland, childbirth in 176
fitness, definition of 210; *see also* sport
Flora Project for Heart Disease Prevention 40–1, 44
Food and Drug Administration, (USA) 15, 247; and estrogen-replacement therapy 125–26, 131, 133–34
food *see* diet
Framingham study 59–62, 74, 79
France, childbirth in 176
freedom, deprivation of, in institutions 105–06
friendship and elderly 88
frustration of clerical workers 59
funding *see* costs

gall-bladder disease 117, 119, 131
gatekeepers, hidden carers as 41
gender bias 44; *see also* sexual division, etc

314 Subject index

General Household Survey (UK) 87, 89, 107–08, 240–42, 262
general practitioners *see* physicians
government response to estrogen-replacement therapy 125–27
gynecology 3

head of family, woman as 154
health *see* women, health, healing
health maintenance organizations 277
health workers *see* workers
heart disease 119
high-risk mothers and babies 175–76
HL versus Matheson, abortion and 163–64, 166
holism and childbirth 183–84, 202–03
Holland, childbirth in 178–79, 195
home: births 195–97, 199, 249; clerical work in 70–1; helps, for elderly 99, 101, 108
hormones *see* estrogen-replacement
hospitals: and abortion 145, 155–56; access to 242–43; birth in 175–76, 194–95, 204, 249, 285, 294–95; work in *see* workers, health
household work 63, 89, 278–82, 289
housing 90, 258, 261
Hyde Amendment on abortion (USA) 143, 147, 156–57, 159

iatrogenesis *see* estrogen-replacement
immigration legislation 247, 252
income: clerical workers 57, 59; elderly 88–9, 107; health workers 250–51, 257, 260, 280–81, 284–85; *see also* poverty
individualism 270–71, 277, 292
inequalities in health care 199, 202, 237–38, 262
informal health care *see* carers, hidden
information, lack of 242, 247
institutional care for elderly 90, 103–06, 252
insurance, health 277
intensive care, neonatal 176
'intrinsic' factors *see* 'extrinsic'
invalidity care: allowance 101; legislation 42
isolation: of computerized clerical work 70–1; of elderly 87–9, 91, 108; of hidden carers 101

knowledge as social construct 8

labor: intensivity of child rearing 36; *see also* birth; employment; sexual division of
Lamaze method of childbirth 190–91, 203
Lane Report (UK, 1974) 245
lay referral system 7, 30–2
Leboyer method of childbirth 192–94
left, political, in feminism 291–92
legislation: abortion 4–5, 139–73 *passim*, 283, 290–91, 293; contraception 289–90; equal opportunities 275; and hidden carers 42–3; immigration 247, 252; maternity services 42; medical 43; sex discrimination 213, 228, 231–32; welfare 292
life: -cycle stages and sport 216–19, 222, 226–27; expectancy 237
loneliness *see* isolation

McRae versus Harris and abortion 159–62, 166, 168–69
male *see* men
malpractice suits 128
management of illness, concentration of research on 29
married women: as carers, hidden 101; clerical workers 56–7, 67; elderly 100; in nursing 254; *see also* mothers
Marxist feminist accounts of reproduction 30, 32–3
mastectomies 2
maternity services 42; *see also* birth
media: and abortion 140; and childbirth 188; and estrogen-replacement therapy 124–25, 130
mediation between public and private domains 42–7
mediators, hidden carers as 26, 34–41
'medical model' and abortion 143–44, 148, 167
'medical necessity' of abortion 142–51
medical profession *see* physicians
medical sociology and hidden carers 27–33
medicalization of birth *see* birth
men: clerical workers 71–2, 77; dominance *see* physicians *below*; elderly 87–90, 100, 105; emulation of, in sport 220; married, and health 288; morbidity rates 241; mortality rates 239; as nurses, senior 254; physicians, dominance of 26, 184–91 *passim*, 249, 253, 260, 274,

286–87, 294; and sport 213, 215
menopause *see* estrogen-replacement
menstruation and sport 218, 230
mental illness of elderly 108
midwives 184, 195, 197, 251, 263
minorities *see* race
misogynism 9
mobility loss of elderly 89
morality, feminist *see* abortion and
    feminist morality
morbidity rates 240–41
mortality rates 238–39, 263; and
    abortion 153–54, 163, 170; and
    cancer 243–44; and childbirth 176,
    178, 195, 201, 239; and class
    239–40; and race 263; and work 240
mothers: in clerical work 56–7, 59, 79;
    depression of 258; in nursing 254;
    perspectives of support relationship
    96–9; working 278; *see also* birth;
    children; family; married women
myocardial infarction 116, 120

National Association of Working
    Women (USA) 58, 69–70, 72–3
National Health Service (UK) 13, 25,
    33, 236–69; access to 236–38,
    242–43,260; and class 238–45, 247;
    comparison with USA 270–303;
    deterioration of 46–7, 199, 256–57,
    261; and elderly 47; inequalities in
    237–38; and race 245–48; resistance
    to 255–60; and social control
    248–50; workers in *see* workers,
    health; *see also* United Kingdom
natural childbirth 189–91
negative imagery of women in drug
    advertisements 2–3
negotiators, hidden carers as 26, 34–41,
    44, 48
neonatal intensive care 176
Netherlands *see* Holland
'New Right' (USA) and abortion
    139–73 *passim*
new technology *see* computers
nuclear family, assumed 42
nursing 3, 9, 105, 280, 285–87; in
    National Health Service 251–54, 259

obesity and sport 219–20, 229
obligation, feeling of 97
obstetrics *see* birth
occupational health *see* clerical
    workers; employment
osteoporosis 121–23; delayed 219

overseas: health workers in UK 251–53,
    261; patients in UK 248, 263

passive responders, elderly as 91–2,
    94–8, 106
patient roles 132
patriarchalism 46; *see also* men
pay *see* income
Peel Report (UK, 1970) 294
pensions 88, 107
personality and sport 221
pharmaceutical companies 125–26,
    131; *see also* drugs
physicians: and abortions 144–46,
    155–56, 165; comparison UK and
    USA 278; elitism 182, 202; and
    estrogen-replacement therapy
    127–32; general practitioners 241,
    262; -patient relationships 130–32,
    146, 189, 204, 242; status of 255;
    women 254–55, 283–84; *see also*
    men, physicians
play 210, 216
playgroup movement 45
policy: on abortion 139–73 *passim*; on
    carers, hidden 27–33, 42–8, 99–103;
    on elderly 99–106; and feminists
    292–95; on sport 212–13, 228–31
political and economic organization
    274–78
politics: of health 46–7; and women in
    sport 225
poverty: and abortion 153–55, 158–59;
    and carers, hidden 34; of elderly
    88–9, 107; of women 77; *see also*
    costs; income
pregnancy and sport 218
premature birth 176
preventive care 243–44, 262; birth risks
    176–80, 200
'privacy, coercion of' 35, 38, 40–1;
    women's rights to 149
private: domain *see* carers, hidden;
    medicine in UK 46–7, 199, 273
Private Patients Plan (PPP) 47
professional medicine: research on
    29–31; *see also* physicians
professional sport 212
profit and health care 273
progesterone added to estrogen 121
'proletarianization' of clerical work
    68–9
providers, hidden carers as 26, 34–41
psychogenic, women's illnesses seen
    as 2
psychological issues and sport 220–22

psychotherapy, feminist 259
psychotropic drugs 3, 39
public and private domains, mediation
    between 42–7

race 5; and abortion 153–55, 158; and
    childbirth 189; comparison UK and
    USA 271–72, 277, 289; and
    estrogen-replacement therapy 131;
    and mortality rates 262; and
    National Health Service 245–48
recipients and providers, division
    between 1, 7, 9; *see also* birth
    practices
recreation 210; *see also* sport
regionalization of Canadian obstetrical
    services 174–83, 200
reproduction, Marxist accounts of 30,
    32–3
reproductive system 5; and
    occupational conditions 54–5;
    cancer of *see* breast, cervical,
    uterine; and sport 218, 229–30
resistance to National Health Service
    255–60
right, political: feminist 291–92; *see
    also* 'New Right'
risks *see* birth; contraception; high-risk
Roe versus Wade and abortion 140,
    142–51, 163–65
role: conflict 222–24, 232; -equity and
    role-change 17; 'strain' 54

satisfaction, job 69, 75
schools and colleges, sport in 211, 213
Seebohm Report (UK, 1968) 43
selectivity v. universalism 273–74
self: -esteem and sport 221–22; -help
    gynecology 10; -perceptions of
    elderly 97–8; -sacrifice of hidden
    carers 37–9
sex: -blindness 32–3; discrimination,
    legislation on 213, 228, 231–32
sexual division of labor 1–2, 13, 25, 89,
    279–80, 283–87, 291–92
single parent families 281
smoking 39–40, 44, 119
social: actor and sport 224–28;
    construct, knowledge as 8; control
    248–50; life of elderly 87; policy *see*
    policy; relationships, clerical
    workers 70–2; security, legislation
    42
sociology 8, 222–24
spatial division of labor 26

sport (USA) 4, 6, 11, 15, 209–35;
    biophysical considerations 214–17;
    changing patterns 210–12; health
    problems 217–20; policy and
    participation 212–13; policy
    implications 228–31; psychological
    issues 220–22; recreation and fitness
    210; and social actor 224–28;
    sociological issues 222–24
status: high, of consultants 255; low,
    of clerical workers 59, 61; low, of
    health workers 3, 250, 255, 257, 260
sterilization 157, 170, 245
stress: coping with, and sport 231; in
    clerical work 54, 58–60, 69, 71, 73,
    76–7, 80; of hidden carers 101
subjective assessments of elderly
    women 90–9; active initiators 92–4;
    passive respondents 94–5; support
    relationships 95–9
'super-fit' syndrome 215
supplementary benefit and elderly 88,
    107
Supreme Court (USA): and abortion
    139–73 *passim*; and contraception
    290
Sweden, childbirth in 176, 178

teachers, women as *see* negotiators
team involvement and sport 223
technology: and birth 249–50; and
    clerical work *see* computers
teenagers: and abortion 163–66; and
    contraception 166, 170–71
temporary clerical workers 61–2
'tending' 103; *see also* carers
'therapeutic' abortions 143–51
thromboembolic accident 116, 121
Toronto *see* birth practices

unemployment 45, 66–7, 77
unions: clerical workers, resistance to
    76, 80; health workers 257, 259
United Kingdom: abortion in 244, 276;
    childbirth in 176, 183–84, 199, 249;
    private medicine in 46–7, 199, 273;
    sterilization in 245; *see also* carers,
    hidden; comparison, health care;
    elderly; National Health Service
United States: childbirth in 184, 188,
    191–92, 197–99; *see also* abortion;
    clerical work; comparison, health
    care; estrogen-replacement; sports
universalism v. selectivity 273–74

uterine cancer 247
victims, women as 145
violence, domestic 258
virginity tests 247
voluntary sector and community care 4

welfare state 271, 274–75; costs of
42–3; legislation for 292; models
274–78; 'retreat from' 261
White Paper on elderly (UK, 1981)
43–4, 99
widows, elderly 87–9
women, health, and healing: abortion
139–73; birth practices 174–208;
carers, hidden 25–52; comparison,
UK and USA 270–303; elderly
88–112; estrogen-replacement
therapy 113–38; National Health
Service 236–69; occupational health
53–85; sports 209–35; theory 1–24
Women's Cooperative Guild 34, 37
women's health movement 132–33,
257–58
women's movement *see* feminists
word processors *see* computers
work, mortality rates and 240
work objects, elderly as 102
workers, health 1–3, 13, 250–55; and
sexual division of labor 282–87; low
income and status 3, 250–51, 255,
257, 260, 280–81, 284–85
working-class families 35, 63, 258
working women: comparison UK and
USA 278–82; numbers of 56–7, 79;
in old age *see* active initiators;
research on 28–9; *see also* clerical
work; workers, health